THE ROYAL CORNWALL POLYTECHNIC SOCIETY TUKE COLLECTION

HENRY SCOTT TUKE

PAINTINGS FROM CORNWALL

CATHERINE WALLACE

POLY
ARTS & SCIENCE

HALSGROVE

First published in Great Britain in 2008

British Library Cataloguing-in-Publication Data
A CIP record for this title is available from the British Library

ISBN 978 1 84114 705 5

HALSGROVE
Halsgrove House, Ryelands Industrial Estate
Bagley Road, Wellington, Somerset TA21 9PZ
t: 01823 653777 f: 01823 216796
e: sales@halsgrove.com www.halsgrove.com

Printed and bound by C&C Offset Printing

Tuke Committee of the Royal Cornwall Polytechnic Society

Anthony Phillips (Chairman)
John Tonkin (Vice-Chairman)
Dolores Banks
Michael Carver
Anthony Fagin
Pamela Lomax

Advisors: Lucinda Middleton (Royal Cornwall Museum)
Brian Stewart (Falmouth Art Gallery)

Consultant Catherine Wallace
Assisted by Adrian Watts, General Manager, RCPS (2003 – 2006)
Richard Glover, Chief Executive, RCPS (2006 –)

Editorial Committee
Brian Stewart, Director, Falmouth Art Gallery
Alex Hooper, Falmouth Art Gallery
Anthony Phillips, Chairman RCPS
John Tonkin, RCPS
Michael Carver, RCPS

Cataloguing
Catherine Wallace

Design
Steve Collinson, Xgraphica

Oil Conservation
Gilly Kinloch
Jim Wray

Paper Conservation
Sue Corfield, Blue Iris

Framing
Sully's Picture Framing, Penryn and Green Ginger Studios, Sancreed

Photography
Steve Tanner, Simon Shawcross and Colin Beer

Catalogue Text

The Royal Cornwall Polytechnic Society's Tuke Collection is available to view by appointment at:
Falmouth Art Gallery
Municipal Buildings
The Moor, Falmouth, Cornwall TR11 2RT.
Tel 01326 313863.
Email info@falmouthartgallery.com www.falmouthartgallery.com

Acknowledgments
The author would like to thank the Tuke Committee of the Royal Cornwall Polytechnic Society for all their support in achieving the conservation, restoration and cataloguing of the Tuke Collection. Particular thanks go to Anthony Phillips, whose enthusiasm, support and determination to achieve our goal never wavered. Thanks also to the editorial committee and especially to John Tonkin for his attention to detail and Michael Carver for his exacting copy-editing. For endless cups of tea and patience, many thanks to the staff and volunteers of Falmouth Art Gallery, and for allowing access to the Collection at any time. Thanks to the exemplary professionalism and miracles performed by the conservation team, Gilly Kinloch and Sue Corfield. The author is most grateful for all those who helped with her research including Brian D. Price whose expertise and knowledge of Tuke and the Collection are unprecedented; John Tonkin for his local knowledge relating to Tuke; Captain George Hogg and volunteers at the library of the National Maritime Museum, Cornwall for their knowledge of ships and help with identifying those in Tuke's paintings; Sir Hugh Fleetwood Hamilton-Dalrymple Bt., G.C.V.O, for his hospitality and generous guided tour of North Berwick; Mrs Ann Willett and Mrs. Susan Wyatt, Tuke's grandnieces, for sharing their memories; Dr. David Crabb for his advice and endless enthusiasm for Tuke; the archivists at the Hyman Kreitman Research Centre at Tate Britain and the National Art Library at the Victoria and Albert Museum.

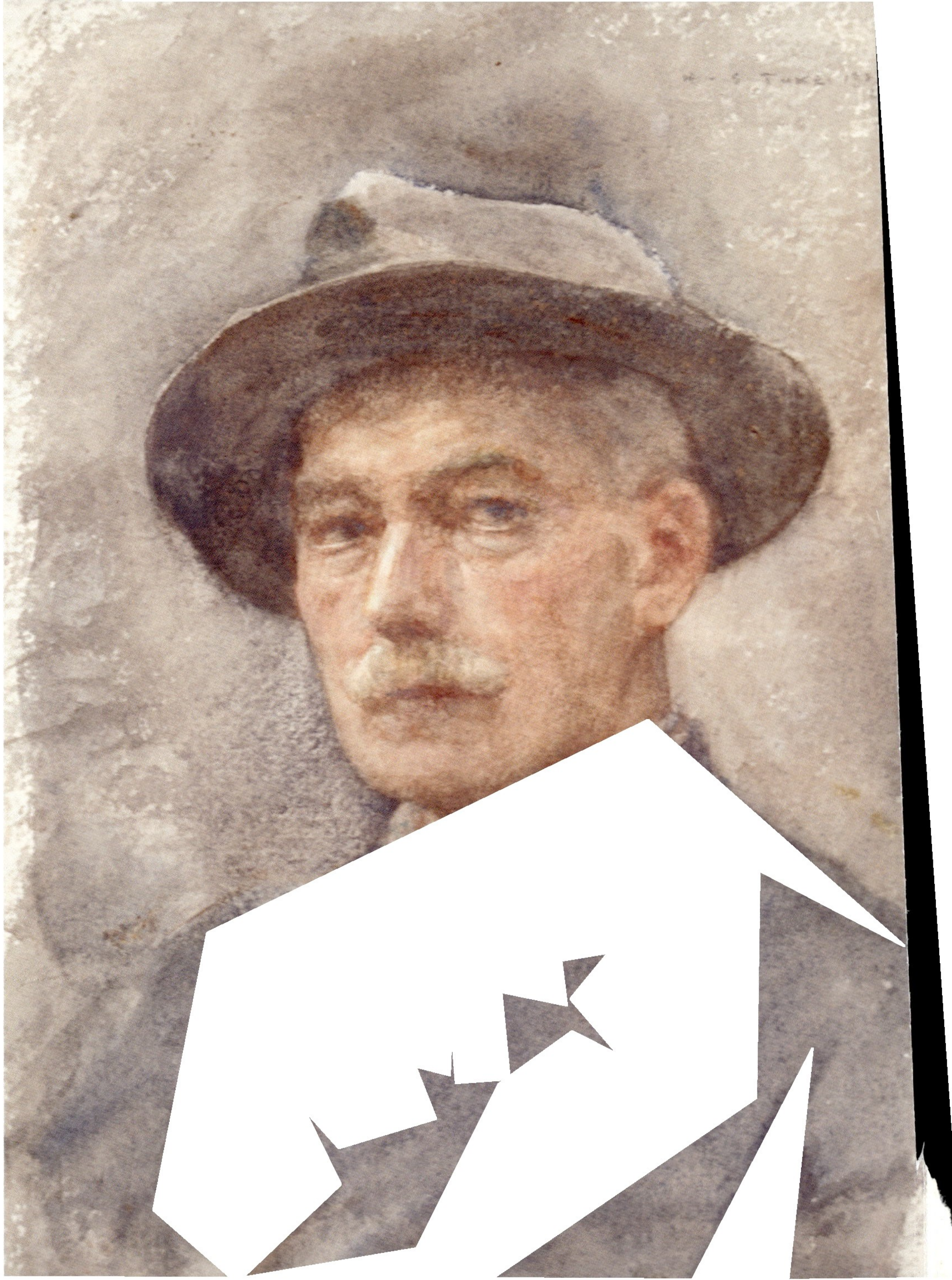

Contents

opposite: Self Portrait, 1927 (A77)

Donations to Tuke Restoration Fund

Charitable Trusts

An Anonymous Trust

The Cornwall Heritage Trust

The Garfield Weston Foundation

The Headley Trust

The Joseph and Nancy Charitable Trust

The Mercers Company

The Pilgrim Trust

The Still Waters Trust

Societies and Clubs

Mullion Old Cornwall Society

St. Agnes Branch Old Cornwall Society

St. Austell Branch Old Cornwall Society

West Cornwall Ladies Luncheon Club

Private Individuals

His Royal Highness The Prince of Wales, Duke of Cornwall

Mr. Jeremy Bird

Viscountess Boyd

Mrs. D.A. Burley for *The Missionary Boat*

Mr. Antony Hichens

Mrs. Mariquita Hichens

Mr. and Mrs. C. Perkins

Dr. Anthony and Mrs. Victoria Phillips

Professor and Mrs. E. Roberts

Mrs. Eileen Stratton

Mr. John and Mrs. Valentine Tonkin

Mrs. Gillian Walker

Preface

HENRY SCOTT TUKE is probably best known for his evocative paintings of naked young men which have won him the reputation as a pioneer of gay male culture. Many of his works focus on the youths he befriended in Falmouth enjoying athletic pursuits – bathing, diving or lounging around on boats or the shore, their pale flesh caressed by the soft, dappled light of the sun. Tuke's fascination with the adolescent male body may seem openly homoerotic today, but in the late nineteenth century would not necessarily have carried that connotation. Not only were scenes of bathers generally acceptable if they did not draw attention to sexual characteristics, but such subjects also conjured up the untainted vitality of a pastoral world, lending conviction to the ideal of public health being advanced at the time by social reformers. Tuke's golden youths appeared to uphold the benefits of fresh air and communal exercise as the antidote to urban squalor, and the artist himself shared with his models a love of boating, cricket, cycling and swimming. The feeling of hearty comradeship generated by Tuke's male nude compositions contrasts with the implications of sexuality, transgression and alienation suggested by their opposite – the female nudes isolated in dingy interiors which made the works of his contemporaries Sickert and Steer far more controversial at the time. It is telling that Tuke's only picture of nudes to be rejected by the Royal Academy was the very heterosexual *The Mermaid's Cave* of 1896, an encounter between a nude boy and a mermaid on a beach. His all-male subjects did not arouse such indignation, but were instead well received, *All Hands to the Pumps* of 1889 (Tate) and August Blue of 1894 (Tate) were both purchased by the Chantrey Bequest for the nation, and *Ruby, Gold and Malachite* of 1902 by the Corporation of London.

The intimacy and directness of Tuke's approach to the body is the single most striking feature of his work. Tuke was unusual in the nineteenth century for treating his models as friends rather than as professionals hired for a job, and his respect for the individuality of his sitters not only comes across in his subject pictures but also in the head studies he produced of local lads, such as the searching portraits of Jack Rolling and William Martin in the RCPS collection. As an exponent of plein air naturalism Tuke was a key contributor to the development of Impressionism in Britain, and both his radical technique and brilliant colour established his reputation as a progressive, a painter who affiliated himself more with the French avant-garde and with alternative exhibiting organisations such as the New English Art Club than with the conservative Royal Academy. In making Falmouth his base, Tuke was also in tune with the Post-Impressionist tendency to work in rural areas in order to obtain an intensity of vision based on a fresh, even naive encounter with nature.

The pictures by Tuke in the Royal Cornwall Polytechnic Society form the largest publicly owned collection of the artist's work in the United Kingdom, spanning his entire career from Slade studies to mature maritime pieces, portraits and nude compositions. The collection is comprised of several gifts, the most significant being the works donated by Brian Price, who gave the other half of his collection (the artist's photographs, sketchbooks, diaries and registers) to Tate in 1990. Both this catalogue and the papers in the Tate Archive provide invaluable sources of information for scholars and members of the public interested in exploring the context in which Tuke worked, not just the locations of his paintings and his relationships with his models, but his artistic allegiances such as his deep friendship with the painter Thomas Cooper Gotch. The catalogue is of further significance in demonstrating the variety of media in which Tuke worked: oil, watercolour, pastel and etching, as well as showing that Tuke was more than a painter of naked young men - his repertoire encompassing portraits, topographical views and marine subjects – all of which disclose his preoccupation with fluctuating patterns of light and colour. He is an artist who deserves more widespread recognition.

Alison Smith
Curator and Head of Acquisitions,
British Art to 1900,
Tate Britain

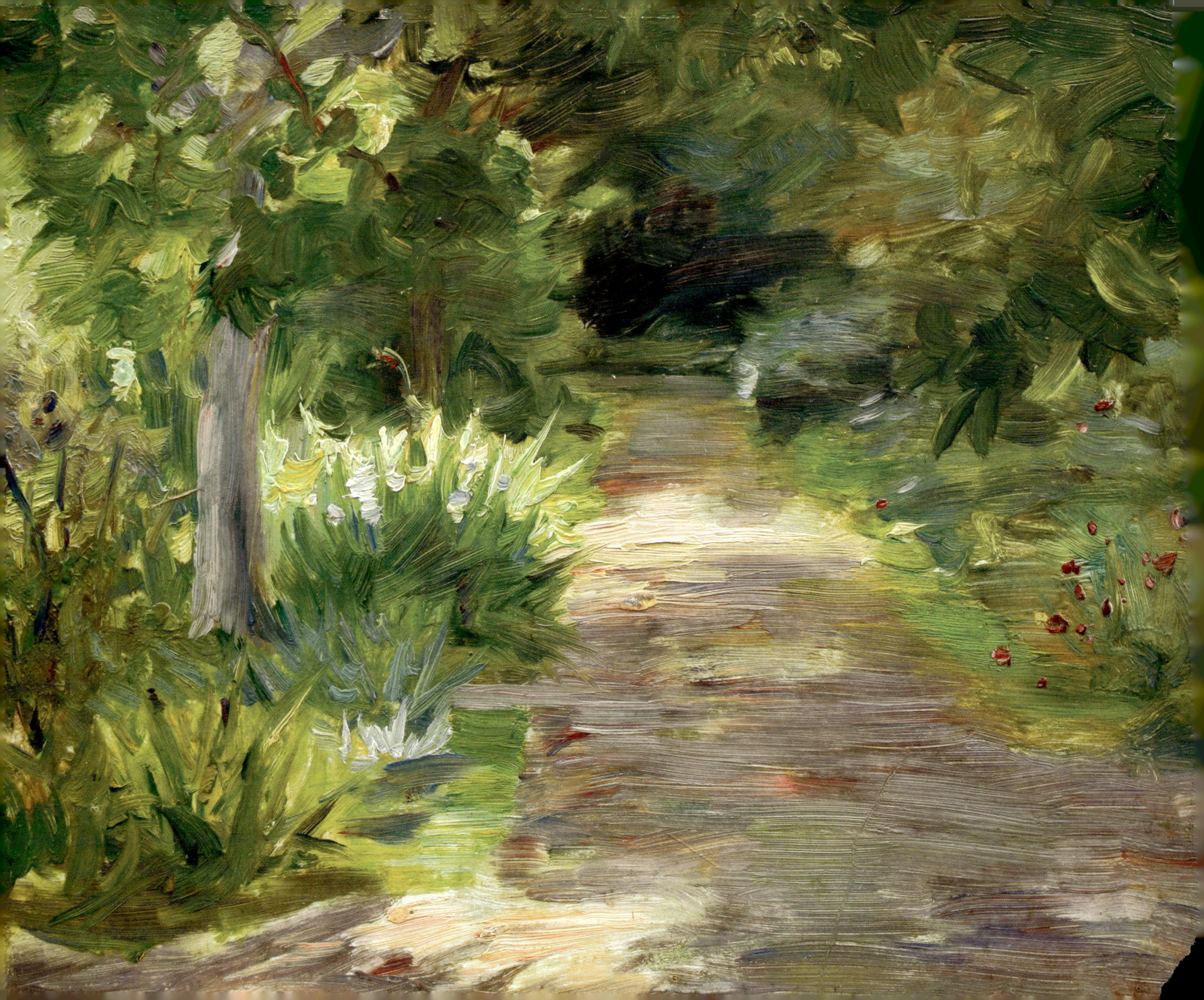

Foreword

The Royal Cornwall Polytechnic Society's collection of the paintings of Henry Scott Tuke (1858-1929) is the largest in public ownership. This Catalogue prepared by Catherine Wallace records all 277 works in the collection, largely the generous gift of Brian Price. It contains oils, watercolours, pastels, etchings and drawings whose execution spans the whole of Tuke's artistic life.

Although sadly neglected for many years after his death, Tuke's importance as a distinguished British Impressionist with his own unique contribution to British art can no longer be ignored. Today he is not only of importance to Cornwall, but nationally and internationally as his works are eagerly sought by galleries and collectors alike.

Tuke's work captures the beauty of that idyllic late Victorian and Edwardian period which was to disappear for ever with the First World War. Although he earned his living through portrait painting, it is with his pictures of ships in Falmouth harbour at the end of the golden age of sail and of naked youths, who would soon face the horrors of the trenches, that he will always be associated.

Unlike many of the Newlyn school of which he was at first a member, Tuke knew Cornwall from earliest childhood; and it was his love of the great bay at Falmouth that after two years drew him away from West Penwith to paint the varied shipping in the harbour, often from his floating studio, the *'Julie of Nantes'*, and the youths on the quiet beaches below his cottage at Pennance Point on the outskirts of Falmouth, his home until his death.

The result is a series of paintings whose warmth, vitality and freshness capture the senses with Tuke's dazzling use of light on sky, sea and flesh. Even if there is about the subject matter an inevitable nostalgia for a world long vanished, the colours of the Cornish waters, rocks and sand captured so brilliantly by Tuke remain to entice the visitor to-day.

Tuke's paintings were not confined to Cornwall, and the Catalogue records many executed on his frequent travels in the United Kingdom and abroad, including his post-war visit to the West Indies where his colouring reached a startling brilliance not seen in earlier works.

While his maritime paintings dominate his output, it is his portrayal of youth which remains his distinct contribution to British art. He was not afraid to express his subject's physical beauty, but always with sensitivity avoiding cheap sensuality. Despite some suggestive poses, there is in the paintings an idealised purity typical of Classical art, which is why it was so warmly recognised in his lifetime and remains so to-day.

It is the Royal Cornwall Polytechnic Society's hope that this Catalogue, which depicts works from all five decades of Tuke's artistic life, will make this unique collection accessible to a wide audience, and be of value to galleries, academic institutions, students, collectors and all who love the beauty of good art. It also indicates beyond doubt that Henry Scott Tuke deserves today that international reputation that is rightly his due, confirmed in his lifetime by his election as a Royal Academician and an Associate of the Royal Watercolour Society.

Anthony Phillips
Chairman, Royal Cornwall Polytechnic Society

opposite: Lyndon Lodge Garden (A65)

The Origins of the Collection

Brian D. Price

The very first Tuke painting I acquired, the watercolour *The Seagirt Wood*, I bought by post from a Japanese dealer, for £15 on 19 May 1962. Those were the palmy days when I advertised for Tukes in Exchange and Mart! In this way I bought *The Missionary Boat* in 1963 for £25. In all, it produced eleven of Tuke's works.

In July the same year I bought some Tuke paintings from John Maggs' shop in Falmouth. They had come from Tuke's model Charlie Mitchell, who had recently died. Other Tuke-bearing shops were Peter Jackson's (Falmouth) and W. Dyer's (Camborne). Over his novelty shop Dyer had a little-known art gallery which was a gold mine of Cornish artists' works in the 1960s. I wish I could turn the clock back and harvest those Newlyn School pictures at such minuscule prices.

The Beginning

I had first become interested in Henry Scott Tuke in 1961, having seen some of his paintings reproduced in Royal Academy Pictures of the Year, such as *August Blue* and *All Hands to the Pumps*. That year I found a copy of Maria Tuke Sainsbury's 1933 memoir on her brother in a second-hand bookshop in Colchester, which I bought for 10/6d and still have. The book fascinated me, as obviously there was a great deal more to find out about the artist than I had realised. It was largely based on Tuke's diaries – where were they now? I was challenged to find out.

The start was to go to Maria's address in Hampstead, mentioned in the memoir, and enquire. I discovered an elderly lady living nearby who had known her, but the only clue she had to offer was that Maria's son Geoffrey Sainsbury had translated some of Maigret's novels from the French. I sent him a letter via the publishers, and eventually went to see him and saw a large number of Tuke works (none big, mostly unframed sketches), and many associated photographs.

Help from Tuke's Relatives

When Tuke died in 1929, the works in his studio at Swanpool had been bequeathed to Maria's four children, Hester, William, Geoffrey, and Philip. Their father Harrington Sainsbury was a medical doctor living in Wimpole Street, then the family home. The four organised a Memorial Exhibition at Cooling's Gallery, Bond Street, in order to sell their paintings, but it was not a financial success owing to the Depression. They needed many of their good pictures to be framed for the exhibition, cash was tight, and they bartered unframed sketches for having pictures framed at the picture-framers Henry Shemilt in Seymour Place, not far from Wimpole Street. This exhibition, I conjecture, was instrumental in creating an unsold cache of 33 of their father's works.

In December 1963 I visited Geoffrey Sainsbury in Hampstead and purchased nine Tukes from him for £38. Afterwards I drove up to Nottingham, where I called on a nephew of Hereward Tresidder, a Falmouth friend of Tuke's. He possessed a Tuke oil painting, and told me rashly that he had spoken to Henry Shemilt, who thought he had some Tuke sketches somewhere. I hared off down the M1 in my dormobile, sleeping somewhere on a side road. It was cold, eggs froze solid, and I had an early-morning visit from the police.

On Christmas Eve I called on Shemilt, who was as vague as he had been with Tresidder, but I engaged him in conversation about Tuke. He disappeared down to his cellar, and brought up that unsold cache of 33 unframed Tukes. I bought the lot for £99, which stretched my resources. One was a portrait sketch for *August Blue*. I bought two more Tukes from a son who was running the Shemilt shop in 1966.

Years later I was told by someone in Falmouth that Tuke had left instructions for his unsigned works to be destroyed after his death, and some were on a bonfire from which that person had salvaged several; but the Shemilt cache, and Geoffrey's residue, showed that those instructions were not completed.

Geoffrey also had Tuke's two manuscript registers of his paintings, and two of his diaries. Avoiding point-blank questioning, I never succeeded in finding out what might have happened to the many other diaries. The registers were on loan to another Tuke-devotee, Glyn Ward, and I had a fruitful task assisting their return. I bought from him a number of Tuke's works, some from Geoffrey's brother Willy, and Glyn gave me one which Geoffrey had given him. Geoffrey gave me all his Tuke registers, which are now in the Tate Gallery Archives, and are frequently consulted by researchers.

Another relative I found was Malcolm Cruickshank, son of Sarah Maria Tylor who was a cousin of the artist. He had his mother's priceless volume of *The Heatherbell Club*, the creation of eight teenage siblings and cousins, including Tuke and his brother and sister, and Sarah. They had hand-bound miscellanies of handwritten stories and poems, sketches and watercolours, with nom-de-plume attributions including *Anther* (HST), *Calyx, Corolla, Pedicel, Root, Sap, Stem*. They must have produced eight copies of everything to make a volume for each member. On my second visit to Malcolm I got as far as photographing the drawings and watercolours for eleven 35mm colour slides, but later attempts to revisit or persuade Malcolm's descendants to photocopy the whole volume failed.

I visited Geoffrey's sister Hester Etchells and her husband twice in 1964-65.

Frederick Etchells had started off as a well-known *vorticist* artist, but he diverted to being a church architect. Hester very kindly gave me a collection of Tuke's juvenilia and three small watercolours, all now in the Tuke Collection. I took to her several of the Shemilt purchases for identifying, one of which was an oils panel of a still-life with an embroidered cloth. That cloth had been her mother's, it was Indian, and she gave it to me.

In 1968 there was a windfall! Geoffrey's brother William Tuke Sainsbury, who had died in 1960 shortly before I came on the scene, had been a golf professional, living in the club-house at Burnham Beeches. That year a dozen or more Tukes were discovered there, secreted in a cupboard under a staircase, and were sent to Geoffrey. They were superior to the remnants which had remained with him, and I bought most of them (by then I was having competition from dealers). Two of them were the fantastically impressionist watercolours *Quay Scamps* and *Scots Guards on Parade*. Fancy buying *Quay Scamps* for a mere guinea! (I never haggled with Geoffrey). After Geoffrey's death, his widow Antoinette told me that a dealer had never paid for several pictures he had bought, but I failed to see what could be done about it, with no written proof.

In 1970 I moved to London, so visiting Geoffrey Sainsbury became much easier for a few years. Over the years, I bought a great many Tukes from him. He gave me five, too, and also a number of photographs which had come from his mother and uncle. He shared what I paid him with Hester, his surviving sibling. Having the pictures framed then was more expensive than buying the pictures themselves!

I last saw Geoffrey in the Royal Free Hospital, Hampstead shortly before he died in 1973. Antoinette survived him, and gave me more photographs (all now in the Tate Gallery Archives). She had a number of quite large unframed watercolours, and offered to give me some, but I thought it not right to accept them, as she was failing. I gathered later that they were destroyed along with other of her possessions, as they were not found by her relatives.

Descendants of Tuke's Friends

I found Sally Jackett, widow of Tuke's model John Jackett, in a bedsit in Islington and she came to live in my bungalow at Tresillian. She gave me her two Tukes. I discovered at Shellingford village a Miss Marshall, from whom I bought three Tukes for a pittance. She had been one of a family who were friends of Tuke, and with whom he had stayed as their guest at Chithurst.

Finally I must mention perhaps the most important Tuke I managed to acquire in all my years of searching. Thomas Cooper Gotch had been at the Slade with Tuke and they became lifelong friends. He had been engaged to Tuke's sister Maria but it was broken off diplomatically, and he married the artist Caroline Yates. Eventually Gotch built Wheal Betsy, a house on Paul Hill, Newlyn, which in the 1960s I discovered was the home of his granddaughter

Deirdre Maclellan. It was from Deirdre that I bought *Our Jack* for £100 (an arm and a leg then) which had been Tuke's wedding present to her grandparents, also etchings of Slade vintage, two certainly by Tuke. Slade Professor Alphonse Legros had been keen on etchings.

Why Tuke?

In hindsight, I believe there have been two reasons for my motivation in collecting Tukes. First and foremost, the beauty and strong subjectivity of his works – just look at the masterly impressionism of watercolours like *Quay Scamps*, in which nevertheless one has no doubt about what they represent – and the intimate feeling put into his portraits. The pittance I paid for the paintings was unimportant to me.

I have always been fascinated by quests to discover things for myself – other long-standing interests still occupy me. Friends have accused me of a 'fixation' about Tuke. One can't have a number of simultaneous fixations!

And why for the Poly?

First, because Falmouth was Tuke's home, and also because earlier in his life he supported the Poly well. In 1899 he was elected Vice President, and when he was elected an Associate of the Royal Academy, the Poly held a banquet in his honour.

Principally I wanted the collection to stay together. This hasn't always been plane sailing, and I am pleased and relieved that a new recognition of the importance of Tuke's work has conserved the collection and produced this catalogue. I hope that the recent awakening of constructive interest in his works heralds emancipation from previous prudery, and ensures the continued preservation of our Tuke Collection.

The works of
Henry Scott Tuke RA RWS

Childhood works

Henry Scott Tuke was born in York on 12 June 1858 to a Quaker family. His great great grandfather William Tuke (1732-1822) founded the Friends' Retreat for 'persons afflicted with disorders of the mind', at York in 1796. William's son Henry Tuke (1755-1814) became a tea-dealer and importer, and married Mary Maria Scott of Norwich (1748-1815) in 1781. This couple with their son, Samuel (1784-1857), carried on the philanthropic works of William, helping to establish Quaker Schools in York and caring for the poor and sick. Samuel's wife Priscilla Hack (1784-1828), daughter of James Hack of Chichester, helped Samuel with all these endeavours and had 13 children, the youngest of whom was Daniel Hack Tuke (1827-1895), Henry Scott Tuke's father. Daniel studied medicine and became a member of the Royal College of Surgeons in 1852. He progressed to be a leading authority on mental health. He married Esther Maria Stickney (1826-1917) in 1853 and they had two sons, William Samuel in 1856 and Henry Scott (known as Harry to friends and family) in 1858.

From the age of two, Harry with his family moved to Falmouth in Cornwall. Their first house was in Woodlane, where Maria was born in 1861. They then moved to Florence Terrace and later back to Woodlane, to a larger house. Tuke's parents were well read and interested in everything from literature to politics. Dr Tuke studied philosophy and psychology and he was a staunch Liberal, while Tuke's mother loved singing and poetry and apparently had a caustic sense of humour. They both made friends easily.

These strong-minded individuals had a big influence on Tuke's development. He too was a Liberal; he loved literature and poetry and became a great socialite. These early days in Falmouth were to supply Tuke with long-lasting happy memories that possibly drew him back to live in Falmouth later in life. Governesses and a tutor taught him and his brother privately until 1872 when they were sent to Irwin Sharp's Friends' School at Weston-super-Mare. As well as lessons, other occupations for Tuke included collecting stamps (a hobby he continued in later life), bathing, croquet, long walks, collecting butterflies, visiting friends' houses and of course, drawing and painting.

The Tuke Collection includes 14 works from Tuke's juvenilia period, all with family provenance.

According to his sister, Tuke's letters from school 'were always full of little drawings'. These included many sketches of ships which he had seen coming in to Falmouth Bay. His early artistic talent probably convinced his parents and himself of his future career.

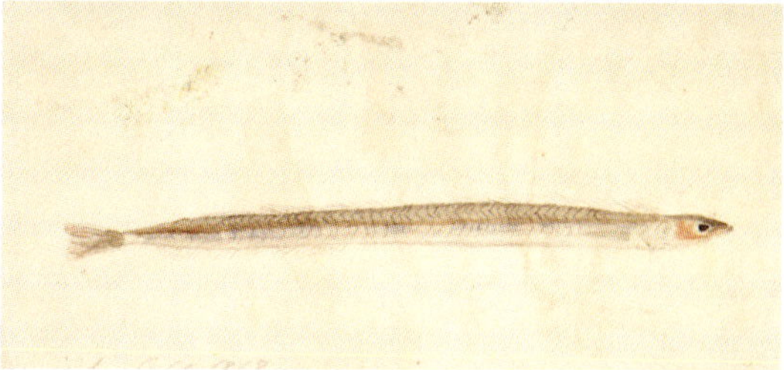

Gersick, Sept.1868
Watercolour and pencil, 9.6 x 20.5cm
Inscribed and dated bottom left: Gersick Sept.1868
Provenance: Given to the Tuke Collection by Hester Sainsbury 27 June1964
RCPS Tuke Collection A225

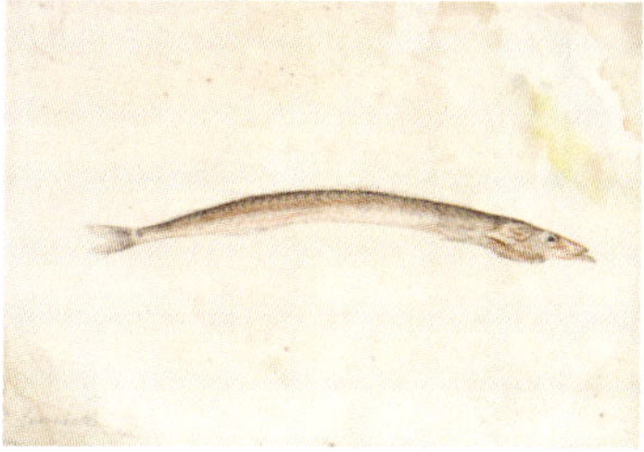

Gersick and Harry's Fish, c.1868
Watercolour and pencil, 14 x 19.6cm
Inscribed bottom left: Guersick (sic)
Inscribed on verso: HARRY'S FISH
Provenance: Given to the Tuke Collection by Hester Sainsbury 27 June 1964
RCPS Tuke Collection A226

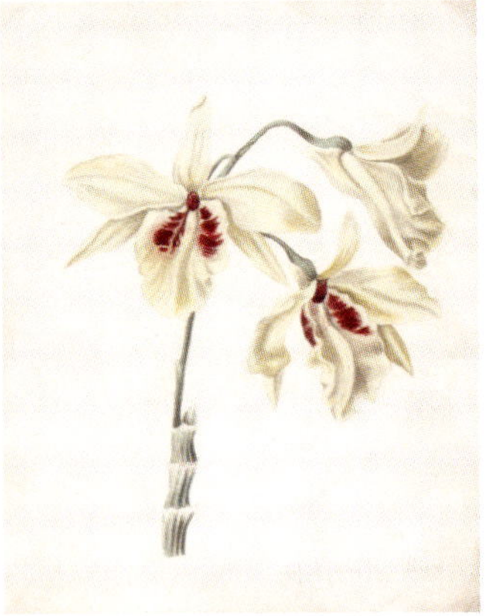

An Orchid, December 1872

Watercolour, 22.9 x 17.5cm
Inscribed bottom right: Copied from Mrs. Ellis
Provenance: Given to the Tuke Collection by Hester Sainsbury
27 June 1968
RCPS Tuke Collection A230

As well as studying art at school, according to his sister Maria, Henry was influenced by their neighbour in Woodlane, Falmouth, Rachael Tregelles, who had been Head of the Friends' Girls' School at York. Maria said, 'She would set us to paint a flower, saying "Paint, dear, paint," which in some mysterious way inspired us to do it.' M.T.Sainsbury p.20*

***Henry Scott Tuke: A Memoir,* M.T. Sainsbury, Martin Secker, London 1933

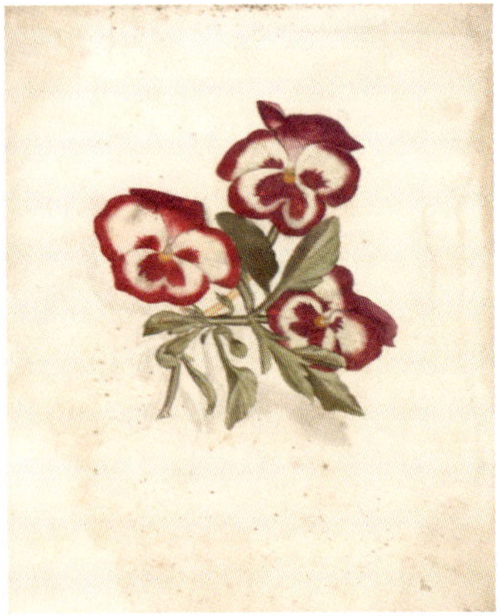

Pansies, 1872

Watercolour, 23 x 17.8cm
Signed in Tuke's nom-de-plume "Phidias" (in Greek) on verso
Inscribed on reverse: *Midsummer Nights Dream Act11 Sc11.*
'It falls (sic) upon a little western flower Before milk white; now purple with love's wound And maidens call it "love in idleness" That is the pansy Calpeppers Botany.'
Provenance: Given to the Tuke Collection by Hester Sainsbury
27 June 1964
RCPS Tuke Collection A229

This picture was painted when Tuke was 14 years old and still studying at school.

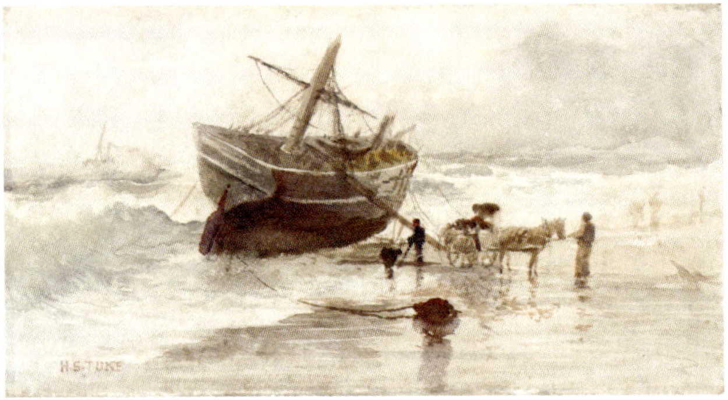

The Wreck

Watercolour, 13 x 24cm
Signed bottom left: H.S.TUKE
Provenance: Purchased from Norman Hall, Newquay
27 Dec 1964
Acquired from W.H. Lane's, Penzance
RCPS Tuke Collection A227

THE SLADE 1875-1879

On January 25th 1875 Tuke entered the Slade School of Fine Art in London at the age of 16. According to his sister Maria, there was much discussion in the family when he left school in 1874 as to his future, but being an artist, for a man, was seen as an acceptable profession by his parents. They did not think it was for a woman, as they denied Maria the opportunity to study there.

'Mr. Poynter A.R.A., is the professor, Mr. Slinger and Mr. Jackson are the assistant professors. There are about 30 students in the Antique room, both male and female, the latter being about three times as numerous. Most of the ladies look somewhat strongminded, and a great many have spectacles, which give them a somewhat imposing appearance.' M.T. Sainsbury p.24.

Tuke's years at the Slade were to be deeply significant to the rest of his life and career as a painter, for it was here that he formed strong friendships with his fellow students such as Thomas Cooper Gotch (1854-1931), George Percy Jacomb-Hood (1857-1929), William Strang (1859-1921) and Walter Dalrymple (1854-1920).

In the academic year 1874/5 he obtained his certificate in Fine Art, Anatomy. In 1875/6 he gained a certificate in General Proficiency in Fine Art and in 1876/7 he not only gained his certificate in painting from the Antique, but he also won First Prize in drawing from the Antique. He came second in Composition.

Works in the RCPS Tuke Collection from 1876-1879 show contrasting styles, which seem to vary according to the medium used. Each term there was a set subject, which Tuke usually undertook in watercolour/body colour. These are early, somewhat naive attempts at using this particular medium, but they allowed him to study composition and light. It is in his drawing and particularly his portraits, which were then translated into etchings, that Tuke's talent as a draughtsman is really seen. In 1876, the French painter and master etcher Alphonse Legros (1837-1911) succeeded Poynter as the Slade's Professor. It was under his influence that many of the students gained the experience of drawing from life and learning etching techniques.

Tuke gained his certificate for drawing from life in 1877/78 and won second prize, equal with Robert Morley, for anatomical drawing. He also gained his certificate in etching that year, and the following year won first prize in etching.

In May 1877 Tuke was one of only two students per year to win the coveted Slade Scholarship which was worth £50 for 3 years.

It was entering the life room, painting directly from the model, that Tuke obviously found his special subject, as the stunning painting in the collection *Portrait of A Youth,* May 1877 (A18) shows. In 1878/79 he gained his certificate and won second prize in painting from life, shared with William Strang. The RCPS Collection has a bold, very accurate portrait etching of Strang (A16) undertaken by Tuke in his student years at the Slade.

A recent gift to the Collection (2006) by B.D. Price of *Seated Nude study* (A253) attributed to Tuke is thought to be one of his paintings from the life model undertaken while at the Slade.

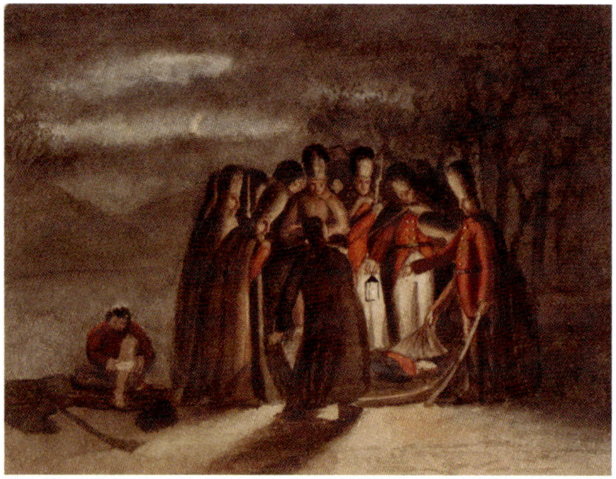

The Burial of Sir John Moore, April 1876
Watercolour, 17.6 x 22.6cm
Skull symbol on reverse in pencil top left inscribed: SKULL xxx, Burial of Sir John Moore subject for April 1876 Original (not quite finished)
Provenance: Gift to the Tuke Collection by Hester Sainsbury
27 June 1964
RCPS Tuke Collection A232

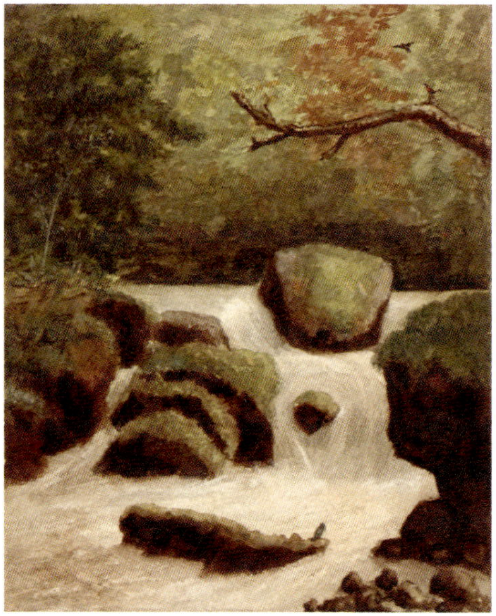

By Fountain, Shade and Rill, November 1876
Watercolour, 22.5 x 17.6cm
Skull symbol and dated on reverse: November 1876
Inscribed on reverse: By Fountain shade and rill. Lycidas Subject for November 1876
From Nature (from a sketch of same)
Provenance: Gift to the Tuke Collection by Hester Sainsbury
27 June 1964
RCPS Tuke Collection A234

In 1876 Tuke visited his relatives, firstly for a month at Saffron Walden, and then to Hull and Danthorpe for a month where he went sketching. He then went to relatives in York, before ending his journey at Exeter, where he stayed with his great uncle George Mennell (M.T.S p.27). From here Harry and Willy Tuke went on a walking tour of north Devon to Clevedon, returning home on 2 October. The sketch from which this painting is taken was probably undertaken either in Hull, or more likely in Devon, as the colours used are clearly autumnal.

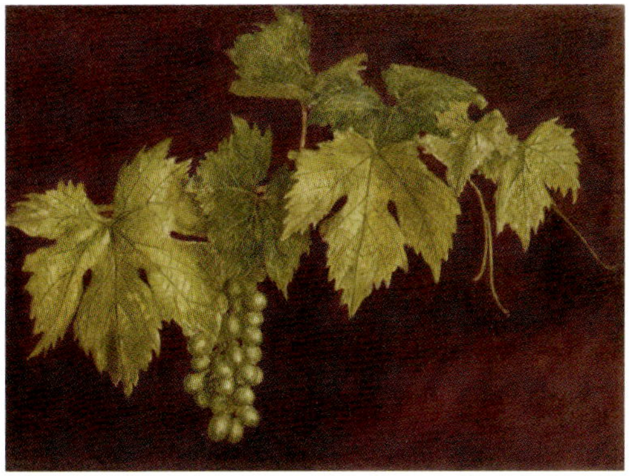

Design for a fan, 1876

Watercolour, 17.5 x 23cm
Skull symbol on reverse dated top right: 1876
Inscribed: Original drawing for a fan subject for October 1876 from Nature
Provenance: Gift to the Tuke Collection by Hester Sainsbury 27 June 1964
RCPS Tuke Collection A233

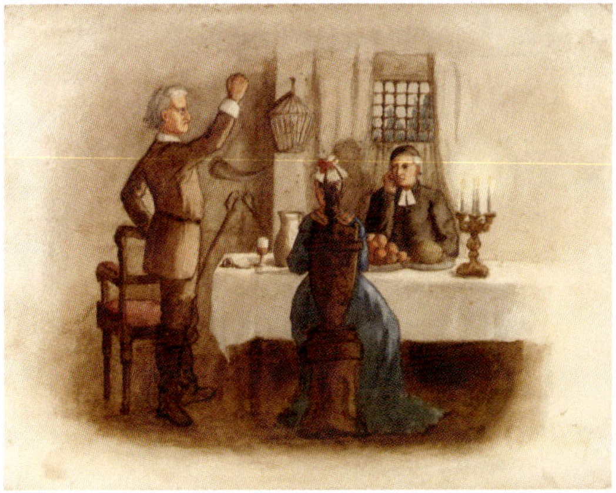

Thus he spake to his guests, January 1877

Watercolour, 17.8 x 22.9cm
Skull symbol on reverse
Inscribed on reverse: Original *'Thus he spake to his guests… After your houses are built and your fields are yellow with harvest No King George of England shall drive you away from your homesteads Burning your dwellings and barns, stealing your farms and your cattle Evanglim Pt.II'* Subject for Jan.1877
Provenance: Gift to the Tuke Collection by Hester Sainsbury 27 June 1964
RCPS Tuke Collection A235

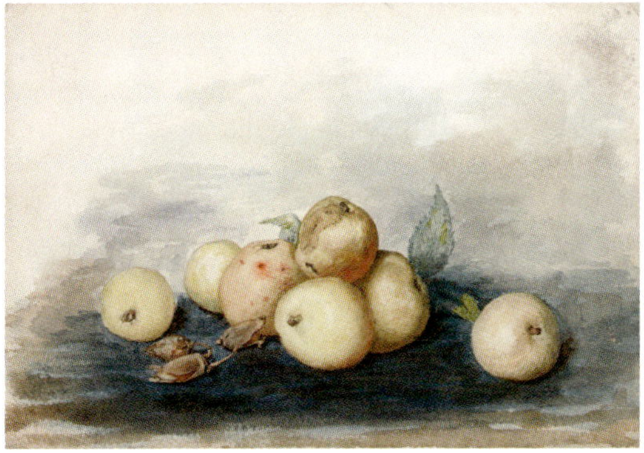

Fruit from Nature, November 1877

Watercolour, 17.8 x 25.5cm
Skull symbol on reverse
Inscribed on reverse: Fruit from Nature subject for November 1877
Provenance: Gift to the Tuke Collection by Hester Sainsbury 27 June 1964
RCPS Tuke Collection A236

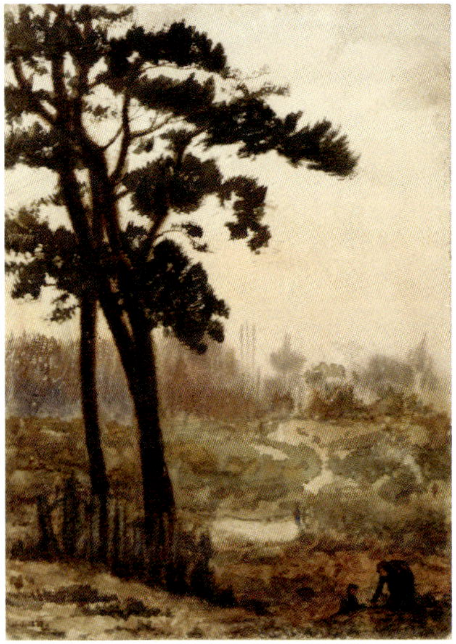

Something Old, December 1877

Watercolour, 25.1 x 17.5cm
Dated bottom left: Dec.1.1877
Skull symbol on reverse and inscribed: Something Old. Subject for December 1877
Some old trees on Hampstead Heath from Nature
Provenance: Gift to the Tuke Collection by Hester Sainsbury 27 June 1964
RCPS Tuke Collection A237

Tuke liked to go sketching on Hampstead Heath; he would often draw the tramps sleeping rough, as well as the trees and surrounding landscape. See Tuke's sketchbook of 1877 in the Tate Archive. TGA9019/1/3.

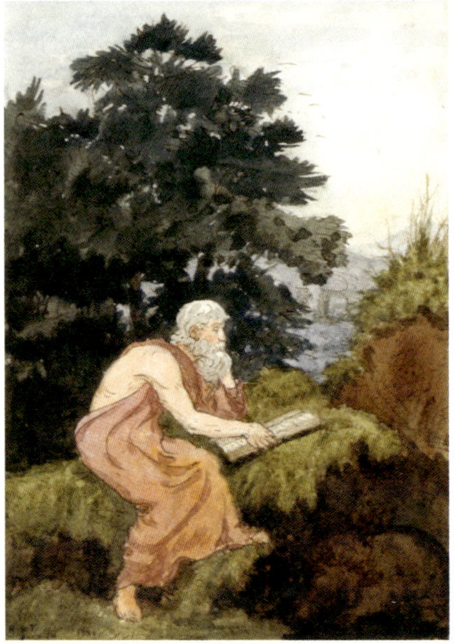

Saint Jerome, 1878

Watercolour, 25.5 x 17.9cm
Inscribed, initialled, and dated bottom left: Saint Jerome H.S.T. 78
Skull drawing and inscribed on reverse: Design for a window subject for July 78
Provenance: Gift to the Tuke Collection by Hester Sainsbury 27 June 1964
RCPS Tuke Collection A240

In July 1878 Tuke went on his second trip abroad to Normandy with Arthur Jacob Tanner (1857 - 1916). They went to Rouen where he drew the cathedral, and then to Bayeux. He went walking and wrote to his sister, 'Walked seventeen miles through a pleasant country; the peasants are a lovely Titian colour.' M.T.S. p.30.

This painting of St. Jerome has something of the Old Master colouring and religious subject matter which were clearly preoccupying Tuke in his artistic tastes at the time.

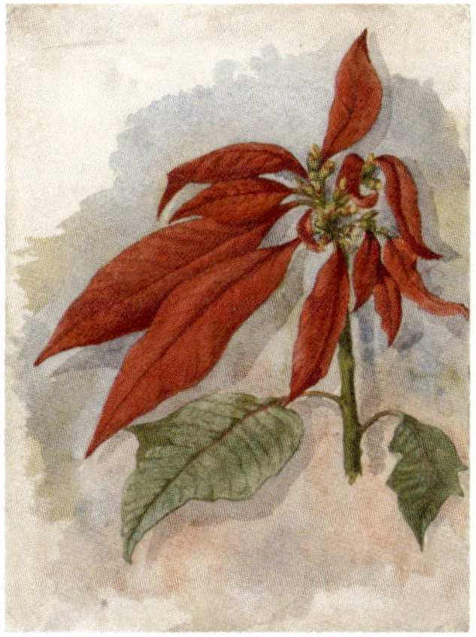

Flowers from nature, January 1878

Watercolour, 25.5 x 18cm
Skull symbol, dated and inscribed on reverse: Flowers from Nature Subject for January 1878
Provenance: Gift to the Tuke Collection by Hester Sainsbury 27 June 1964
RCPS Tuke Collection A238

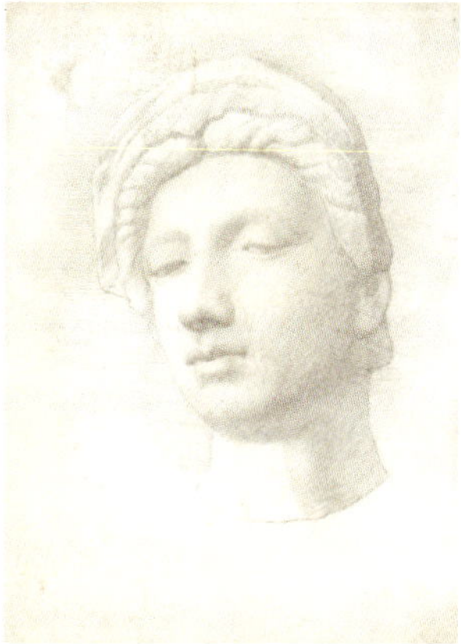

Sculpture from the Object, March 1878

Pencil on paper, 25.5 x 18cm
Skull symbol top right and inscribed on reverse: Sculpture from the Object Subject for March 1878, (Mask of Madonna by Michaelangelo)
Provenance: Gift to the Tuke Collection by Hester Sainsbury 27 June 1964
RCPS Tuke Collection A239

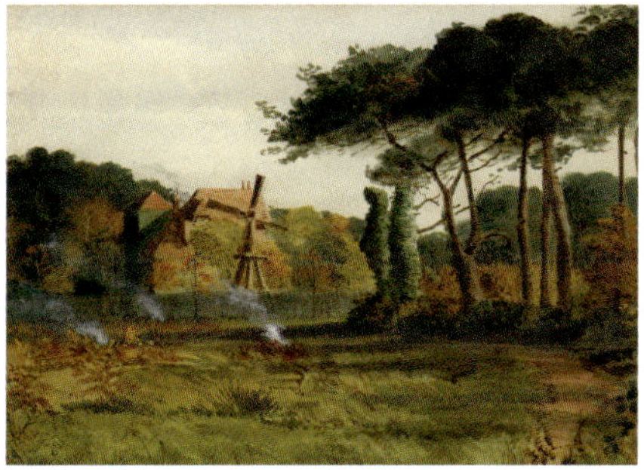

Chill October

Watercolour, 17.2 x 23.4cm
Inscribed on reverse: Felis Subject for ..oo? Chill October
Provenance: Purchased from Geoffrey Sainsbury 8 September 1968
RCPS Tuke Collection A231

Etchings

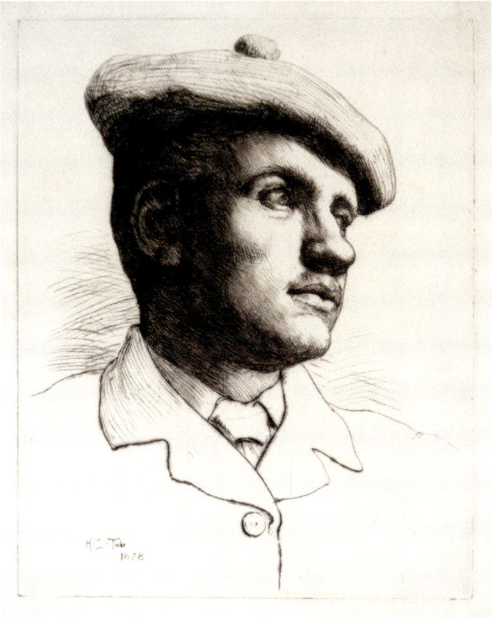

George Percy Jacomb-Hood described the etching classes at the Slade:

'Legros also rigged up the top floor of the building as an etching room, and there, every Saturday, Goulding, the "master – printer", attended, and some of us started cheerfully on spoiling many copper and zinc plates.' *With Brush and Pencil,* Jacomb-Hood, p.12. Tuke won first prize for etching at the Slade, and he possibly would have continued had he had the finances to set up a print studio.

A Highland Boy, 1878

Etching, 28.2 x 22.4cm
Signed and dated bottom left: H.S.Tuke 1878
Exhibited: The Royal Academy 1879
Provenance: Purchased from Geoffrey Sainsbury 27 February 1966
RCPS Tuke Collection A16

This is a portrait of fellow student at the Slade, William Strang (1859-1921), who became a Royal Academician and spent from 1880-1900 producing over 750 etchings and prints.

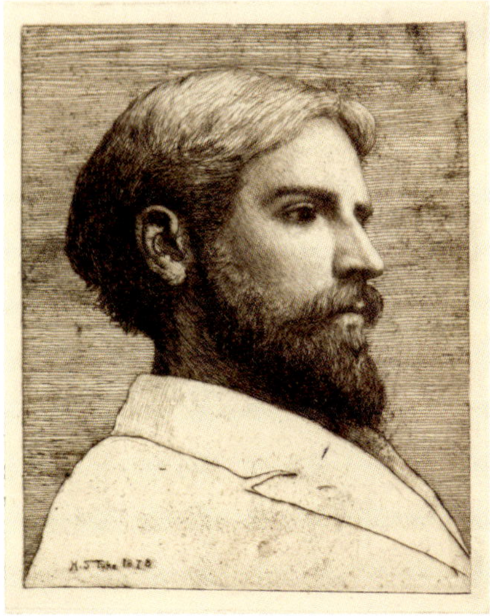

Willy Tuke, 1878

Etching, 17.4 x 13.7cm
Signed and dated bottom left: H.S.Tuke 1878
Provenance: Purchased from Mrs. D. McClellan
6 January 1965
RCPS Tuke Collection A75

This etching was probably taken from a drawing of Tuke's older brother, William Tuke (b.1856), which is reproduced in Maria Tuke Sainsbury's biography of Tuke op. cit. page 32. William Tuke was a brilliant medical student at the University College London, and studied with Harrington Sainsbury who became Maria's husband. He organised a debating society which included Tuke and Gotch and some female students from the Slade. He was however to die from tuberculosis at the age of 27 in 1883.

A Young Man, 1878

Etching, 25.2 x 19.8cm
Initialled bottom right: HST
Inscribed: Competition Summer 1878
Provenance: Purchased from Geoffrey Sainsbury
27 February 1966
RCPS Tuke Collection A88

This was an etching for a competition set by Alphonse Legros – etching master at the Slade. The model appears West Indian African in origin, the challenge to the art student presumably being how to depict a darker complexion in the medium of etching. Tuke has kept the background fairly light with the back of the head and neck in shadow, but the face is depicted as white against the semi-dark background.

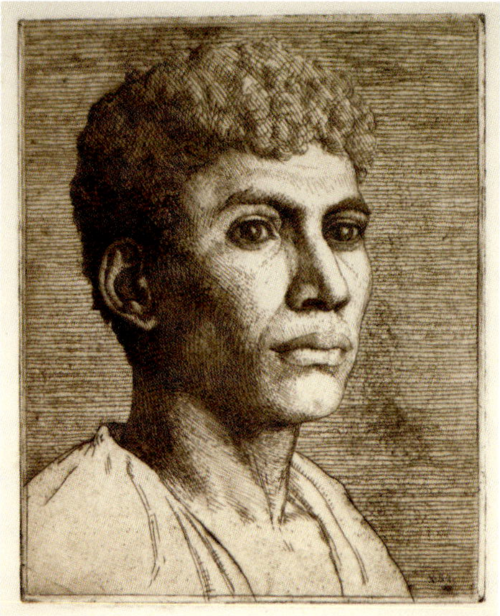

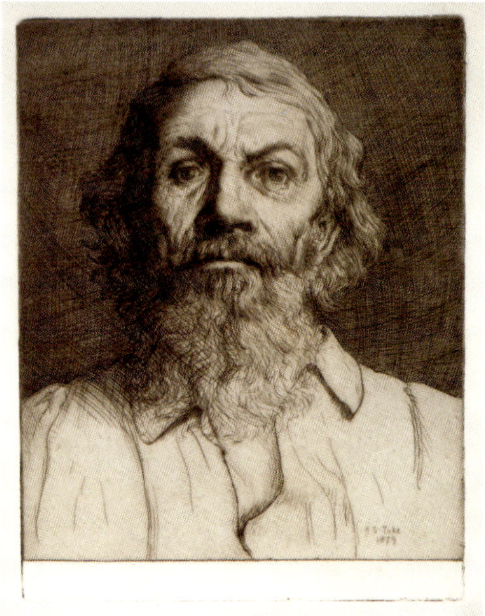

Portrait of an Old Man, 1879

Etching, 22.7 x 18.7cm
Signed and dated bottom right: H.S.Tuke 1879
Provenance: Purchased from Mrs D. McClellan
18 August 1965
RCPS Tuke Collection A74

This etching was completed while Tuke was at the Slade and was probably set by Alphonse Legros.

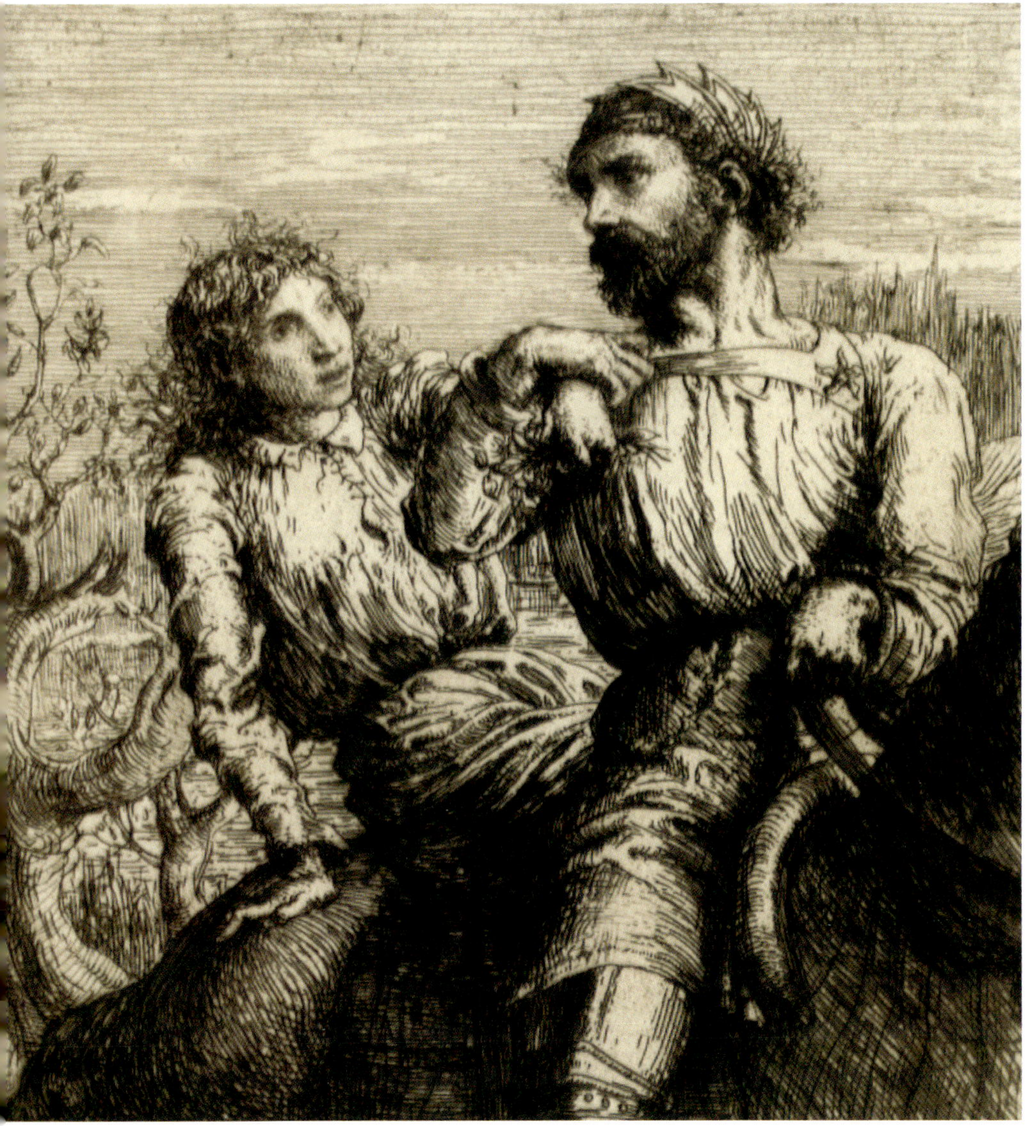

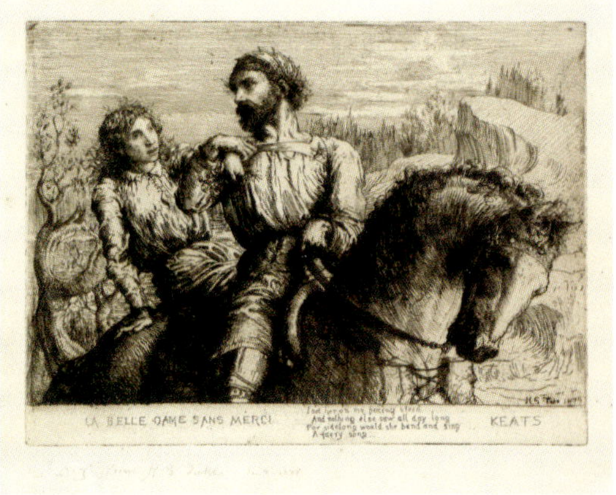

La Belle Dame Sans Merci, 1879

Etching, 14.9 x 20.2cm
Signed and dated bottom right: H.S.Tuke 1879
Inscribed underneath plate: C.B.Y. (Caroline Burland Yates) from H.S.Tuke Jan 8 1880. Inscribed on plate the title: La Belle Dame Sans Merci and a verse from the poem of the same name by Keats is written 'I set her on my pacing steed, And nothing else saw all day long, For sidelong would she bend and sing, A faery song...' Followed by the word 'KEATS'
Provenance: Purchased from Mrs. D. McClellan 6 November 1965 (Caroline Gotch (nee Yates) and T.C. Gotch's granddaughter)
RCPS Tuke Collection A76

According to George Percy Jacomb-Hood, it was he who 'propounded a great scheme of a Slade School edition of Spenser's "Faery Queene" illustrated by etchings, and persuaded my fellow-scholars Tuke, Gotch, J.B.Clark (and, I think, William Strang), to co-operate. I led off with a plate of The Gentle Knight "pryking o'er the plaine" for the first canto, and Gotch did one of La Belle Dame sans Merci, but the other fellows were so dilatory about starting that nothing came of it.' *With Brush and Pencil* p.12.

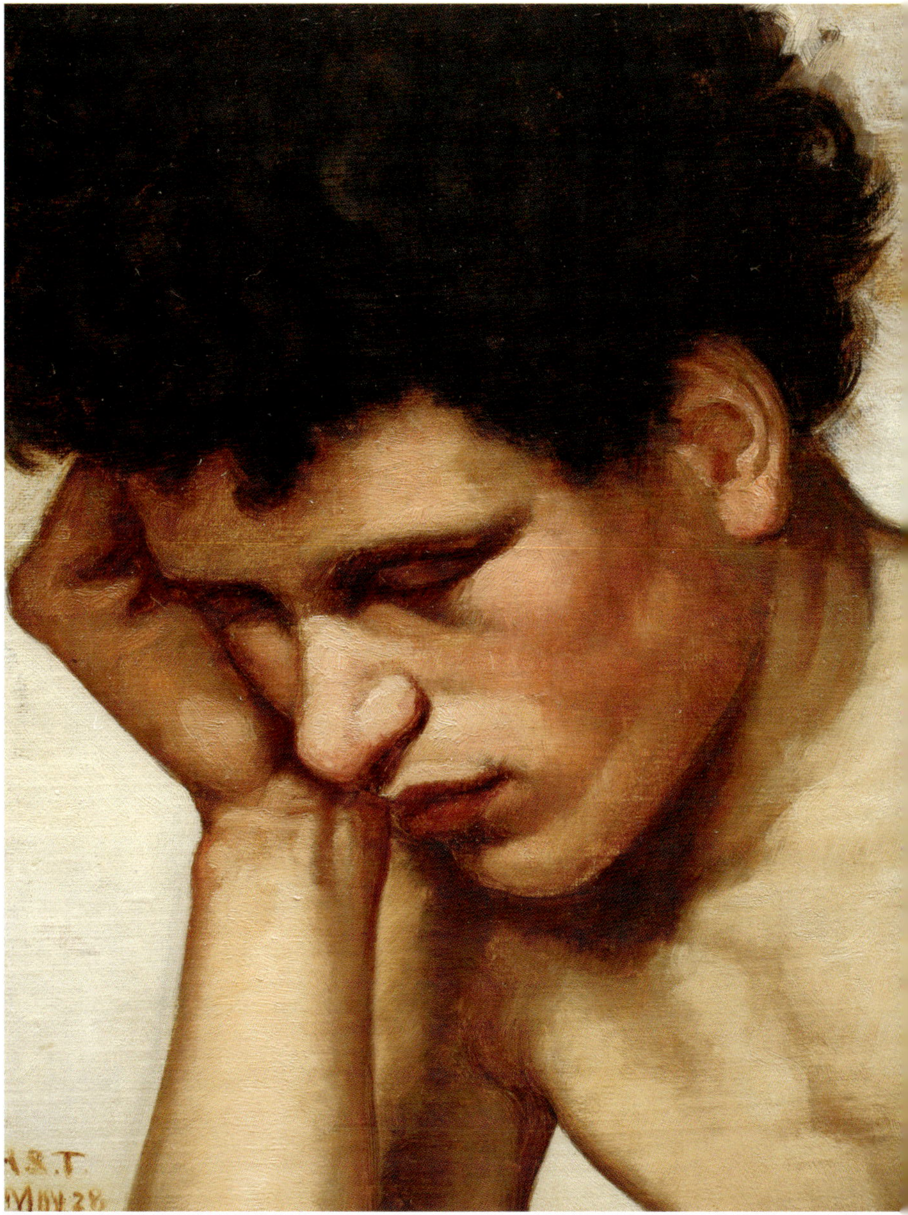

Portrait of a Youth, May 28 1877
Oil on canvas, 32 x 23.6cm
Initialled and dated bottom left: H.S.T. May 28 1877
Provenance: Purchased from Glynn Ward 1 June 1964
RCPS Tuke Collection A18

Painted while Tuke was at the Slade studying painting from life.

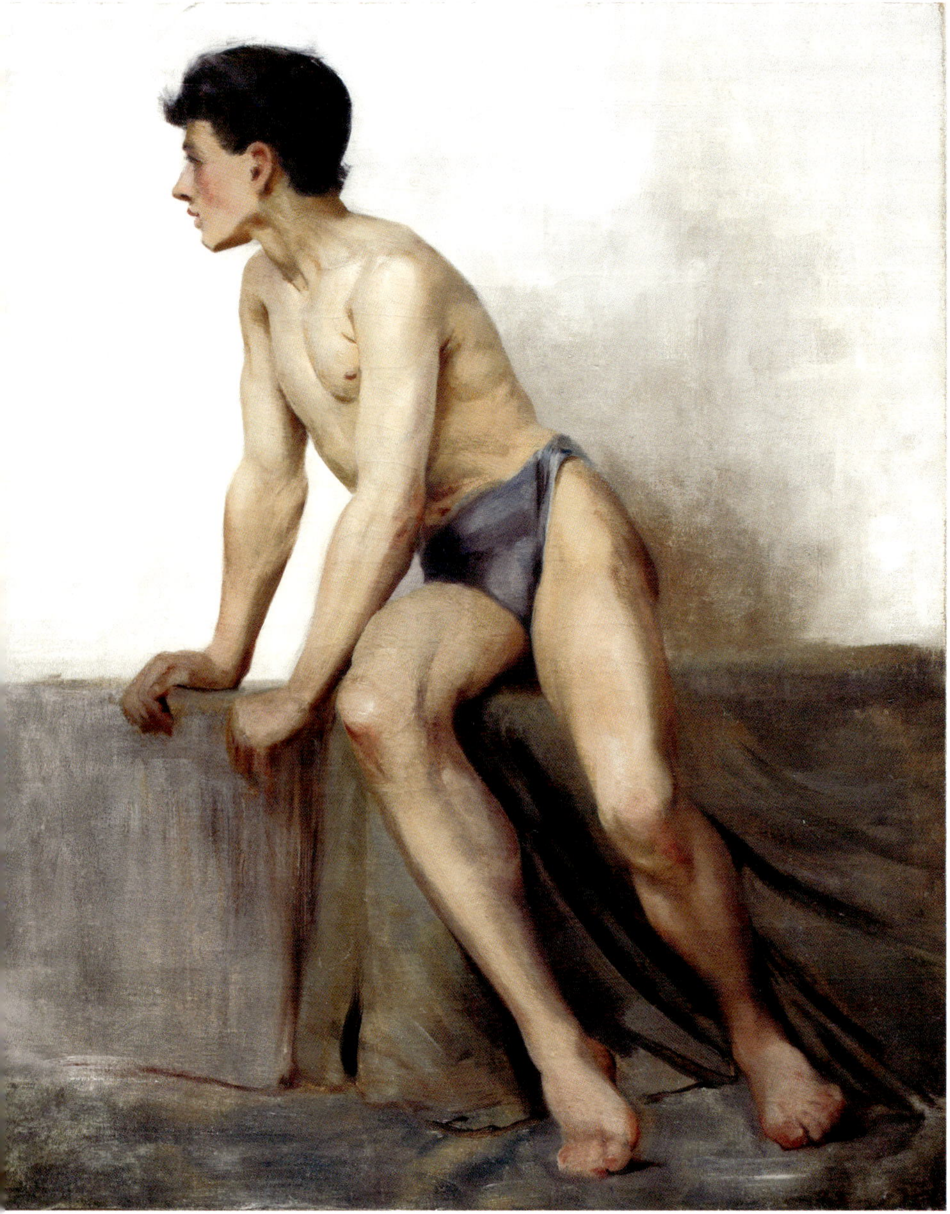

Seated Nude Study

Oil on canvas, 66 x 53cm
Provenance: Purchased from Lily Corbett,
Portobello Road, 9 March 1974
Gift to the Tuke Collection by B.D. Price
February 2006
RCPS Tuke Collection A253

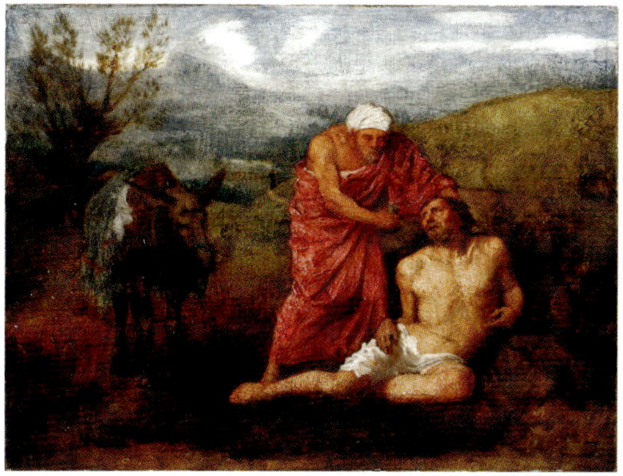

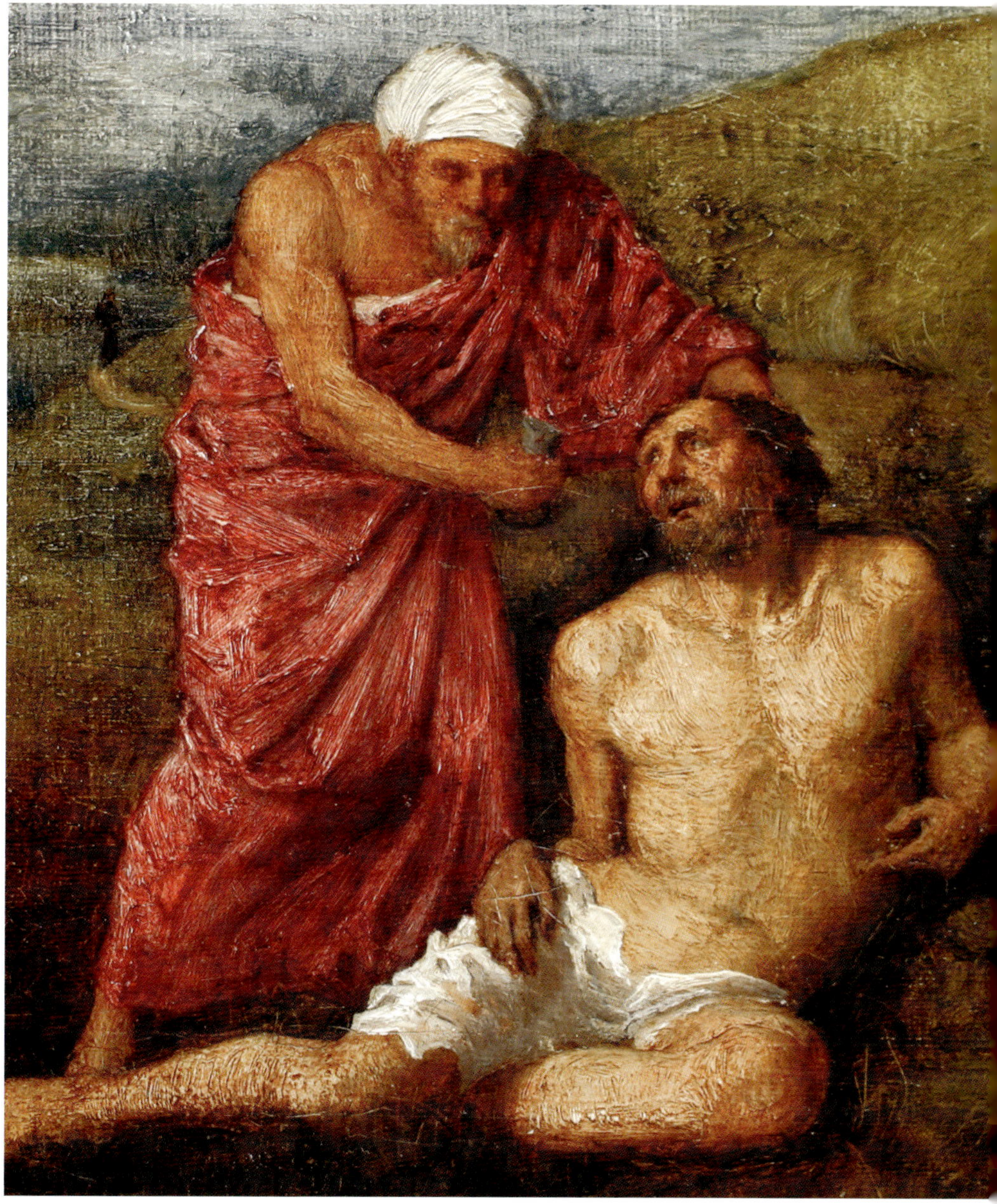

The Good Samaritan, 1879

Oil on canvas, 20.5 x 25.7cm
Signed and dated H.S.Tuke 1879 bottom left
Previous address labels on reverse: The Good Samaritan, Henry Scott Tuke 1879, 5 Provost Road N.W.3
On stretcher: H.S.Tuke. 4 Charlotte Street, Bedford Square
Exhibited: The Royal Academy 1879
Provenance: Purchased from Geoffrey Sainsbury 14 December 1967
RCPS Tuke Collection A11 R1

This is one of the important early works in the Tuke Collection – it was the first Tuke exhibited at the Royal Academy. According to Wainright and Dinn, Tuke was in later years 'much ashamed' of this painting. 'His mother, naturally was immensely proud of it and hung it where she could always see it.' *Henry Scott Tuke 1858-1929: Under Canvas*, by David Wainright and Catherine Dinn p.14.

ITALY 1880-1881

In November 1880 Tuke went to Italy to study at the Florence Academy. While there he took rooms initially at a pensione overlooking the Ponte Vecchio, 49 Via Ricasoli, and he obtained a pass allowing him to copy Old Masters from the major galleries.

Tuke found Italy an inspiration, 'subjects reek on every hand, such landscapes beyond the heart of man to conceive. The gradation of the sky is something astonishing...' Letter to T.C. Gotch 11 Feb. 1881.

He spent a great deal of time on a large painting called *The Bronzista Shop*. He wrote to his friend and fellow artist Tom Gotch, 'I have been struggling with the arrangements of my pots and pans hanging in the shop, having got all the figures in their places, I can put the "machines" just where they fit; but how to find where they fit cost me much thought. I spent two days sketching in the streets, trying to the nervous nature.' Letter dated 6 Feb 1881. Tuke even rigged up 'a sort of shed' in his studio to 'represent the shop'. While undertaking the work for this picture, which was rejected by the RA in 1881, Tuke wrote to his sister, 'I feel I must have another long spell at the nude before long, in some place where I shall not be disturbed and where models are cheap.'

While in Florence, Tuke met Arthur Lemon (1850-1912), an artist whom Tuke found 'A delightful man, I am glad I came here, if only to make his acquaintance. I don't know anyone who has influenced me so much of late years, for good let us hope.' Letter to T.C. Gotch 12 March 1881.

In June 1881, Tuke went with Arthur Lemon to the coast where they also met William Heath Wilson (1849-1947). He wrote to Maria on May 30th, 'Here we are at last by the sea. This place lies about half way between Livorno and Spezia so we are some 60 miles from Florence. It is very small and unsophisticated, there being no other visitors besides ourselves, so we just make ourselves at home in the inn...'

He spent four weeks there and he wrote again on June 16, 'We have done several nude boys on the beach which is more useful than anything for me. They sit till they are incapable of keeping still any more, and are richly repaid with 2d.' These weeks spent in Italy on the coast gave Tuke the blueprint for the lifestyle and subject of his art that he would follow for the rest of his life; that is, living the outdoor life, painting, bathing, boating and mixing with like-minded companions.

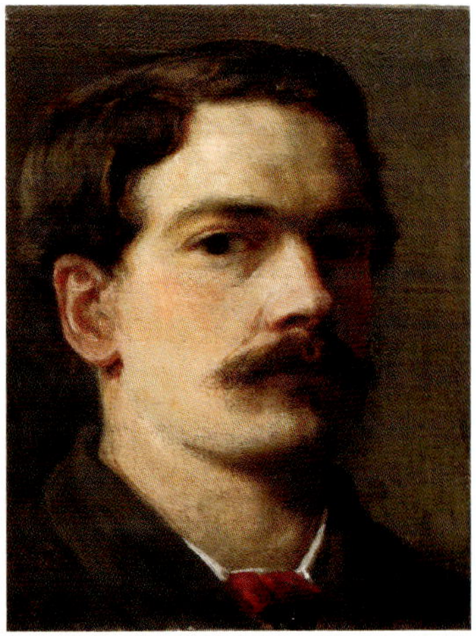

Self Portrait, 1881
Oil on canvas, 23 x 17cm
Verso: small piece of original canvas inscribed in pencil 'Florence 1881'
Provenance: Gift to Tuke Collection by Geoffrey Sainsbury 5 March 1965
RCPS Tuke Collection A6

Tuke undertook this self portrait while studying in Florence in 1881. It shows Tuke slightly sallow-skinned, which may be because he used a technique that was taught to him by a Florentine teacher Acquarolli. As he wrote to Maria, 'Had a long lecture from old Acquarolli on his theory of green underpainting (tutto verde, tutto verde, punto giallo) – Painted my portrait in the tutto verde method.' Letter 18 December 1880 M.T.S. page 47. Tuke also mentions an old man in the Academy in Florence going round the gallery telling the students how Titian painted 'tutte verde'. Letter to T.C.Gotch Dec.22 1880.

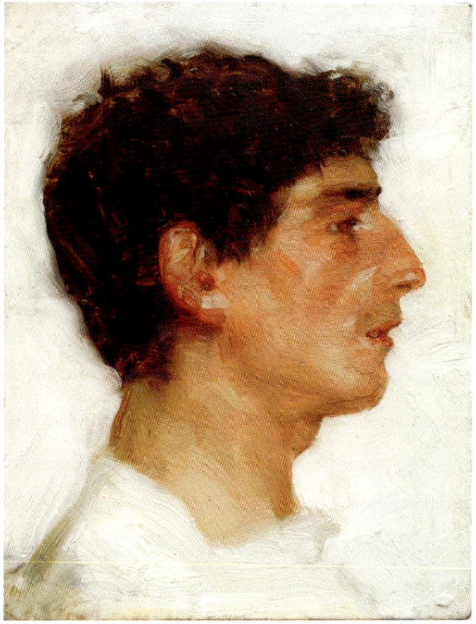

Portrait of Italian Youth, 1881

Oil on mahogany panel, 16.4 x 12cm
Inscribed on reverse: Head. Italy 1881, H.S.Tuke
Provenance: Gift to the Tuke Collection by
Geoffrey Sainsbury 4 October 1965
RCPS Tuke Collection A3

'Some of the boys wrote to him afterwards, addressing him as "Stimatissimo Signor Enrico" and he composed Italian letters to them – Aristide, Oreste, Egidio, Lorenzo, Canfino – all their names fascinated him, and they escorted him as far as they could...' M.T.S. p.52

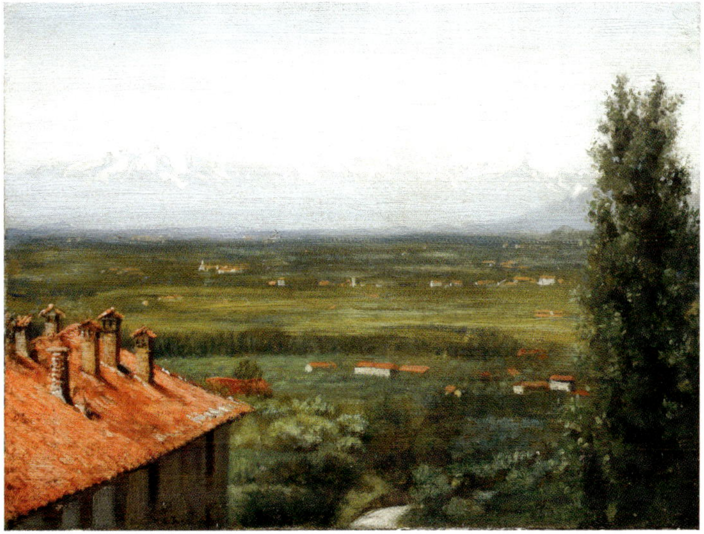

Italian Landscape, 1881

Oil on canvas, 18.6 x 25.4cm
Signed and dated H.S.Tuke 1881 bottom left
Provenance: Purchased from W. Dyer 30 May 1967
RCPS Tuke Collection A122

At the end of May 1881 Tuke went with Arthur Lemon and William Heath Wilson to Pietra Santa near Forte dei Marmi (between Livorno and La Spezia) and he described it as 'one of the principal places for shipping the marble from the quarries in the mountains behind us.' Letter to T.C. Gotch 6 June 1881. The mountains in this painting suggest it was painted near where Tuke was staying, and the quarries in the mountains he refers to would have been those at Carrara where marble has been quarried for centuries.

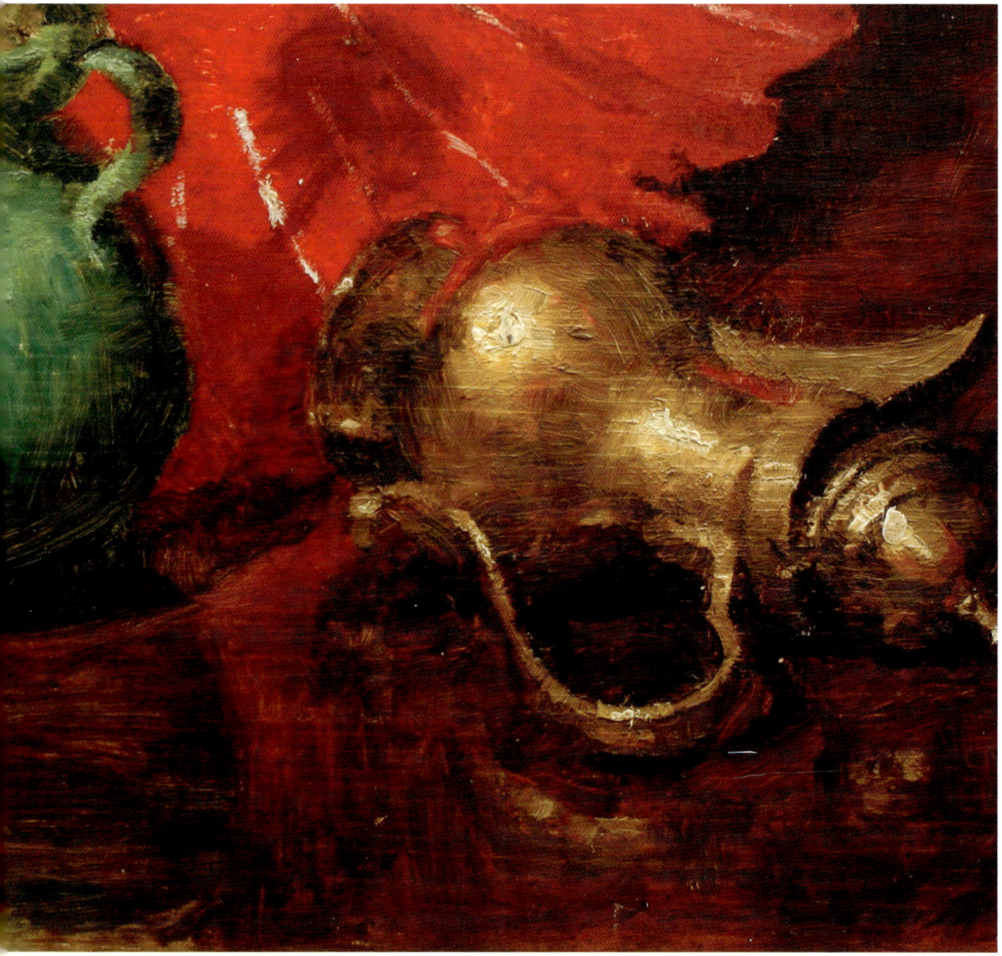

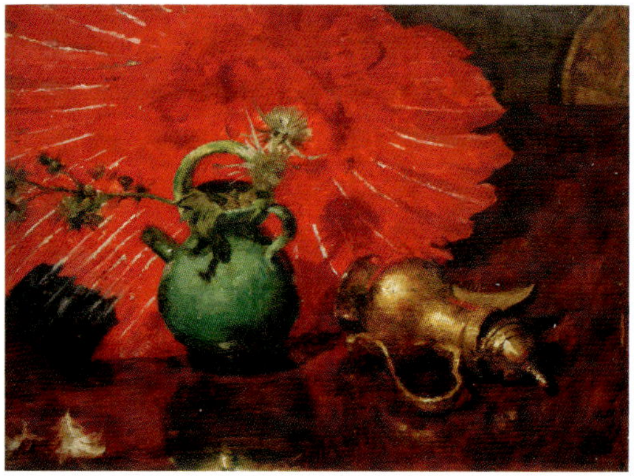

Still Life

Oil on panel, 26.7 x 35cm
Signed in pencil bottom right: H.S.Tuke
Provenance: Purchased from Henry Shemilt
9 August 1966
RCPS Tuke Collection A135

While studying in Florence in 1881, Tuke undertook a major oil of a brass pot and pan shop called *The Bronzista Shop.*[1] In his letters to his friend Tom Gotch, he describes the difficulties and challenges he faced with this painting: 'Tonight I have been resting my eyes having rather strained them with long hours in the studio doing fine brass-work. Metal painting is very interesting and is full of fat things. I find it takes a great deal longer than I had calculated, so that I feel I shall not get done comfortably, but it is no use beginning by doing such things with bravura. I see no other way than to master the details and gain facility by much practice.' Letter dated 11 Feb 1881, quote written on 15th Feb. Although not dated, it seems that this particular painting could be one of Tuke's studies of 'metal' paintings.

[1] The Bronzista Shop *was rejected by the RA in 1881, together with works by Clark, Gotch and Lemon. The picture was later sold for £10.*

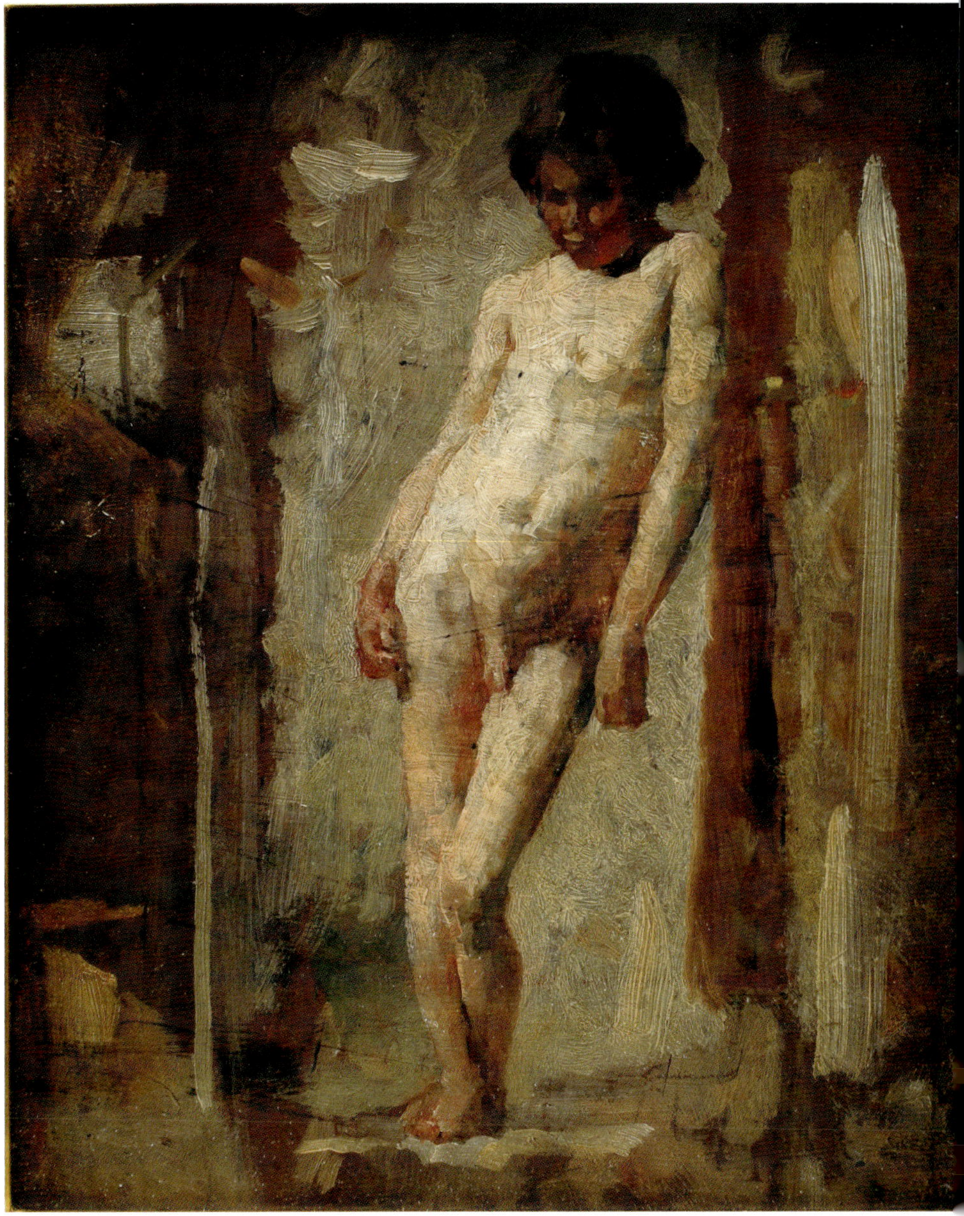

Nude Italian Boy, c.1881
Oil on sketch block end, 21.6 x 17.4cm
Provenance: Purchased from Henry Shemilt
9 August 1966
RCPS Tuke Collection A4

In June 1881 Tuke was on the North Italian coast at Pietra Santa between Livorno and La Spezia, with Arthur Lemon, whom he had met in Florence, and William Heath Wilson. He wrote to Tom Gotch, 'We are going to paint nude boys on the shore in a few days. We began yesterday in a small way by sketching one in the sea, but the approach of females put a stop to further operations. Both these men (Lemon and Wilson) are great tonists so I hope to learn lots.' Letter dated June 6 1881.

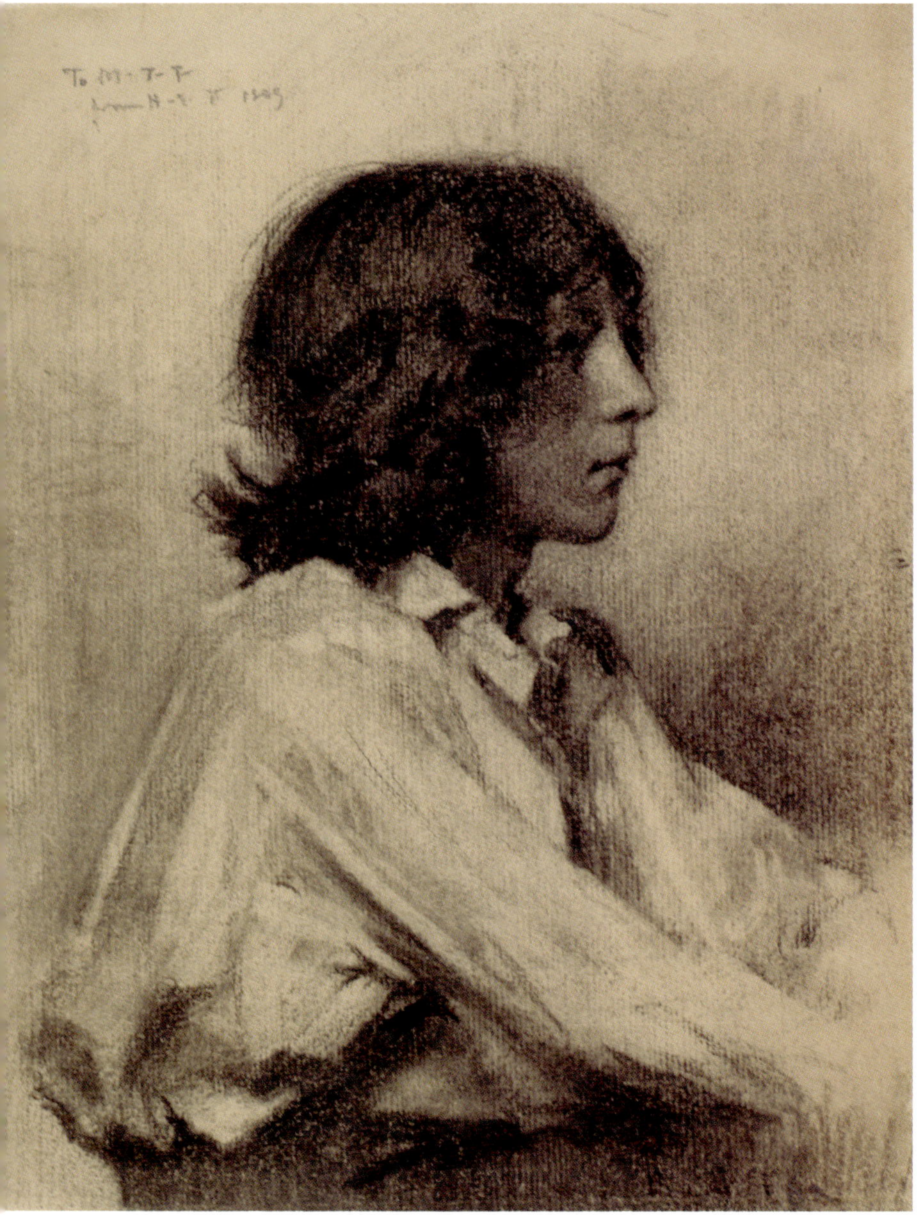

Portrait of an Italian Youth, c.1880/81

Charcoal on paper, 30 x 23.2cm
Inscribed top left: To M.T.T from H.S.T 188
On reverse of original sheet is a sketch (A14a) for *Un Jour de Paresse* see also A132
Provenance: According to Brian Price's notes it was in the possession of Maggie Tuke Tyler all her life.
Purchased from Geoffrey H Sainsbury
RCPS Tuke Collection A14

The date on this work 1889 relates to the date the work was given to Margaret Tuke Tyler (d. 1944), Tuke's cousin. The recent discovery of a drawing on the reverse makes this work more likely to have been undertaken in Italy in 1880-1881 (see A14a).

Torcross, Devon, 1882

In 1882 Tuke was still studying at Jean-Paul Lauren's studio in Paris, but that summer he was invited to stay at Torcross by George Percy Jacomb-Hood (1857-1929), who was also studying at Lauren's studio, along with artists Joseph Benwell Clark (1857-1938) and Albert Chevallier Tayler (1862-1925). Jacomb-Hood recalls the summer of 1882 in his autobiography *With Brush and Pencil*, 1925: 'Every late summer found my brothers and myself living a simple and semi-amphibious life at a Devonshire fishing village in Start Bay. Here, after my second winter in Paris, I lured Tuke, J.B. Clark, and Chevallier Tayler for a couple of months "messing about" in fishing boats. Tuke, in his methodical and persevering way, started, and worked steadily on, a largish canvas, en plein air and sunlight, a picture which was referred to in the village as "Dally in the Apple Tree," "Dally" being one of the village lads in his blue jumper, seen against the blue sky beyond, in the boughs of a small fruit-laden apple tree on the hillside above the butcher's. I regret to say that I spent nearly all my days on – or in – the sea, loving it and the handling of an open boat. When I first took Tuke out sailing without a "professional" in charge, I remember his exclamation that "if his father and mother knew it they would have a fit." However, he soon became as much enamoured of the sea and a boat as myself, so much so that he has remained a devoted lover ever since, and has given his life and his art to it.' pp. 26 and 27.

The painting Jacomb - Hood refers to is *Un jour de Paresse* (Lazy Day) R19 which was exhibited in the Paris Salon of 1883. Tuke describes it in a letter to his sister: 'I have found a very beautiful spot, a boy sits asleep in an apple tree, in shadow, relieved by the village and sea in bright sunlight seen through the branches.' Letter to M.T.S. p. 62. It was a large canvas which Tuke goes on to describe as, 'A beautiful scene in reality but almost impossible to paint. The difficulties of coping with the monster canvas in the wind and sun are immense, though I am generally surrounded by a willing band of gamins ready to run for stick or ropes as required.' Maria describes the final picture as, 'not entirely successful but had been a most instructive exercise in outdoor painting.' p.63.

Tuke clearly enjoyed Torcross: 'I am quite in love with the place, there are lots of charming things to be done, a great deal more than we can hope to broach', and the fact that Tuke found 'the village people... extremely amiable and were on the best terms with nearly all' meant that he had 'an inexhaustible supply of models.' M.T.S. p.62.

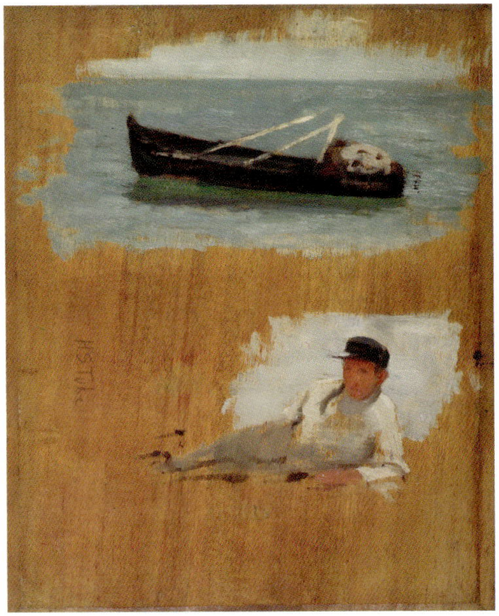

Sketch of a Boat and Sketch of Boy reclining – Torcross, c.1882
Oil on wood panel, 35.1 x 27cm
Provenance: Purchased from Henry Shemilt
17 January 1964
RCPS Tuke Collection A123

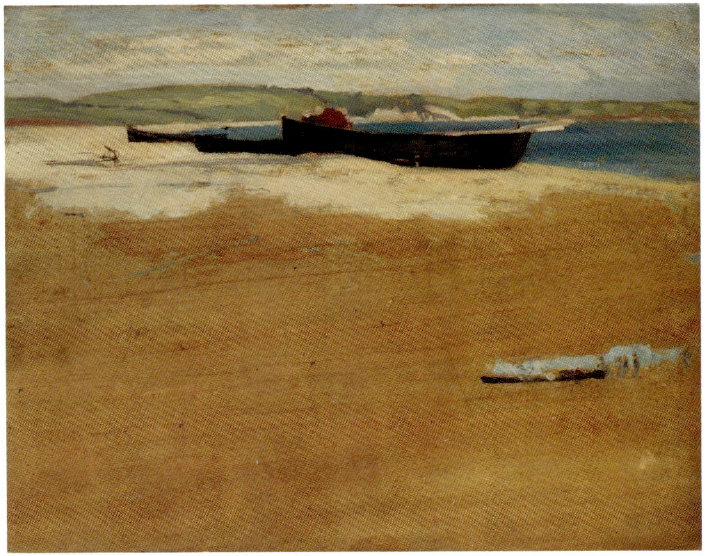

Sketch of Three boats on a beach, Torcross, c.1882
Oil on wood, 27 x 35.1cm
Provenance: Purchased from Henry Shemilt
17 January 1964
RCPS Tuke Collection A123a (Verso of A123)
These sketches may be studies for two paintings in Tuke's register R14 *Torcross Evening* and R15 *Jack and Jim Dimond on the beach.*

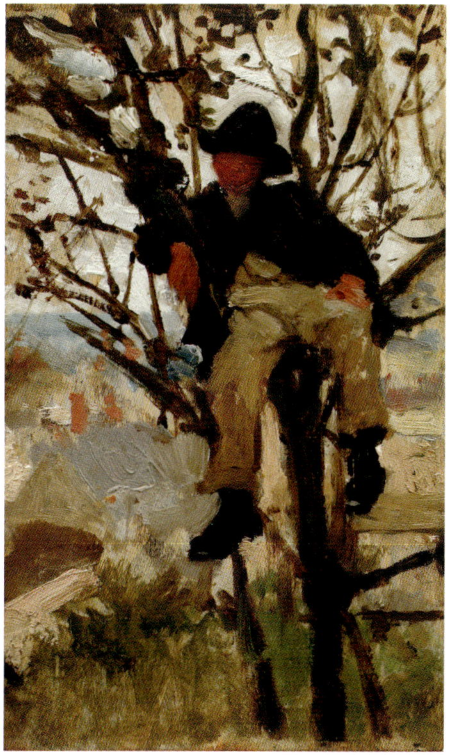

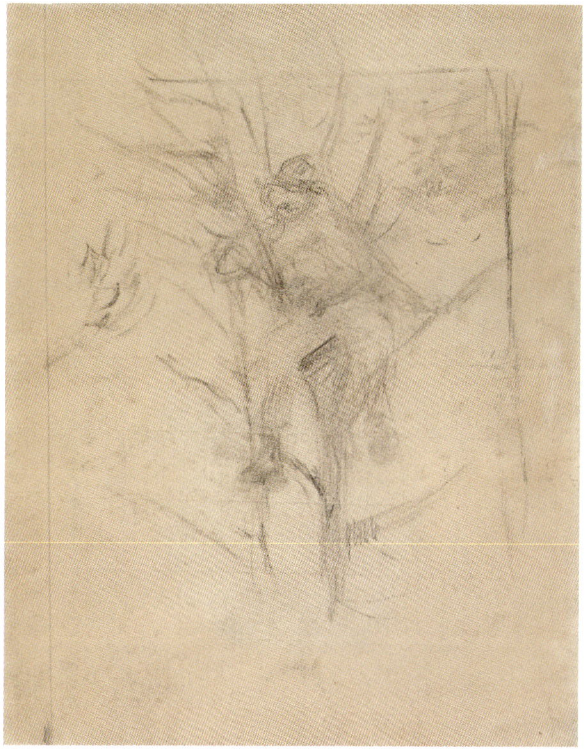

Boy in Tree (Study for Un Jour de Paresse), c.1882
Oil on panel, 21.6 x 12.4cm
Inscribed on reverse: Tuke
Provenance: Purchased from Henry Shemilt 17 January 1964
RCPS Tuke Collection A132

This oil sketch was undertaken in Torcross, Devon in the summer of 1882 and is a study for the painting *Un jour de Paresse* (Lazy Day), R19, 1882, a large oil Tuke painted en plein air and which was exhibited at the Paris Salon in 1883. The model was Dally Hutchings, a local lad, up an apple tree. This picture relates to *Boy asleep in a Sou' Wester* (A92) and (A14a) in the Collection.

Boy in Tree (Study for Un Jour de Paresse), c. 1882
Charcoal on paper, 30 x 23.2cm
RCPS Tuke Collection A14a (Verso of A14)

This recently discovered sketch for *Un Jour de Paresse* R19 is on the reverse of (A14). It was drawn in 1882 in Torcross, Devon, and is the same composition as the oil study *Boy in Tree* (A132), and also relates to *Boy asleep in a Sou' Wester* (A92).

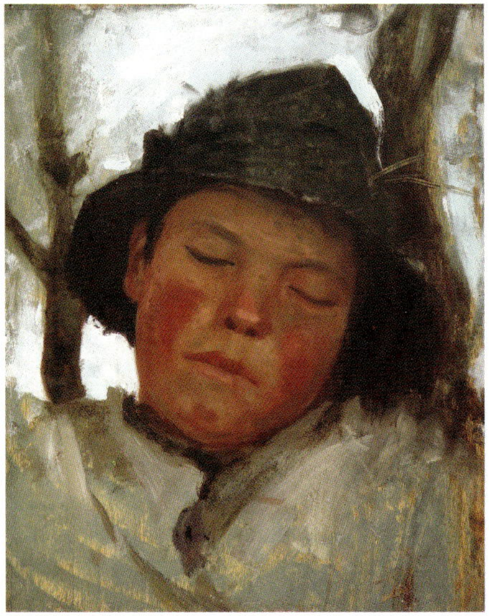

Boy Asleep in a Sou' Wester (in a tree), c.1882

Oil on wood panel, 31.9 x 25cm
Provenance: Purchased from Henry Shemilt
24 December 1963
RCPS Tuke Collection A92

Study for *Un Jour de Paresse*, R19 which was painted in Torcross, Devon in the summer of 1882. Although Dally Hutchings was the model for the final painting, this study seems to be a portrait of Jim Dimond in a tree as identified by a photograph of Jim in the Tate Gallery Archive. Jim Dimond was one of two sons, the other being Jack, of William Dimond, a local fisherman. Jim was 11 years old at the time. The small oil sketch *Boy in Tree* (A132) shows the overall composition of the bigger painting. On the reverse of this painting is another oil sketch of a boy standing in a boat, sculling.

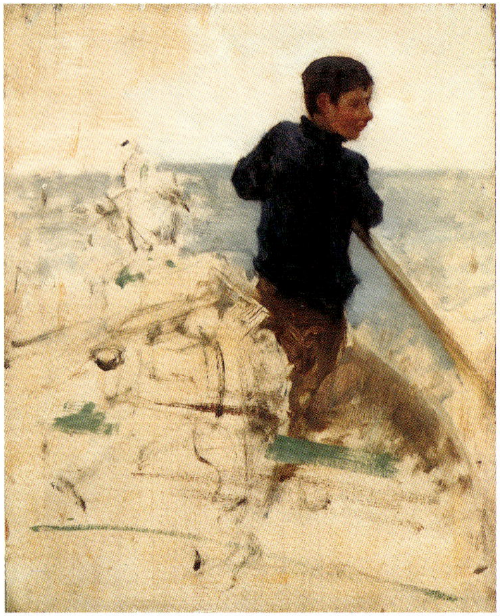

Boy sculling a boat, c.1882

Oil on wood panel, 31.5 x 21.5cm
Provenance: Purchased from Henry Shemilt
24 December 1963
RCPS Tuke Collection A92a (Verso of A92)

NEWLYN 1883-1885

Tuke first came to Newlyn on a visit in 1879 with Tom Gotch to visit Caroline Burland Yates – the future Mrs. Gotch. He returned to stay for two periods in 1883 and 1884. By this time Tuke had reached a watershed in his life after travelling and studying abroad, and returning to face the death (at the age of 27) of his elder brother William from tuberculosis. He came to Newlyn to paint and be with his friends, Chevallier Tayler, Tom and Carrie Gotch, Frederick Millard (1857-1937) and William John Wainwright (1855-1931), who had all been at the Slade.

Tuke found a room with a view across Newlyn harbour in Trewarveneth Street in the home of a local fisherman Philip Harvey[1] (1843-1932) and his wife Jane. Tuke exchanged portraits of Philip and his cousin Tom for a small sailing boat and a model yacht. The RCPS Collection has an early pastel by Tuke of Philip Harvey in his cellar (A102, R39). In the time that Tuke spent in Newlyn he recorded ten oil paintings in his register, two of which were set in Harvey's linney cellar. One was *Ship-Builders*, R26, 1883; the second was *Dinnertime*, R29, 1883. This was Tuke's first experience of this kind of environment as a subject for his art: 'I have found a very fascinating cellar under our house, which is alive with subjects', he wrote to his sister. The painting *Ship-Builders* was to be important for Tuke, as he sent it to London to be shown at the Nineteenth Century Art Society in Conduit Street. It was bought by the dealer Dowdeswell, which was the beginning of a profitable relationship between artist and dealer.

Maria notes that Penzance afforded Tuke with 'many opportunities for sociability, besides the daily intimacy with Newlyn artists. George Tregelles, at the Bank, was an old friend, and he soon made others.' M.T.S. p.70. It was while based at Newlyn that Tuke went to Bournemouth to paint a portrait of a Dr Falls. He returned to Newlyn in May to find it 'looking more bewitching than ever, I only wonder I didn't come here sooner, as it is now simply reeking with subjects.'

Tuke's first painting of boys in boats, which was to become one of his motifs, was completed in Newlyn in 1884. It was called *Summertime* (R44) and depicts two local boys, John Wesley Kitching and John Rouffignac Cotton, in Philip Harvey's punt 'Little Argo'. While in Newlyn, until the winter set in and he returned to London to paint, Harry Tuke seemed to spend most of his time sailing, fishing, swimming and seeing his friends. Tuke was photographed at the time with the Newlyn School artists Frank Bramley, Blanford Fletcher, Ralph Todd, Edwin Harris, Stanhope Forbes and others. However, he did not stay long in Newlyn; his own style of painting was more impressionist than many of the Newlyn painters, and therefore his artistic allegiances were different from theirs. However, he would remain close friends with many of the artists who came and went from Newlyn and Lamorna for the next thirty years.

1. From a manuscript of the Harvey family tree – private collection.

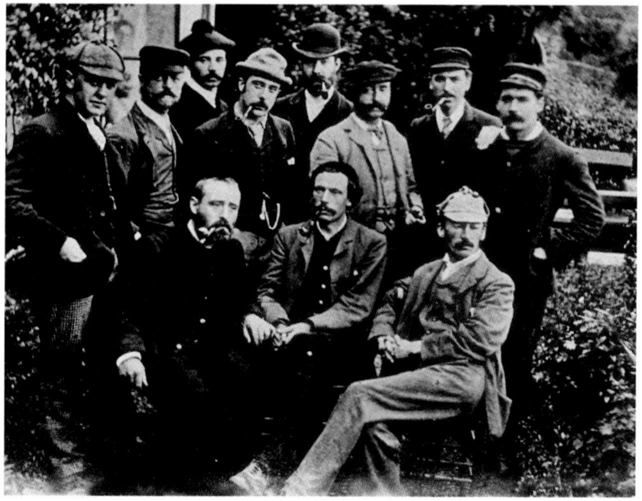

H.S.Tuke – (first right standing) with Newlyn School painters
From M.T.S. op cit p.74

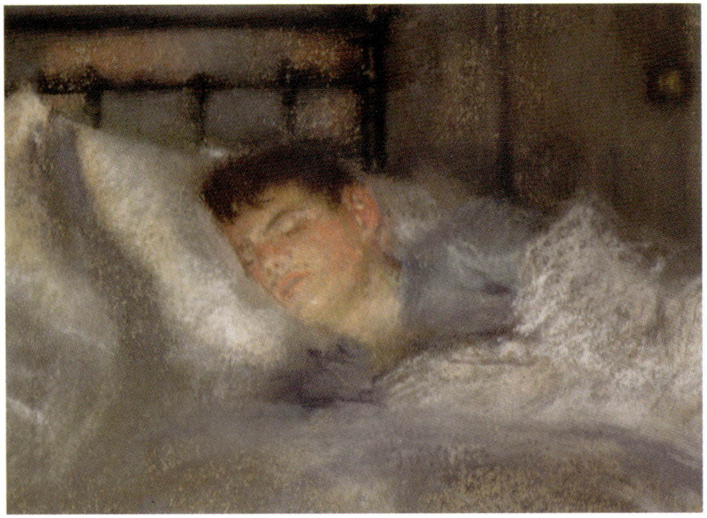

Ambrose, c.1884

Pastel on paper, 18.5 x 25cm
Exhibited: The Nineteenth Century Art Society May 1885
Provenance: Purchased from Glyn Ward
17 November 1962
RCPS Tuke Collection A8 R40

In Tuke's register he writes, 'In my room at Trewarveneth Street, Newlyn. Head of Ambrose Rouffignac.' Tuke came to paint in Newlyn from September to November 1883 and between May and December 1884. Ambrose also modelled for another painting Tuke undertook in Newlyn called *Dinner Time* or *Ambrose in the Loft*, R29 illustrated on p.70 of M.T. Sainsbury's book. Maria described him: 'the model has the fine name of Ambrose Ruffignac [sic], of a family of French extraction. If you have got so grand as to keep a tiger, he would do very well, he is very paintable and has a nice Cornish accent.' M.T.S. p.70.

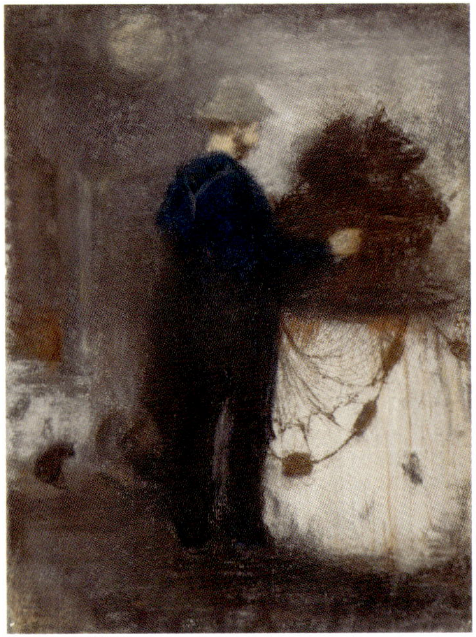

Philip Barking Nets, c.1884

Pastel on paper, 29 x 21.5cm
Exhibited: The Nineteenth Century Art Society May 1885
Provenance: Purchased from Geoffrey Sainsbury
13 March 1965
RCPS Tuke Collection A102 R39

According to Tuke's register, 'Philip Harvey stood for me in the cellar', which would have been at Trewarveneth Street, Newlyn where he lived in 1884.

Sketch (Newlyn)

Oil and pastel on wood panel, 20.3 x 45.9cm
Provenance: Gift to Tuke Collection
by Geoffrey Sainsbury 1965
RCPS Tuke Collection A127a
(Verso of A127)

This sketch shows a portrait of a child in a wide-brimmed hat with a yellow background.

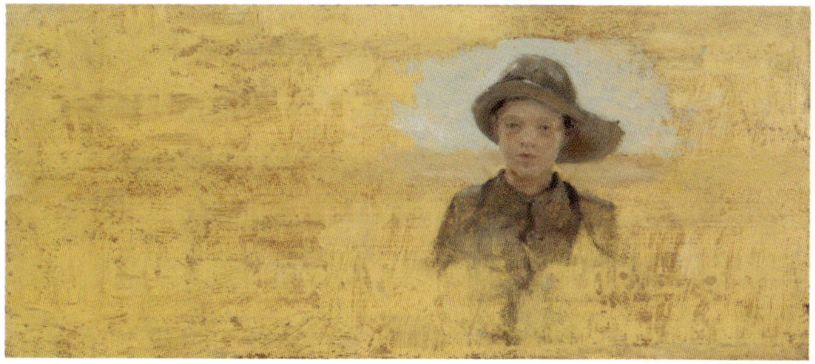

Sketch (Newlyn)

Oil and pastel on wood panel, 20.3 x 45.9cm
Provenance: Gift to Tuke Collection
by Geoffrey Sainsbury 1965
Verso to *Sketch Newlyn* (A127a)
RCPS Tuke Collection A127

This sketch in pastel, pencil and oil is of a typical Newlyn group gathered on the sea front with adults and children.

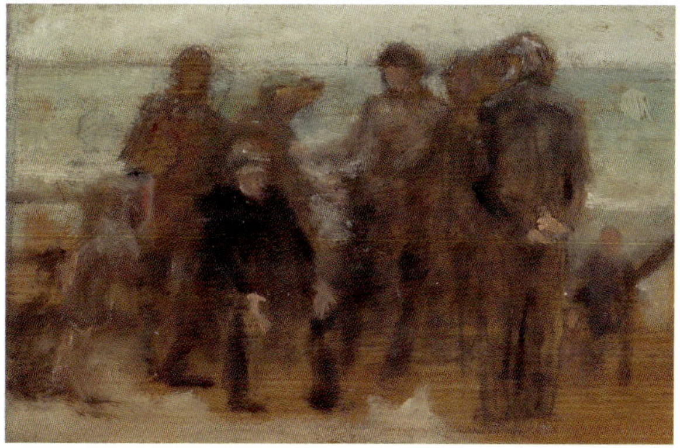

Portrait of Liz, c.1884

Oil on wood panel, 29.1 x 23.9cm (panel size)
Liz image 18.6 x 21.6cm Signed: H.S.Tuke
Provenance: Purchased from Henry Shemilt
17 January 1964
Verso to 'Julie of Nantes' (A39a)
RCPS Tuke Collection A39

This is a portrait of one of Philip Harvey's daughters, Elizabeth Harvey who was born in 1881, which would make her approximately three years old in this picture. Tuke wrote to his sister Maria that he liked all the Harveys' children and thought Liz 'a very fine little maid.' He didn't like them however 'when they come and chump apples in my ear.' M.T.S. p.69

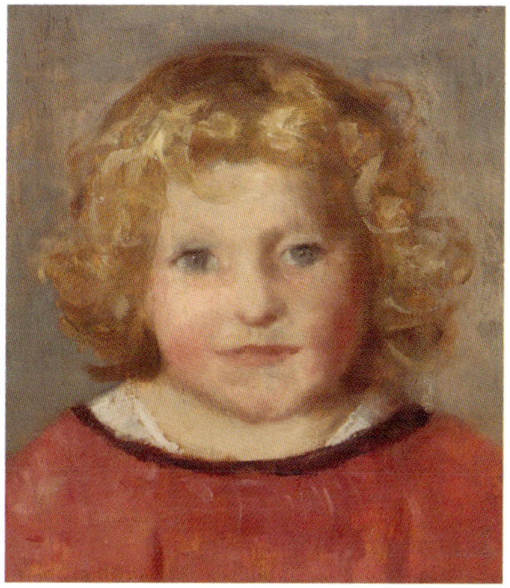

Falmouth from 1885

Tuke returned to his childhood haunt of Falmouth, east of Newlyn, on June 8th 1885. It was an important decision as it remained his 'painting home' until he died 44 years later. Although Falmouth did not have the same artistic colony as Newlyn, it was the home of several important artists of the time such as Charles Napier Hemy (1841-1917) who was a well-known maritime artist and undertook many of his paintings on a floating studio. Tuke was to follow his example and in 1886 purchased an old French brigantine, the '*Julie of Nantes*', to use as a studio. Although unseaworthy, Tuke used it as a backdrop for many of his figure paintings from 1886-1891. After initially using models from London, he later relied mainly on local men and boys. They were to feature regularly in such paintings as *All Hands to the Pumps!*, 1889, R118, the first painting by Tuke to be bought by the Chantrey Bequest. Tuke, as well as living on board the '*Julie*', also rented rooms at Pennance Cottage, initially as a tenant with a housekeeper, Mrs Fouracre. Later he had a studio built in the grounds. It was adjacent to the sea and had a view of Pendennis Castle. Its other advantage was its close proximity to Newporth beach which was a secluded and a 'truly enchanted spot' where Tuke was able to undertake all his outdoor nude painting. Falmouth allowed him to indulge in all his favourite sports of yachting, tennis, cricket, boating and bathing. He had become a skilled yachtsman and bought many sailing craft during his life in Falmouth, including the '*Lily*'. It was onboard this particular boat Tuke was to paint one of his most endearing portraits of Jack Rolling – *Our Jack* (A2)(R62) in the Tuke Collection. Jack was what Tuke called a 'quay scamp', a term used to describe one of the many children who could be found in Falmouth playing on the quays by the water. Tuke helped found the Falmouth Sailing Club. He was also very keen on cricket and played for the Falmouth Church Institute Cricket Club. He set up the first Falmouth Art Gallery at Grove Place with fellow painter William Ayerst Ingram (1855-1913) and John Henry Eva Downing. It was around this time that his long association with the Royal Cornwall Polytechnic Society in Falmouth began. In 1890 he arranged an exhibition of contemporary art at the Poly and judged the local art competition for many years. He was elected Vice President in 1899, and when he was elected as an Associate of the Royal Academy in 1900, the Poly held a banquet in his honour. Although he travelled a great deal and spent several months every year at his family home in Hanwell, London, Tuke always regarded Falmouth as his home and when he died he was buried in Falmouth Cemetery.

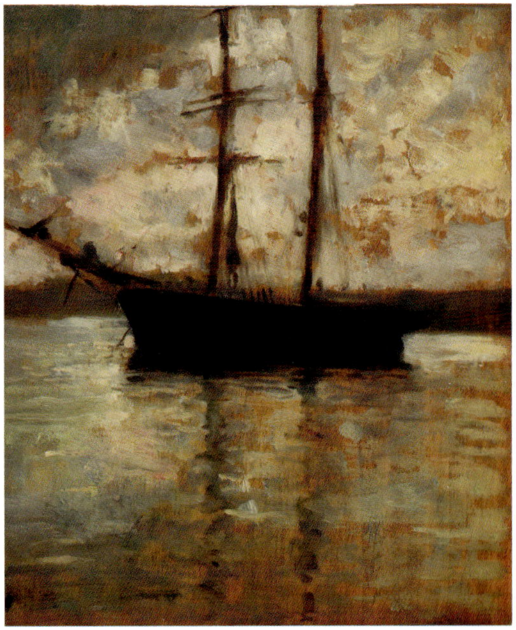

'Julie of Nantes', c.1886
Oil on wood panel
29.1 x 23.9cm (panel size)
Provenance: Purchased from Henry Shemilt 17 January 1964
RCPS Tuke Collection A39a (Verso of A39)

Local Models

Tuke's painting register reads, 'Begun April 28 1886. The first of many I painted of Jack Rolling. Done on the *Lily*.' This painting was given to Thomas Cooper Gotch and Caroline Burland Yates, artist friends from the Slade, as their late wedding present. Between 1886-1887 Tuke lists over 13 paintings of Jack in his register. Painted on Tuke's quay punt '*Lily*', it shows Falmouth in the background with the Church of King Charles the Martyr clearly visible. Tuke depicts another tall-masted ship on its moorings, with the smoking funnel of a tug also moored at the quay in the middle ground. Jack Rolling (a.k.a. Rowling) was described by Maria Tuke Sainsbury as a 'loveable young barbarian who could look like an angel and behave like a demon', which seems to sum up these two aspects of his personality. Tuke gets Jack standing in a jaunty pose with his hip thrown out to one side as he casually leans on the edge of the boat, one hand in his pocket and using his other hand to hold onto the rigging. It is a pose of relaxed boredom and the somewhat hard, penetrating, unsmiling stare indicates toughness despite the ruddy-cheeked angelic complexion. It is a typical Newlyn style painting with subtle tones of grey and blue, a grey overcast sky reflected in the sea. Jack Rolling left Falmouth for London in 1890, and he wrote to Tuke when both he and Tuke were ill. It is a very touching letter in which Jack repeatedly calls Tuke 'My dear Sir' and asks if he can help him out with money for a ticket to get him back to Falmouth. (Letter 15 January 1890, No.166, Tate Gallery archive)

Jack Rolling became a diver and went on his first dive in 1891, and it was to be the making of him. He dived on the '*Mohegan*' wreck off the Manacles in 1898 while he was working for the Liverpool Salvage Company. Tuke watched him at work and said in a letter, 'he is now a very expert hand at work, and earns anything between two and ten pounds a week.' Tuke never painted Jack without clothes, although he painted his brother William in the nude. The diving took its toll on Jack's health and he died at the relatively young age of 49.

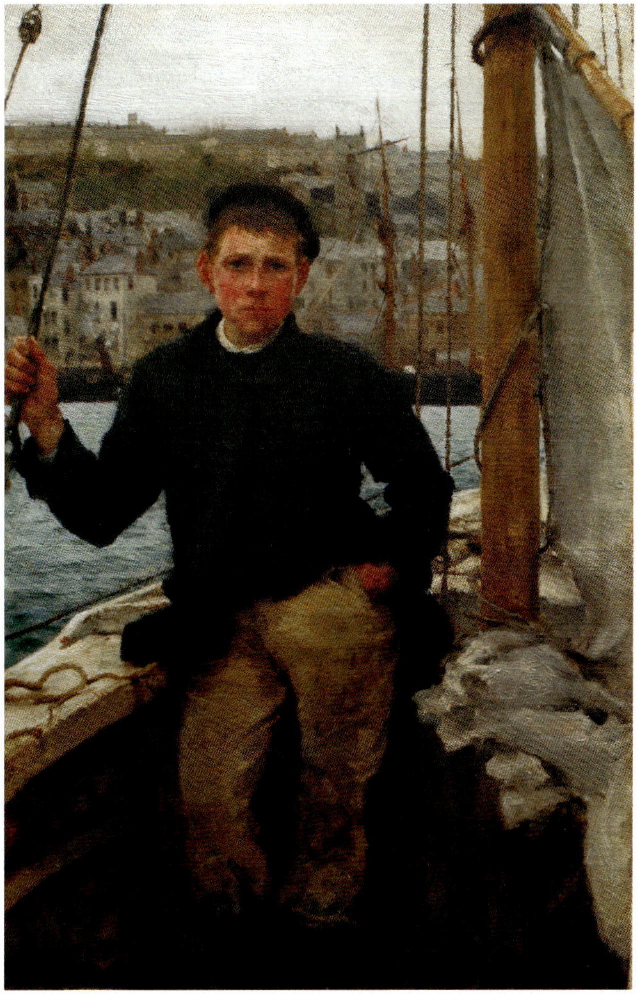

Our Jack, 1886
Oil on canvas, 50.5 x 32cm
Exhibited: Liverpool 1886
Provenance: Purchased from Mrs D. McClellan
4 September 1966
RCPS Tuke Collection A2 R62

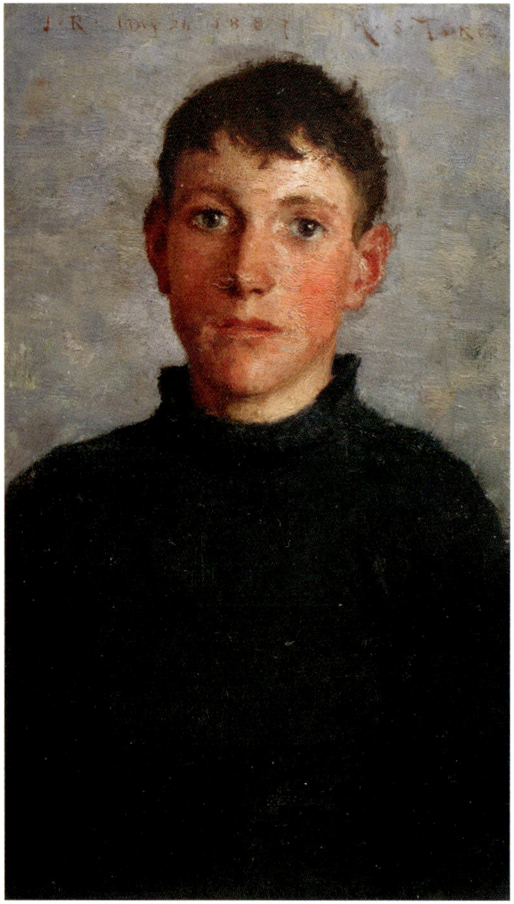

Portrait of Jack Rolling, 1887
Oil on panel, 21.8 x 12.4cm
Inscribed, dated and signed top: J.R. May 26 1887 H.S.Tuke.
Provenance: Purchased from Geoffrey Sainsbury
19 December 1963
RCPS Tuke Collection A31, R81

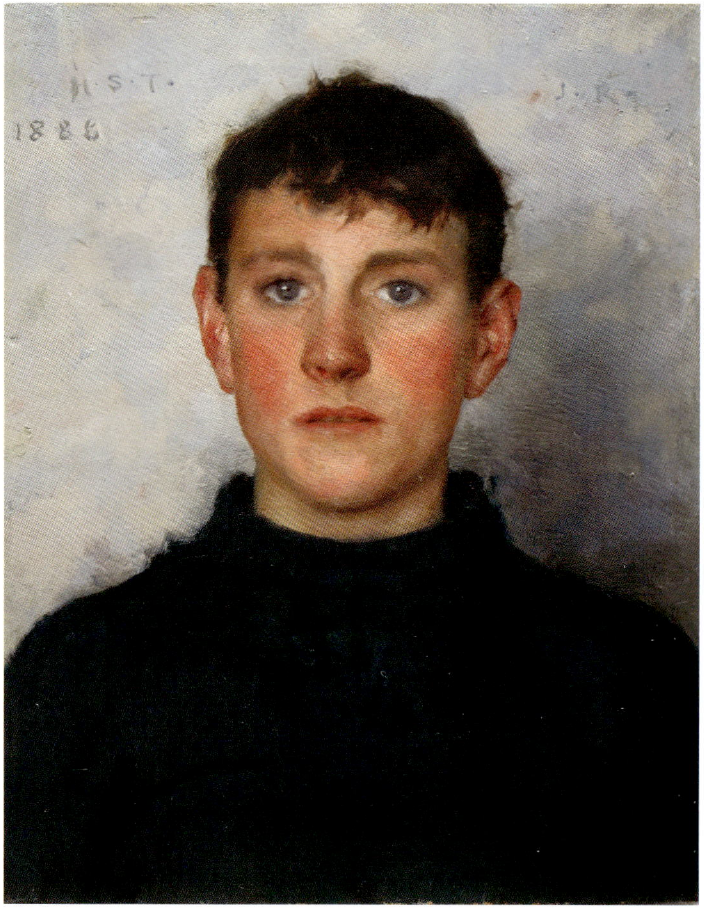

Portrait of Jack Rolling, 1888
Oil on board, 30 x 23.6cm
Initialled and dated top left: HST 1888
Inscribed top right: J.R.
Provenance: Purchased from Glyn Ward
28 April 1965
RCPS Tuke Collection A15

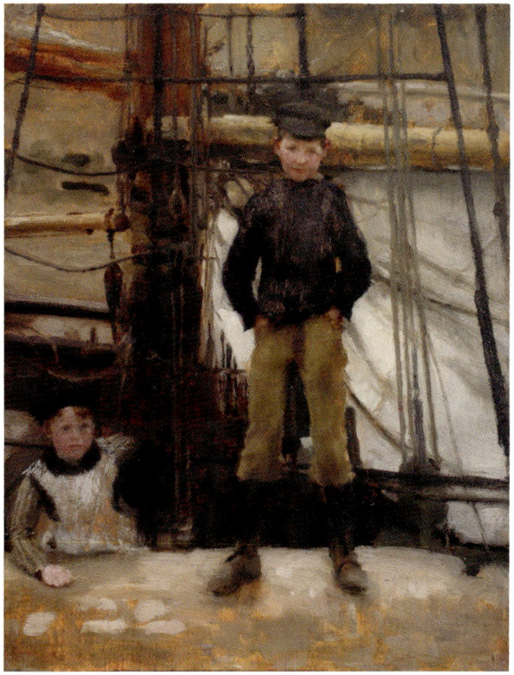

Two Children on Deck

Oil on wood panel, 35.5 x 26.5cm
Provenance: Purchased from Henry Shemilt
24 December 1963
RCPS Collection A66

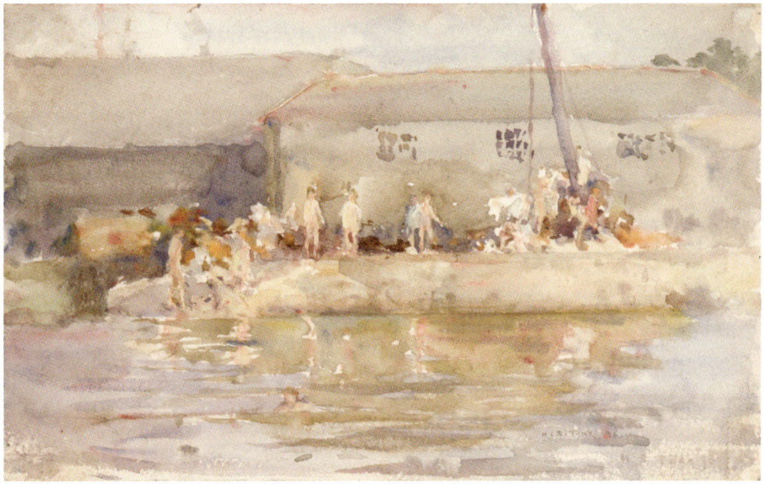

Quay Scamps, 1896

Watercolour, 13.9 x 21.5cm
Signed and dated bottom right: HSTuke '96 (twice)
Provenance: Originally William Sainsbury's. Purchased from Geoffrey Sainsbury 29 May1968
RCPS Tuke Collection A214

This impressionistic watercolour depicts children playing on one of the many quays around Falmouth harbour in the summer. It is possibly in one of the boatyards, as there is a crane on the quay and a slipway for the boats. The children can also be seen swimming in the water after jumping off the quay.

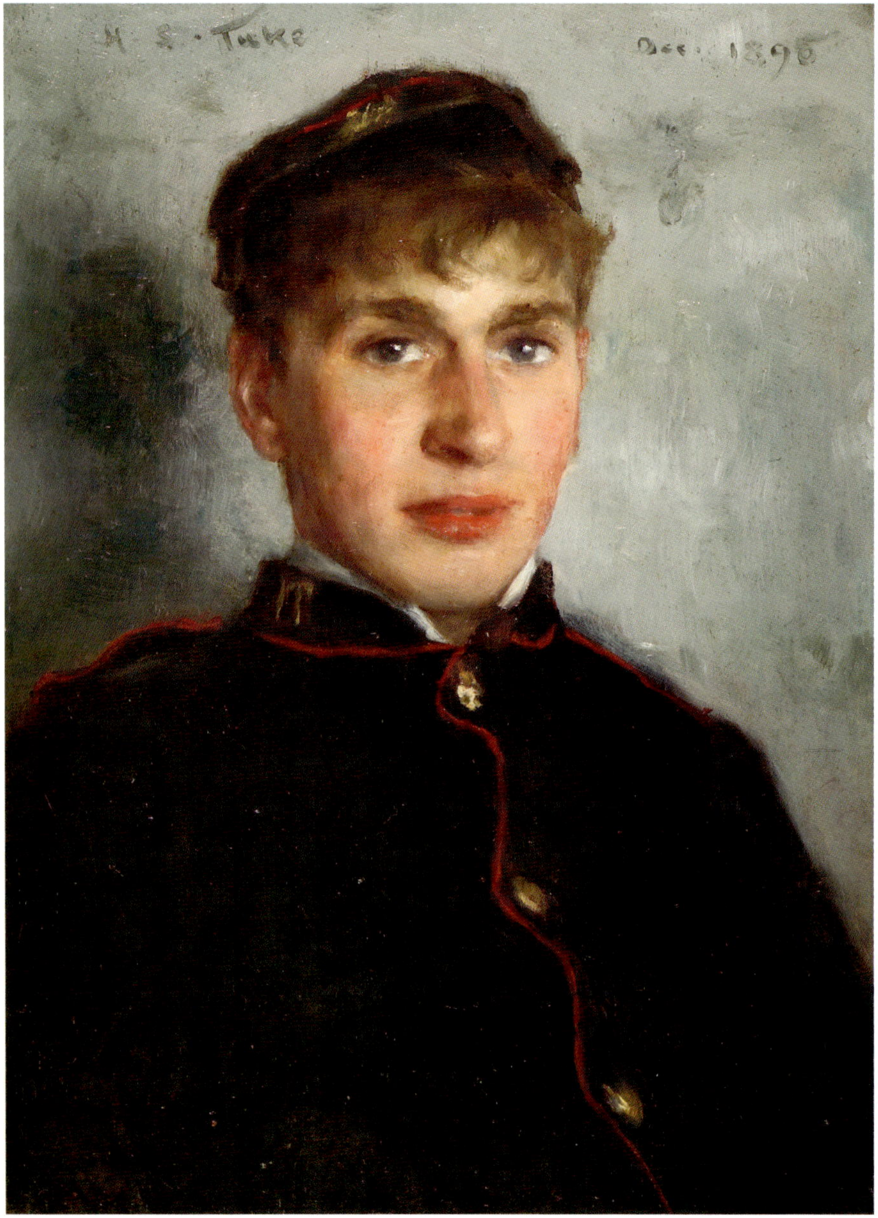

Portrait of William J. Martin, 1890

Oil on mahogany panel, 35.8 x 26cm
Signed top left: H.S.Tuke Dated top right: Dec 1890
Provenance: Given to William J Martin by Tuke. Donated to RCPS by his daughter Betty Whittingham
April 1993
RCPS Tuke Collection A405, R154

This painting of the postman William John Martin (b.1870), who features in Tuke's large painting *The Message* R152 (Falmouth Art Gallery), is of Tuke's postman in real life who delivered his mail to the cottage at Swanpool. There are two other studies of William Martin in the Tuke Collection (A24 and A93). They are all of Martin in his uniform, but this is the most finished and most sympathetic portrait of the three. In this portrait Martin's eyes sparkle, and Tuke models the nose and lips in a soft way emphasising their structure. His postman's hat on the back of his head at a jaunty angle allows greater emphasis on the wavy brown hair and long fringe which covers his forehead. According to Martin's reminiscences, he had been happy to pose for Tuke for nothing, but he did ask whether he could have a portrait of himself 'for a wedding present' as he was getting married in a few months' time. Martin had his own stamp dealing business and an office in Killigrew Street. 'I did quite well, and I got connections all over England and on the continent, numbering at one time the King of Portugal among my clients.' Tuke painted Martin many times, and as he was a keen stamp collector himself, they must have had a lot in common.

William Martin was born in Falmouth the son of a master mariner who was drowned at sea when William was very young. His mother married again, but William refused to take his step-father's name. He went to the British School in Falmouth, and when he left school he started work in a grocer's shop but got the sack. He took on the job of postman for his health, as his doctor had advised him to walk more. The post office offered him an early morning round walking from Falmouth to Swanpool, which allowed him to do a day's work in his office. This is how William Martin came to meet Tuke on his post round.
(From William John Martin's 'Reminiscences', written by his daughter Betty Whittingham, and reproduced in the Poly Magazine, 1983 pp. 16-17.)

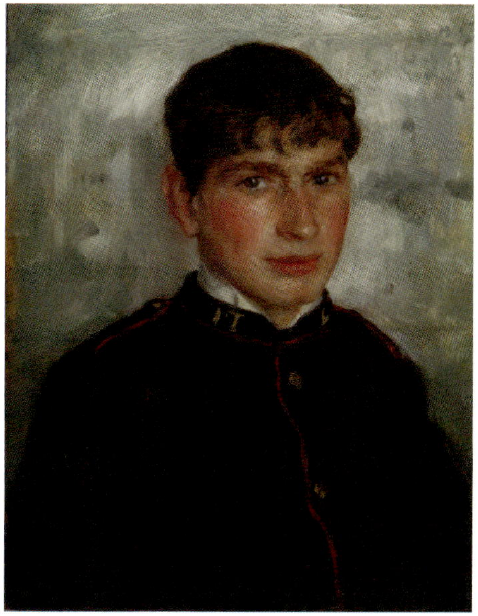

Head of Martin (Portrait of William J.Martin), 1890

Oil on panel, 34.8 x 26.4cm
Signed and dated top right: April 25 1890
Provenance: Purchased from Henry Shemilt
24 December 1963
RCPS Tuke Collection A93 R131

This study of William Martin, the postman in *The Message* (R152) and in real life, is mentioned in Tuke's register as being undertaken in April 1890 in the studio. This study features Martin in his uniform but without his cap. It is showing Martin from his right side as with the painting A405/R154. Tuke portrayed him standing showing the left side of his face in the final painting as in the study A24.

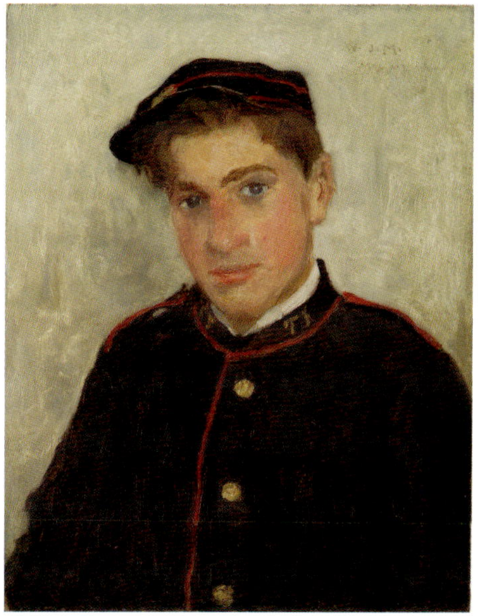

Head of William J.Martin, 1890

Oil on wood panel, 27.3 x 20.9cm
Initialled and dated top left: HST 90
Inscribed and dated top right: WJM May 12. 90
Provenance: Purchased from John Maggs
14 July 1962
RCPS Tuke Collection A24

Of all the studies of William Martin as the postman, this is the closest pose to that in *The Message* (R152): the tilt of his head and the cap are almost exactly the same as that of the final painting.

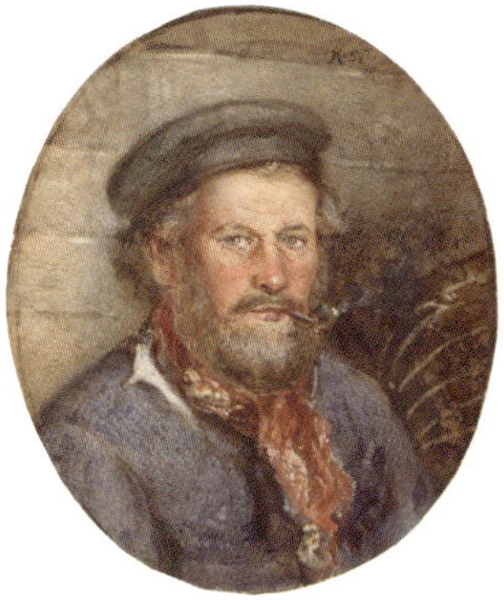

Head of Tom Tregenza, 1890

Watercolour, oval 30.8 x 25cm
Initialled and dated top right: HST '90
Exhibited: Devon and Cornwall Exhibition, Plymouth 1891
Provenance: Purchased from P. Theelke, Bristol 28 February 1968
RCPS Tuke Collection A101 R129

This is a portrait of a local Falmouth man who modelled for several paintings including *At the Wheel* (R113), *The Fisherman* (R119) (Nottingham City Art Gallery), and *Euchre – or The Dog Watch* (R122) (Neue Pinakothek, Munich). In the Falmouth census of 1871, Thomas Tregenza was listed as a 30 year old blacksmith living in Beacon Street, Falmouth with a son also called Tom aged 4.

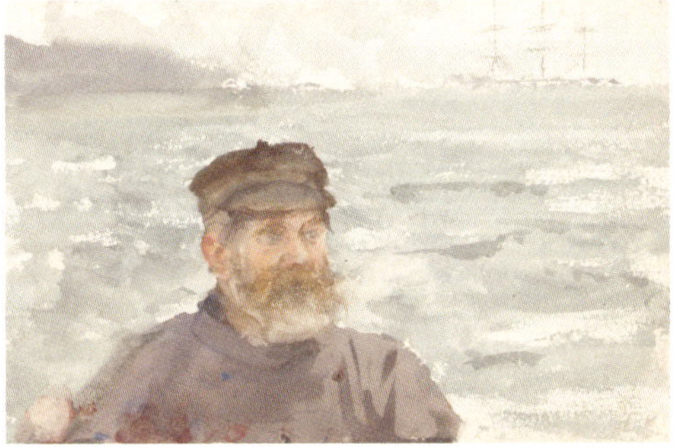

Portrait of a Fisherman (Neddy Hall), c.1892

Watercolour, 13.9 x 21.6cm
Provenance: Purchased from Geoffrey Sainsbury 30 April 1967
RCPS Tuke Collection A217

This is a similar pose by model Neddy Hall to that of *The Steering Lesson* (R183 1892) a painting commissioned by an Australian but never paid for. It shows Neddy on board with a tall ship at sea in the background. This may have been a study for the final painting. *The Steering Lesson* also features Neddy Hall's son Freddy, who was to become one of Tuke's most frequent nude models.

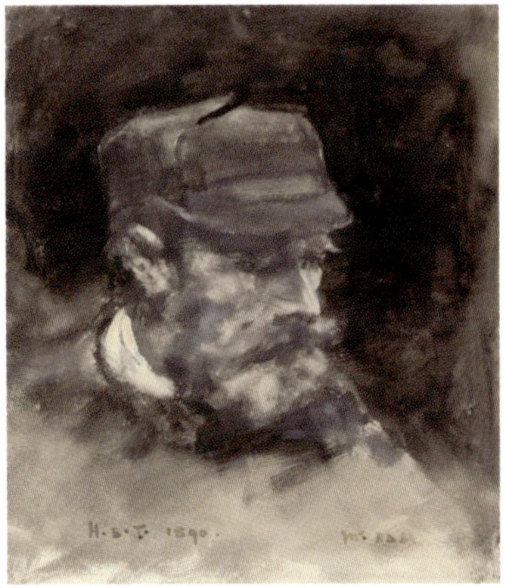

Mr Hall, 1890

Body colour wash, 25 x 21cm
Initialled and dated bottom left: H.S.T 1890
Inscribed bottom right: Mr Hall
Cut out inscription 'Wishing you all a Happy Xmas'.
Provenance: Purchased from Miss Barbara Marshall 21 November 1964. Originally a Christmas present to Kenneth and Edith Marshall, her grandparents.
RCPS Tuke Collection A43

Neddy Hall was a local fisherman from Falmouth who posed for many of Tuke's paintings, especially those on board the *'Julie'*, including *Land in Sight* (R93 1888), *In the Foc's'l* (R103), *'What do you make of her?'* (R111 1888), *All Hands to the Pumps!* (R118 1888), *Euchre* (R122 1889), *Reefing the Mainsail* (R136 1890), *Hoisting the Mainsail* (R145 1890), *The Lamp Cleaners* (R164 1891). He nearly always appears in his fisherman's peaked cap.

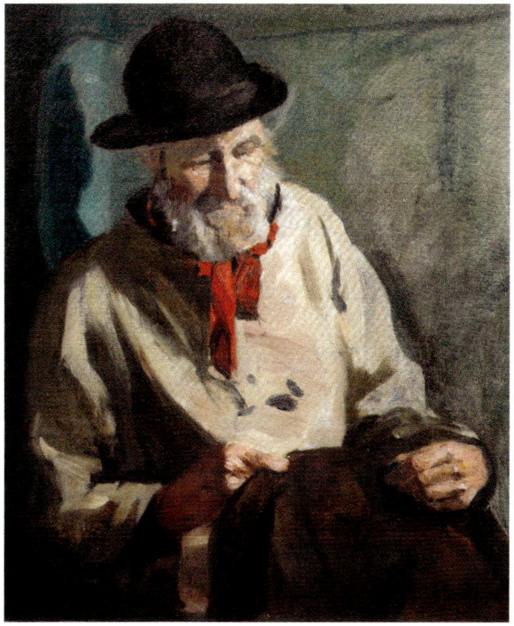

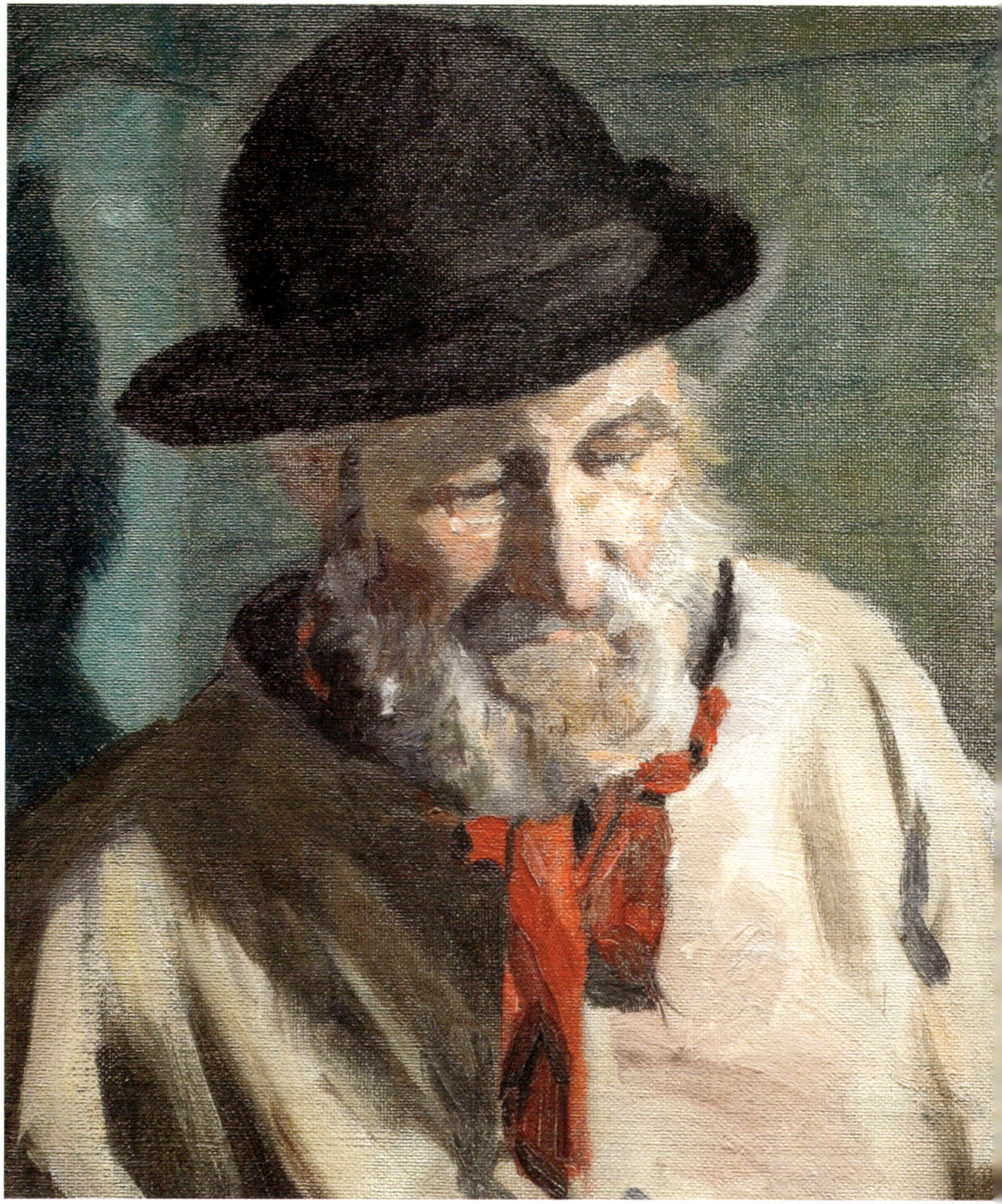

Denny mending sail, c.1890

Oil on canvas, 62.6 x 47.6cm
Signed top right: H.S.Tuke
Provenance: Purchased from A.A. Ballard, Warminster 25 May 1967
RCPS Tuke Collection A23 R127

This is a portrait study of Falmouth fisherman Denny Morrison, seated mending a sail. Denny Morrison was another local model whom Tuke used regularly for his major oils including *All Hands to the Pumps!* (R118). He also posed for a small watercolour with the title *'Yes Sir, I'm a Teetotaller'* (R116 c.1889).

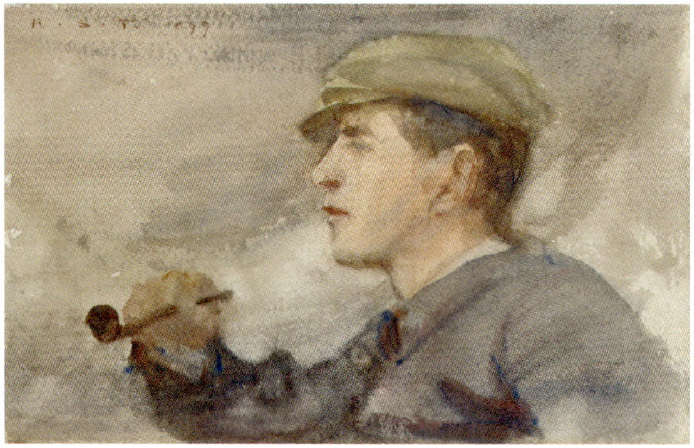

Portrait of a Young Man
with a cap and pipe, 1899
Watercolour, 13.7 x 21.5cm
Initialled and dated top left: H.S.T 1899
Provenance: Purchased from Peter Jackson, Falmouth
14 February 1966
RCPS Tuke Collection A51

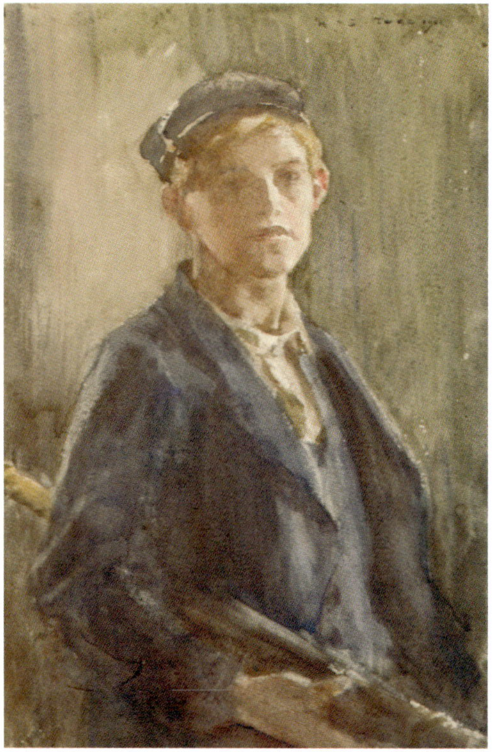

Bert White with Oar, 1901
Watercolour, 21.2 x 13.7cm
Signed and dated top right: H.S.Tuke 1901
Provenance: Purchased from Geoffrey Sainsbury
18 December1964
RCPS Tuke Collection A90

Bert White was an apprentice at Falmouth docks, and was a friend of Harry Cleave and Thomas Tiddy. He and Cleave got into trouble for playing pranks at the docks or pretending to be injured, and frequently were laid off, which allowed them to model for Tuke. Bert features in many of Tuke's paintings between 1901 and 1904 including *Ruby, Gold and Malachite* (R374 1901), *The Run Home* (R380 1901-2), *Noonday Heat* (A402 R382 1902), *The Stowaway* (R396 1903), and *The Three Companions* (R484 1905).

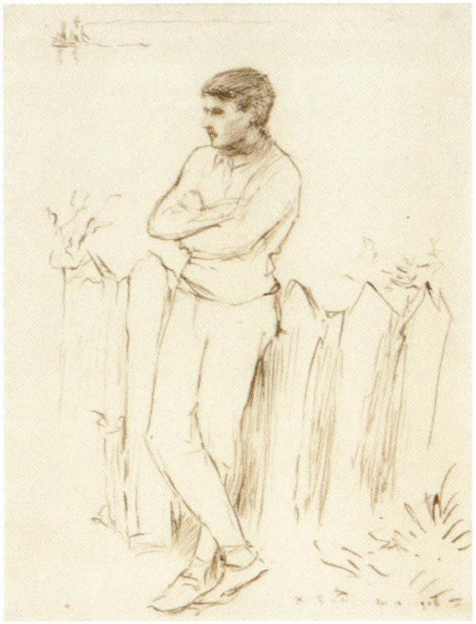

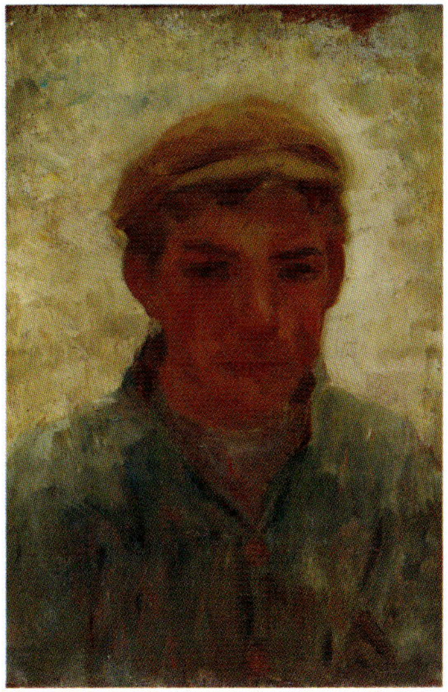

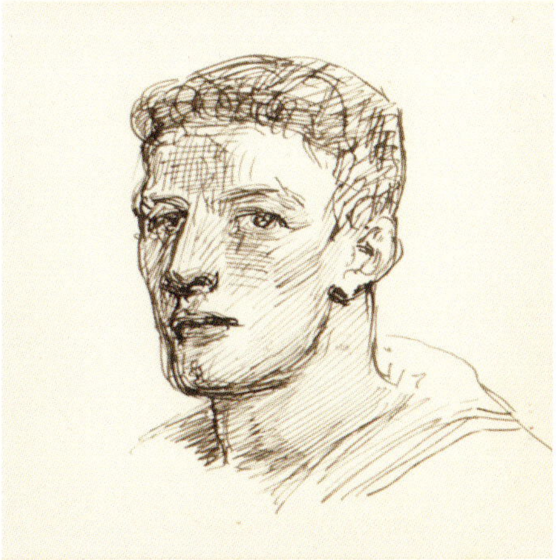

Johnnie Jackett, 1904

Pen and iron gall ink on paper, 25.4 x 18.9cm
Initialled and dated H.S.T. Cot. 12.1904 bottom right
Provenance: Given to the Tuke Collection by Sally Jackett 20 June 1965
RCPS Tuke Collection A81

Edward John Jackett (1878-1935) was the son of Thomas Jackett, a Falmouth boatbuilder. Johnnie, as he was known, modelled for Tuke on many occasions. This drawing was done, according to Sally Jackett, John's future wife, with Tuke's first fountain pen which Johnnie gave him as a present. Johnnie was devoted to Tuke and the gift of a fountain pen shows how much Tuke meant to him. The drawing depicts Johnnie leaning against the wooden fence at Pennance Cottage. Johnnie used to cycle with Tuke and he became a great cyclist and rugby player, representing Cornwall and England. Tuke went to see him play whenever he could.

Johnnie

Oil on panel, 24 x 16cm
Inscribed 'Johnnie' in pencil top right
Provenance: Purchased from Henry Shemilt 24 December 1963
RCPS Tuke Collection A130

This is a very rough sketch of Johnnie Jackett wearing a cloth peaked hat.

Sketch for Portrait of Ginger Carne, c.1908

Pen and iron gall ink on paper, 8.9 x 8.8cm
Provenance: Gift from Geoffrey Sainsbury 15 July 1965
RCPS Tuke Collection A49

Ginger Carne is depicted here in his sailor's cadet uniform. He was one of the many local boys to join the *'Foudroyant'* which was moored in Falmouth harbour bewteen 1907 and 1930 and used as a sea cadet training ship. It was not rigged as a sailing ship and had only one dummy mast. It was owned by George Wheatley Cobb (d. 1930). Tuke later undertook several portraits in pastel and one in oil of the cadet sailors on board the ship in the main cabin. This pen and ink sketch could be a study for a pastel portrait of *Ginger Carne* (R574 1908), bought by Wheatley Cobb.

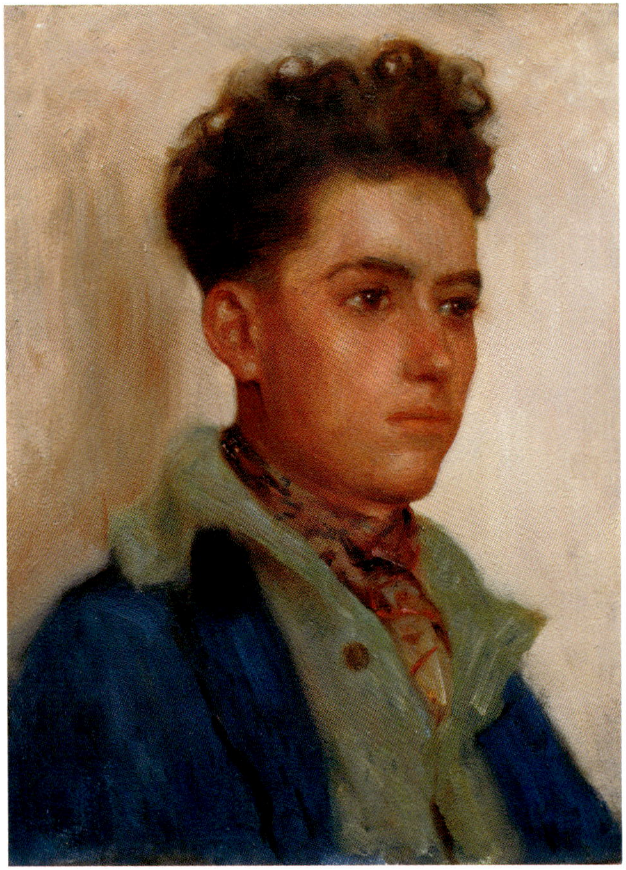

Portrait of Youth
Oil on wood panel, 33 x 24cm
Inscribed in pencil on reverse: H.S.Tuke
Provenance: Purchased from Henry Shemilt
24 December1963
RCPS Tuke Collection A59

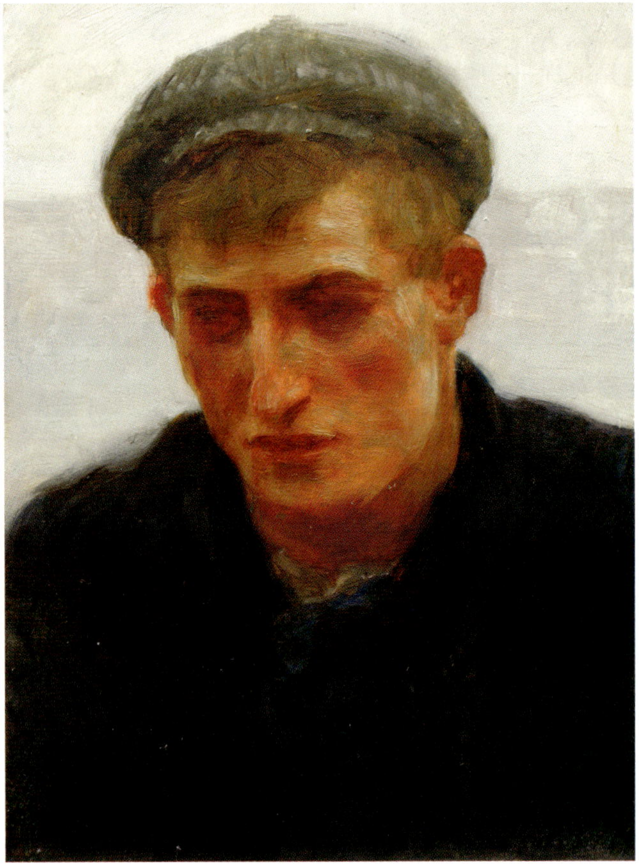

Sketch for *Summer Evening*, (Portrait of a Youth)
Oil on wood panel, 26.6 x 18.9cm
Provenance: Purchased from Henry Shemilt
24 December 1963
RCPS Tuke Collection A35

This is a portrait of Georgie Fouracre with a hat and coat. It is thought to be a study for the painting *Summer Evening* (R336) illustrated in M.T. Sainsbury on op.cit p.132. Although not the same pose, Georgie is wearing the same hat and coat as in the final painting. Georgie Fouracre was the son of Tuke's housekeeper, Mrs Elizabeth Fouracre.

Portraits of Family and Friends

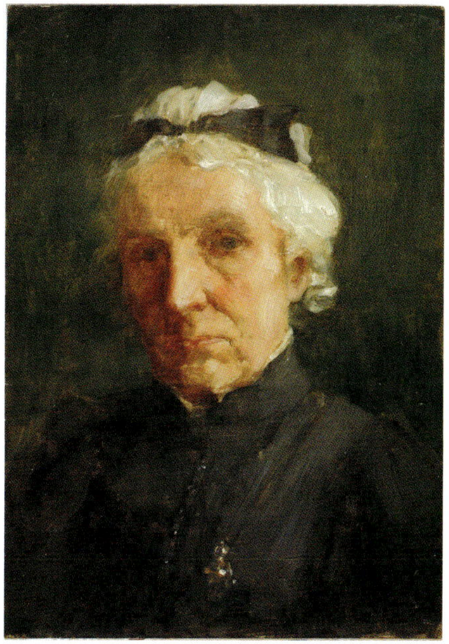

Sketch for Portrait of E.M.T, c.1903

Oil on wood panel, 27.2 x 18.8cm
Provenance: Gift from Geoffrey Sainsbury 2 February 1964
RCPS Tuke Collection A52

This is a sketch study of Tuke's mother, Esther, for the portrait R346, when she was 77 years old. It was painted at the family home in Lyndon Lodge, Hanwell. Born Esther Maria Stickney (1826-1917), she was the eldest daughter of Joseph (1792-1866) and Eliza Stickney (née Mennell), who was the daughter of Isaac Mennell (1770-1829) of Scarborough. Brought up on the Ridgmount Estate, Holderness, Esther was the eldest of 12 children and was educated at the Quaker Friends' School in Micklegate, York founded by William Tuke (1732-1822) and Esther (née Maud) Tuke in 1785. She married Daniel Hack Tuke (1827-1896) in 1853 at the small Friends' Meeting House in Pickering, near Whitby. They lived in Lawrence Street in York, while Daniel was visiting physician to the Retreat before they moved to Falmouth.

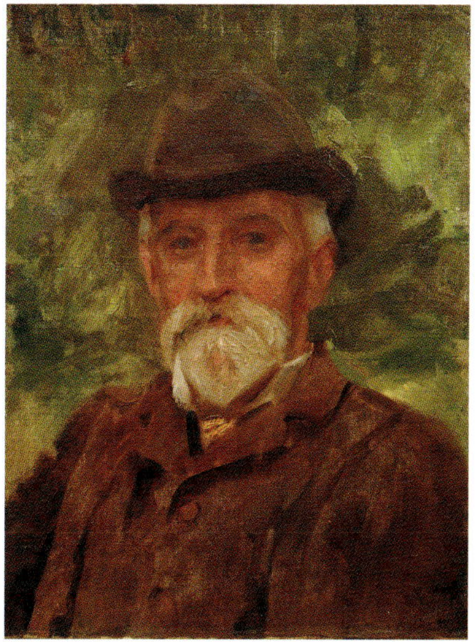

Howard Fox, c.1909

Oil on canvas board, 36.5 x 26.9cm
Provenance: Purchased from Lane's Auction house
by Norman Hall for the Tuke Collection
RCPS Tuke Collection A121

This is a sketch for a larger portrait of Howard Fox (R647) completed in 1909 which was exhibited at the Royal Academy in 1910. Both the works were painted in the garden at Rosehill, Falmouth, and Tuke was 'often interrupted by rain'.

Howard Fox (1836-1922) was a member of the important and influential Fox family who were Quakers and owned Rosehill House and gardens at the time. They also owned many other large houses and gardens in and around Falmouth including Penjerrick and Glendurgan.

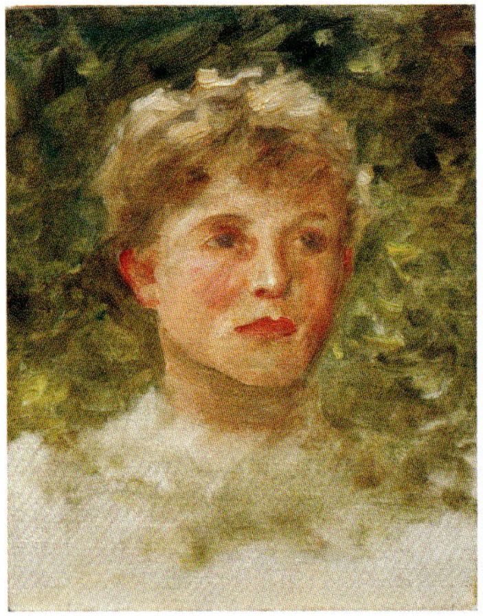

Head of Colin Goodwyn, c.1903

Oil on canvas board, 34.2 x 26.5cm
Provenance: Purchased from Henry Shemilt 24 December 1963
RCPS Tuke Collection A62

According to Tuke's diary, he painted a study of Colin Goodwyn on 25 August 1903 while he was staying in Cornwall at Carbis Bay and came over to sit for Tuke at Falmouth. But Tuke had also painted Colin's head as a study for *Coming of Day* (R345) in April 1903 at Hanwell when he was repainting this picture. He had already exhibited *Coming of Day* at the Royal Academy in 1901 but was obviously not happy with it. Diary entry for 28th April 1903 reads, 'Painted study in the garden, from Colin Goodwyn for *Coming of Day*.'

This study in the Tuke Collection could be either of the works mentioned above. Colin Goodwyn was the son of a neighbour at Tuke's family home, Lyndon Lodge, in Hanwell. Colin's father was an architect.

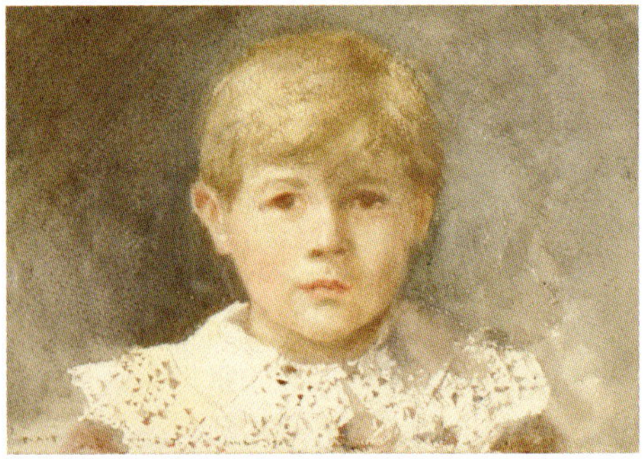

Philip Sainsbury, 1904

Watercolour, 13.6 x 18.7cm
Inscribed, initialled and dated bottom left: P.A.S, H.S.T Jan 3 1904
Provenance: Purchased from Geoffrey Sainsbury 18 December1964
RCPS Tuke Collection A47

This is a portrait of Tuke's youngest nephew in lace collar. Tuke's diary entry for 3 January 1904 reads, 'Painted watercolour sketch of Philip, who sat very well for nearly an hour and then got fidgetty.' Philip Anthony Sainsbury (1899-1937) was the fourth child of Maria Tuke Sainsbury. He remained a bachelor all his life.

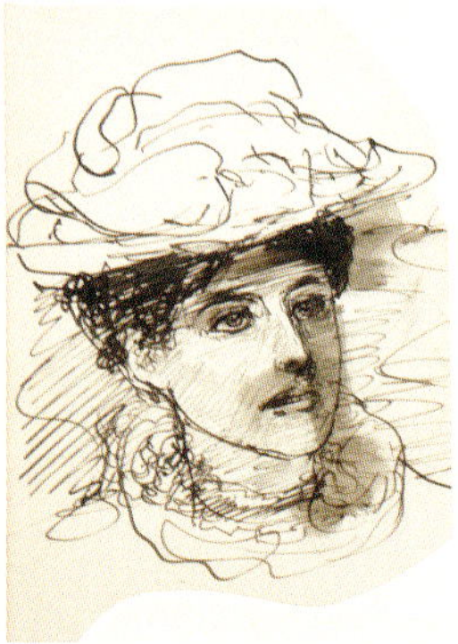

Sketch of a Lady, c.1908

Pen and iron gall ink on paper, 12.5 x 8.9cm
Provenance: Gift from Geoffrey Sainsbury 15 July 1965
RCPS Tuke Collection A50

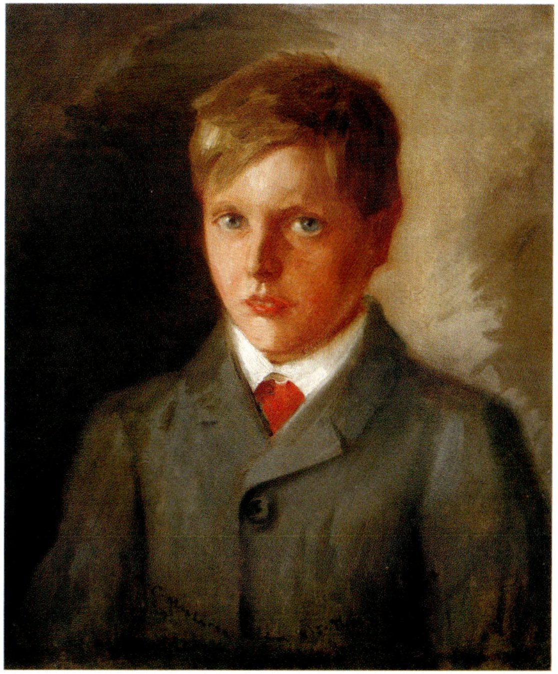

Portrait of A.J. MacLaren, 1908

Oil on canvas, 53 x 42.8cm
Signed and dated and inscribed twice:
To A.C. MacLaren from H.S.Tuke June 1908
Provenance: Purchased from W. Dyer 26 May 1966
Dyer acquired it from Abbot and Holder.
RCPS Tuke Collection A120

This portrait was painted at Shillinglee Park near Chiddingford on the Surrey – Sussex border where the Indian cricketer Prince Ranjitsinjhi (1872-1933) lived for several years and where Archibald Campbell MacLaren (1871-1944), known as Archie, was his private secretary. Archie MacLaren was himself a cricketer and played between 1890 - 1923, was captain of the England cricket team, and wrote several books on cricket. Tuke obviously painted this portrait for Archie while he was painting Ranjitshjhi's portrait at Shillinglee. The sitter was Archie MacLaren's son, A.J. MacLaren, who went into the army and rose to the rank of major. He resigned in 1957 and became a stockbroker in Edinburgh. (From *'Notes on H.S.Tuke and his Associates'* by B.D. Price.)

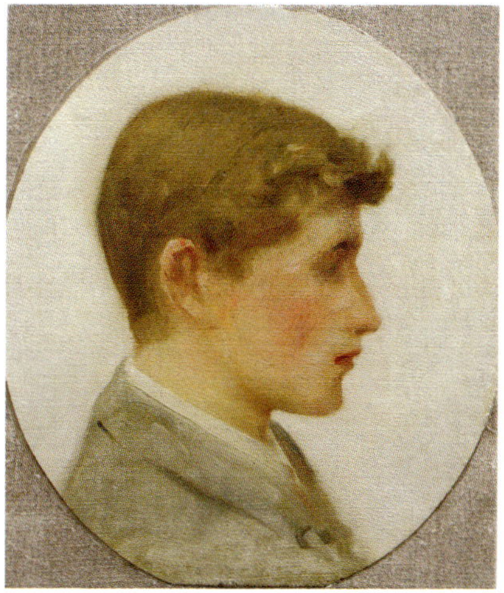

Portrait of a Youth

Oil on canvas, 24.5 x 20.4cm
Provenance: Purchased from Henry Shemilt
24 December 1963
RCPS Tuke Collection A33

This picture is thought to be a portrait of Henry Allen who was a neighbour of the Tukes in Hanwell. His father was the Rev. Solomon W. Allen. Henry Allen was a model for Tuke's painting *To the Morning Sun* (R473 1904). He is approximately 18 years old in this picture. He was a clerk for London City Council from 21 December 1903-13 November 1912. He later became a major in the army and then ran a school in Clevedon. (From *'Notes on H.S.Tuke and his Associates'* by B.D. Price.)

Portrait Studies for Paintings

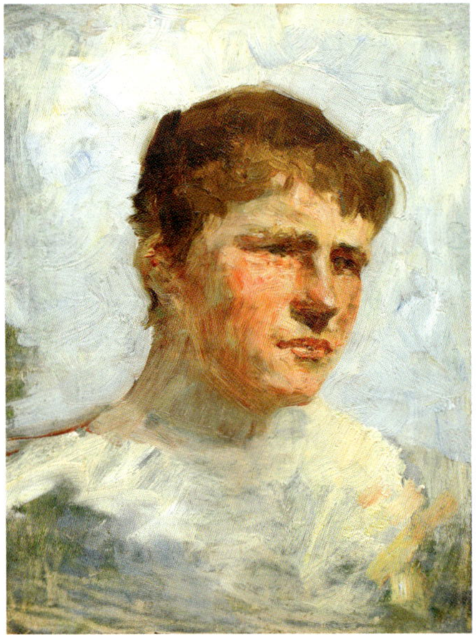

Study for *August Blue*, c.1893

Oil on panel, 21.5 x 16cm
Provenance: Purchased from H. Shemilt
24 December 1963
RCPS Tuke Collection A7

This is a sketch for the head of the boy standing in the boat on the far right in *August Blue* (R210 1893). The final painting was bought by the Chantrey Bequest from the Royal Academy in 1894 for £525. The sitters included Tonkin, Creba, Gregory Rolling, Freddy Hall, Hamley and Ruffy Harris. It is not known which of these models features in this portrait.

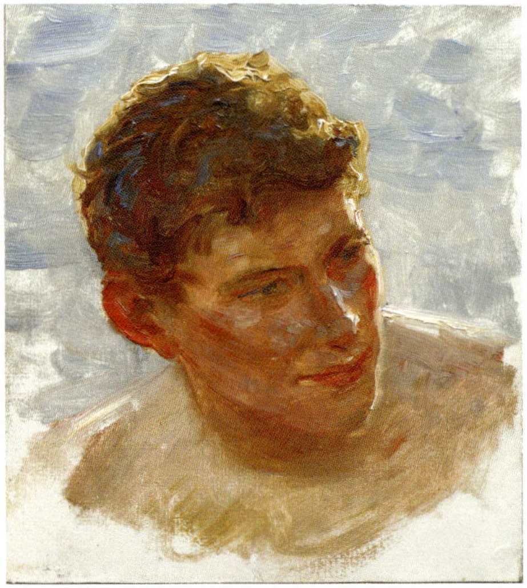

Head of T.C. Tiddy (Study for *Midsummer Morning*), c.1907

Oil on canvas, 21.7 x 19.4cm
Provenance: Purchased from Glyn Ward
17 November 1962
RCPS Tuke Collection A26

This is a study for a major oil *Midsummer Morning* (R593 1907) – a group of five young boys catching fish on the rocks at Newporth beach, Falmouth. This sketch is for the head of the furthest figure on the left hand side who is looking over the rocks to see what his friends have caught. Thomas Charles Tiddy (b.1886) was a dockyard apprentice at Falmouth and a friend of Bert White and Harry Cleave. In '*Tuke Reminscences*' by Brian D. Price, Thomas recalls going out to the boat '*Mazatlan*' after work, where he posed with the others for paintings such as *Foc's'l Gossip* and *Sailors Yarning*, 1906. He also remembered posing for *Midsummer Morning* on Newporth beach early on Sunday mornings before breakfast.

Sketch Portrait for *Under the Western Sun*, c.1918

Oil on canvas board, 36.6 x 26.8cm
Provenance: Purchased from Henry Shemilt
24 December 1963
RCPS Tuke Collection A103

This is a portrait study for *Under the Western Sun* (R876 1918), one of Tuke's most significant paintings of the time, and is of Tom White. He was a local boy who became one of Tuke's regular models, due to many of his usual models having been called up for service in the war. Tom was born 11 March 1901. According to Brian Price's interview with Tom White in 1971, Tom did not pose for Tuke until he left school in about 1914. On leaving school, Tom was a messenger boy for the Post Office from March 1915 for about 6 months, then became a telegraphist. Tom lived in Erisey Terrace and Tuke asked Tom's neighbour, Webber who was a shop assistant at Grose's, to invite Tom to pose for him after seeing him swim at Sunny Cove. Tom was paid 2/6d for posing for Tuke's paintings. This was for an hour session. He would also be paid for the time it took him to walk from Falmouth out to Newporth where the modelling was done, and back. Later Tuke gave him an old bicycle to make the journey quicker. Tuke apparently always carried the easel, canvas and paints down to the beach from his studio at Pennance Cottage. Sometimes Tom would get out to Swanpool too late and Tuke would say it was 'No good now, tide too far gone'. So instead Tom would sometimes stay in the studio and listen to Tuke talking about techniques of painting – the importance of clouds, sky and light being correct. On other occasions they would laze around the beach and bathe, and from these sessions Tuke would get ideas for poses for his paintings. Tom moved to London in January 1919, but returned in the summer to help Tuke finish his bathing paintings.

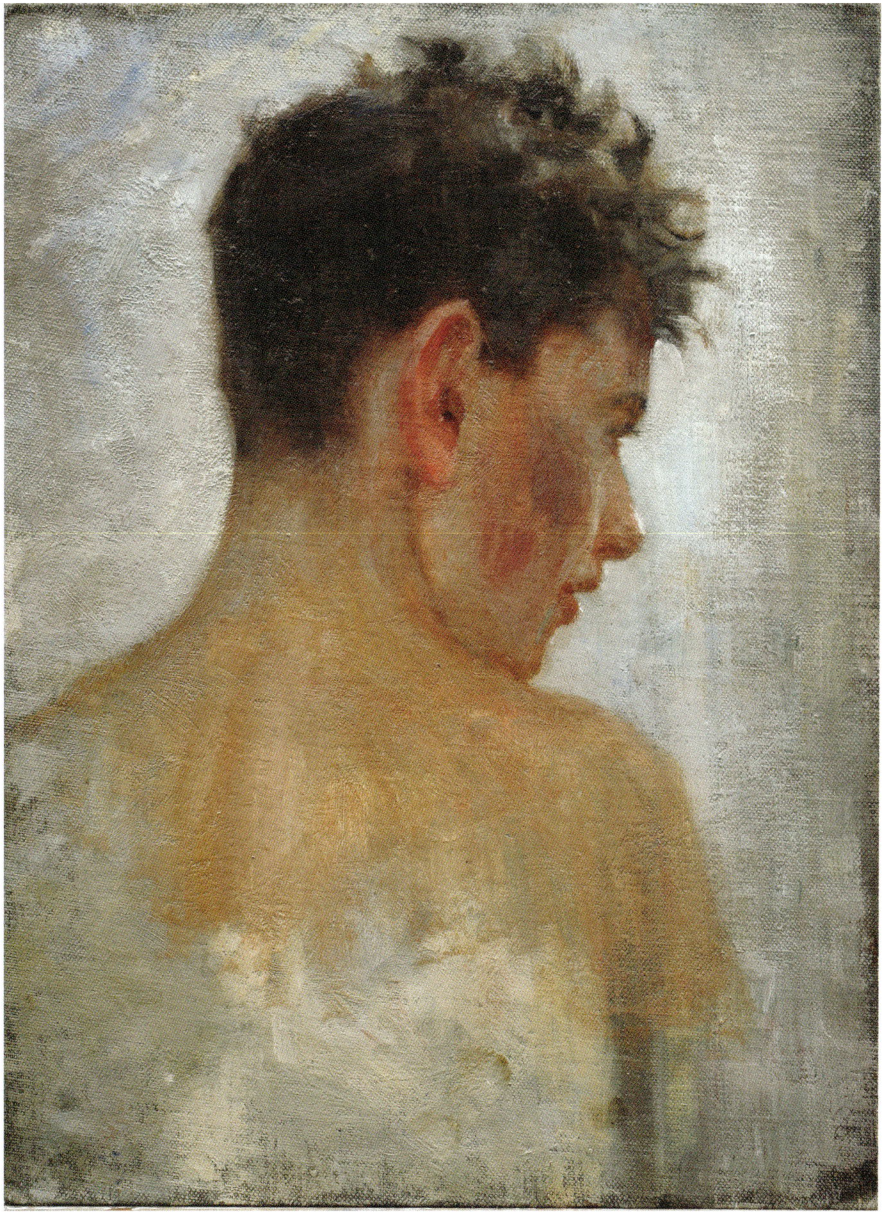

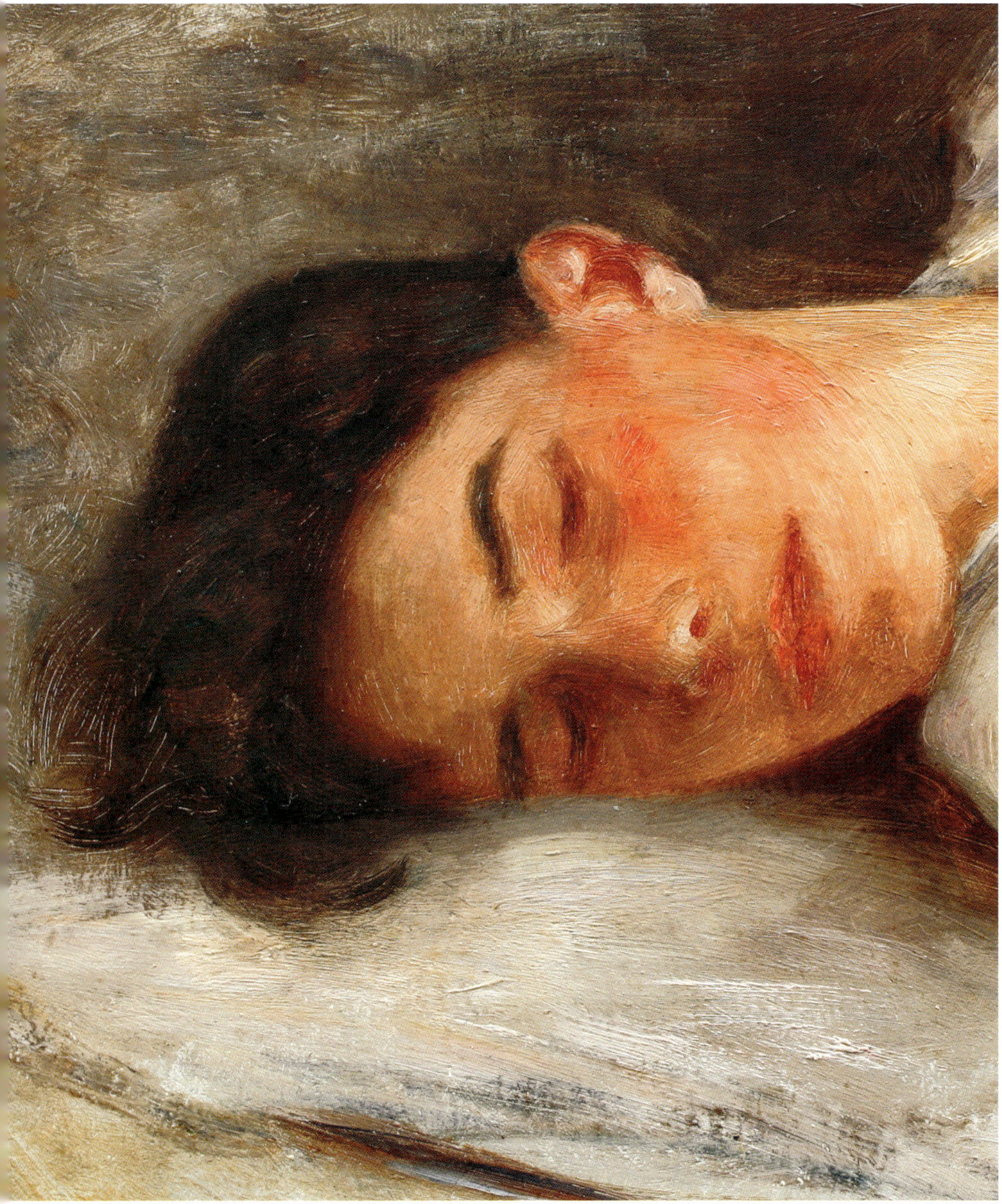

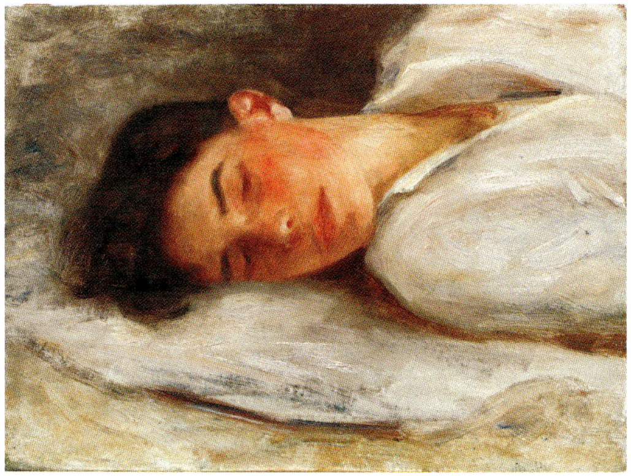

Sketch for *Summer Dreams*, c. 1919
Oil on board, 26.5 x 35cm
Provenance: Purchased from Henry Shemilt
24 December 1963
RCPS Tuke Collection A97

This is another portrait of Tom White, asleep on the beach at Newporth. In Tom's reminscences he thinks he might have fallen asleep as he had been on night duty as a telegraphist at Falmouth Post Office. Tuke asked him to keep the pose so he could paint a full nude version which was called *Summer Dreams* (R898), and was exhibited at the Royal Academy in 1919, Pittsburgh and Aberdeen in 1921, Rome in 1923 and Wembley in 1925.

The Nude

Today Tuke is mainly known for his paintings of bathing boys in the nude painted in Falmouth on the beach near his cottage. However, it actually took many years for him to arrive at this *oeuvre* which made him so notorious. Whatever his motivations for these paintings, they were first and foremost an artistic challenge.

He started painting the nude outdoors in Italy in 1880/81 with artist Arthur Lemon. Most of his first nudes were disguised as mythological subjects such as *Leander, Perseus and Andromeda*, and *Hermes at the Pool.* A friend John Addington Symonds (1840-1893), who gave Tuke some advice regarding these nude paintings, may have influenced his decision to change his approach: 'I should say you ought to develop studies in the nude without pretending to make them "subject pictures"... Your own inspiration is derived from nature's beauty. Classical and Romantic mythologies are not your starting point. Number your pictures Op.1.2.3.etc. Do not find titles for them.' (Letter 10 Jan. 1893) Although Tuke was always to give his nude paintings titles such as *August Blue, Morning Splendour, Noonday Heat,* he did drop the pretence of mythological subjects. In fact 1893 was to be a pivotal year, as in it he produced *August Blue* (R210) which featured a very natural figure composition of four boys, three of them nude on a rowing boat in the sea in Falmouth harbour surrounded by sailing ships. This painting was one of the first that could be said to herald Tuke's 'Impressionist' style. Tuke's palette became, on the whole, lighter and brighter from then on. Tuke always painted the nude outdoors but not always in the warmest weather. 'When I first began painting nudes out of doors the model sat out till mid – November, and I used to watch him going pink and blue in patches. But he was a professional and knew what to expect. Latterly I have worked with amateurs, and am much more careful to preserve them. They are very plucky generally, and if you let them swear a little now and again, it seems to revive them.' (From 'The Life story of a Famous Painter' by Flora Klickmann, *Windsor Magazine*, 1895 p.606) In the same article, Tuke states that the reason he lived in Falmouth was 'primarily to paint the nude in the open air'. He felt that this approach seemed 'to open up fresh vistas, and certainly gave new interest to the study of the undraped figure. To depict it with the pure daylight upon it, instead of the artificial light of the studio'.

The RCPS collection mainly includes small studies of nudes for Tuke's larger oils, with the exception of his Royal Academy exhibit *Noonday Heat* (A402 R382). The studies show how Tuke developed his composition, skin tone colours, and paint handling technique in both oils and watercolour.

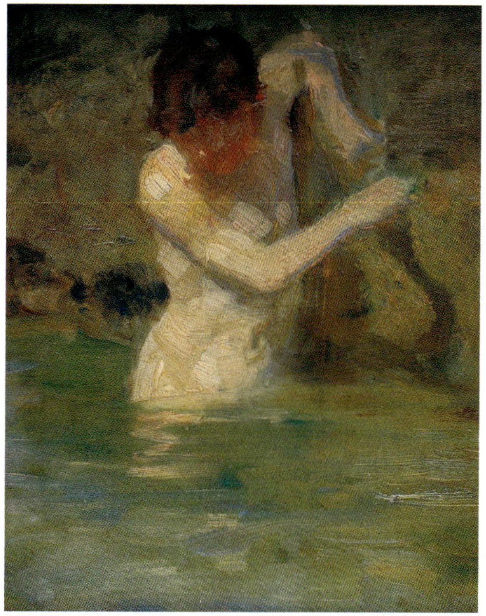

Study for *A Summer Morning*, (Boy Bathing), c.1886
Oil on panel, 27.4 x 21.9cm
Provenance: Purchased from Geoffrey Sainsbury 16 September 1962
RCPS Tuke Collection A10 R72?

This is a study for *A Summer Morning (or Small Bathers)* (R77 1887) which featured Jim Dimond and Jack Rolling; this is thought to be Jim Dimond and could be R72 *Jim*.

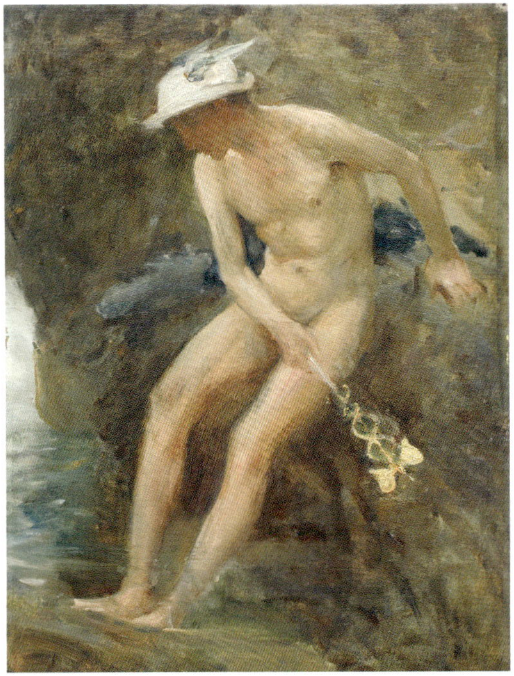

Sketch for *Hermes at the Pool*, c.1900

Oil on canvas, 48 x 36cm
Provenance: Presented to the Tuke Collection by Sally Jackett 6 December 1965
Originally given by Henry Scott Tuke to Johnnie Jackett
RCPS Tuke Collection A114

This is a study for a major oil exhibited at the Royal Academy in 1900, *Hermes at the Pool* (R338). It was poorly received at the exhibition. Even after making alterations, Tuke did not like it: 'The first varnishing day at the RA Hermes looks worse than in my studio.' Diary entry 26 April 1900. The model was Johnnie Jackett.

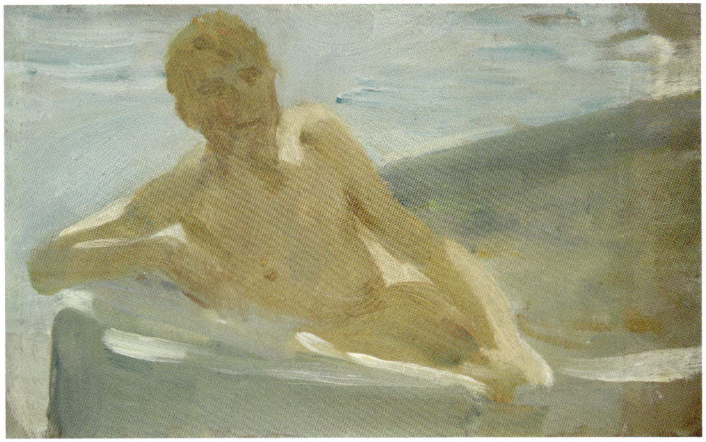

Sketch for *Morning Splendour* (previously *August Blue*)

Oil on panel, 12.3 x 20.6cm
Provenance: Purchased from Henry Shemilt 17 January 1964
RCPS Tuke Collection A133

This sketch could be for the painting *Morning Splendour* (see A19) and not *August Blue* as previously thought, as the boy is in the bow of the boat.

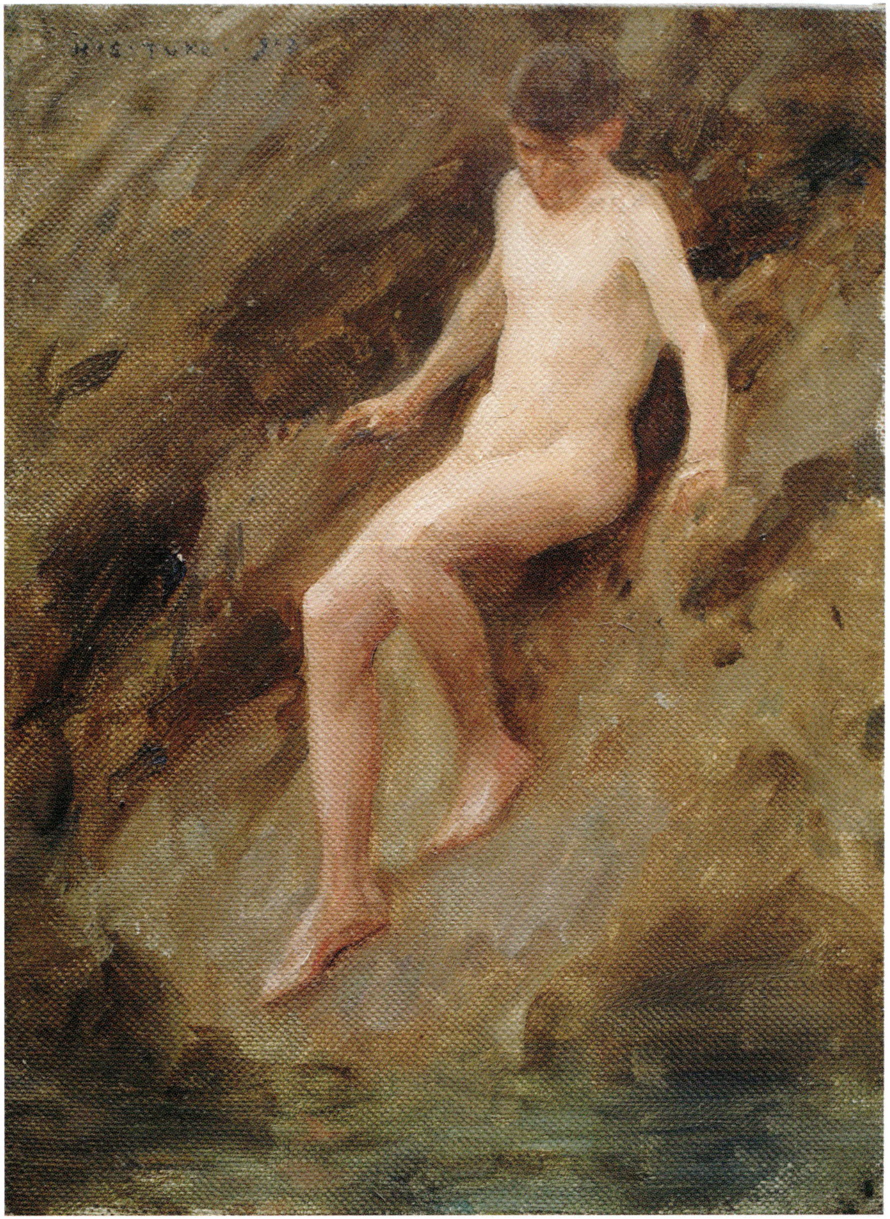

Nude boy on rock
Oil on canvas, 38.2 x 28cm
Signed and dated top right: H.S.Tuke ca. 1895 or 1905
(partially erased)
Provenance: Purchased from Henry Shemilt
24 December 1963
RCPS Tuke Collection A94

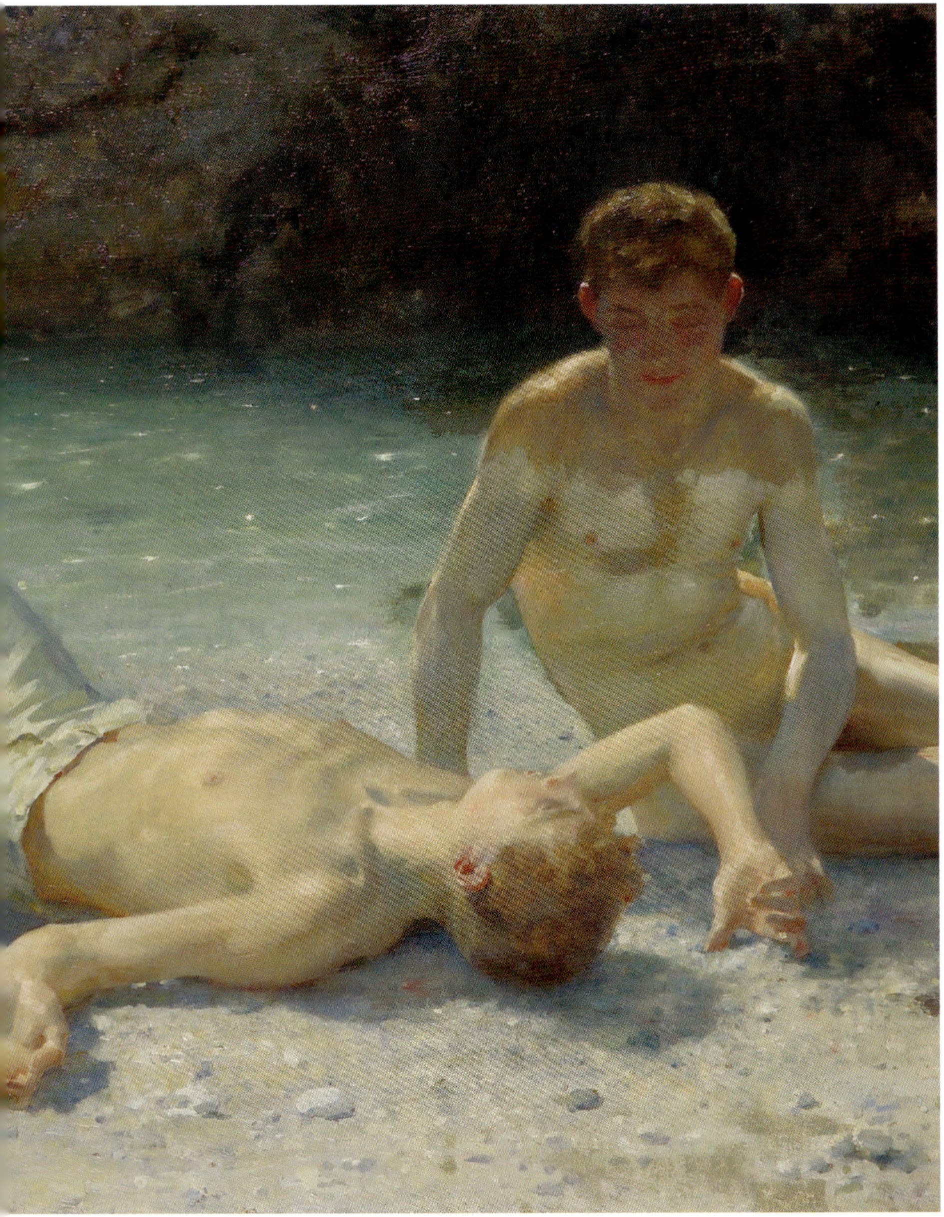

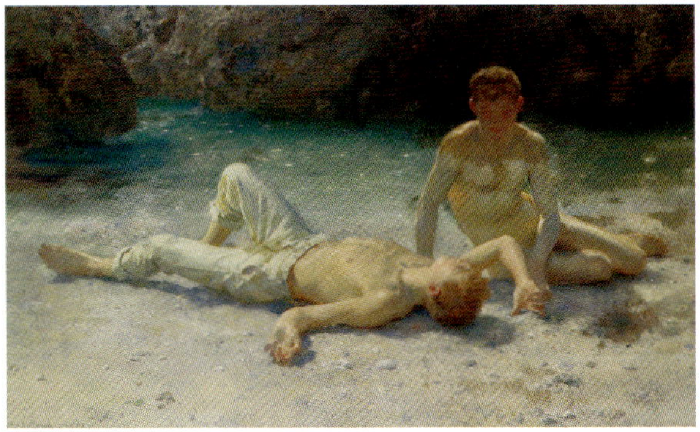

Noonday Heat, 1902/03

Oil on canvas, 82 x 134cm
Signed and dated bottom left: H.S.Tuke 1903
Exhibited: Royal Academy 1903, Liverpool 1903
Provenance: Bought by Colonel Sydney Lomer in 1922
Bought by H.S.Tuke and Jack Hone in 1926
Jack Hone (1895-1978) owned it and gave it to the RCPS November 1965
RCPS Tuke Collection A402 R382

This picture of models Georgie Fouracre and Bert White was painted in the summer of 1902 at Falmouth, on the beach at Newporth. According to his diary entries, the painting took over five months to complete and gives a unique insight into how he developed a painting. On 12 July, 'Stretched canvas and blocked in new picture of basking'; 13 July, 'Painted Georgie and White in new picture'; 3 August, 'Bert and Georgie out at Newport[h]'; 24 August, 'A good sitting with Bert White'; 25 August, 'Repainted rock and water on fresh canvas'; 7 September, 'A fine day on White's torso'; 9 September, 'Bert having a week off...Study of head and breast'; 13 September, ' ... got on with legs'; 18th September, 'A most lovely day, decided to alter George's head to *profile perdue*'; 19 September, 'Did a good study of [George Fouracre's] head in new position and worked it into the picture in the afternoon'; 30 September, 'Did some good touches on G's head'; 12 October, 'Work all the morning at Newport[h] on Bert W's torso'; 17 October, 'Got White's head nearly right'; 26 October, 'A lovely morning, two good hours with Bert'; 9 November, 'An hour in the sun with B[ert] W[hite]. Painted dongaree [sic] pants in picture.' Tuke was later commissioned to undertake a nude version of this painting in watercolour for Leonard Duke in 1911.

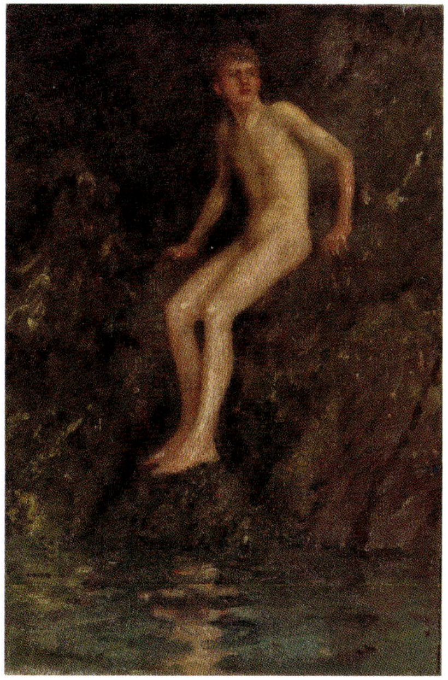

Nude Boy on Rocks, 1907

Oil on canvas, 55.5 x 36cm
Signed and dated bottom left: H.S.Tuke 1907
Provenance: Purchased from Glyn Ward 29 April 1964 via Henry Shemilt, who bought it from Mary Owens-Thurston before she went to South Africa. It had belonged to her mother Mary Henderson Bull.
RCPS Tuke Collection A117

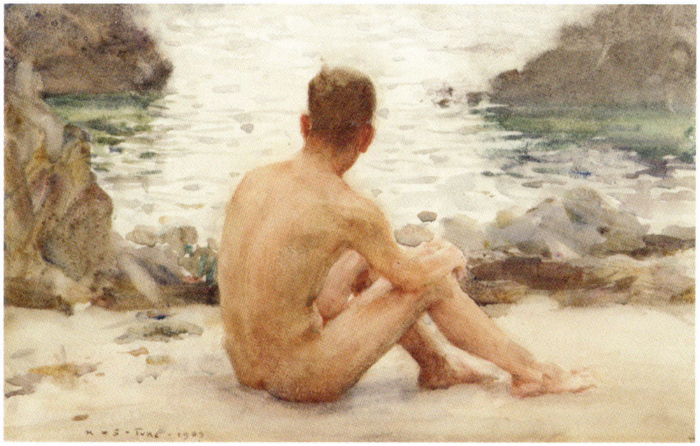

Charlie Seated on the sand, 1907

Watercolour, 14 x 21.5cm
Signed and dated bottom left: H.S.Tuke 1907
Provenance: Purchased from Rev. H.Y. Ganderton 7 April 1966
RCPS Tuke Collection A158 R587

Charlie Mitchell (1885-1957) was born in Falmouth and first appears as a nude model in *Ruby, Gold and Malachite* (R374 1901), when he was 16 years old. Charlie was a regular model for Tuke for many years and appeared in numerous major paintings and many studies. He looked after Tuke's boats until he died, and used to row Tuke out from Swanpool into the bay so he could paint the ships.

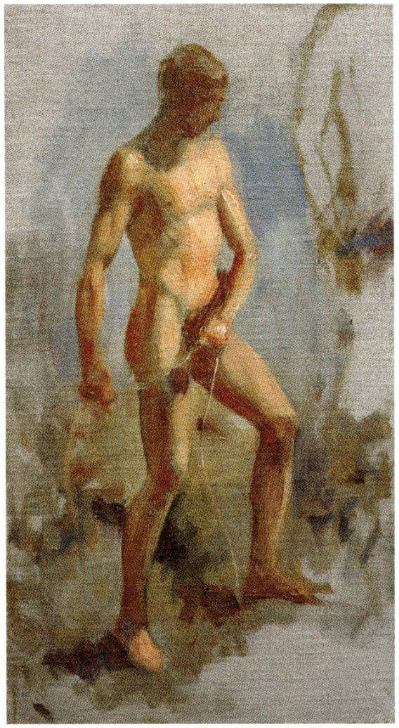

Study for *Charlie Throwing Line*, c.1907
Oil on canvas, 31.8 x 17.2cm
Provenance: Purchased from Glyn Ward
17 November 1962
RCPS Tuke Collection A27

It is assumed this oil sketch is a study for a watercolour of the same title (R564) *Charlie (Mitchell) Throwing Line* exhibited at the Royal Watercolour Society in 1907.

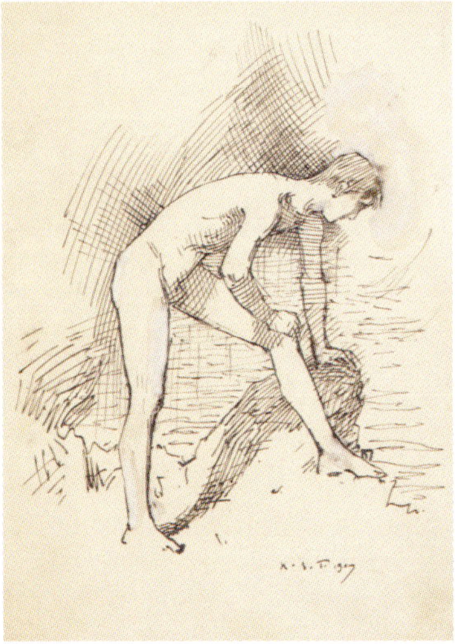

Sketch for *The Diving Place*, 1907
Pen and iron gall ink with watercolour on paper, 19.9 x 13.7cm
Initialled and dated bottom right: H.S.T 1907
Inscribed on reverse: H.S.Tuke ARA The Pool
(written by Willy Sainsbury)
Provenance: Purchased from L. Justinian Delany
6 June 1962
Previously owned by W. Dyer of Camborne
RCPS Tuke Collection A252

This is a sketch of Charlie Mitchell on the rocks at Newporth used for a final painting called *The Diving Place* (R563), which was exhibited at the Royal Academy in 1907, Glasgow in 1907 and Pittsburgh in 1911.

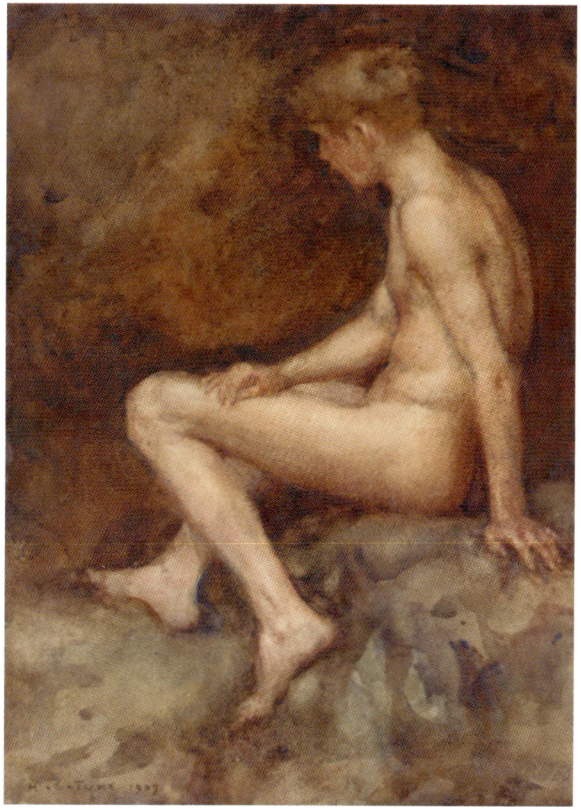

Nude Seated in a Cave, 1909
Watercolour, 26.3 x 18cm
Signed and dated bottom left: H.S.Tuke.1909
Exhibited: Royal Watercolour Society Spring 1910
Provenance: On back of frame was written in pencil: 'Purchased from Tuke by Laurence Murray Ogilvy. 6 of May 1945 [sic]'.
Purchased from Mrs M. Kemp, 1 June 1963 for Tuke Collection
RCPS Tuke Collection A5 R666

As this picture was exhibited at RWS in 1910, Tuke must have regarded it as a good example of his work. It features a familiar pose of a boy sitting on a rock against a dark background. It dates from the same year as *Two Boys on a Beach (A Study in Bright Sunlight)* (R662) which is in the Ashmolean Museum, Oxford. These two works show an opposite approach to the use of light.

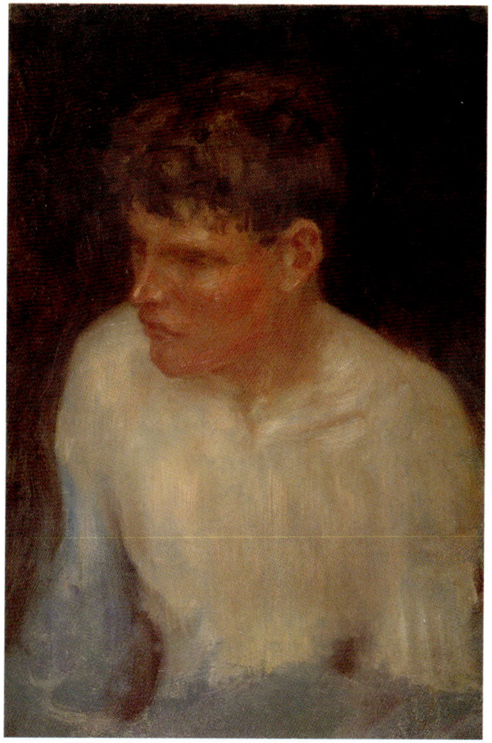

Portrait of a Boy
Oil on board, 30.5 x 20cm
Provenance: Purchased from Henry Shemilt 24 December 1963
RCPS Tuke Collection A37

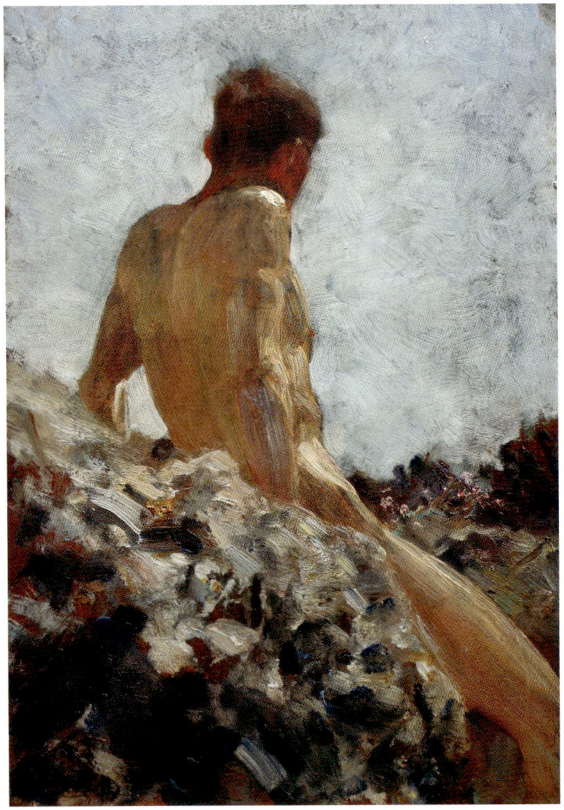

Nude Study

Oil on wood panel, 29.2 x 19.9cm
On reverse original Royal Academy label: H.S.Tuke R.A. Nude Study (small panel) oil, Executors of the Late H.S.Tuke.
Exhibited: Posthumously Royal Academy 1929
Provenance: Purchased from Glyn Ward 15 October 1963
Glyn Ward had purchased it from Willy Sainsbury.
RCPS Tuke Collection A29

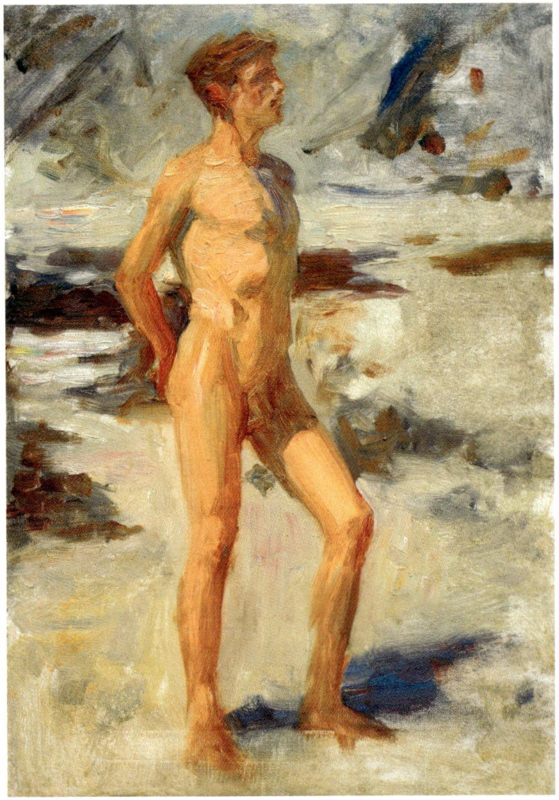

Boy on beach

Oil on canvas, 45 x 30.7cm
Provenance: Purchased from Glyn Ward
17 November 1962
RCPS Tuke Collection A106

Broad brush worked study of male nude on beach in strong sunlight. Pictures like this show Tuke using his best Impressionist style.

Sketch of Nude Youth (Study for *Morning Splendour*), c.1921

Oil on panel, 31.6 x 40cm
RCPS Tuke Collection A403

Sketch of Charlie Mitchell in the nude seated on the beach. This is a very similar pose to seated figure in *Morning Splendour* (R986 1921).

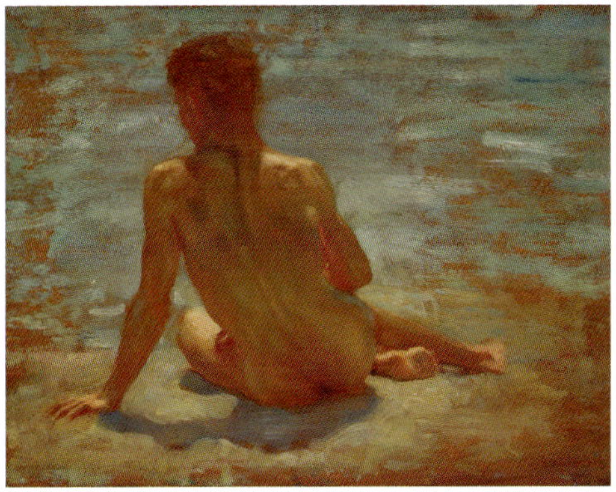

Sketch of Seated Boy

Oil on panel, 31.8 x 40cm
Signed bottom middle: H.S.Tuke 1917
RCPS Tuke Collection A403a (Verso of A403)

This painting is on the reverse of A403. It is a landscape with a lake and trees and is signed bottom left by W.H. Humphries, an artist whom Tuke knew. Tuke has overpainted this work with a sketch of a male nude on a rock.

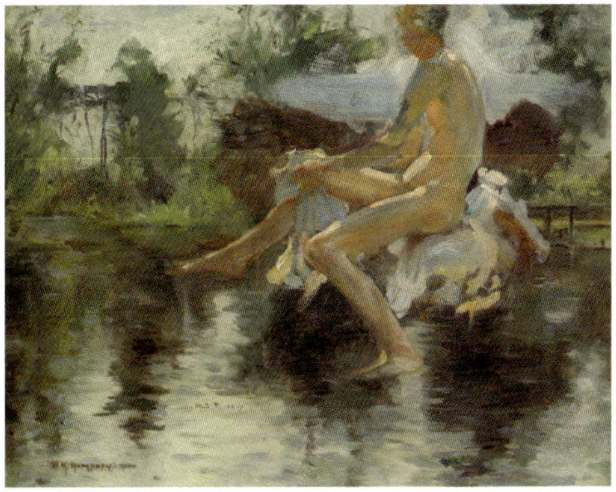

Charlie on the Beach

Watercolour, 14 x 21.6cm
Signed bottom right: H.S.Tuke
Provenance: Purchased from Geoffrey Sainsbury 18 December1964
RCPS Tuke Collection A91

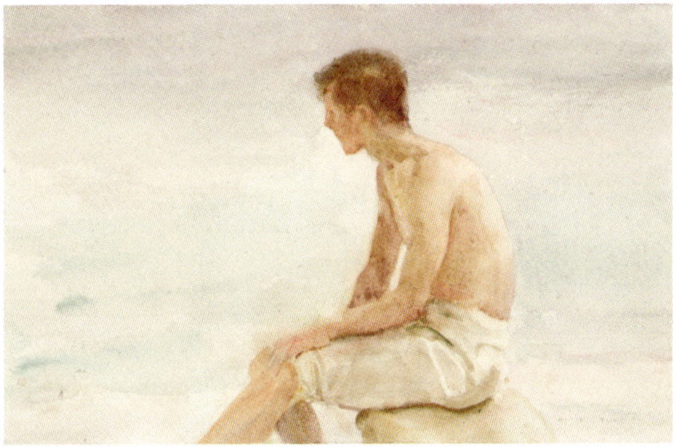

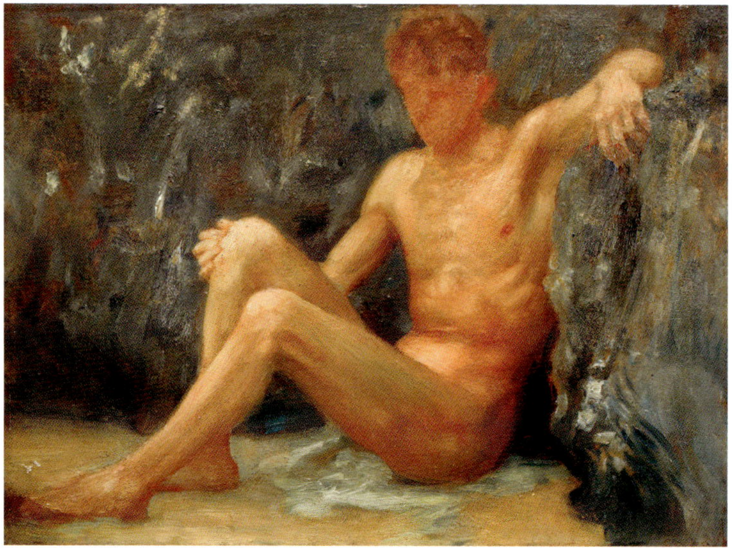

Bather Seated
Oil on panel, 26.5 x 35.5cm
Provenance: Purchased from Geoffrey Sainsbury
19 December 1963
RCPS Tuke Collection A118

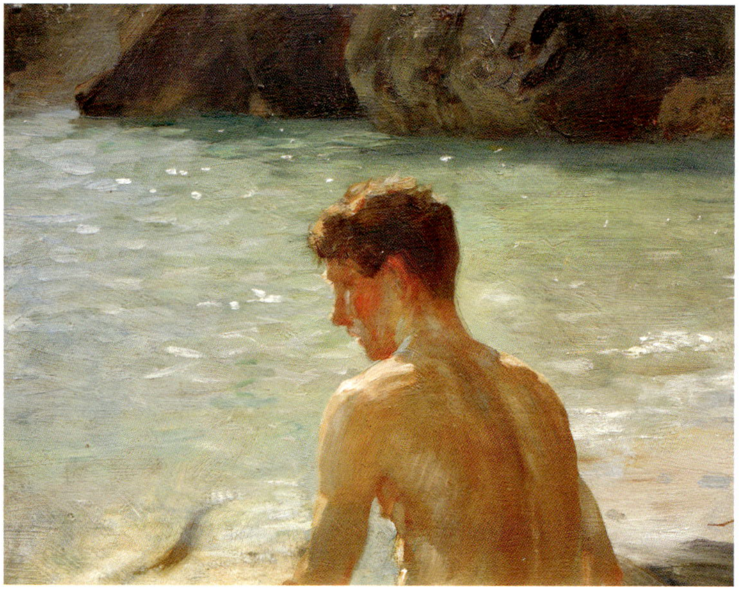

Sketch for *The Critics*, c.1928
Oil on board, 28.6 x 36.3cm
Provenance: Purchased from Geoffrey Sainsbury
13 July 1963
RCPS Tuke Collection A69

Sketch for major oil *The Critics* (R1231 1928)
Charlie Mitchell on the beach

Nude Group Sketches

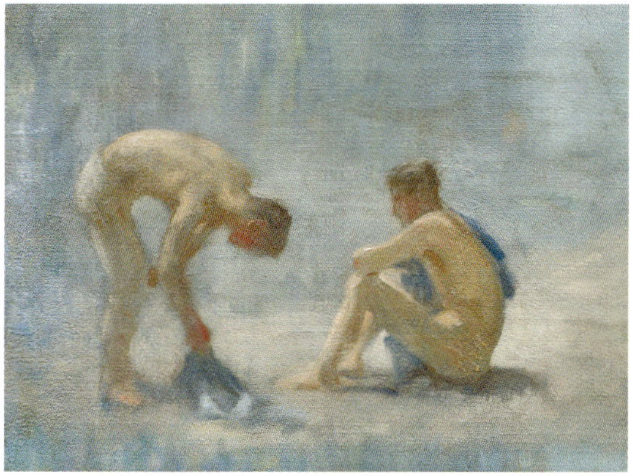

Study for *Aquamarine*, c.1927/28

Oil on canvas, 25 x 33.5cm
Provenance: Purchased from Geoffrey Sainsbury
13 July 1963
RCPS Tuke Collection A61

This is a study for *Aquamarine* (R1262 1928) which must have been one of the last paintings of nudes on the beach that Tuke undertook before he died. It was exhibited posthumously at the Royal Academy in 1929 and in 1933.

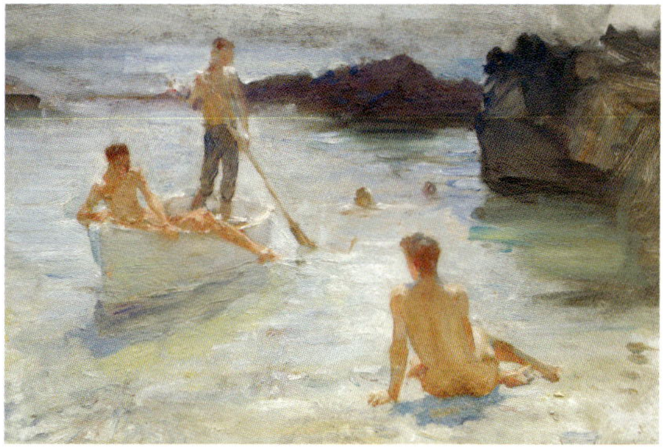

Study for *Morning Splendour*, c. 1921

Oil on canvas, 26 x 39.9cm
Provenance: Purchased from Geoffrey Sainsbury
20 December 1962
RCPS Tuke Collection A19

This is a study for the major oil *Morning Splendour* (R986 1921) which was painted on Newporth beach, Falmouth in the summer of 1921 and exhibited at the Royal Academy in 1922. The models were Charlie Mitchell, William Sainsbury, Leo Marshall and Georgie Fouracre. *Morning Splendour* used to hang in Baden-Powell House, the headquarters of the Scout and Guide movement in London.

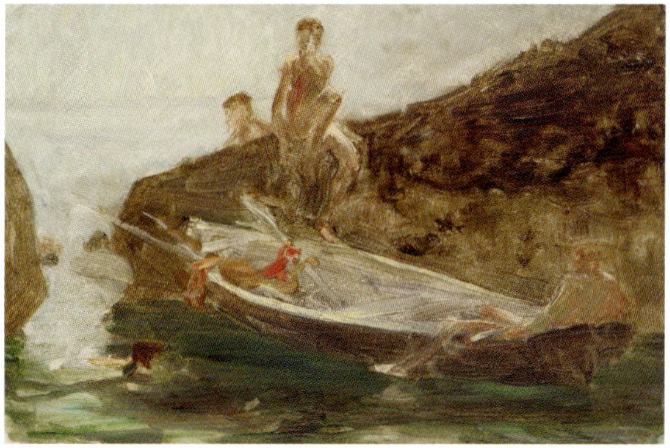

Sketch for *The Swimmer's Pool*, c.1895

Oil on panel, 24.5 x 36cm
Provenance: Purchased from Geoffrey Sainsbury
9 October 1966
RCPS Tuke Collection A79

A sketch for a major oil of 1895 *The Swimmer's Pool* (R226 1895) where one boy sits in the stern of the boat, another sits on the rock holding the boat with a toe, another boy is behind the rock, and there are two boys in the sea. Tuke used Georgie Rolling, and Johnnie Jackett's and William Martin's heads as the models.

The Clothed Figure

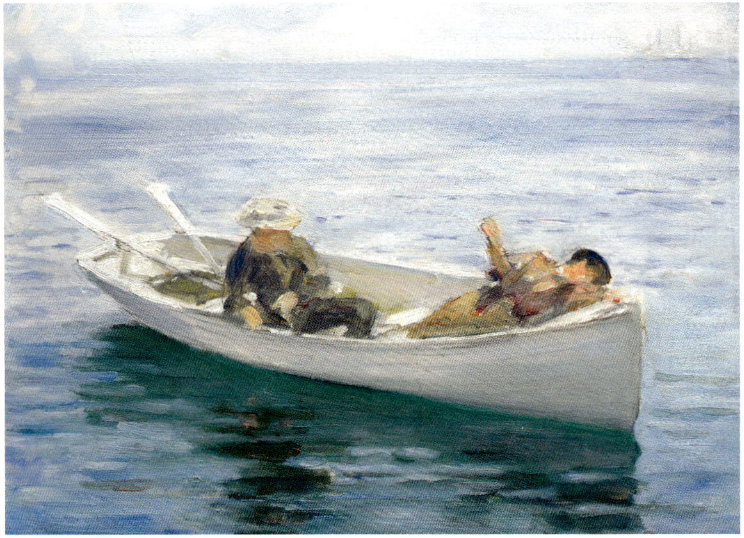

Study for *The Idyll of the Sea*, c.1897
Oil on canvas, 25.3 x 35cm
Provenance: Purchased from Frank Jackett
11 January1965
RCPS Tuke Collection A111

This was a study for the major oil *The Idyll of the Sea* (R301 1897) and was exhibited at the Royal Academy in 1898, Liverpool 1898, Paris International 1900 where it won the Silver Medal, and Sheffield 1901. The models were Lily May and Johnnie Jackett.

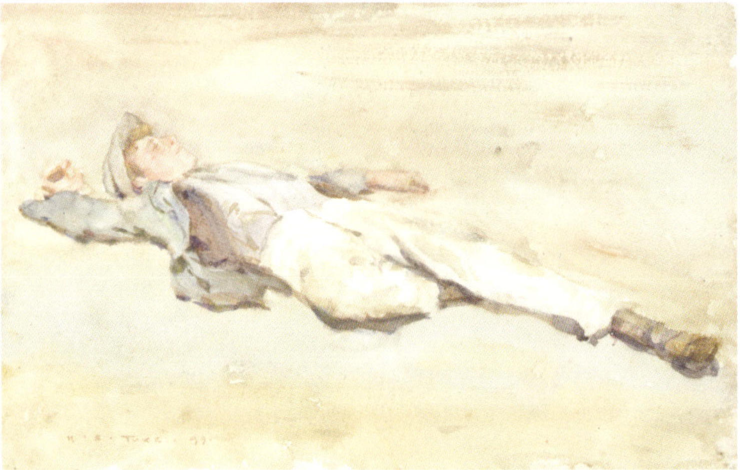

Basking, 1899
Watercolour, 13.9 x 21.4cm
Signed and dated bottom left: H.S.Tuke.99
Provenance: Purchased by Captain C.E. Parkes
21 December 1922 from Brook Street Art Gallery
and purchased from him on 13 September 1965
by B.D. Price
RCPS Tuke Collection A100 R329

Sketch for *The Three Companions*, c.1904

Oil on panel, 20 x 29.2cm
Provenance: Purchased from Henry Shemilt
24 December 1963
RCPS Tuke Collection A125

This is a sketch for a major oil *The Three Companions* (R484), which was exhibited at the Royal Academy in 1905. In the finished work, two boys, one nude and one clothed, are sitting on rocks and a dog is swimming in the water. The models for the final painting were Bert White, Johnnie Jackett, Charlie Mitchell and Harry Cleave.

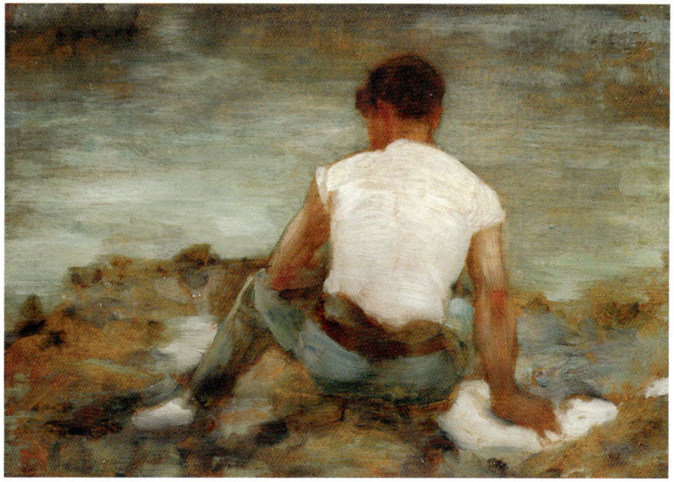

Boy leaning on a boat

Watercolour, 18 x 25cm
Provenance: From the sketchbook given by Hester Etchells
to the Tuke Collection 27 June 1964
RCPS Tuke Collection A85

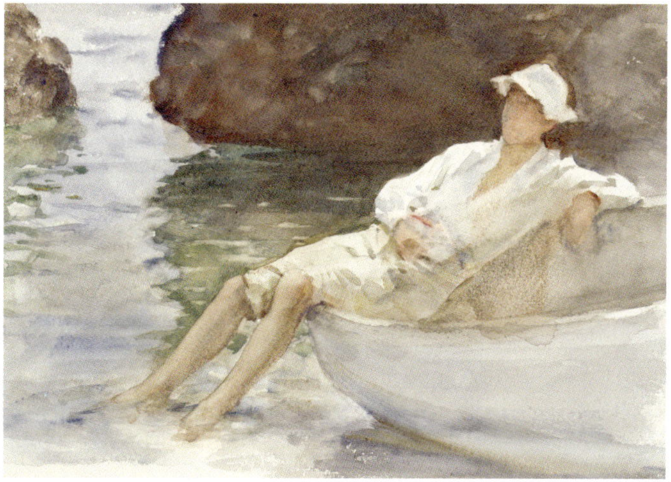

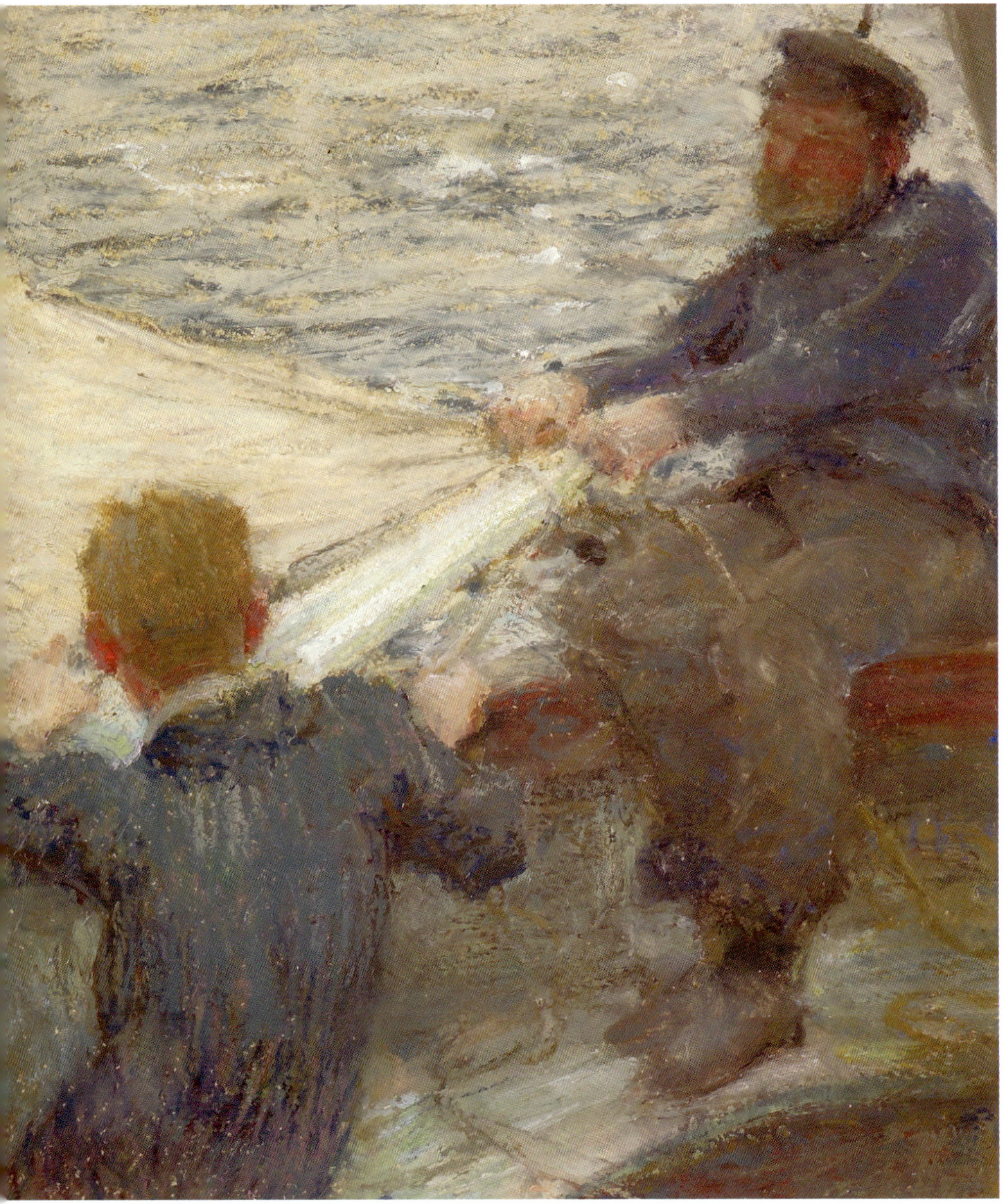

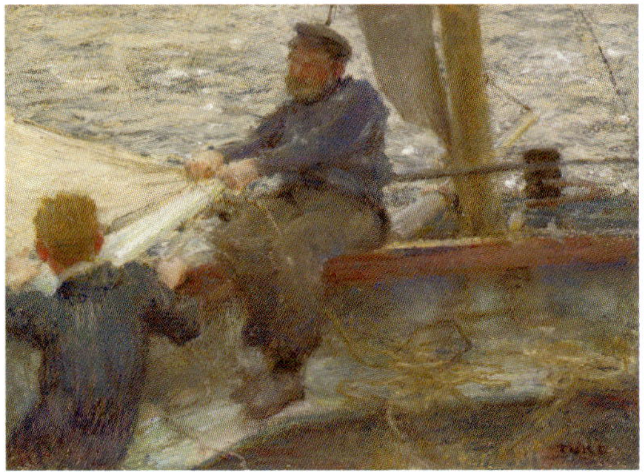

Sketch for *Reefing the Mainsail*, c.1903
Raffaelli oil sticks on panel, 26.6 x 36cm
Signed bottom right: TUKE
Provenance: Purchased from Geoffrey Sainsbury
20 December 1962
RCPS Tuke Collection A58

This study for a larger work *Reefing the Mainsail* (R386), also in oil sticks, was of Neddy Hall and Will Rolling taking in a reef. Tuke's diary entry of 23 January 1903 reads, 'Started a new Raffaelli, Hall and Billy Rowling taking in a reef, from a former sketch. Got most of it done.'

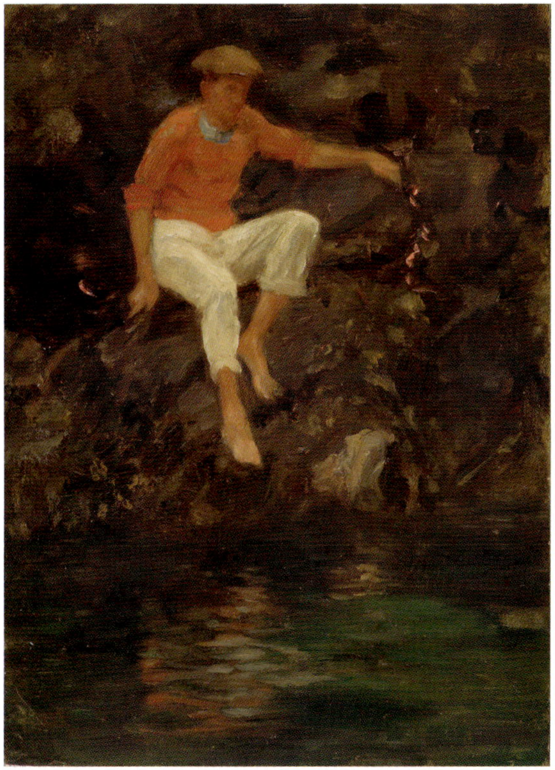

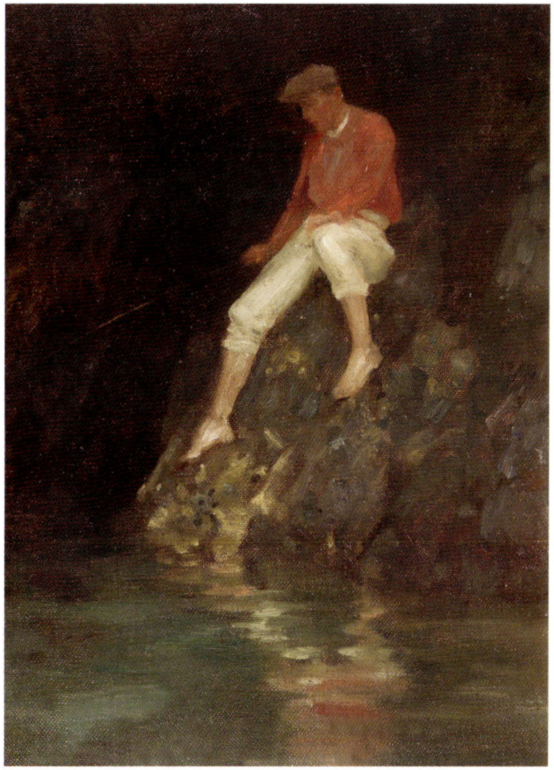

Charlie Mitchell on the Rocks

Oil on panel, 38.5 x 27.3cm
Provenance: Purchased from Geoffrey Sainsbury
29 May1968
RCPS Tuke Collection A136

The model is Charlie Mitchell, painted on rocks on Newporth beach, Swanpool, Falmouth. This picture is less dark than a very similar pose in A108. This version also has more pink flowers on the rocks.

Boy Fishing on Rocks

Oil on canvas board, 36.7 x 26.4cm
Provenance: Purchased from Geoffrey Sainsbury
13 July 1963
RCPS Tuke Collection A108

This is also Charlie Mitchell posing on the rocks. It is a slightly different version of A136.

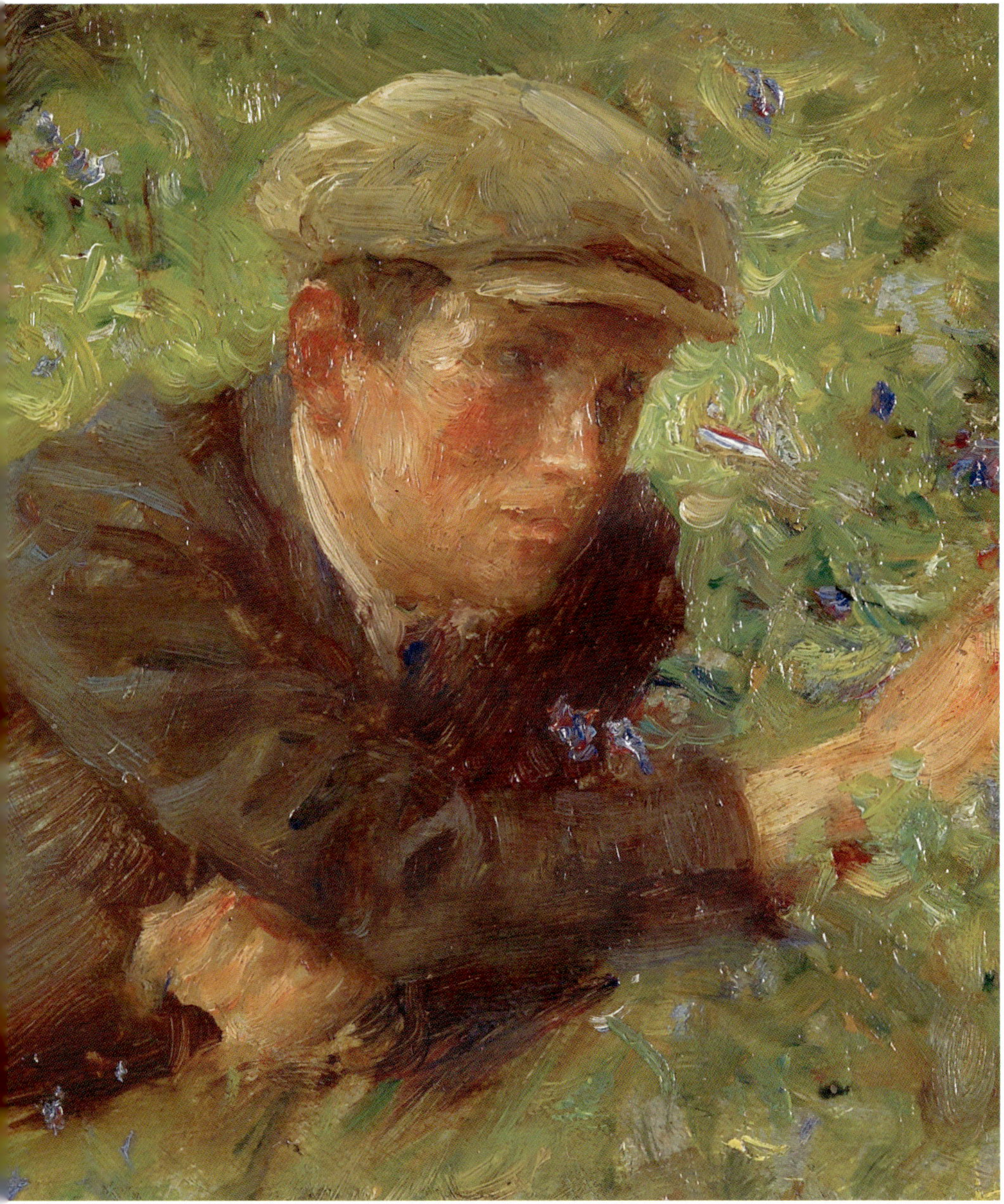

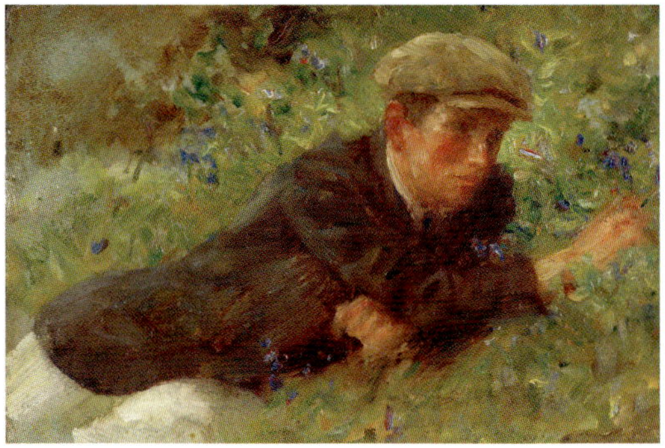

Bluebells
Oil on board, 20 x 29.1cm
Provenance: Purchased from Henry Shemilt
24 December1963
RCPS Tuke Collection A98

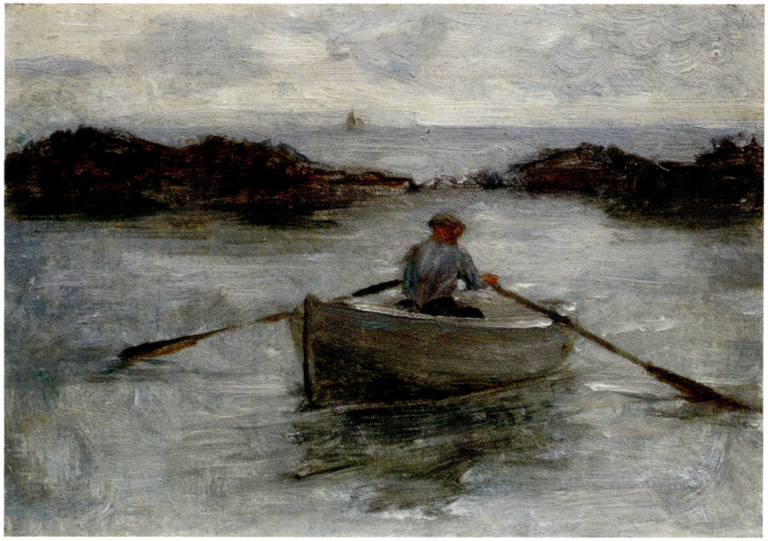

Man rowing a Dinghy
Oil on panel, 18.8 x 26.6cm
Provenance: Purchased from Geoffrey Sainsbury
19 December 1963
RCPS Tuke Collection A128

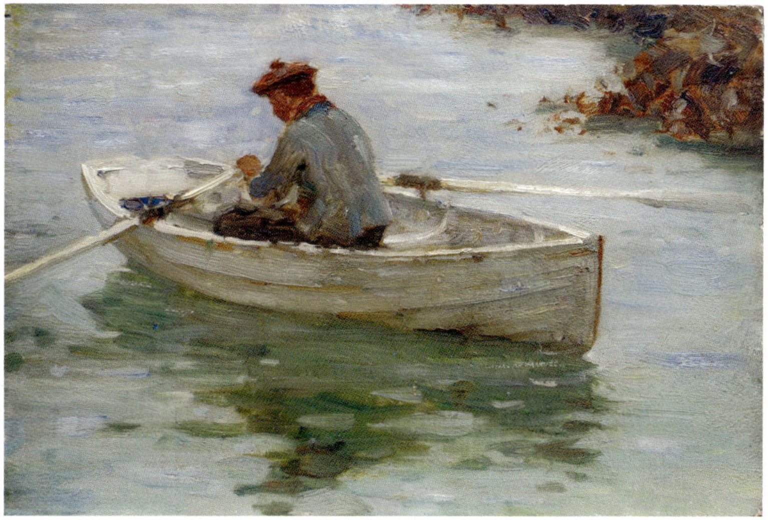

Boy in a Dinghy
Oil on board, 19.9 x 29.1cm
Provenance: Purchased from Henry Shemilt
24 December 1963
RCPS Tuke Collection A36

The model is probably Charlie Mitchell who rowed and looked after Tuke's boats for him.

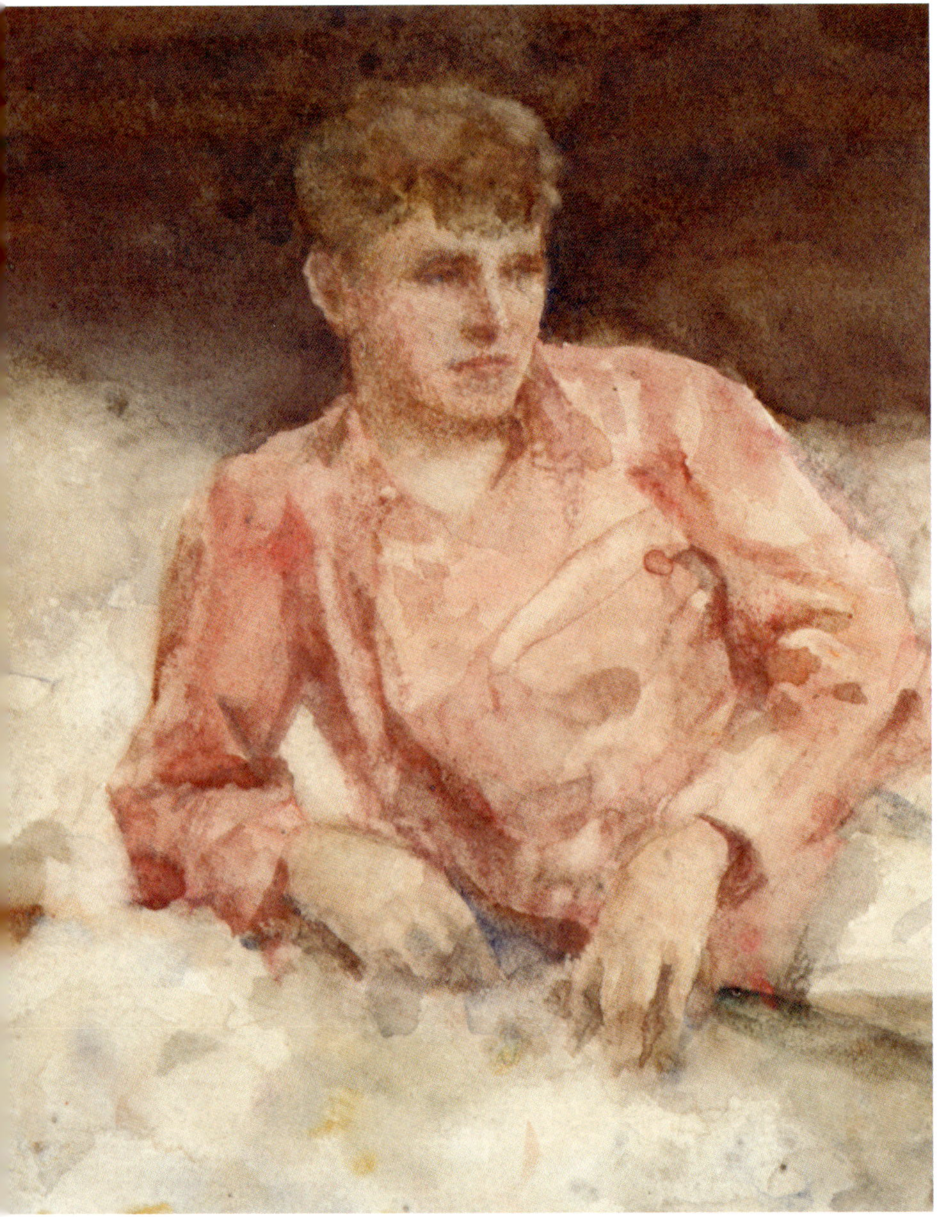

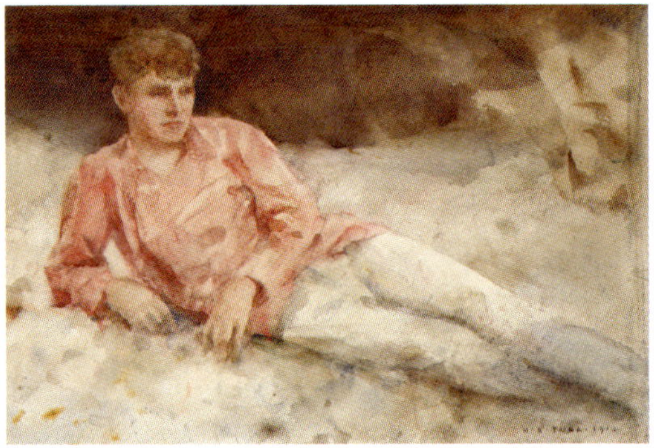

Boy in a Red Shirt, 1914

Watercolour, 13.7 x 19.5cm
Signed and dated bottom right: H.S.Tuke 1914
Provenance: Purchased from Geoffrey Sainsbury
29 May 1968
Originally owned by Willy Sainsbury
RCPS Tuke Collection A54

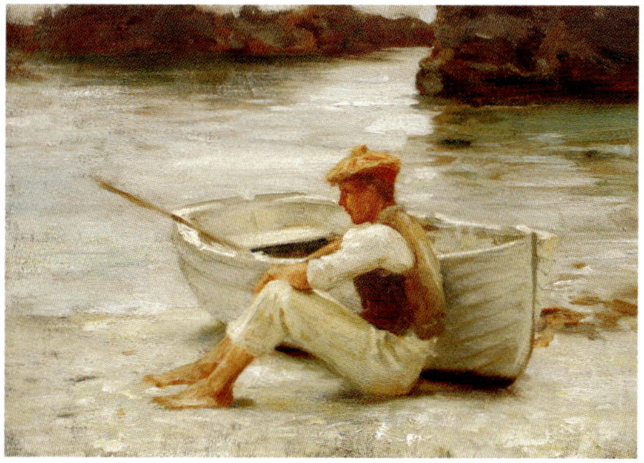

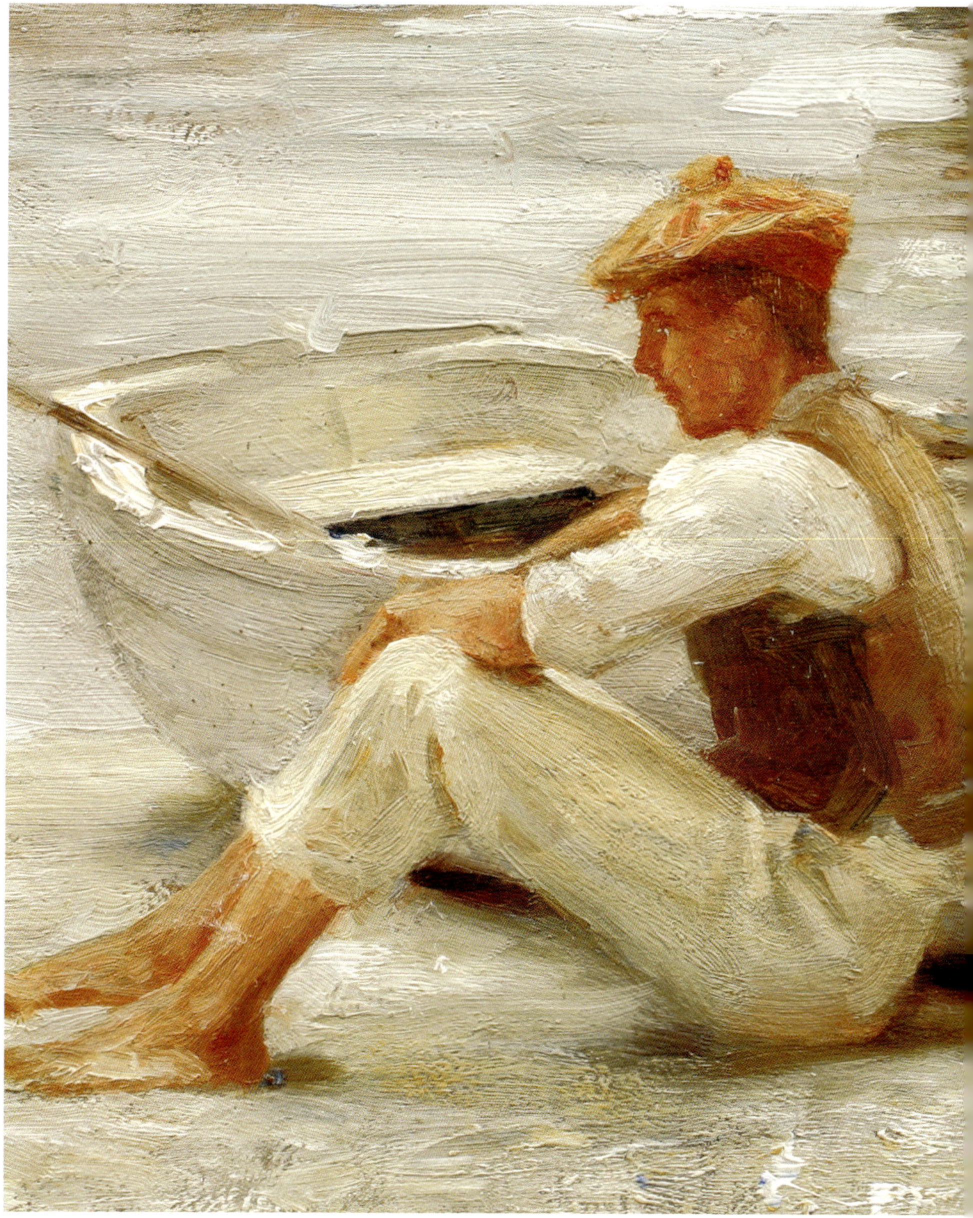

Boy and Boat

Oil on panel, 24 x 33cm
Provenance: Purchased from Henry Shemilt for the Tuke Collection 24 December 1963
RCPS Tuke Collection A80

This is of Charlie Mitchell sitting on the sand beside Tuke's rowing boat and wearing a red tam o'shanter, on Newporth beach at Swanpool, Falmouth.

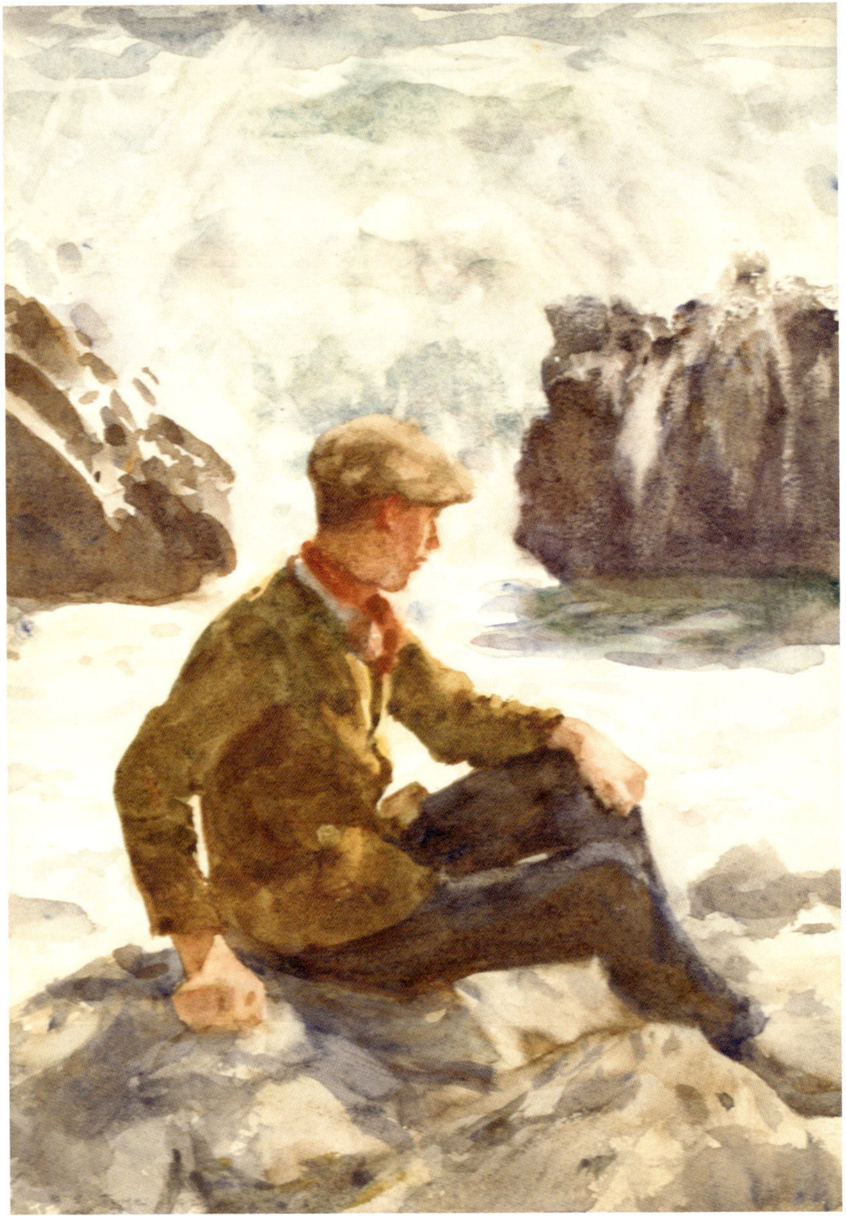

Breakers, 1923

Watercolour, 26 x 17.7cm
Signed and dated bottom left: H.S.Tuke 1923
Labels on reverse hand written:
New Zealand Ex/25, Breakers, H.S.Tuke RA, Swanpool, Falmouth, England.
Printed label: International Exhibition of the Fine Arts, New Zealand and South Seas International exhibition, Dunedin, 1925/1926,
Ernest Marsh Director.
Small label: N.Z.S.S. Ex.266
Exhibited: Royal Academy 1923;
The International Exhibition of the Fine Arts – New Zealand and South Seas International exhibition Dunedin, 1925/26
Provenance: Purchased from Geoffrey Sainsbury 18 December1964
RCPS Tuke Collection A110 R1233

There is a photograph of this painting pasted into Tuke's register. It is of Charlie Mitchell clothed in a cap and scarf, sitting on a rock by the breaking sea.

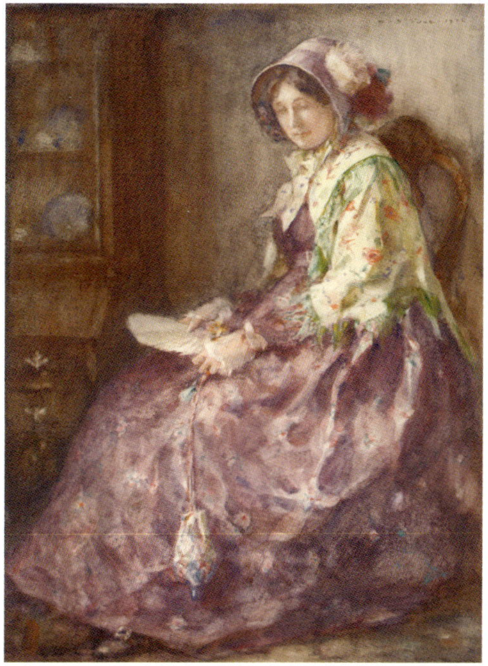

Lady in Period Costume, 1922

Watercolour, 35.3 x 25.3cm
Signed and dated top right: H.S.Tuke 1922
Inscribed in pen on reverse bottom right:
Mrs Sainsbury, 5 Provost Road, South Hampstead NW3
Purchased from Geoffrey Sainsbury 18 December 1964
RCPS Tuke Collection A78

According to Maria's granddaughter Anne Willett, this could be Maria's maid who acted as the model, dressed in period costume. It would not be Maria, as she would have been 51 years old in 1922. Tuke possibly painted it for Maria.

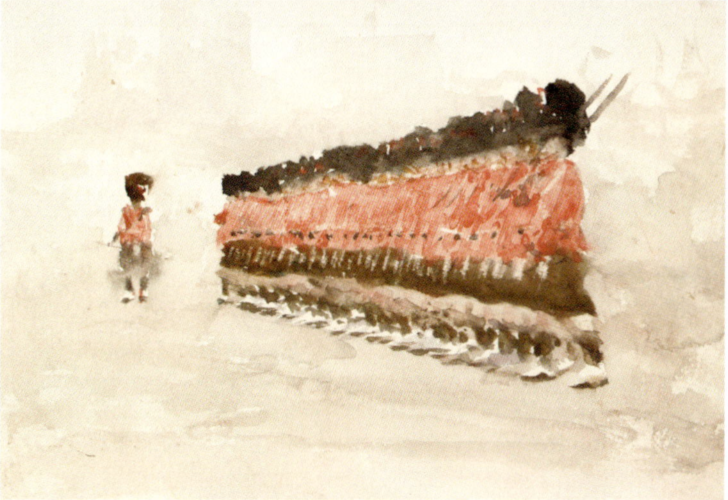

Scots Guards on Parade

Watercolour, 17.5 x 25cm
Provenance: Purchased from Geoffrey Sainsbury
29 May 1968. Previously Willy Sainsbury's
RCPS Tuke Collection A165

Ships and Working Boats

For Tuke, one of the main attractions of Falmouth was its very active harbour, with ships of all shapes and sizes coming and going all over the world. Ships came to Falmouth for their orders as to where to deliver their cargo, and would anchor in the bay while waiting for instructions or for a more favourable price on their cargo. From the 1880s through the 1920s Tuke witnessed the last great age of sail and captured every aspect of it in his work, from the windjammers to topsail schooners, from local fishing boats to rowing boats and training ships to steamers. His home at Pennance Point, just before the entrance to Falmouth harbour, was a good vantage point for him to observe the movement of shipping in and out of the bay. He also knew many owners of sailing ships and boats, being a yachtsmen himself, and this gave him access to sailing on the tall ships and being able to paint from the deck. When the weather would not allow him to paint outdoors, he rented a small store on Customs House quay that doubled as a harbourside studio.

Although he did not regard himself as a marine artist, Tuke's paintings of ships account for a large proportion of his overall output and are reflected in the large number of works on a maritime theme in the RCPS Tuke Collection.

Tuke had made observations of tall ships when he first came to Falmouth at the age of 10[1]. When he returned to Falmouth he learned to sail and began to develop his skills as a watercolour artist. Watercolour was the main medium he used for capturing the ships directly from observation, usually at anchor or coming into Falmouth or being pulled by a tug out of the Carrick Roads to catch the wind. He would use the ship studies as a backdrop to some of his major oil paintings such as *August Blue* (R210) and *The Run Home* (R380), but the majority of the watercolours stand as works of art in their own right. From 1887-1894 Tuke had exhibited his watercolours at the Royal Institute of Painters in Watercolour, but in February 1904 he gained entry into the highly prestigious Royal Watercolour Society. The works he showed there were demonstrations of an artist at the peak of his artistic talent and technical ability. The RCPS Tuke Collection contains several works that were exhibited at the Royal Watercolour Society over a period of 20 years, and some still have their original gilt frames.

1. *See MTS p.21 illustration.*

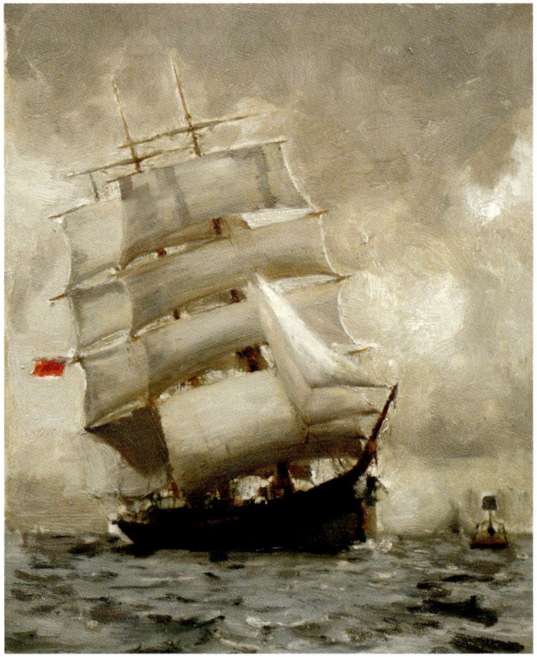

Rounding the Manacle Buoy, 1888
Oil on panel, 35 x 26.8cm
Signed and dated bottom left: H.S.Tuke 1888
Exhibited: The RCPS and the RBA in 1888
Provenance: Purchased from Geoffrey Sainsbury 20 June 1965
RCPS Tuke Collection A13 R108

The Manacles are a series of rocks of great danger to shipping 6.3 nautical miles due South of Falmouth, and 8.4 nautical miles North East from the Lizard Point.

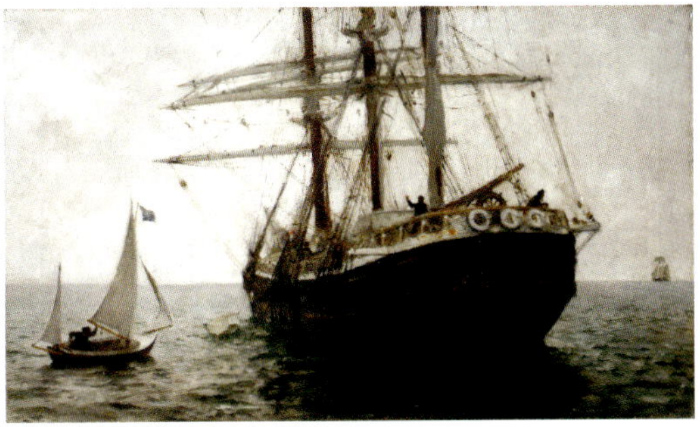

The Missionary Boat, 1894

Oil on canvas, 56 x 92cm
Signed and dated bottom right: H.S.Tuke 1894
Provenance: Originally sold to Mr J. B. Burchett
as a wedding present to Mr Lithgow
Purchased from Mrs M. Kemp
14 August 1963
RCPS Tuke Collection A1 R209

This painting is of a French barque *'Verveine of Marseilles'* in Falmouth Bay being met by the mission yawl *'Clarice'*, sailed by Chaplain James Badger of the British Sailors' Society in March 1894. Ships visited by the chaplain on Sundays would hoist the blue burgee of the British Sailors' Society to the masthead. Crew of other ships on seeing this would row across for a service held on deck.

In an interview he gave to the *Windsor* magazine, 1895, Tuke recalls the 'plucky' nature of his sitter: 'There was the harbour missionary. A man wanted a sketch of the mission boat going alongside a French barque. To give it a final air of verisimilitude, I persuaded the missionary to come off and sit in his boat. Soon it came on to blow and drizzle, but he stopped until I had finished. I think we were both wet through, but he was a good fellow and didn't mind.' *Windsor* magazine p.606.

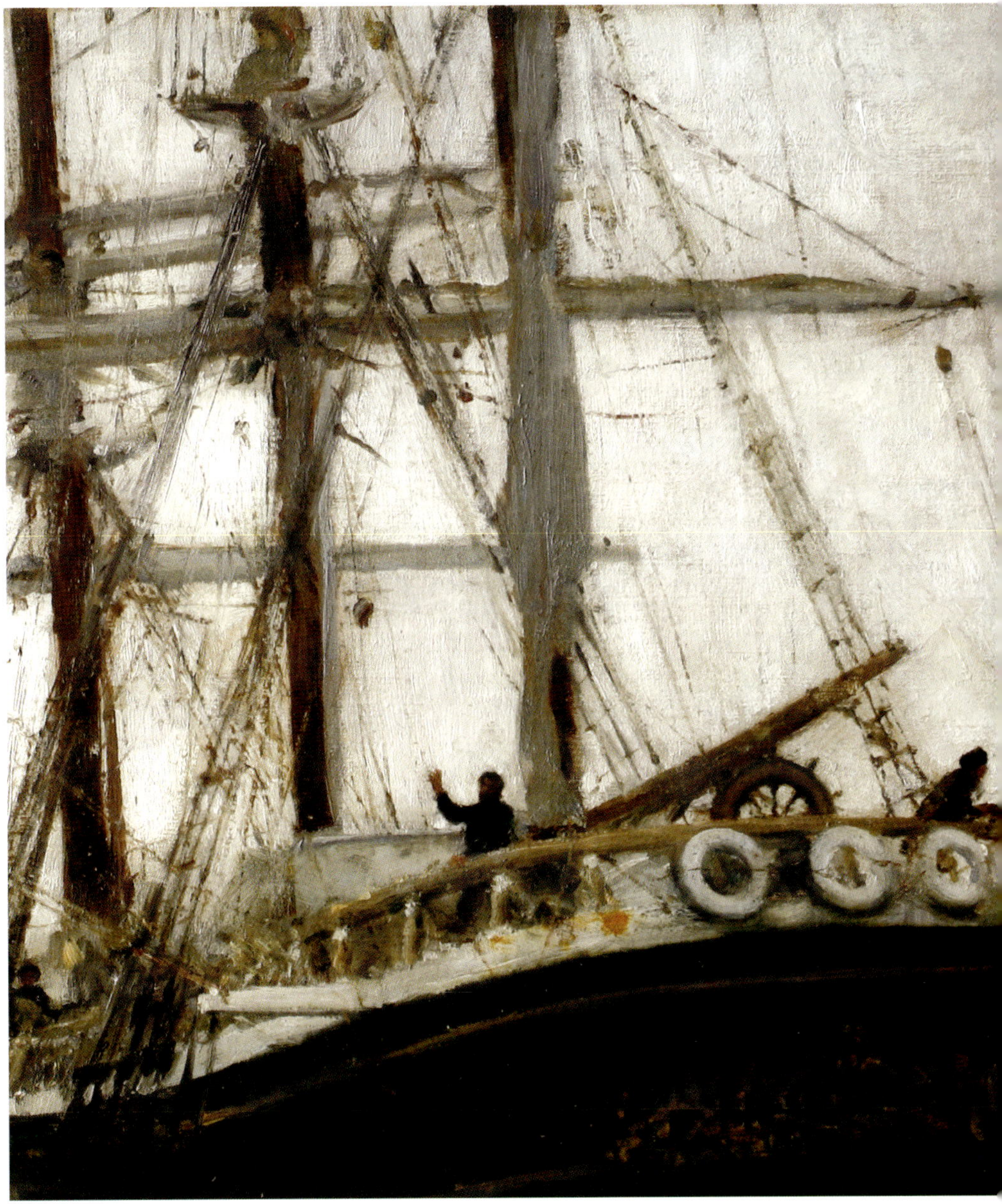

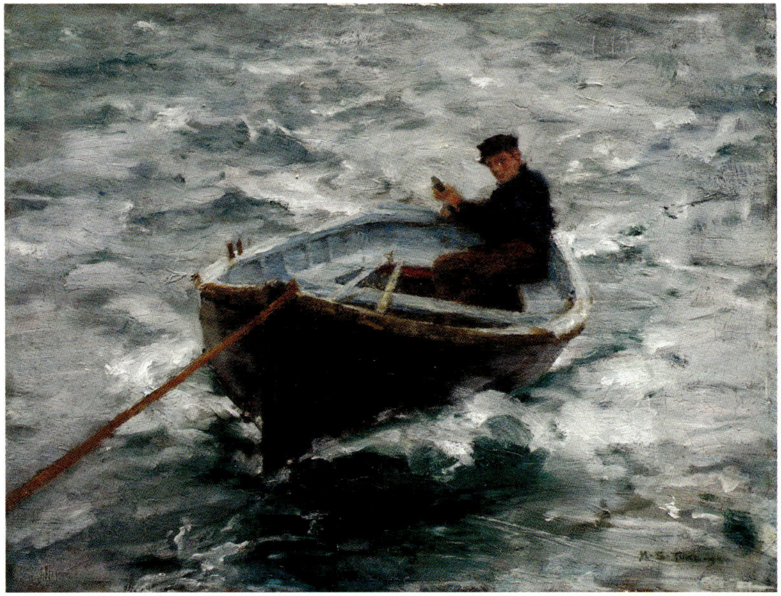

In Tow, 1893

Oil on panel, 26.5 x 35cm
Signed bottom right: H.S.Tuke .93
Exhibited: The RCPS Falmouth 1893
Provenance: Purchased from Sir John Hedges, 22 October 1964
RCPS Tuke Collection A71 R199

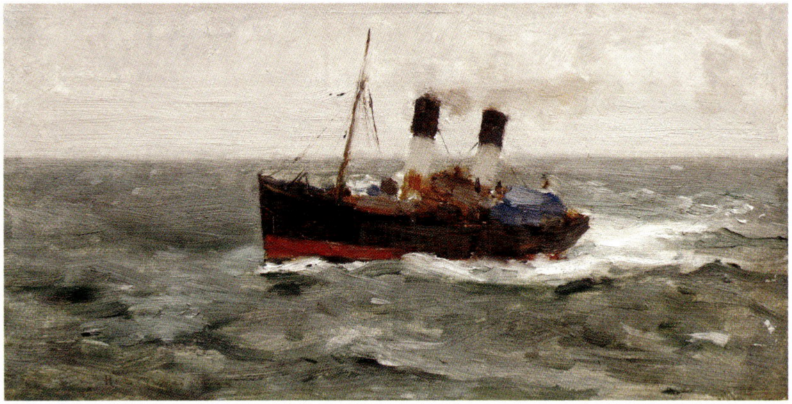

Two-funneled Steamer, 1894

Oil on canvas board, 12.4 x 25.1cm
Signed and dated bottom left: H.S.Tuke 1894
Provenance: Purchased from Geoffrey Sainsbury 19 December 1963
RCPS Tuke Collection A30

This is a paddle steamer, possibly the first of two boats called *'Penguin'* built by Cox and Co., owned by the Falmouth Steam Tonnage and Passenger Company. This assumption is based on the fact that (as far as is known) the *'Penguin'* was the only locally made paddle steamer that had two funnels. These steamers were used around Falmouth to transport goods and passengers.

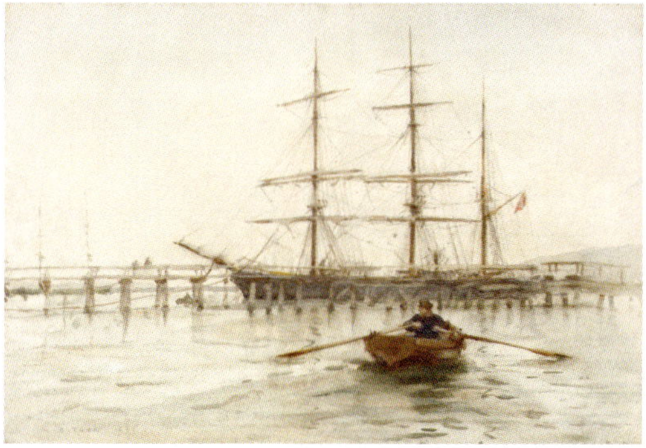

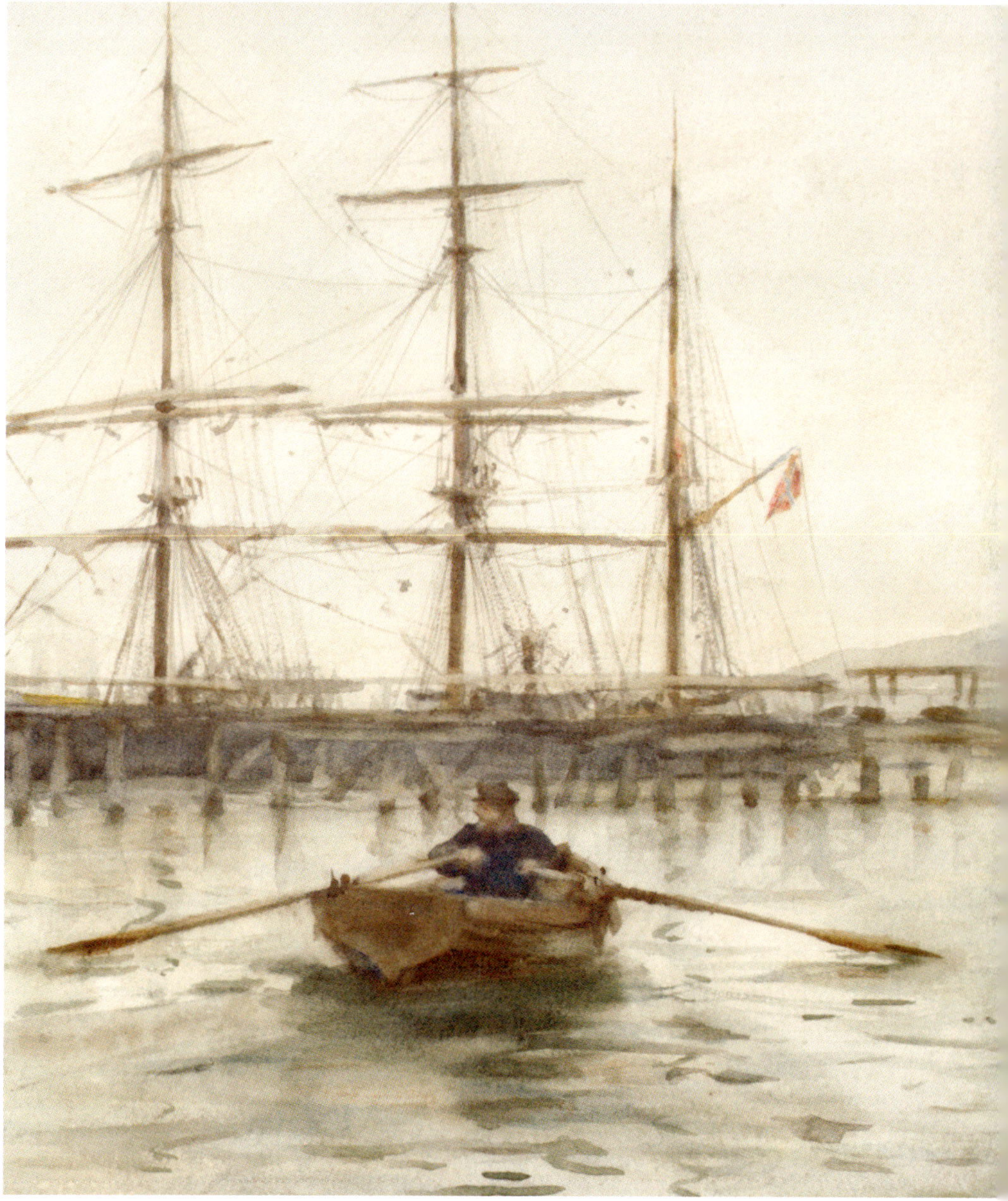

Barque *'Jorgen Bang'*, 1899

Watercolour, 28.4 x 41cm
Signed and dated bottom left: H.S.Tuke 1899
Provenance: Gift to Tuke Collection by Mrs Connor September 1963. Tuke originally sold it to Mrs Davies, sister of Alfred De Pass
RCPS Tuke Collection A109 R310

According to Tuke's diary, he sketched the barque *'Jorgen Bang'* on 27 March 1899. The *'Jorgen Bang'* was a Norwegian wooden barque built in 1892. It was travelling from Larvik, Norway to Sydney in Australia with a cargo of boards when it came into Falmouth on 24 March 1899. It was in for repair as its port bow had been damaged after a collision with another boat in a snow storm.

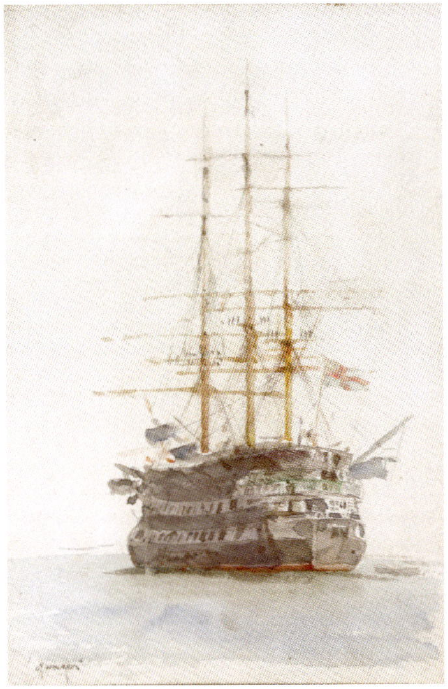

H.M.S *'Ganges'*

Watercolour, 21.5 x 13.8cm
Provenance: Purchased from Geoffrey Sainsbury
8 September 1968
RCPS Tuke Collection A191

HMS *'Ganges'* arrived in Falmouth in 1866, was anchored off St. Just Pool, and was run from the former Naval dockyard at Mylor. It was used as a sea cadets' training ship for young boys, and trained up to 400 cadets at once. It had its own sports team and music band. It was, however, a tough life, the punishments given out were brutal by today's standards, and there were fatalities over the years. There is a memorial in Mylor Churchyard to those who lost their lives while serving on the ship.

Tuke sailed on its final voyage when it was taken to Shotley, Plymouth, as his diary entry for 29 August 1899 reads, 'Went off early aboard the *'Ganges'* with Downing, Bassett Smith having invited us to go to Plymouth in her. Heavy squalls of rain and wind delayed our start. When we got out a bit most of the sail was set, and we boomed along about 7 knots reaching the breakwater about 5, a 6 hour passage. Towed right up to the Hamoaze with band playing and all the training boys looking on.'

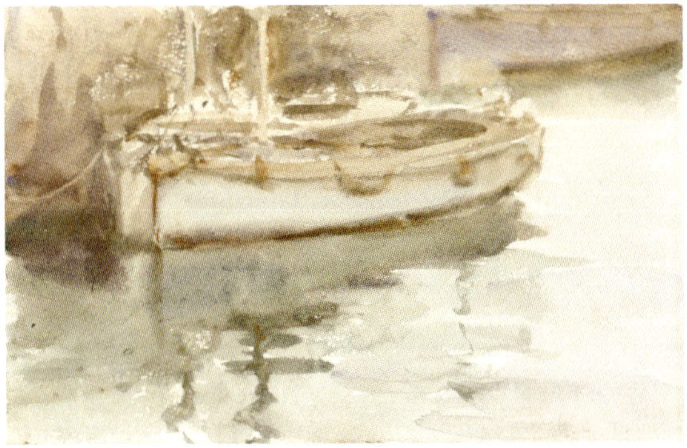

Boats at Falmouth

Watercolour, 14 x 21.5cm
Initialled bottom right: H.S.T
Inscribed on reverse: Boats at Falmouth
Provenance: Bequethed to the Tuke Collection by Honor Carveth Price
9 March, 1990
RCPS Tuke Collection A404

As well as the big ships, Tuke often painted the small rowing craft that were moored around the quays in Falmouth; his studio in a storehouse at the end of Customs House Quay was an ideal location for making these studies.

Green Barque

Watercolour, 26.5 x 36.6cm
Signed bottom left: H.S.Tuke
Provenance: Purchased from Geoffrey Sainsbury
20 June1965
RCPS Tuke Collection A144

Boats with green hulls were one of Tuke's favourite subjects.

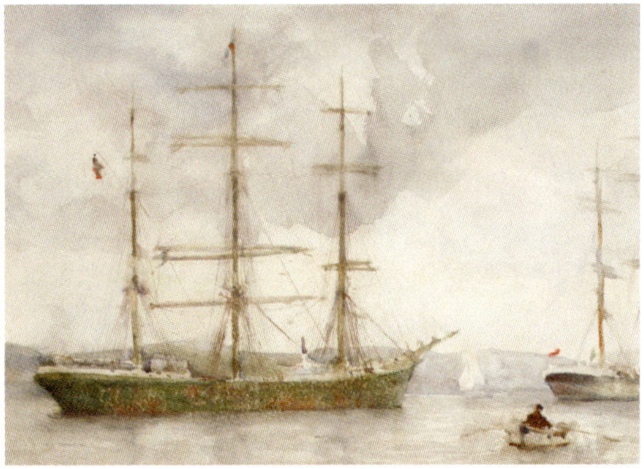

Ship, 1900

Watercolour, 14 x 21.4cm
Signed and dated bottom left: H.S.Tuke 1900
Provenance: Purchased from Peter Jackson
14 February1966
RCPS Tuke Collection A157

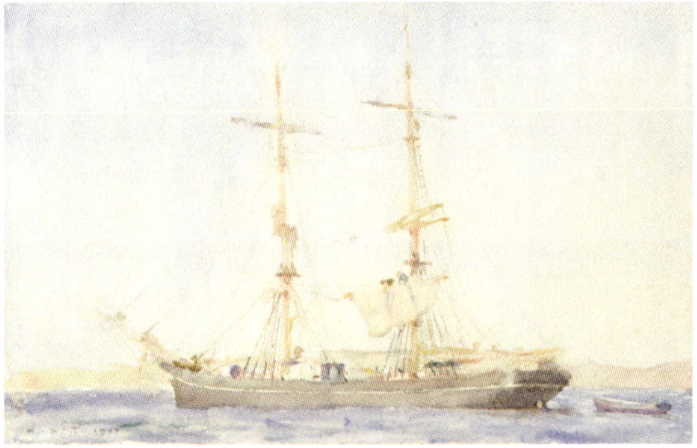

Green Ship

Watercolour, 13.8 x 21.4cm
Provenance: Purchased from Geoffrey Sainsbury
8 September 1968
RCPS Tuke Collection A186

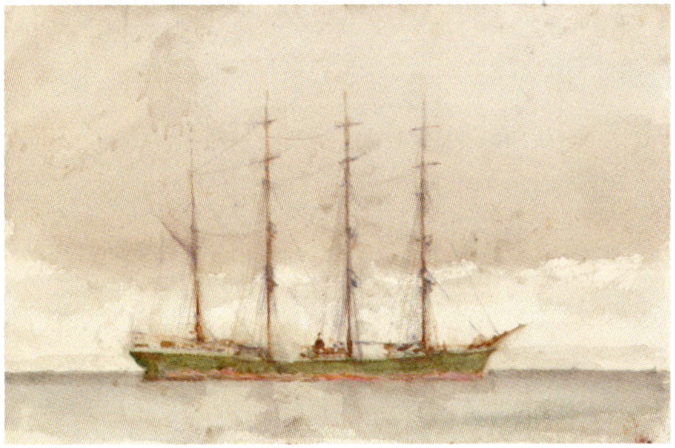

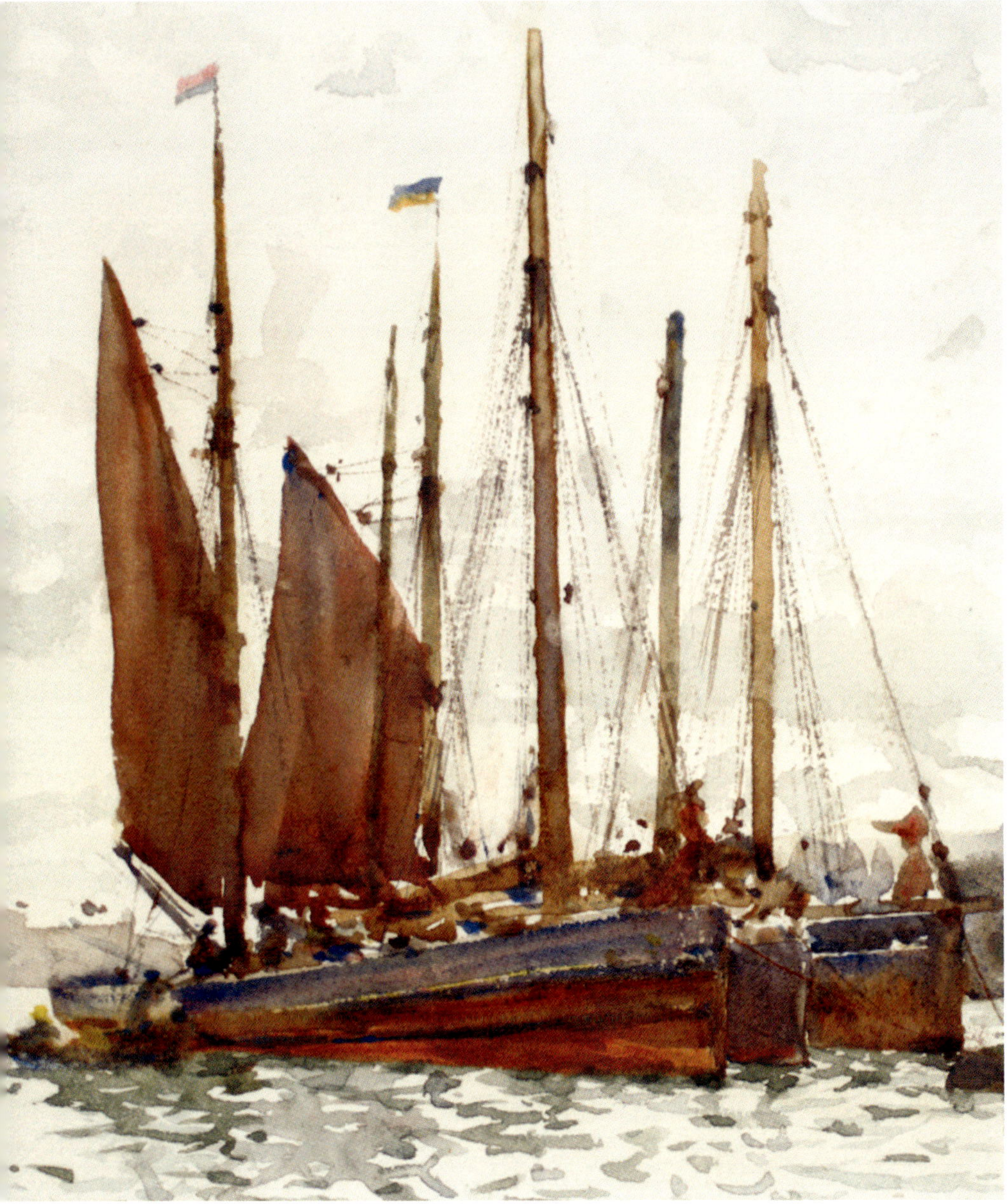

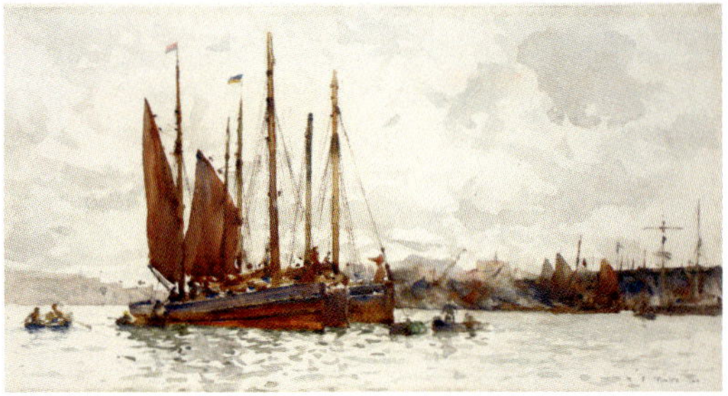

Lowestoft Drifters
(previously known as *Ships*), 1903

Watercolour, 25 x 45cm
Signed and dated bottom right: H.S.Tuke 1903
Provenance: Purchased from Robin Eden's Antiques, Pickwick, 27 November 1965, who purchased it from Cowlin's, Clifton R.E. Netherdown, August 1960
RCPS Tuke Collection A105

In 1903 Tuke painted several watercolours of Lowestoft boats that could be seen in Falmouth and Newlyn at the time. This picture is of Lowestoft fishing boats or drifters moored in a harbour which does not appear to be Falmouth. Tuke went to Lowestoft in 1905 and did sketches there.

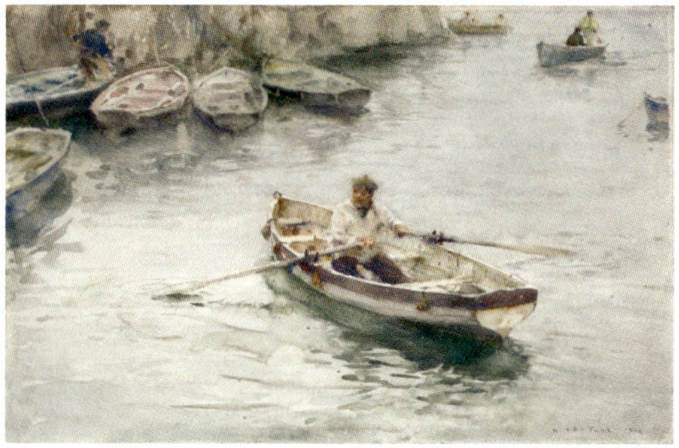

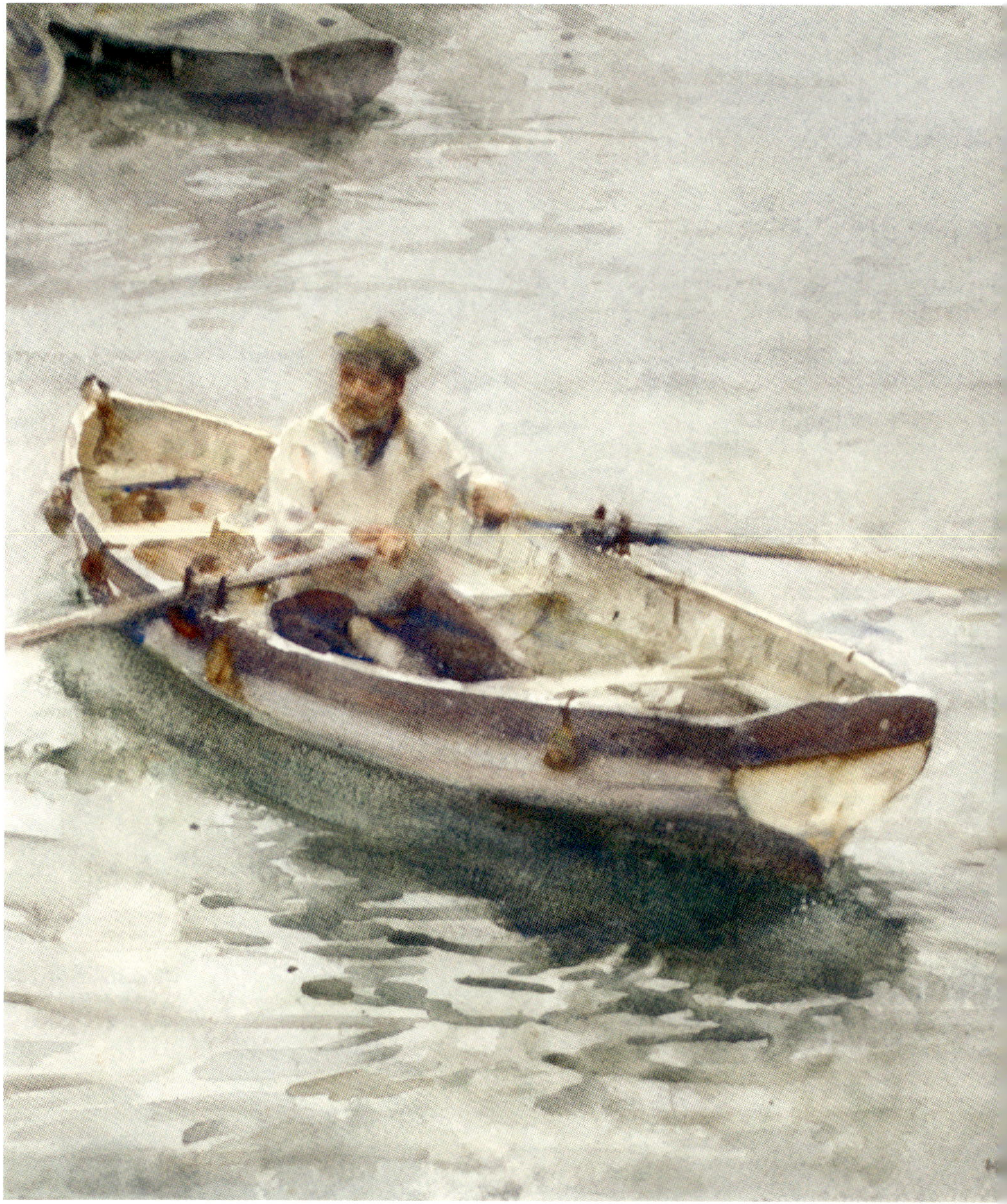

The Quay Steps, 1904

Watercolour, 30.5 x 45.8cm
Signed and dated bottom right: H.S.Tuke 1904
Provenance: Purchased from Ernest Lette
13 November 1967
Exhibited: The Royal Watercolour Society, winter 1904
RCPS Tuke Collection A119 R476/R521

Painted from Tuke's store/studio on Customs House Quay in Falmouth, where he had a seaward window inserted for painting the view in bad weather. This watercolour shows a man, probably local fisherman and frequent model for Tuke, Neddy Hall, in a green tam o'shanter and a white smock rowing a jolly boat in the harbour, with quay punts tied up against the harbour wall. The horizon is just visible on the far right.

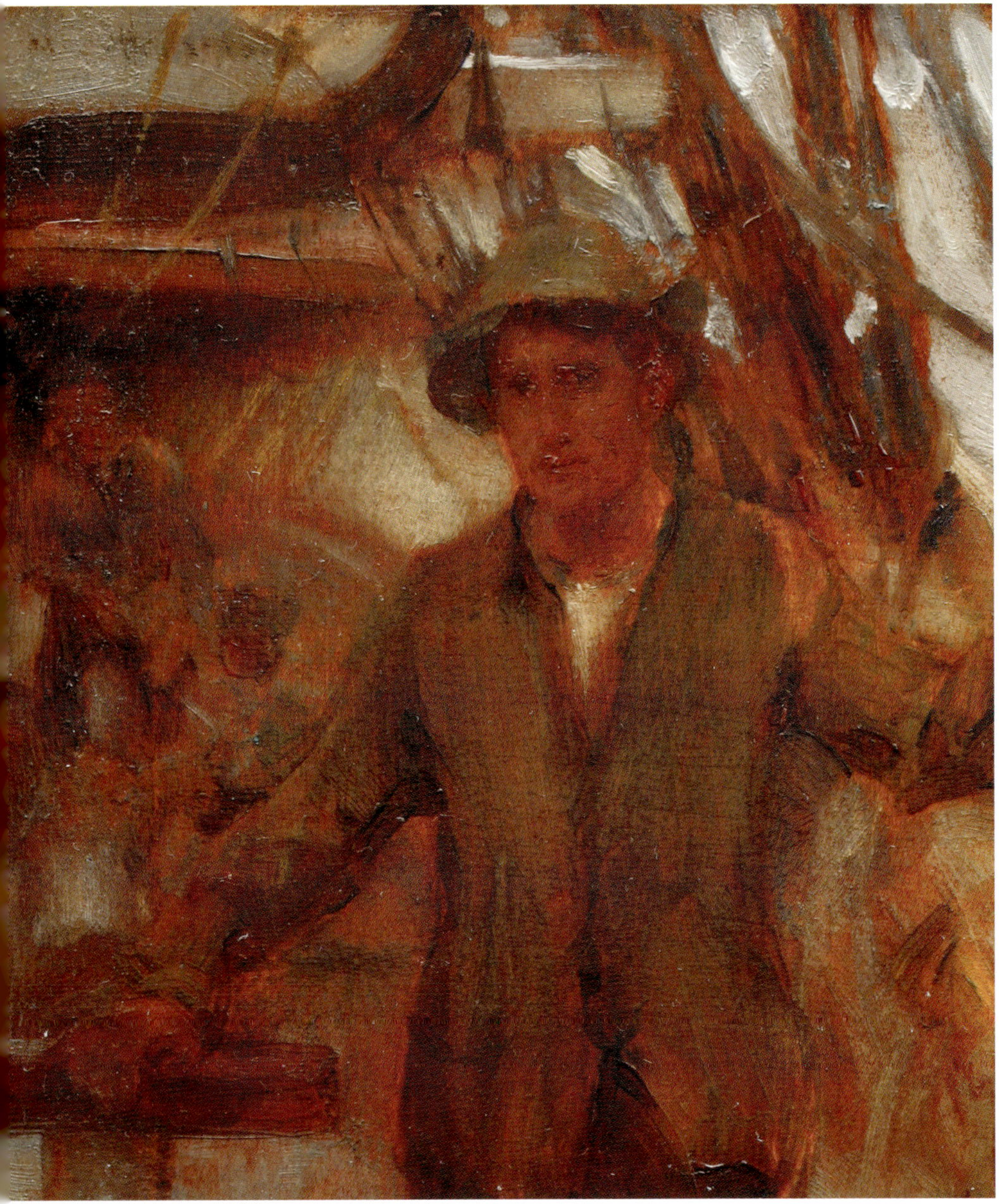

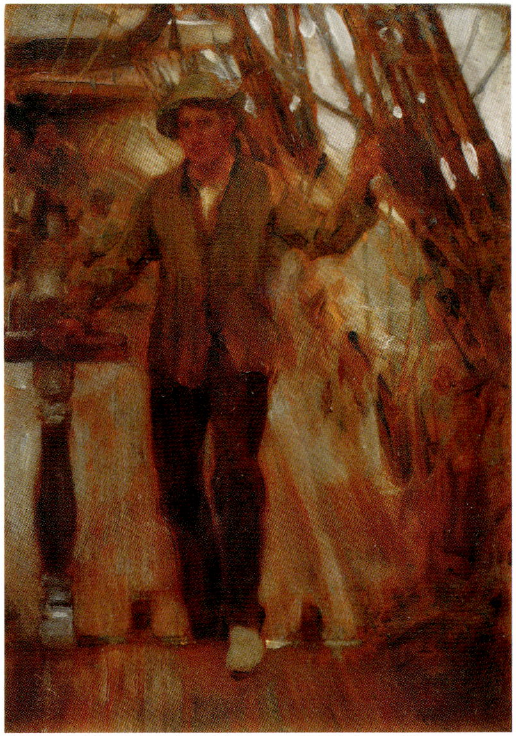

Study for *'At the break of the Poop'*, c.1905
Oil on panel, 29 x 19.9cm
Provenance: Purchased from Arthur J. Cole
4 December 1963
RCPS Tuke Collection A124

This is thought to be a sketch undertaken on the French barque *'Mazatlan'* which was for sale in Falmouth Harbour in 1905. The boat was sold for £400. The bigger picture for which this was a study was called *At the break of the Poop* (R508 1905). In 1914 Tuke undertook another painting of a similar subject called *On the Poop Deck* (R780).

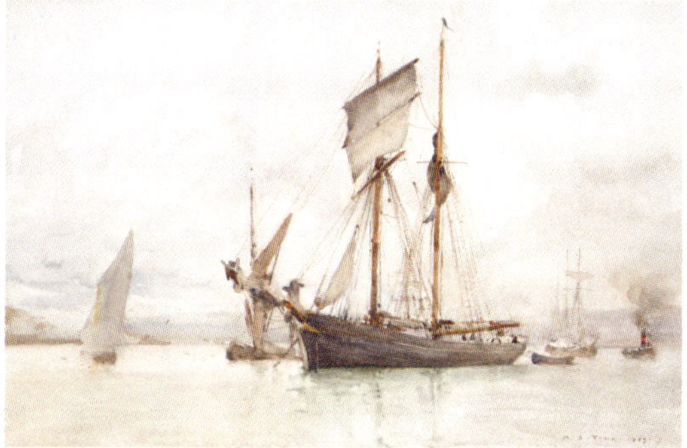

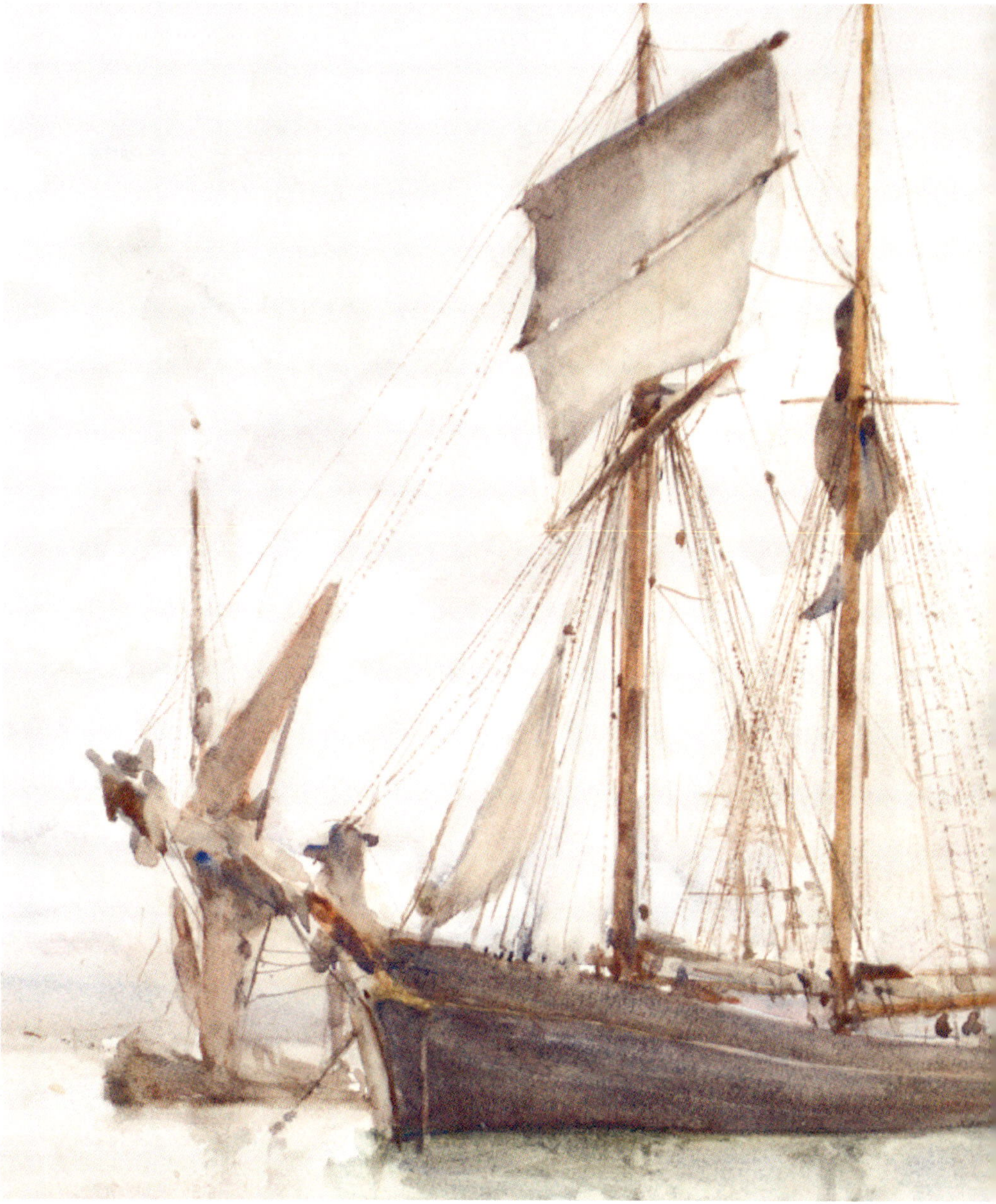

Group of Vessels and Tug, 1907

Watercolour, 30.5 x 46cm
Signed and dated bottom right: H.S.Tuke 1907
Provenance: Originally sold to Archie Montgomery
Purchased from J.T. Hyde 12 October 1963
RCPS Tuke Collection A67 R558

Tuke met Archie Montgomery, the purchaser of this picture, in May 1904 in London. He was the son of the owner of a boat called the *'Lynton'*.

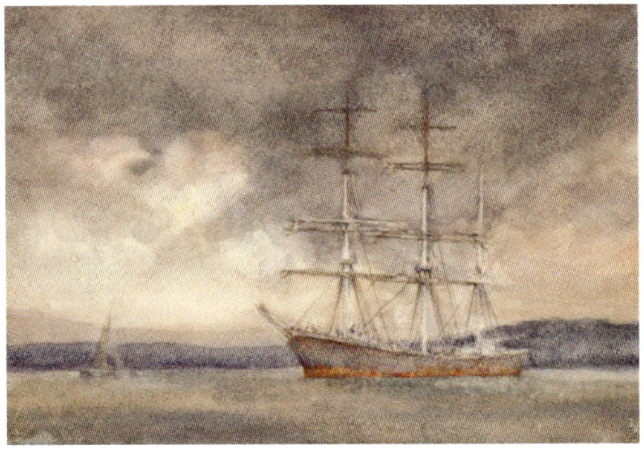

Barque at Sunset

Watercolour, 17.9 x 25.5cm
Inscription in faint pencil bottom left: Vinga or Vigor
Provenance: Purchased from Geoffrey Sainsbury
19 December 1963
RCPS Tuke Collection A55

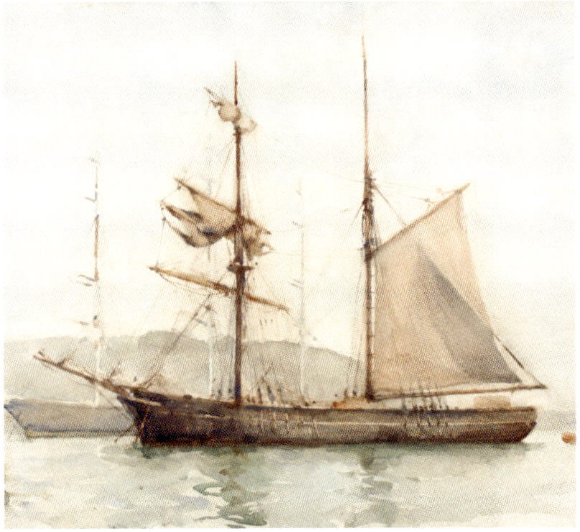

Brigantine Drying Sails

Watercolour, 30.5 x 33.5cm
Initialled bottom right: H.S.T (in Willy Sainsbury's hand)
Inscribed on reverse in biro: Charlie Mitch
Provenance: Purchased from John Maggs 14 July 1962
– reputedly from Charlie Mitchell's brother
RCPS Tuke Collection A113

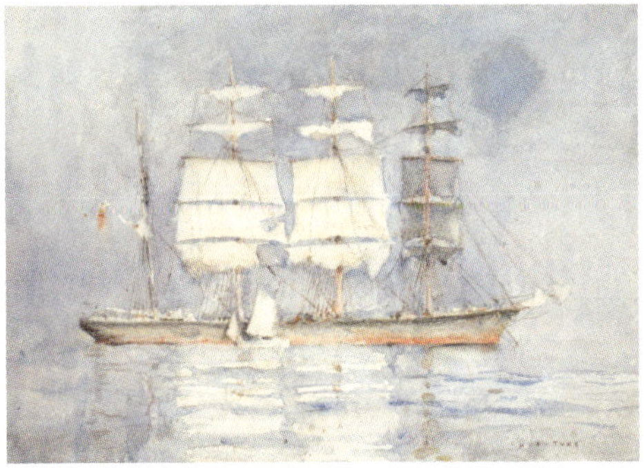

In Falmouth Bay

Watercolour, 25.5 x 35.3cm
Signed bottom right: H.S.Tuke
Provenance: Purchased from Geoffrey Sainsbury
20 June 1965
RCPS Tuke Collection A20

This watercolour of a 3 masted barque is illustrated as a colour plate in Maria Tuke Sainsbury's biography of Tuke. op. cit. p.116.

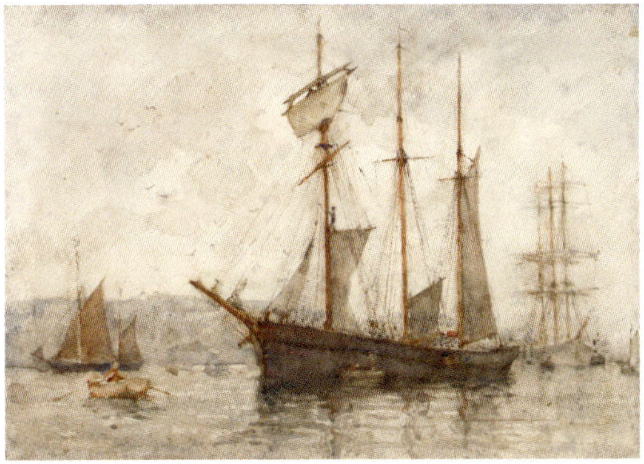

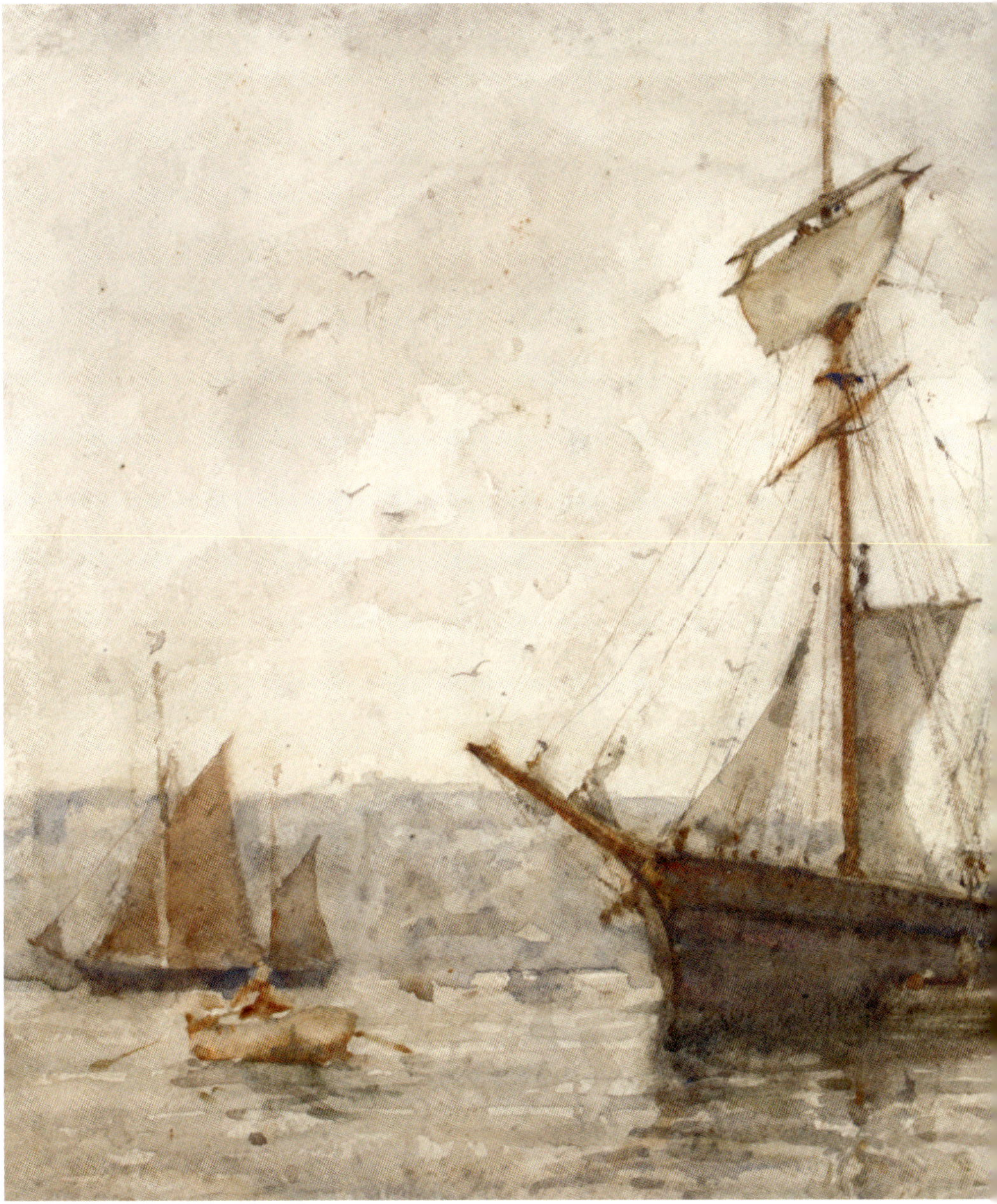

Topsail Schooner

Watercolour, 25.3 x 35.5cm
There is a watercolour sketch of a tall ship on the reverse A170a
Provenance: Purchased from Geoffrey Sainsbury 29 May 1968
RCPS Tuke Collection A170

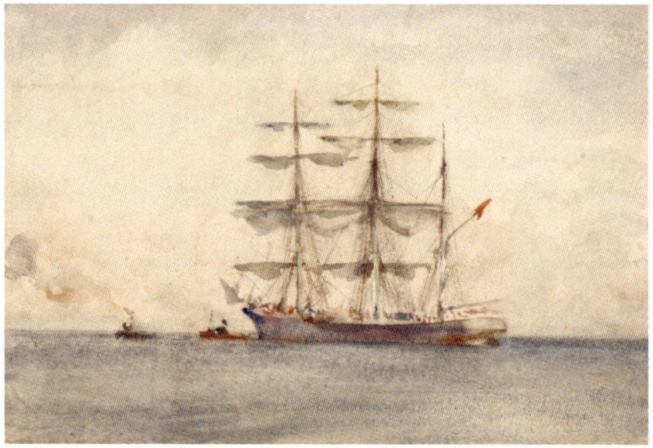

Sailing Ship

Watercolour, 17 x 24.6cm
Initialled bottom right: H.S.T.
Provenance: Purchased from Geoffrey Sainsbury
8 September 1968
RCPS Tuke Collection A188

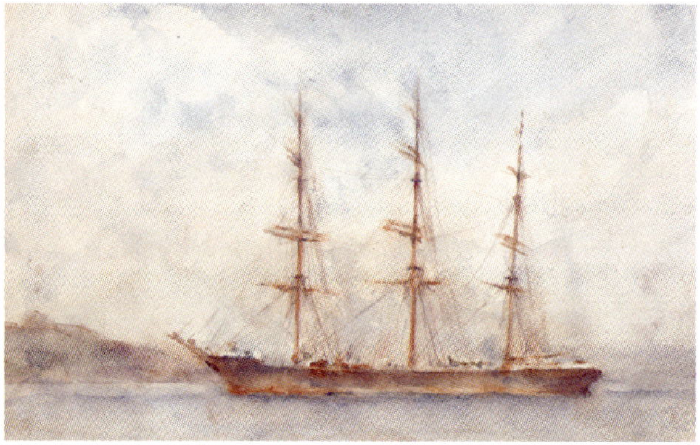

Sailing Ship

Watercolour, 14 x 21.7cm
Provenance: Purchased from Geoffrey Sainsbury
8 September 1968
RCPS Tuke Collection A192

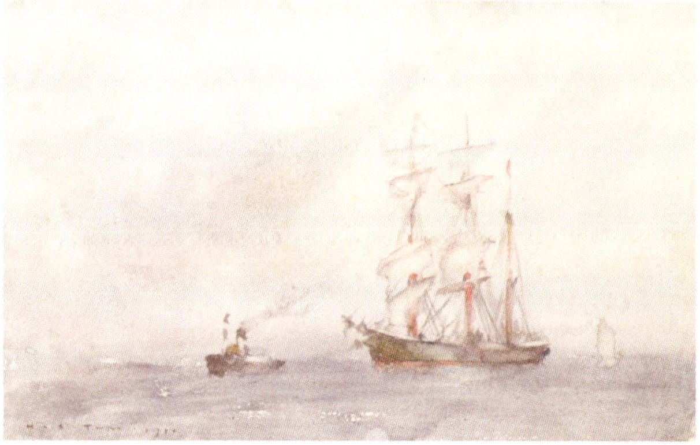

Sailing Ship and Tug, 1911

Watercolour, 13.5 x 21.7cm
Signed and dated bottom left: H.S.Tuke 1911
Provenance: Given to Tuke Collection by Miss Barbara Marshall
15 July 1965
RCPS Tuke Collection A228

Sailing Ships and Tug

Oil on canvas, 23 x 34cm
Provenance: Purchased from Geoffrey Sainsbury 29 May 1968
RCPS Tuke Collection A161

This was probably painted in Falmouth harbour. The ship on the right is under tow from a Falmouth tug.

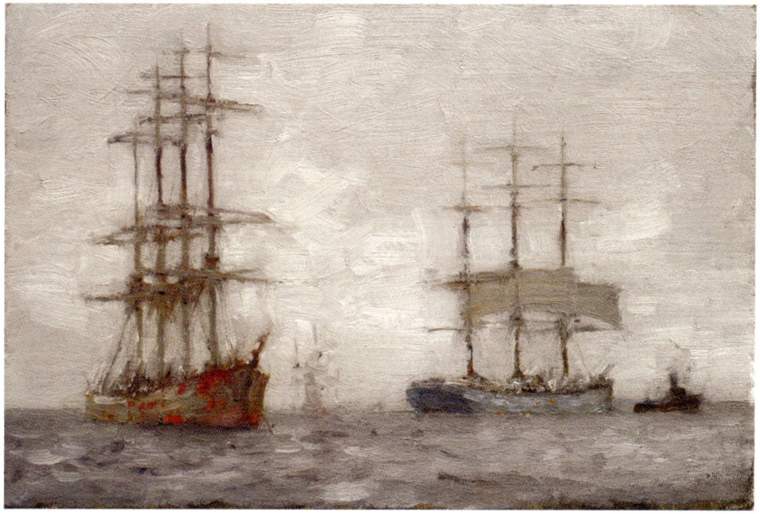

White Barque

Oil on canvas, 36 x 48.6cm
Provenance: Given to Johnnie Jackett by Tuke, then to his wife who gave it to the Tuke Collection 6 December 1965
RCPS Tuke Collection A68

An Italian Barque in the Carrick Roads.

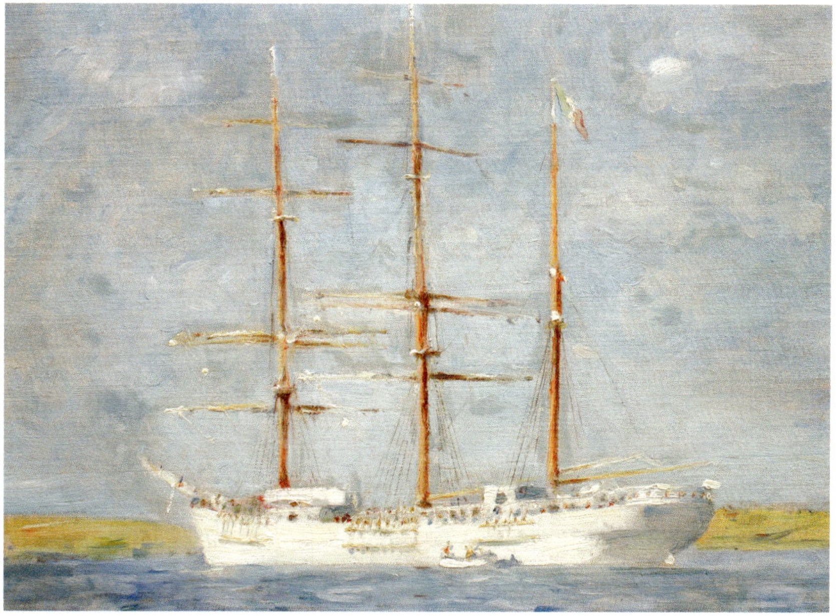

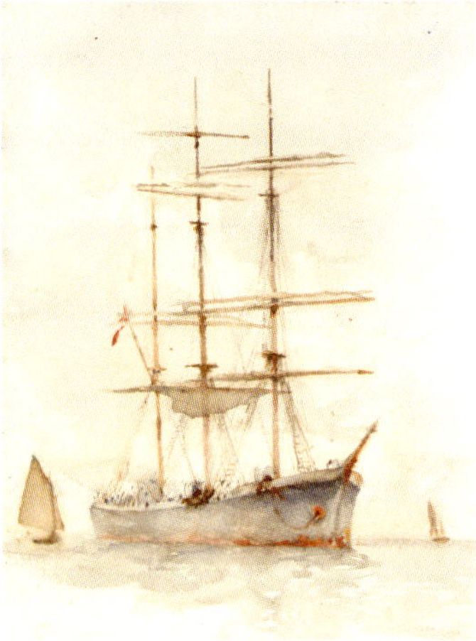

Three Masted Ship

Watercolour, 35.5 x 25.5cm
Signed bottom right: H.S.Tuke
Provenance: Purchased from Geoffrey Sainsbury
30 April 1967
RCPS Tuke Collection A149

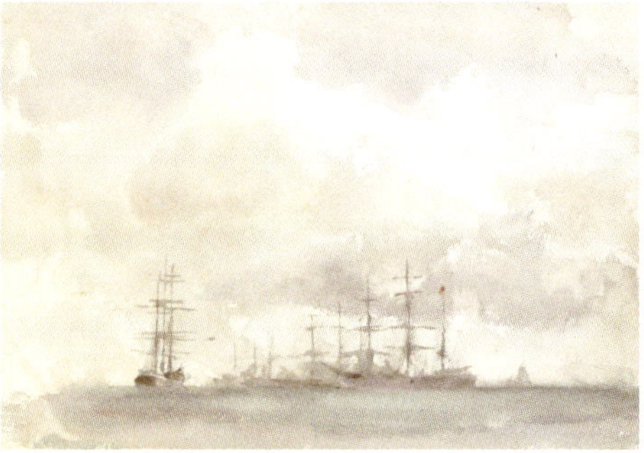

Sailing Ships at Anchor

Watercolour, 16.6 x 25cm
Provenance: Purchased from Geoffrey Sainsbury
8 September 1968
RCPS Tuke Collection A179

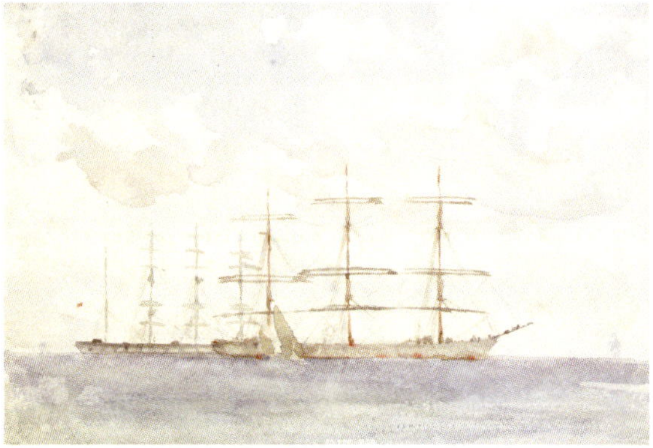

Sailing Ships

Watercolour, 16.3 x 23.8cm
Provenance: Purchased from Geoffrey Sainsbury
8 September 1968
RCPS Tuke Collection A195

Three Masted Barque

Watercolour, 17.9 x 26.1cm
Initialled bottom right: H.S.T.
Provenance: Purchased from Geoffrey Sainsbury
8 September1968
RCPS Tuke Collection A162

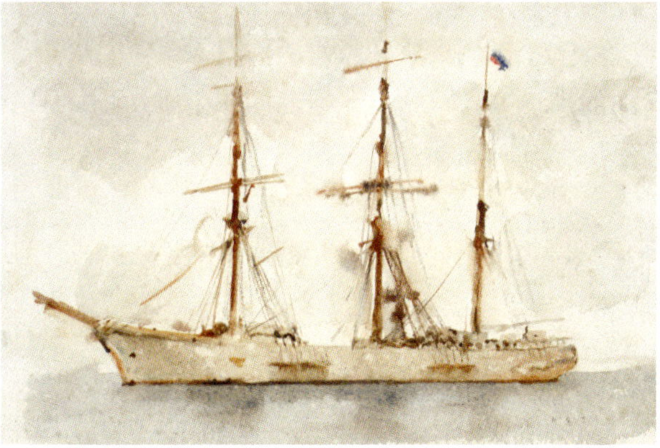

Sailing Ships

Watercolour, 30.3 x 45.5cm
Signed bottom left: H.S.Tuke
Pencil drawing of a tall ship on reverse A177a
Provenance: Purchased from Geoffrey Sainsbury
30 April 1967
RCPS Tuke Collection A177

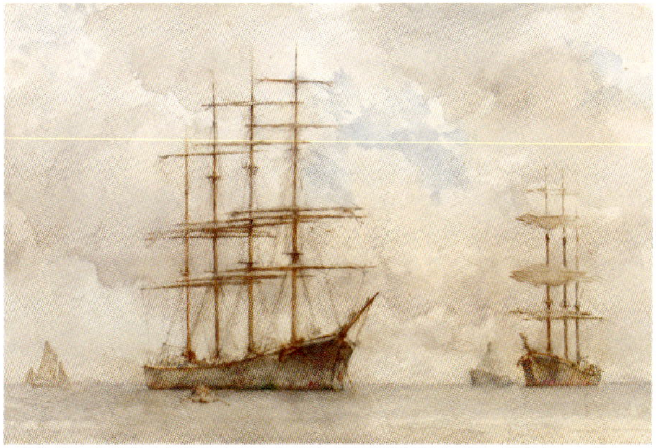

Brigantine

Watercolour, 25.7 x 35.5cm
Provenance: Purchased from Geoffrey Sainsbury
8 September 1968
RCPS Tuke Collection A155

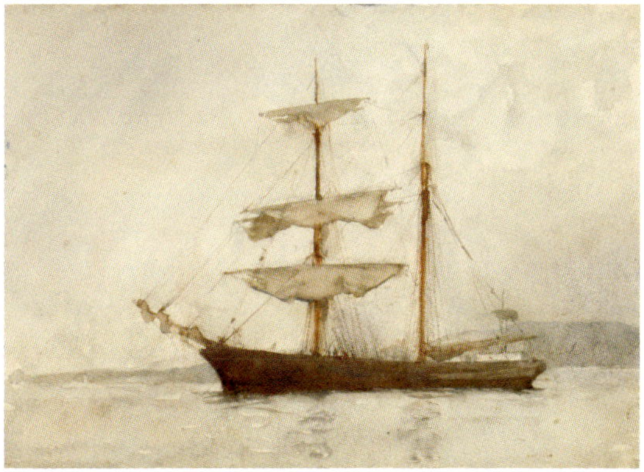

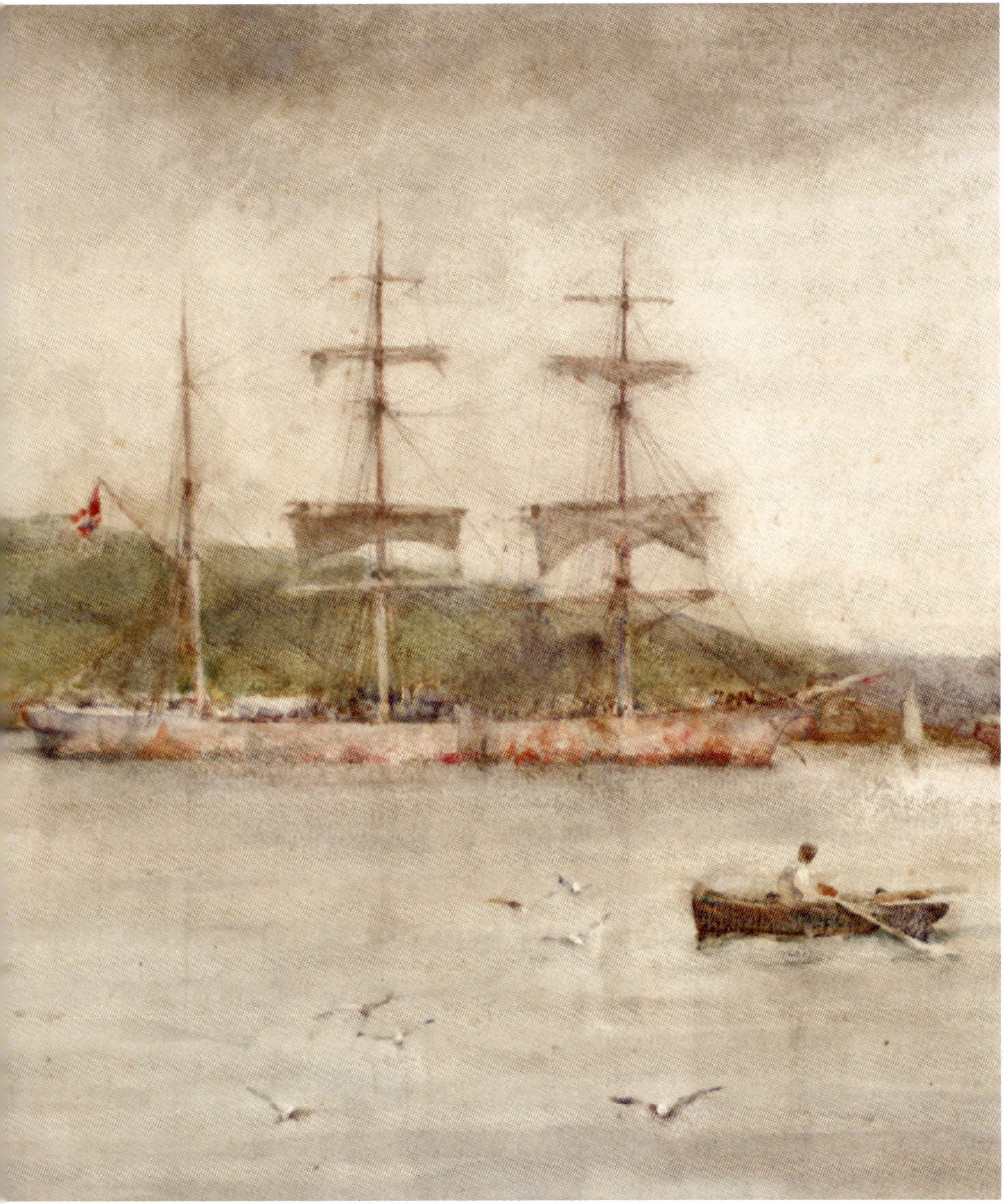

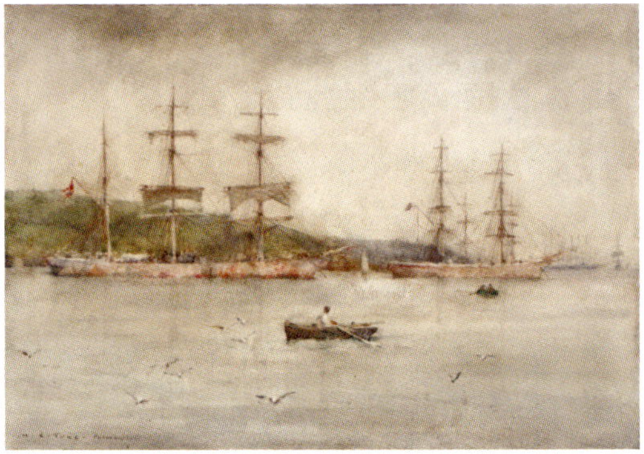

Ships at Falmouth

Watercolour, 35.5 x 25.3cm
Signed bottom left: H.S.Tuke Falmouth
Inscribed bottom right: Falmouth
Provenance: Purchased from Mrs Alice H. Mallet
27 February 1966
RCPS Tuke Collection A146

This watercolour shows several barques moored off Trefusis Point opposite Falmouth.

Smacks in Falmouth Harbour

Watercolour, 13.8 x 21.6cm
Initialled bottom right: H.S.T.
Inscribed on reverse: Smacks in Falmouth H.S.Tuke RA
Provenance: Purchased from Geoffrey Sainsbury
29 May 1968
RCPS Tuke Collection A203

A smack is a small boat used for fishing. These are seen moored in front of the town of Falmouth.

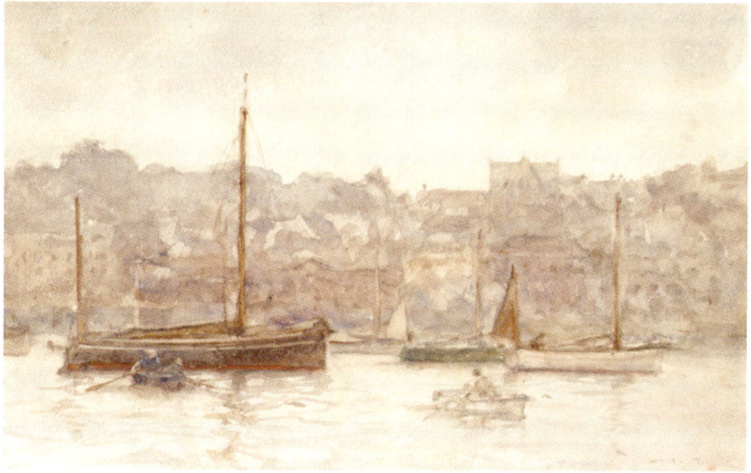

Ships in Falmouth Harbour

Watercolour, 18 x 25cm
Provenance: From the sketchbook given by
Hester Etchells to the Tuke Collection
27 June 1964
RCPS Tuke Collection A82

This is a very impressionistic watercolour of two brigantines, with ships in the background in Falmouth harbour.

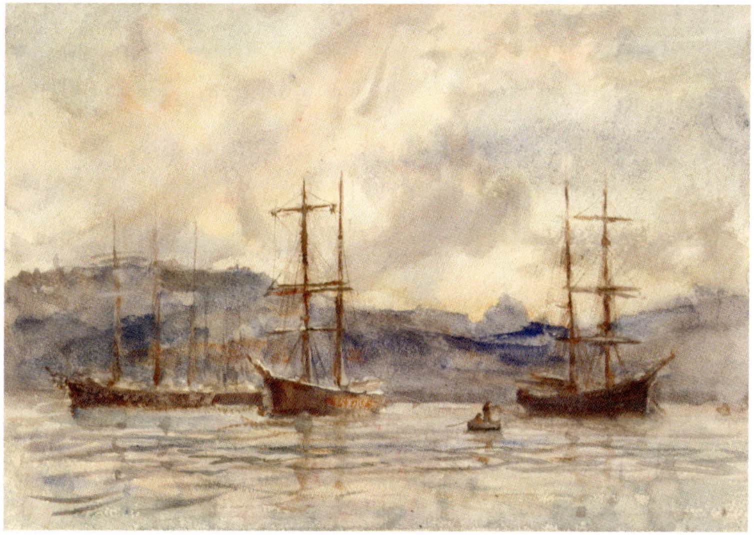

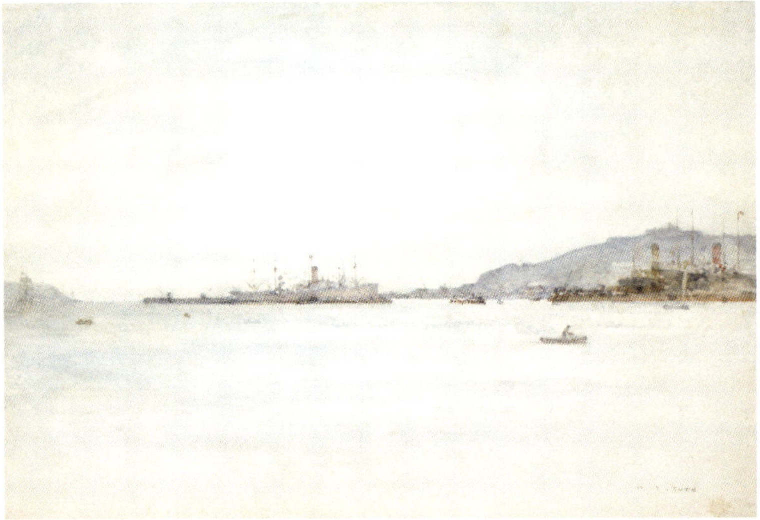

Ships in Falmouth Harbour

Watercolour, 27 x 38.9cm
Signed bottom right: H.S.Tuke
Provenance: Purchased from Geoffrey Sainsbury
29 May 1968
RCPS Tuke Collection A140

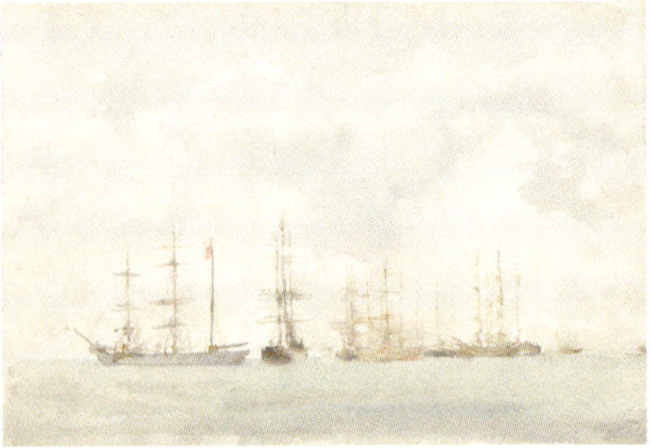

Ships at Anchor

Watercolour, 16.5 x 23.5cm
Provenance:Purchased from Geoffrey Sainsbury
8 September1968
RCPS Tuke Collection A193

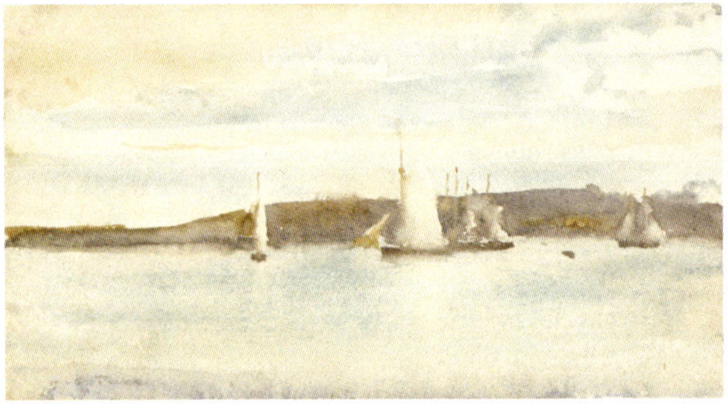

Ships at Falmouth

Watercolour, 9.7 x 17.3cm
Initialled bottom left: H.S.T.
Provenance: Purchased from W. Dyer, Camborne
12 January 1965
Previously owned by Leonard Duke
RCPS Tuke Collection A48

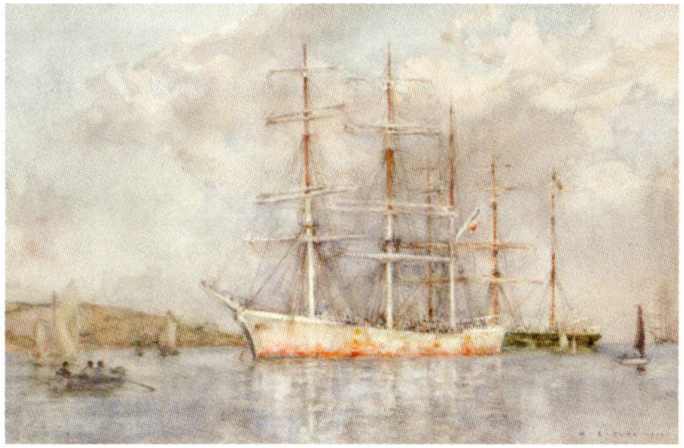

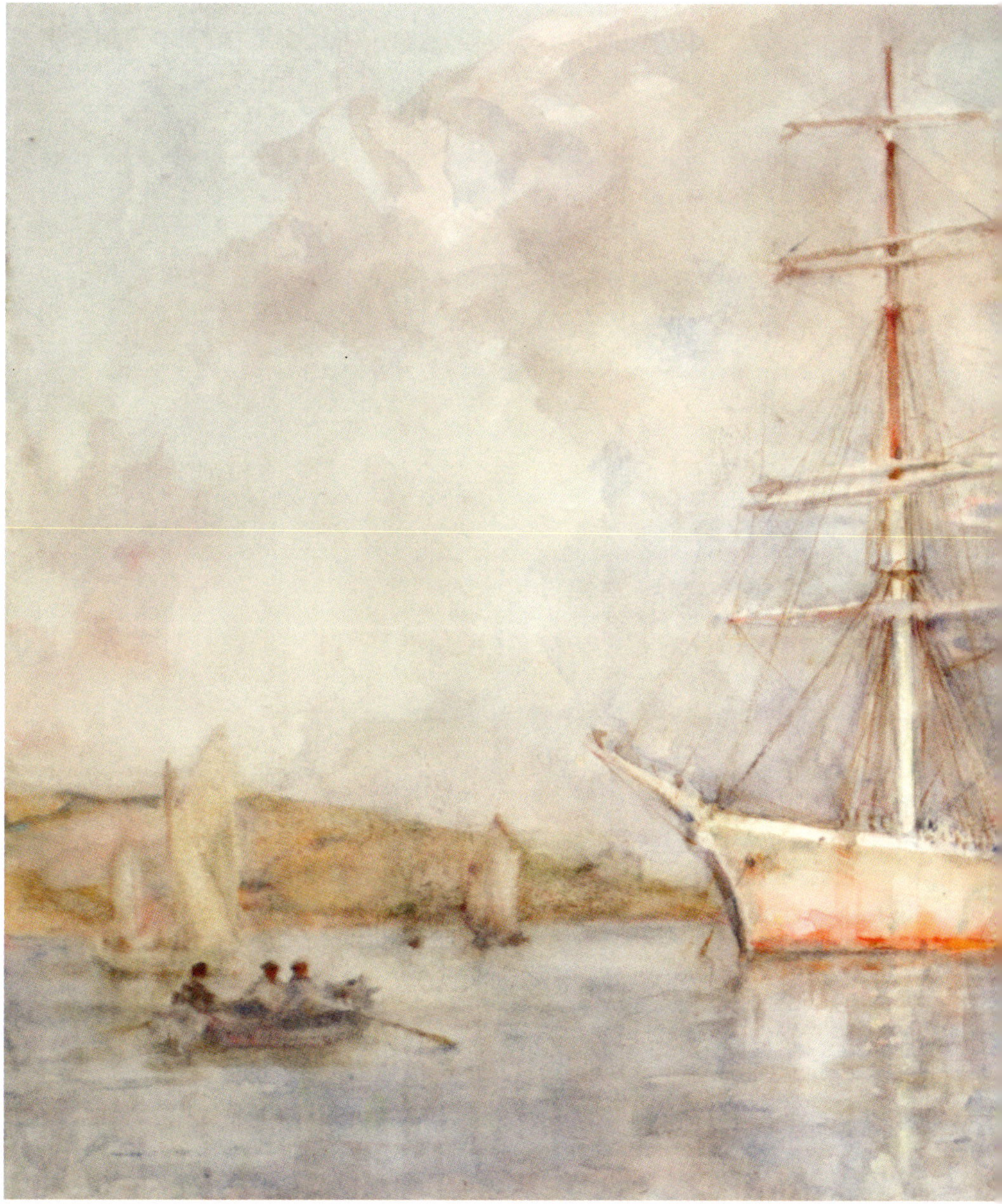

Sunset in the Harbour, 1911

Watercolour, 30.4 x 45.9cm
Signed bottom right: H.S.Tuke 1911
Exhibited: The Royal Watercolour Society 1911
Provenance: Purchased from Mrs Kemp, Witnesham
21 November 1966
RCPS Tuke Collection A175 R 689

This watercolour shows a metal-hulled French barque moored in front of a green-hulled Italian barque off St. Mawes, surrounded by small sailing dinghies. St. Mawes castle is shown on the end of the Roseland Peninsula on the left of the picture.

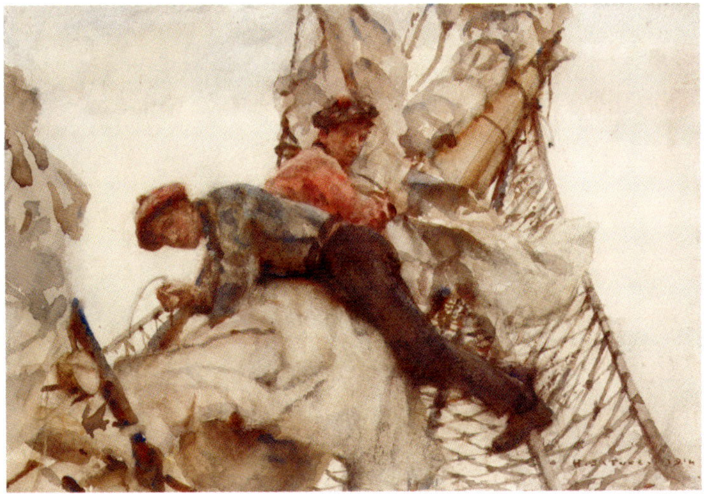

Stowing Head Sails, 1914

Watercolour, 17.8 x 25.8cm
Signed and dated bottom right: H.S.Tuke 1914
Exhibited: The Royal Watercolour Society, 1914
Provenance: Purchased from Geoffrey Sainsbury 29 May 1968
RCPS Tuke Collection A201 R786

Painted on the captured German ship *'Ponape'* anchored off King Harry Ferry, with Charlie Mitchell and Harry Giles posing. The *'Ponape'* came into Falmouth harbour on 21 September 1914 on its leaving Antwerp, when it was captured by British warships. According to his register, Tuke kept the painting at Lyndon Lodge, Hanwell, as a souvenir. The register also says it was reproduced in 'Colour' (this probably refers to the magazine *Colour*).

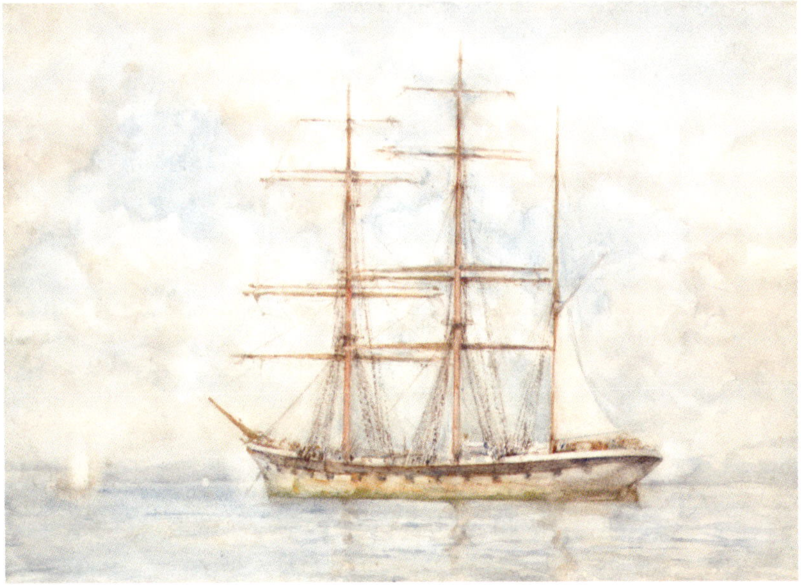

'Killoran', c.1915

Watercolour, 27.7 x 38cm
Initialled bottom right: H.S.T.
Inscribed 'Killoran' on reverse of old mount board
Provenance: Purchased from Geoffrey Sainsbury 20 June1965
RCPS Tuke Collection A143

The *'Killoran'* was a steel-hulled barque built at the Ailsa Shipbuilding Company at Troon in Glasgow in 1900. It is possible this picture was painted in January 1915 when the *'Killoran'* came to Falmouth on its way back to Rotterdam.

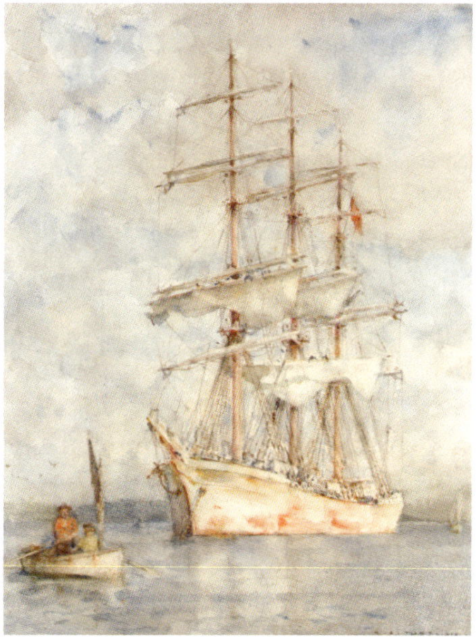

White Ship, 1915

Watercolour, 35.5 x 25.4cm
Signed and dated bottom right: H.S.Tuke 1915
Provenance: Purchased from John Maggs, Falmouth 7 November 1964, who purchased it from auction July 1964
RCPS Tuke Collection A22

During the First World War, Tuke benefited from the number of sailing ships that were either captured or ordered into Falmouth by the British Navy patrolling the waters nearby. It gave him a far greater variety of subjects to choose from. He gained permission to use them as a set for his models. However, according to letters to his sister, Tuke did not like the way German ships were captured: 'Sept. 15. [1914] Three large German sailing ships have been towed in at intervals, as prizes, flying the English naval flag over the German. It seems rather mean to capture them like that, none of them had heard of the war till they arrived off the Scilly islands, but it is all part of the horrible business.' MTS p.153.

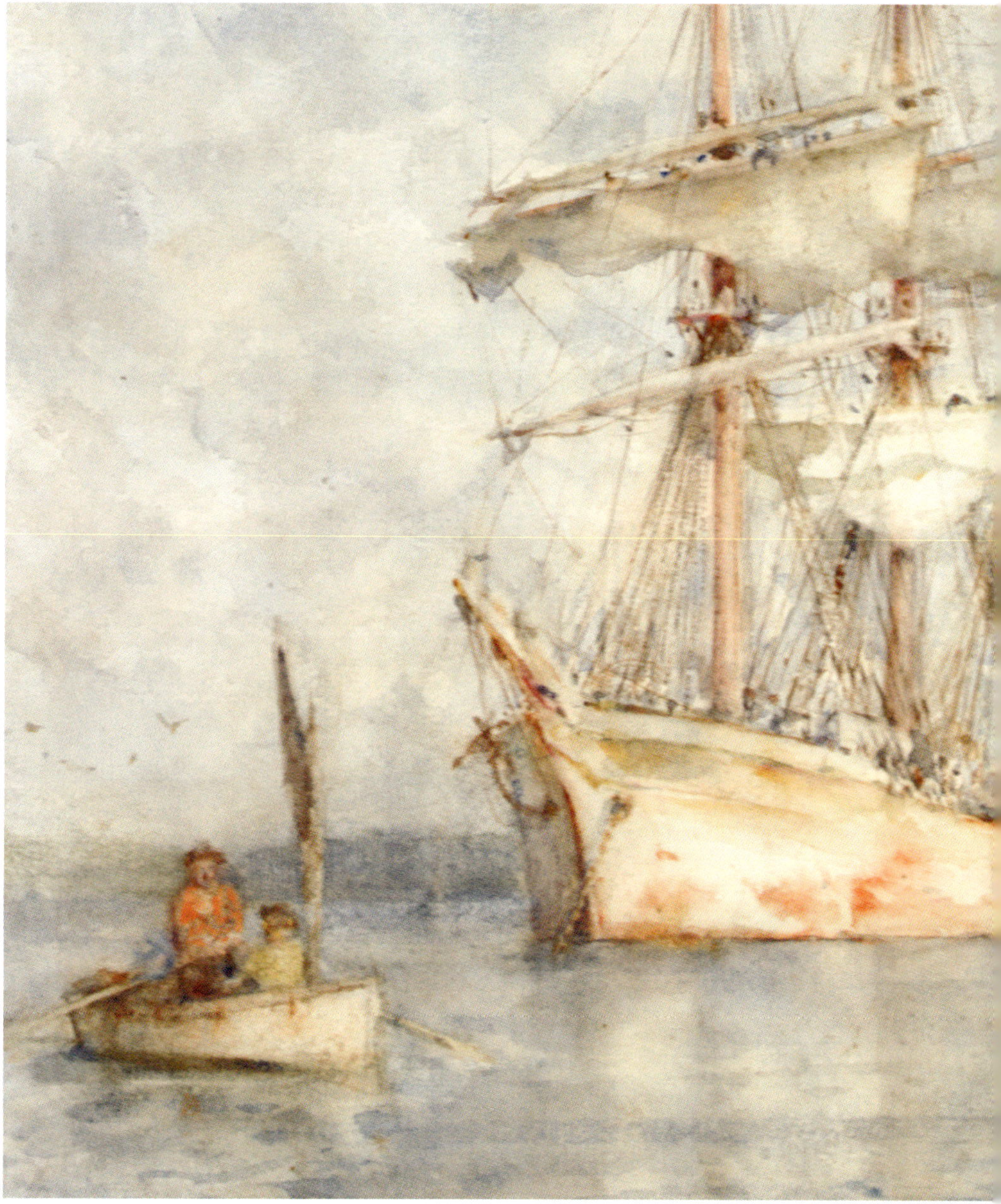

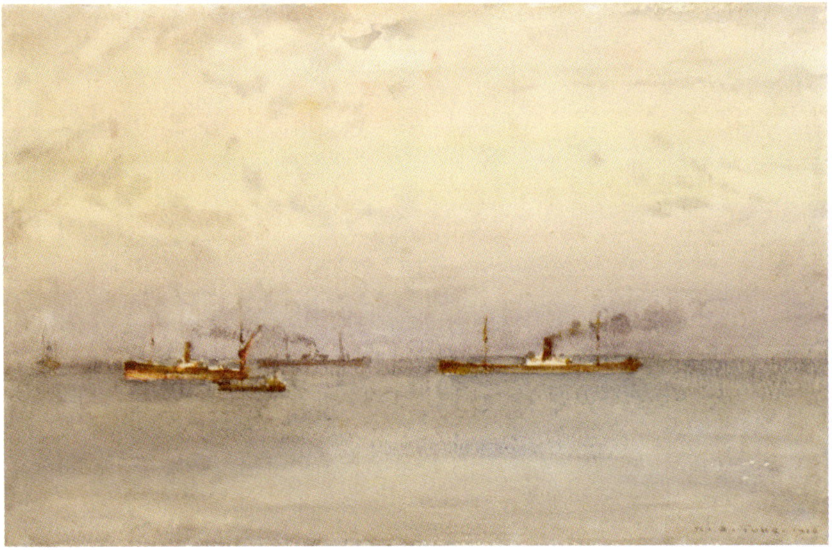

Ships at Sea, 1916

Watercolour, 13.8 x 21.4cm
Signed and dated bottom right: H.S.Tuke 1916
Provenance: Purchased from
Geoffrey Sainsbury
8 September 1968
RCPS Tuke Collection A180

According to Tuke's sister Maria, 'He hated the war, but on the other hand could not tolerate the pacifist attitude. Most of the boys he knew went out, and he knew they were right to go, although he was deeply distressed when tragic news came of any of them. His models went to sea, and whenever they came home on leave would come out and sit for him and tell him all their adventures...' MTS p.154

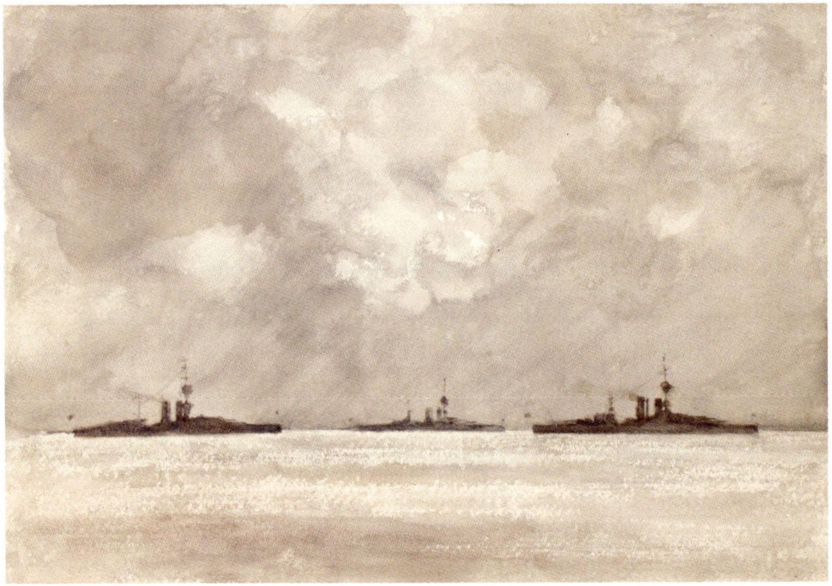

Warships, c. (1914-1918)

Watercolour, 25.4 x 36.2cm
Provenance: Purchased from
Geoffrey Sainsbury
8 September 1968
RCPS Tuke Collection A152

During the First World War, Falmouth and the docks were principally used to repair ships that had been damaged by German submarines. Tuke sent four watercolours in aid of the Red Cross to the Royal Watercolour Society; they raised £67 when sold by auction at Christies at the close of the exhibition.

Harbour Scene

Watercolour, 25.4 x 35.5cm
Provenance:
Purchased from Geoffrey Sainsbury
8 September 1968
RCPS Tuke Collection A151

This paintings shows steamers moored at Falmouth docks. There was a great surplus of shipping just after the First World War, and because of its deep water both in the harbour and up the river Fal, Falmouth was used to store ships.

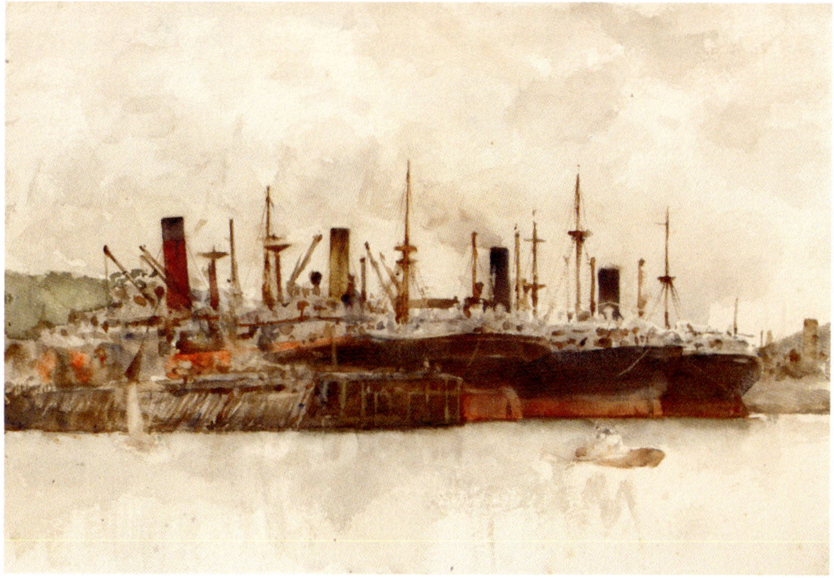

Steam Vessels, Falmouth

Watercolour, 17.8 x 36cm
Signed bottom right: H.S.Tuke
Provenance:
Purchased from Geoffrey Sainsbury
27 Feb 1966
RCPS Tuke Collection A173

This painting shows steam ships moored in Falmouth at the docks, with Pendennis in the background.

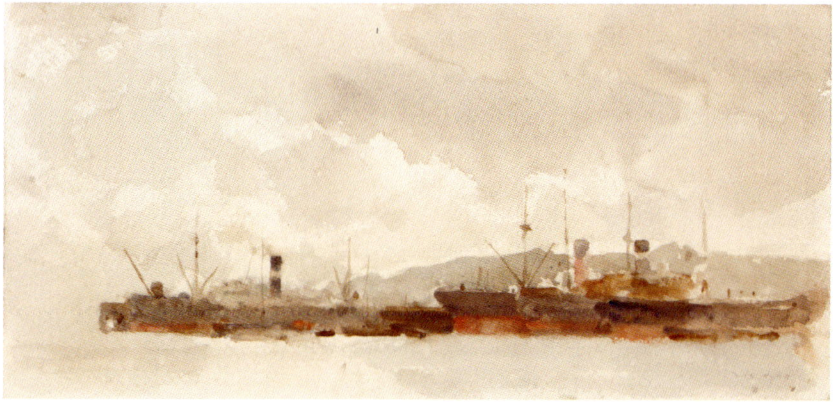

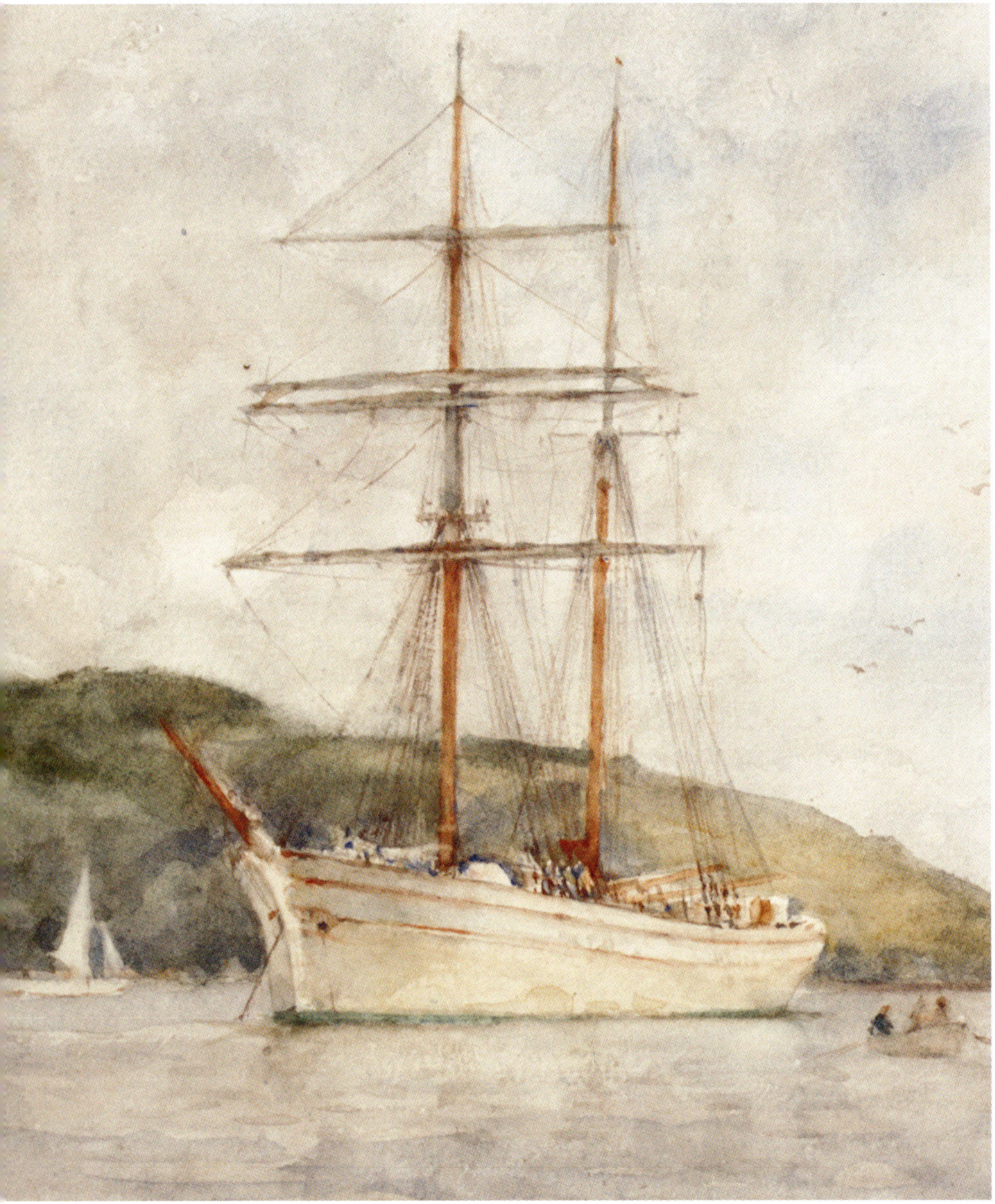

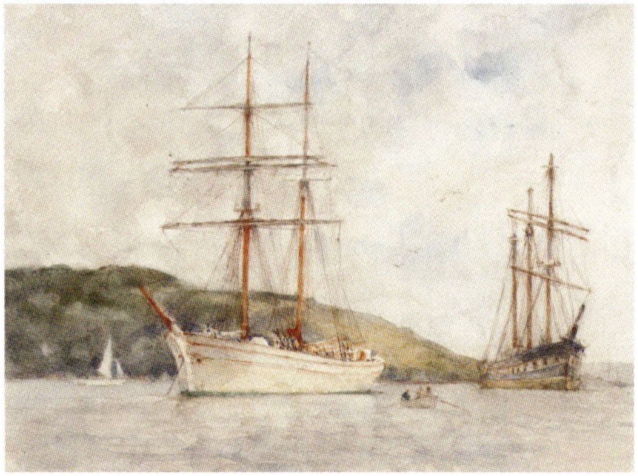

'Lady of Avenel', c. 1919/1920
Watercolour, 24 x 32cm
Inscribed on reverse: Lady of Avenel
Provenance: Purchased from Geoffrey Sainsbury
8 September 1968
RCPS Tuke Collection A160

This brig of 163 tons was the most famous of the ships of Henry Stevens of Trethowan, who launched her at Little Falmouth in July 1874 as a topsail schooner. First owned by E.D. Anderton of Falmouth, she was later re-rigged as a brigantine. In 1920 she was fitted out by Captain W.H. Dowman as a school training ship for Devitt and Moore, prior to his buying and re-rigging the *'Cutty Sark'*. This watercolour shows the ship moored off Trefusis Point, opposite Falmouth. It was towed into Falmouth on 27 July 1919 by the tug *'Triton'* with a fire in the hold. This watercolour was probably completed c.1919/1920 when Captain Dowman bought it, as he and Tuke were great friends.

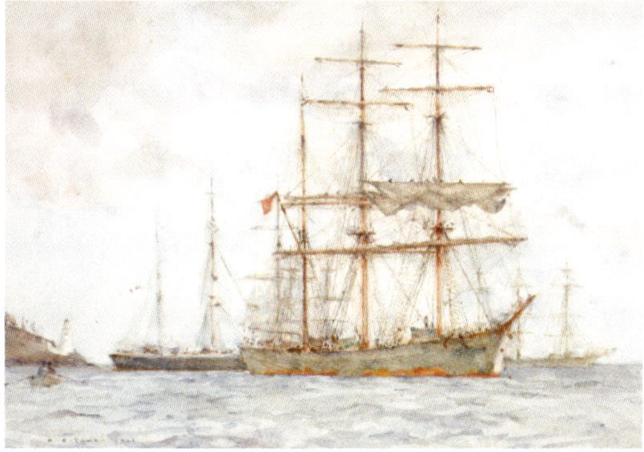

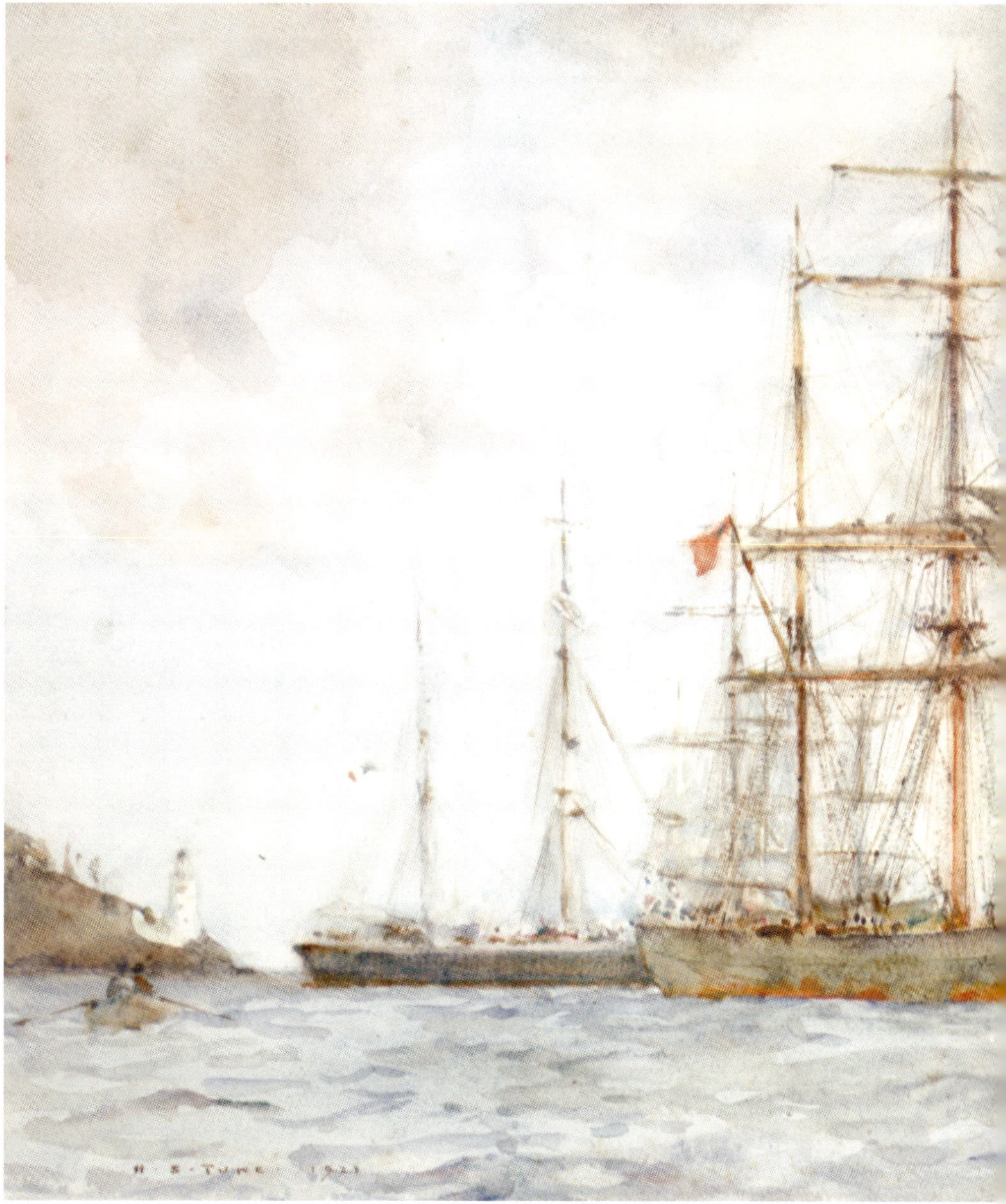

Just Arrived, The *'Bellas'*, 1921

Watercolour, 25.4 x 35.6cm
Signed and dated bottom left: H.S.Tuke 1921
Exhibited: The Royal Watercolour Society 1921
Provenance: Purchased from Eric W. Phipps
10 November 1964
RCPS Tuke Collection A21 R974

The *'Bellas'* was an iron-hulled barque built in 1875 in Whitehaven. It was originally called *'Routenbeck'* and was German owned. During the First World War it was taken over by H.M. Government and managed by Stewart and Co. It came to Falmouth on September 10 1921 on its way from Sydney, Australia to Barry carrying a cargo of wheat. This watercolour shows the *'Bellas'* moored off St. Anthony's Head, with the lighthouse depicted on the far left.

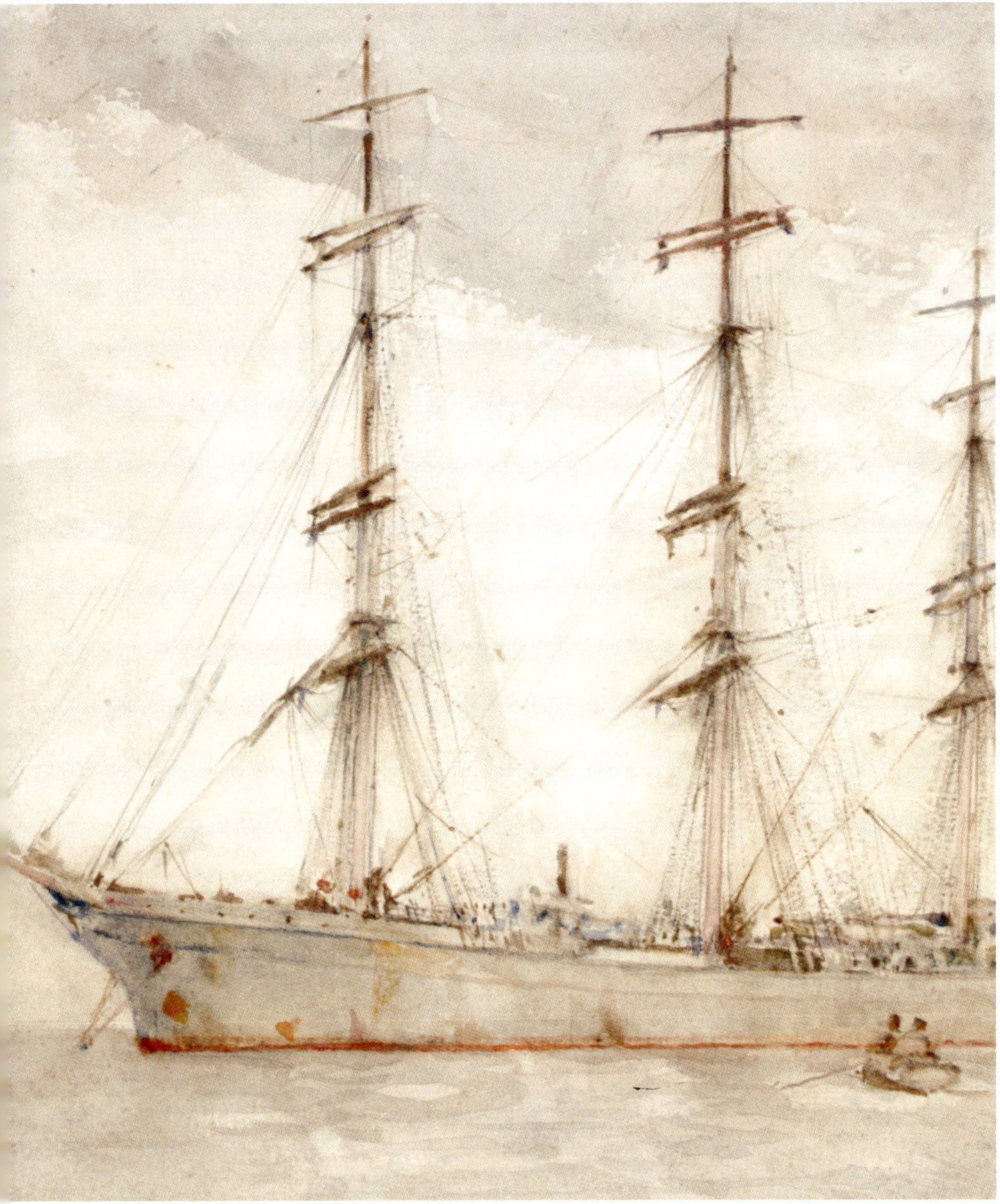

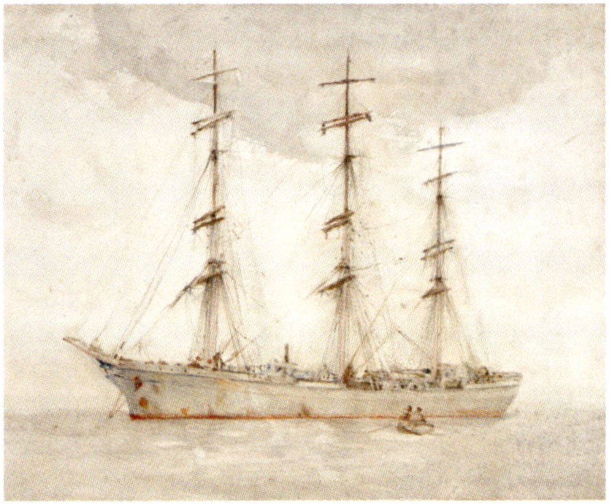

'Desaix', c.1920
Watercolour, 30.6 x 35.7cm
Inscribed on reverse: 'Desaix'
Provenance: Purchased from Geoffrey Sainsbury
8 September 1968
RCPS Tuke Collection A154

'Desaix' was a French-built ship and came into Falmouth on August 18th 1920 on its way from Dublin to Buenos Aires. This is probably when Tuke undertook this watercolour.

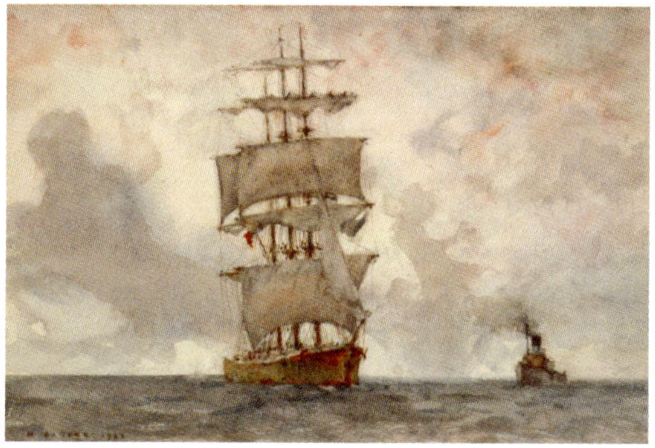

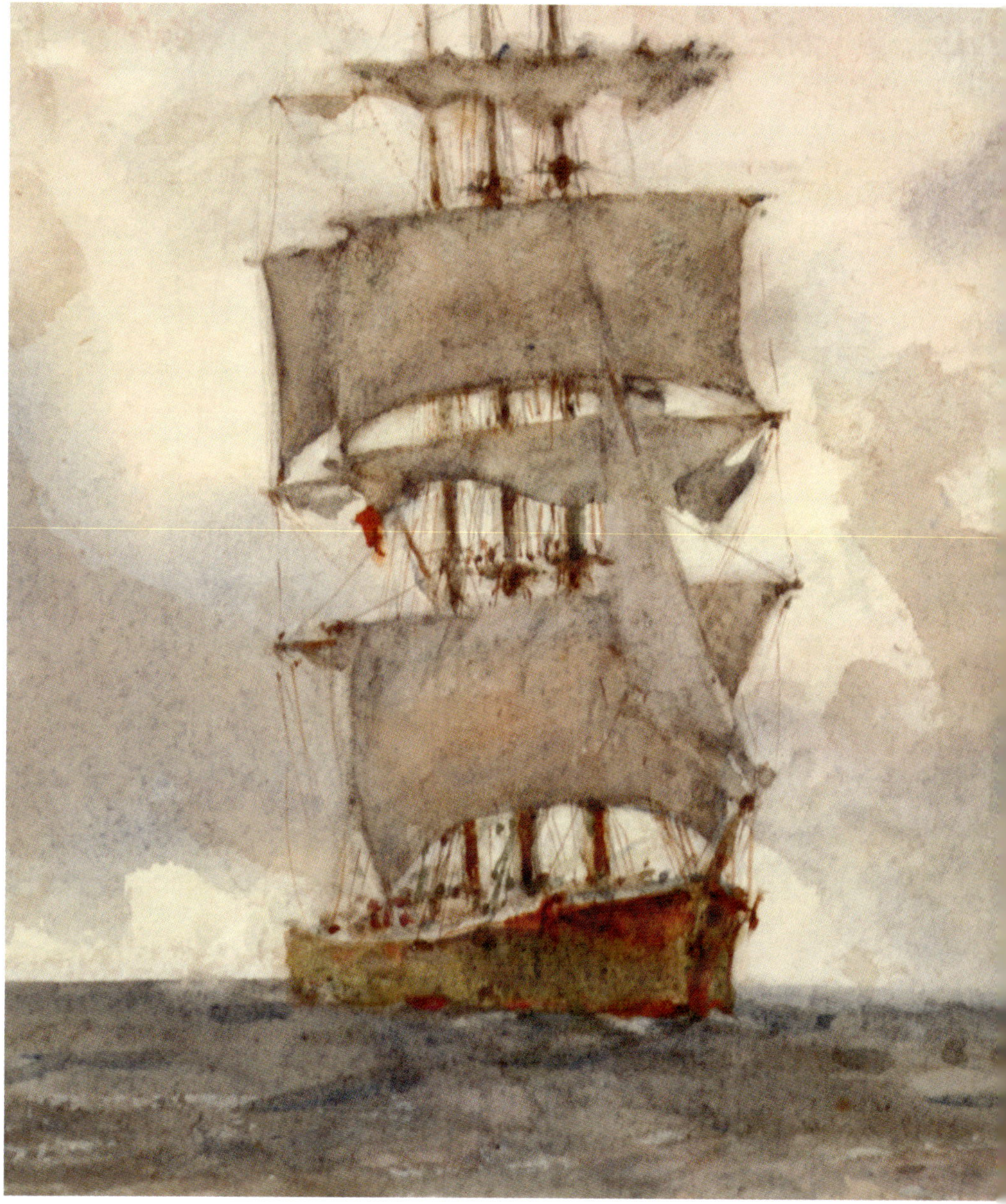

Barque and Tug, 1922

Watercolour, 17.6 x 25.4cm
Signed and dated bottom left: H.S.Tuke 1922
Provenance: Purchased from W. Dyer of Camborne 13 August 1966. Dyer had bought it from the Christies' sale of the Princess Royal's paintings.
RCPS Tuke Collection A176

Tuke's contribution to the portfolio of watercolours presented by the Royal Watercolour Society to the Princess Royal on her coming of age.

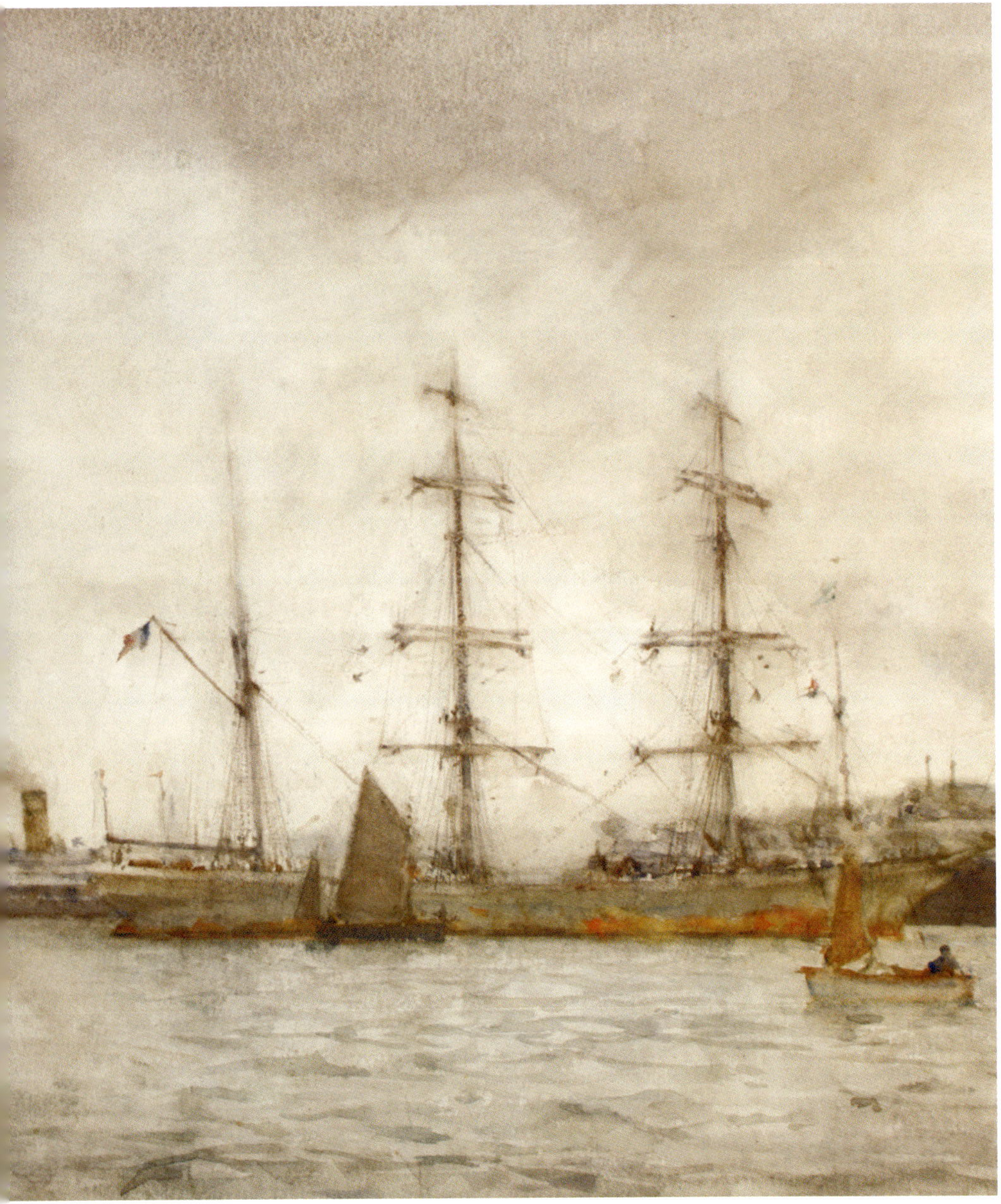

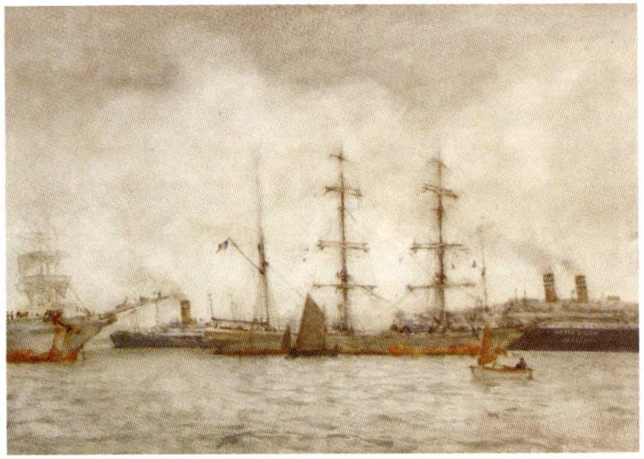

Ships in Harbour, c.1919

Watercolour, 36 x 50cm
Provenance: Purchased from Geoffrey Sainsbury
27 Feb 1966
RCPS Tuke Collection A174

This watercolour shows shipping in Falmouth harbour with a French barque at centre, and a Falmouth quay punt alongside. The liner SS *'Rotterdam'* is on the right. It is possible to date this watercolour from when the *'Rotterdam'* came into Falmouth harbour, which was just after the First World War, on June 20th 1919 on its way from New York to Rotterdam. It was a passenger and mail liner of the Holland-America line and had stopped in Falmouth to drop off passengers.

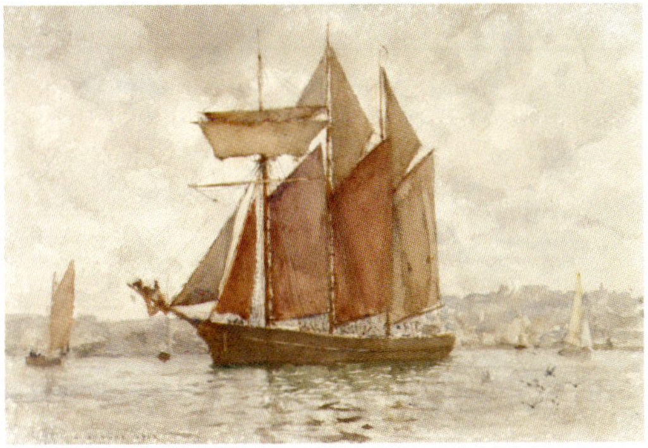

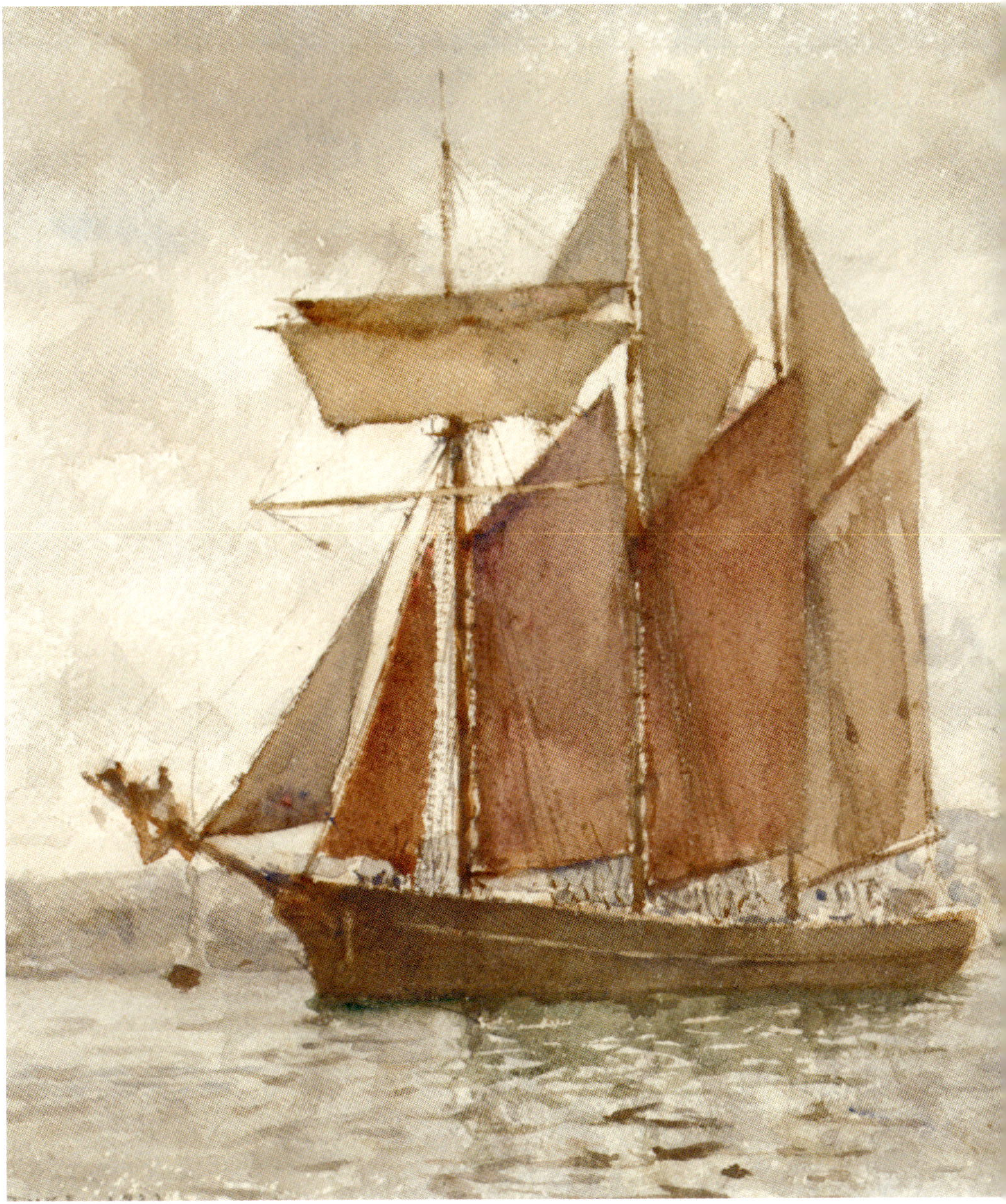

Drying Sails, 1922
Watercolour, 25 x 34.8cm
Signed and dated bottom left: H.S.Tuke 1922
Exhibited: The Royal Watercolour Society Winter 1922 and the Royal Scottish Watercolour Society 1922-23
Provenance: Purchased from Peter Jackson 10 November 1964
RCPS Tuke Collection A115 R985

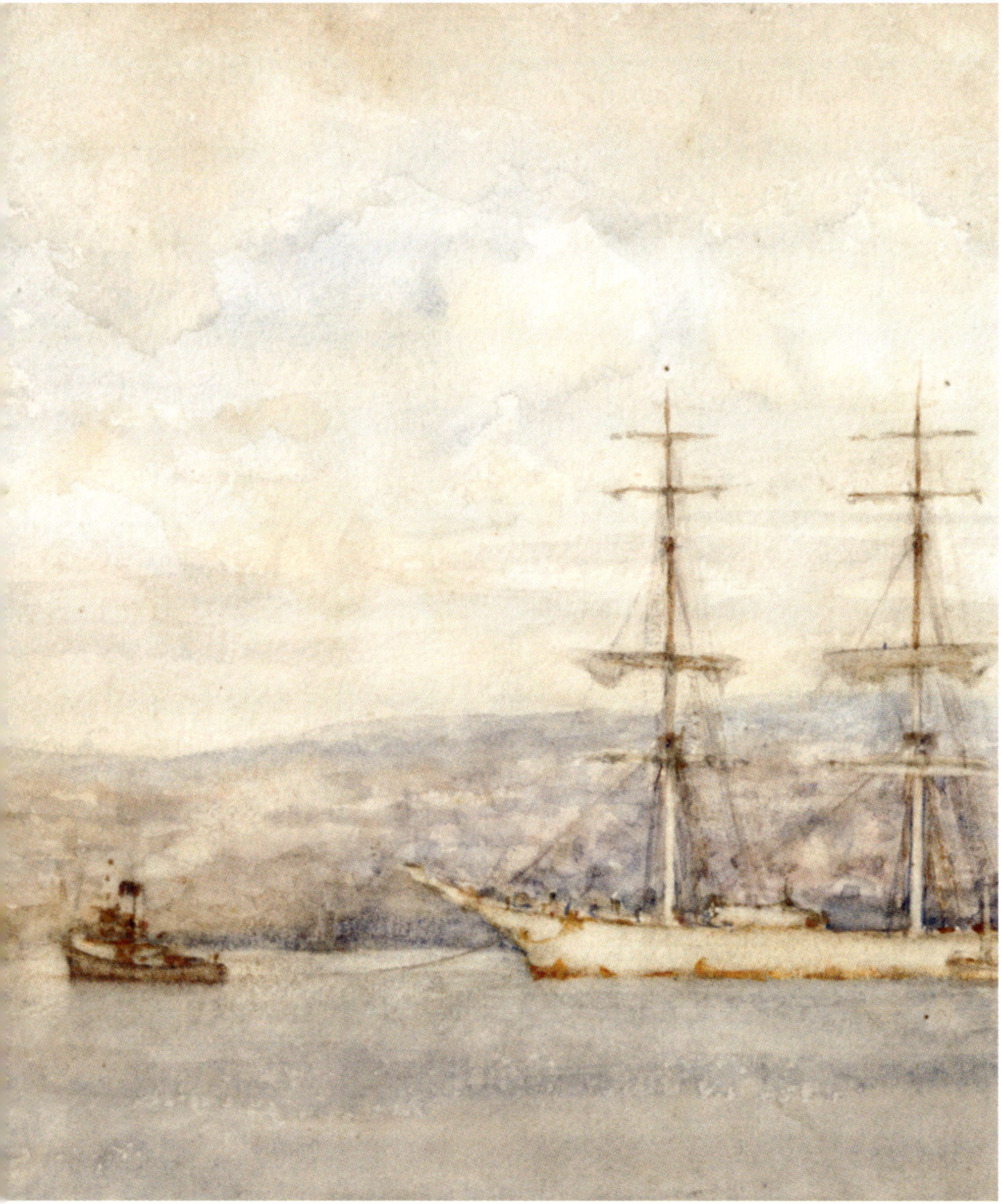

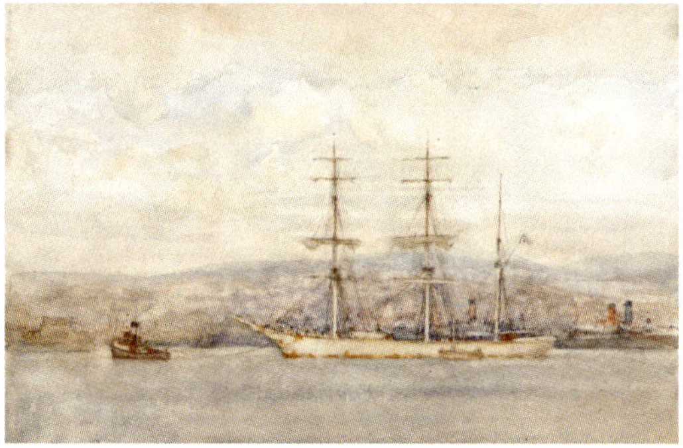

'Favell', c.1920s

Watercolour, 17.7 x 25.4cm
Inscribed on front and reverse of old mount in MTS's hand: 'Favell'.
Sketch on reverse A156a
Provenance: Purchased from Geoffrey Sainsbury 8 September1968
RCPS Tuke Collection A156

The *'Favell'* was a steel-hulled 3 masted Finnish barque of 1363 tons, built by Hill and Son of Bristol in 1895. She was originally Russian-owned, then after 10 years was sold to Gunnar Rydman of Helsingfors, Finland. In 1925 she sailed from Adelaide to Falmouth in 125 days. She was also recorded to have come into Falmouth on June 8th 1927. According to Maria, Tuke wrote in his diary 9 June 1927, 'Went out in the bay to meet the Finnish Barque Favell sailing up slowly in a light west wind with all sail set.' M.T.S p.179. The picture shows the *'Favell'* being towed into Falmouth Harbour by a tug.

'Kobenhavn', c. 1927

Watercolour, 25.4 x 35.4cm
Inscribed on original mount by MTS: 'Kobenhavn'
Provenance: Purchased from Geoffrey Sainsbury
29 May 1968
RCPS Tuke Collection A166

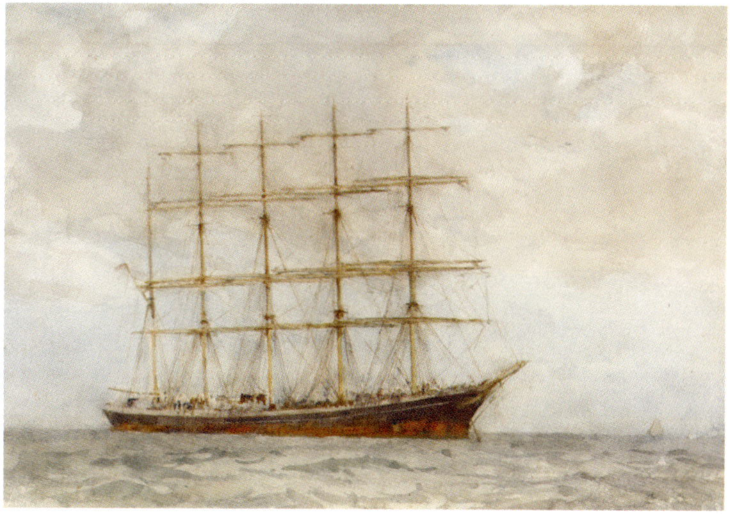

The *'Kobenhavn'* was a five-masted barque built by Ramage and Ferguson c. 1919. 'It was the largest sailing ship ever built in the British Isles' (*The Last of the Windjammers*, by Lubbock, p.335). It also had a four cylinder diesel engine which was capable of driving her at about six knots. She came into Falmouth from Adelaide, Australia in 109 days on June 17th 1927. This is probably when Tuke undertook this watercolour. In June 1927 he noted in his diary the *'Kobenhavn'* coming in, describing her as a 'great Danish cadet ship... five masts, too far out in the bay for me to do much.' M.T.S. p.179. According to Maria, Tuke did manage to get several notes and sketches of this ship.

'Britannia', c. 1926

Oil on canvas paper, laid down on canvas, 22 x 26cm
Inscribed on reverse: 'Britannia'
Provenance: Purchased from Brian Wells
14 May 1967
RCPS Tuke Collection A134

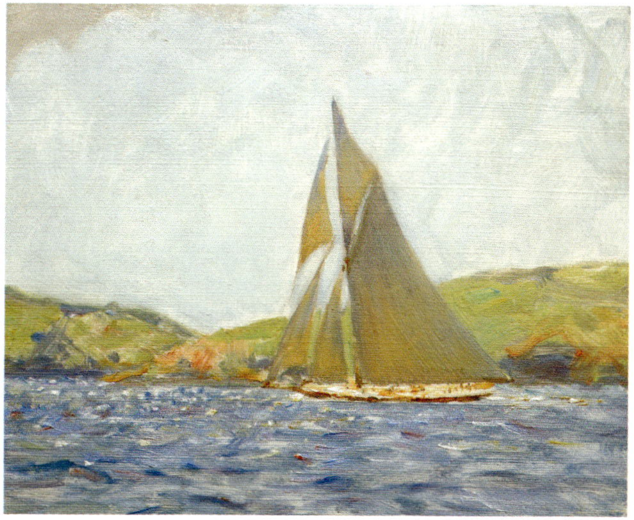

A rough oil sketch which shows King George V's yacht *'Britannia'* in full sail off a headland. It is known from photographs of the time* that *'Britannia'* came to Falmouth for races in June 1926, which is when the first races were held there for the world's largest yachts. As Tuke was not very well in 1926, this may account for the rough handling of the paint in this work.

* *'Ships and Shores around old Cornwall'* by Fisher Barham.

Views of Falmouth and environs

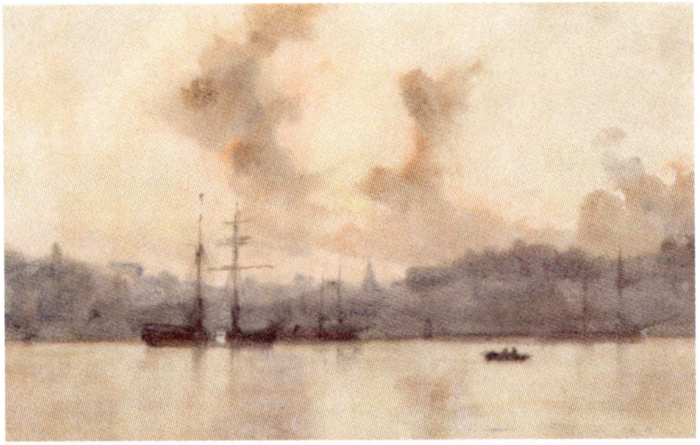

Falmouth from Flushing, 1906
Watercolour, 13.9 x 21.6cm
Signed and dated bottom left: H.S.Tuke 1906
RCPS Tuke Collection A401

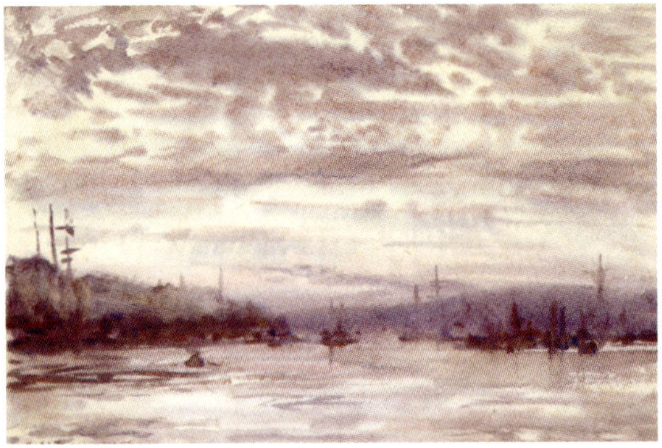

Twilight, 1911
Watercolour, 18.8 x 26.3cm
Signed and dated bottom left: H.S.Tuke 1911
Provenance: Purchased from J.T. Hyde
21 October 1963
RCPS Tuke Collection A32 R697

A sunset over the Penryn River, seen from Falmouth with Trefusis Hill on the right.

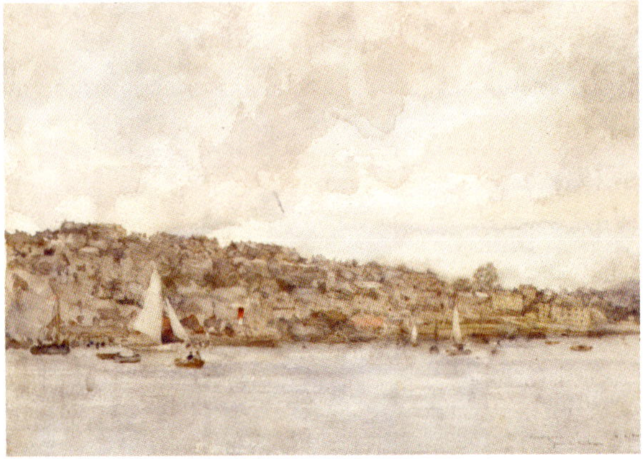

Falmouth from the Harbour
Watercolour, 25.2 x 35.3cm
Signed and inscribed bottom right: H.S.Tuke Falmouth from the Harbour
Provenance: Purchased from Geoffrey Sainsbury
29 May1968
RCPS Tuke Collection A142

This watercolour was probably painted on board a vessel in Falmouth harbour. It shows the Greenbank Hotel and boats around the Royal Cornwall Yacht Club.

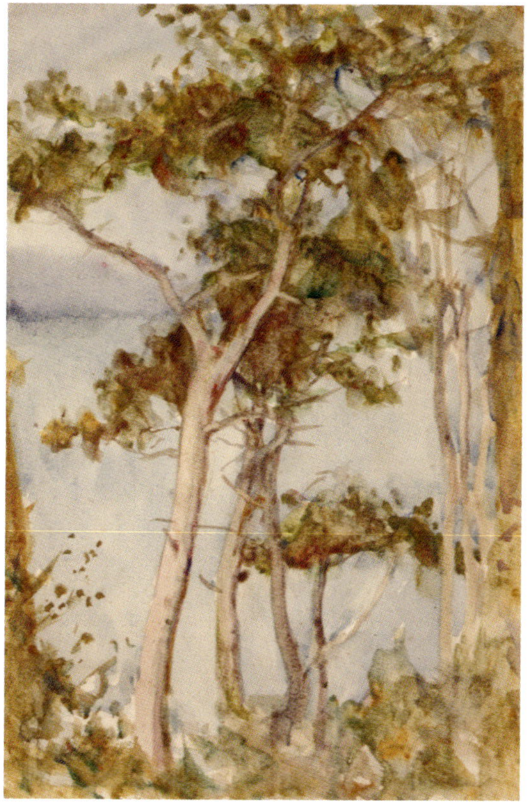

Trees at Stack

Watercolour, 21.5 x 13.8cm
Signed bottom right: H.S.Tuke
Inscribed on back: Charlie Mitch.
Provenance: Reputedly from Charlie Mitchell's brother
Purchased from John Maggs
14 July 1962
RCPS Tuke Collection A25

A watercolour of trees on Stack (Pennance Point) with the sea in the background. Tuke lived nearby in Swanpool, Falmouth. Comparison with R1035 would indicate it was painted c. 1923.

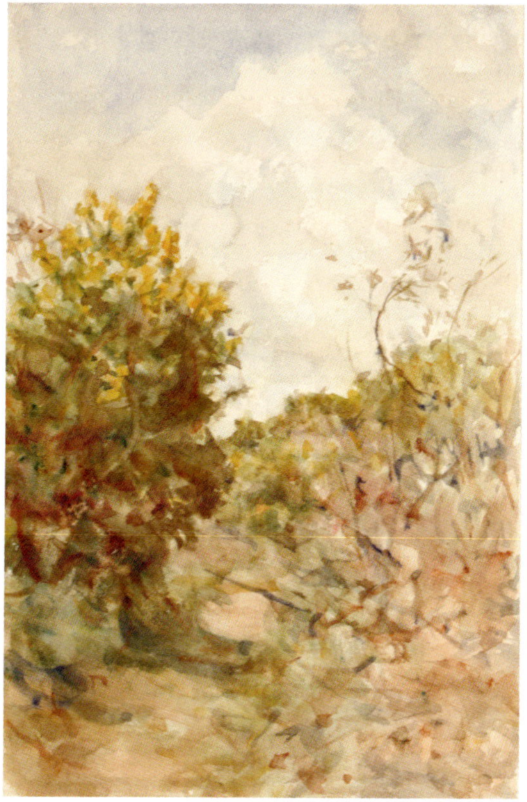

Stack

Watercolour, 21.5 x 13.7cm
Provenance: Purchased from Geoffrey Sainsbury
30 April 1967
RCPS Tuke Collection A218

Painted from the coastal path from Swanpool to Maenporth, south of Falmouth, near Pennance Cottage where Tuke lived.

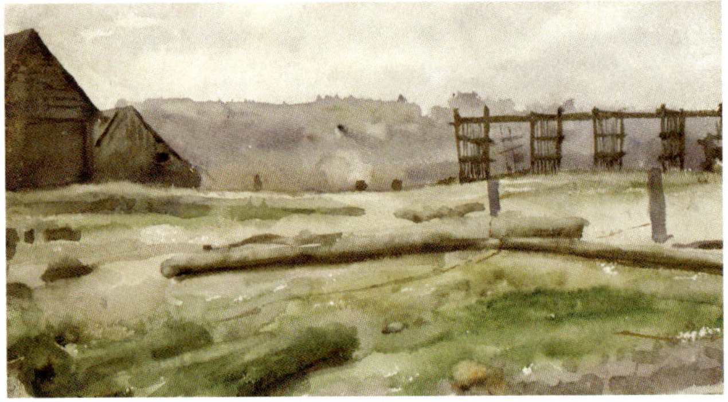

The Bar Pool, Falmouth

Watercolour, 14 x 25.9cm
Provenance: Purchased from Geoffrey Sainsbury
14 December 1967
RCPS Tuke Collection A209

The Bar Pool in Falmouth was originally created for a tidal mill which ceased to operate in 1862. The pool continued to be used for seasoning wood for local boatyards nearby. The balks of timber are visible in the foreground of this watercolour, and the mast of a sailing ship is visible in front of the town in the background.

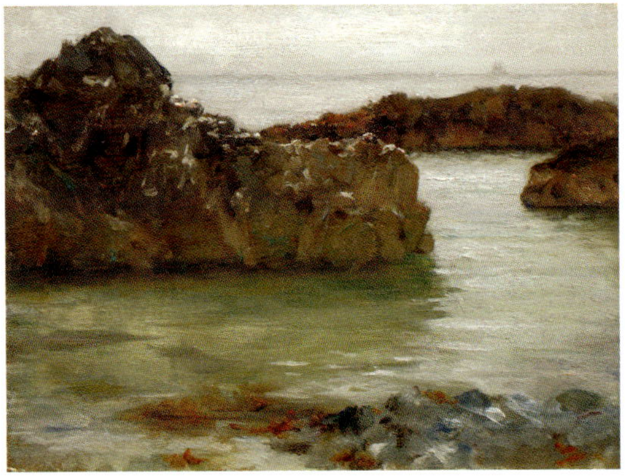

Rocks at Newporth

Oil on board, 26.5 x 35cm
Provenance: Purchased from Henry Shemilt
24 December 1963
RCPS Tuke Collection A96

Painted in Falmouth at Newporth beach. This beach featured as a backdrop to many of Tuke's major paintings. It was ideal as it is difficult to access by land, and is more easily accessible by boat. It is very sheltered, as the back of the beach is a steep cliff and cannot be viewed by passers-by, giving Tuke privacy while painting his male models.

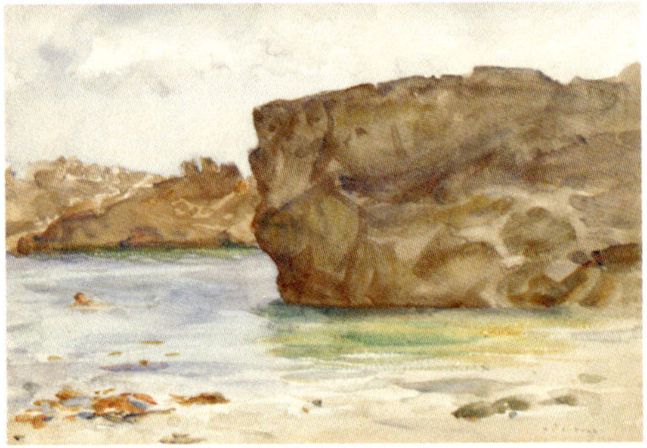

Newporth Beach

Watercolour, 17.8 x 25.7cm
Signed bottom right: H.S.Tuke
Provenance: Purchased from Geoffrey Sainsbury
31 March 1964
RCPS Tuke Collection A83

Rocks at Pennance Point

Watercolour, 17.7 x 25.6cm
Initialled bottom left: H.S.T
On reverse another watercolour of a rock at Newporth beach
Provenance: Purchased from W. Dyer of Camborne
28 October 1967
RCPS Tuke Collection A213

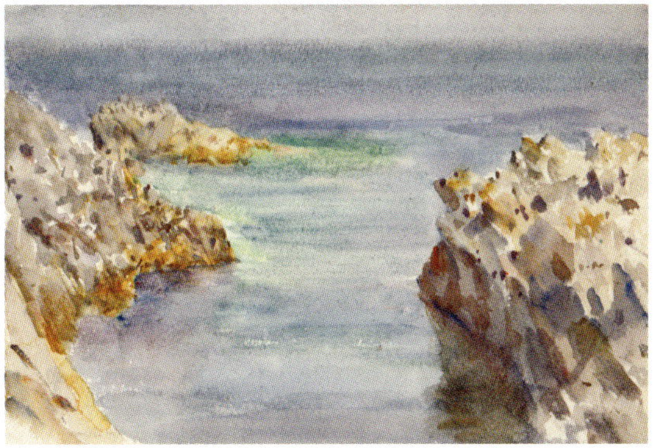

Rock on Newporth beach

Watercolour, 17.7 x 25.6cm
Provenance: Purchased from W. Dyer of Camborne
28 October 1967
RCPS Tuke Collection A213a

This watercolour is on the reverse of A213.

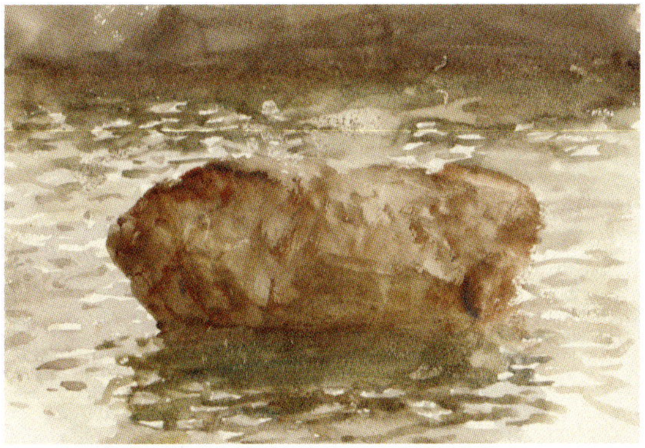

Sunrise from Swanpool, 1910

Watercolour, 11.5 x 20.3cm
Signed and dated bottom left: Tuke 1910
Incribed on the mount: Sunset from Swanpool
Provenance: Purchased from Geoffrey Sainsbury 8 September1968
RCPS Tuke Collection A185

Swanpool is an inland pool just south of Falmouth, divided from the sea only by a road and sand bar. It was originally a sea inlet, but storm waves built up sand on the beach and closed the inlet to create the pool. It has brackish water which allows swans and other wildlife to thrive, hence the name. Tuke lived just outside Swanpool along the coast at Pennance Point.

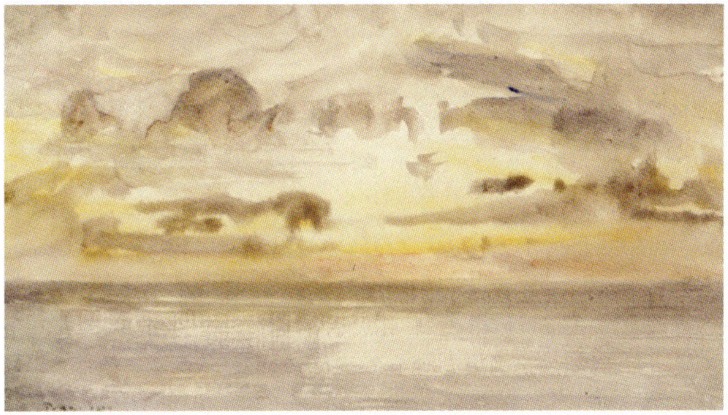

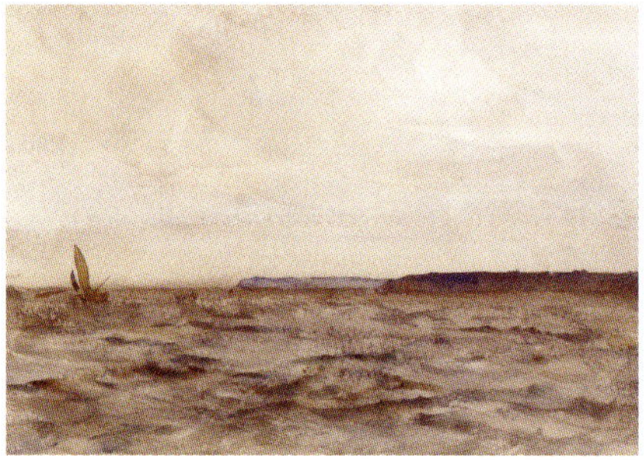

Aft o' the Lizard

Watercolour, 17.8 x 25cm
Provenance: From the sketchbook given by Hester Etchells to the Tuke Collection 27 June 1964
RCPS Tuke Collection A84

This view was probably painted on board a boat, looking back at the top of the Lizard from the Helford River.

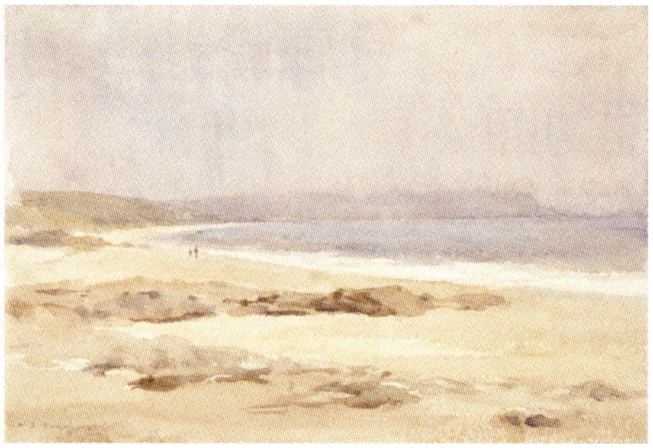

The Sands – Porthleven, 1923

Watercolour, 17.6 x 25.8cm
Signed and dated bottom left: H.S.Tuke 1923
Inscribed on back of original mount: Porthleven, Cornwall
Exhibited: Hull, Spring 1930
Provenance: Purchased from Geoffrey Sainsbury 30 April 1967
RCPS Tuke Collection A99

This watercolour seems to be the view looking south from Porthleven to Loe Bar – a sand bar which cuts off the tidal inlet which used to go up to Helston and is now a pool. Porthleven is a coastal town with an inlet leading to a harbour 13 miles to the west of Falmouth.

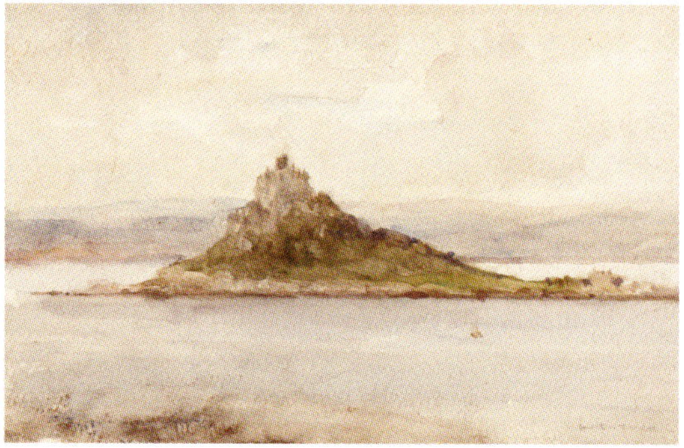

St. Michael's Mount

Watercolour, 14 x 21.7cm
Signed bottom right: H.S.Tuke
Provenance: Purchased from Geoffrey Sainsbury 29 May 1968
RCPS Tuke Collection A215

This view of St. Michael's Mount, which is in the bay opposite Penzance, Cornwall, is painted from east of Marazion. The causeway connecting the Mount to the mainland at low tide is just visible. The hills behind Penzance and Newlyn are in the distance. Tuke would often cycle down to Newlyn and Lamorna to visit other artists with whom he remained friends, including Tom and Carrie Gotch and Lamorna Birch.

Mounts Bay

Watercolour, 10 x 15.5cm
Inscribed bottom left: Mount's Bay
Provenance: Purchased from Geoffrey Sainsbury 14 December 1967
RCPS Tuke Collection A205

Restronguet

Watercolour, 17.9 x 25.6cm
Inscribed bottom left: Restronguet
Provenance: Purchased from Geoffrey Sainsbury
31 March 1964
RCPS Tuke Collection A40

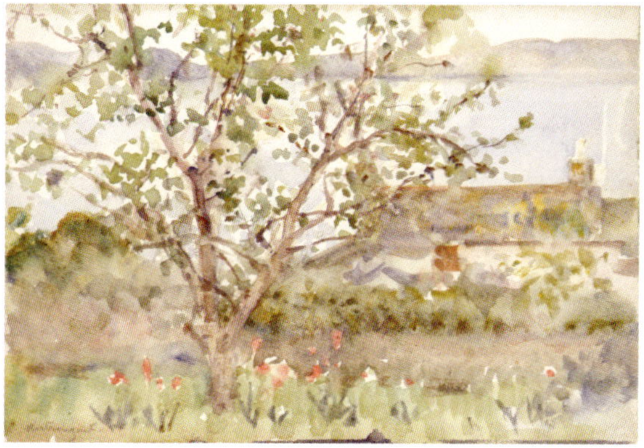

This soft, impressionistic watercolour is of the small hamlet of Restronguet, at Restronguet Creek off the River Fal, approximately three miles north east of Falmouth. It is famous for the Pandora Inn which used to serve an old ferry which brought traffic across in medieval times from the quay at Restronguet Point.

Hulk in Sailor's Creek

(previously know as *Sketch at Lastingham*)
Watercolour, 17.7 x 36.2cm
Initialled on reverse bottom right: H.S.T.
Inscribed on old mount on reverse: *Sketch at Lastingham*
(but this is now thought to be incorrect.)
Provenance: Purchased from Geoffrey Sainsbury, 8 September1968
RCPS Tuke Collection A159

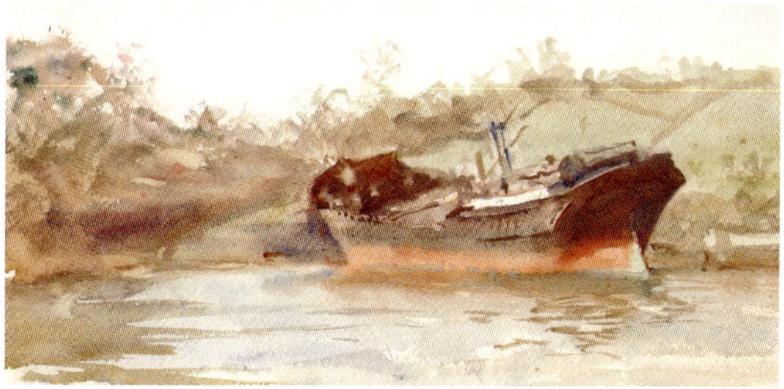

This sketch was previously thought to be titled *Sketch at Lastingham* – but Brian Price notes this seems incorrect as it is obviously of a hulk in a creek; he gives a diary entry of 21 April 1925, 'Afternoon with the '*Nada*' to Sailor's Creek... Did a slight sketch of the hulk in the creek.' Sailor's Creek is on the Penryn River which flows into Falmouth harbour.

River Gannel, Newquay

Watercolour, 17.5 x 25.4cm
Inscribed bottom left: River Gannel from de P's estate, Newquay
Provenance: Purchased from Geoffrey Sainsbury
29 May 1968
RCPS Tuke Collection A216

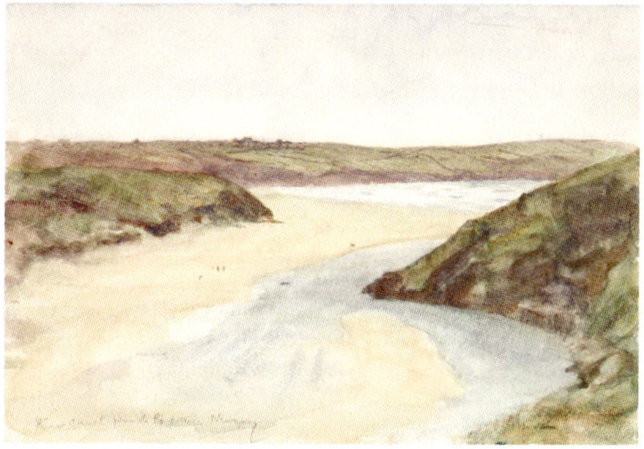

Apparently there is some question as to whether this is by Tuke or George Beldam [1](1868-1937). Tuke certainly knew Alfred De Pass well and would have been invited to visit him at his estate at Newquay.

[1] George Beldam was an amateur artist, photographer and cricketer who was a great friend of Tuke.

Coastal Scenes

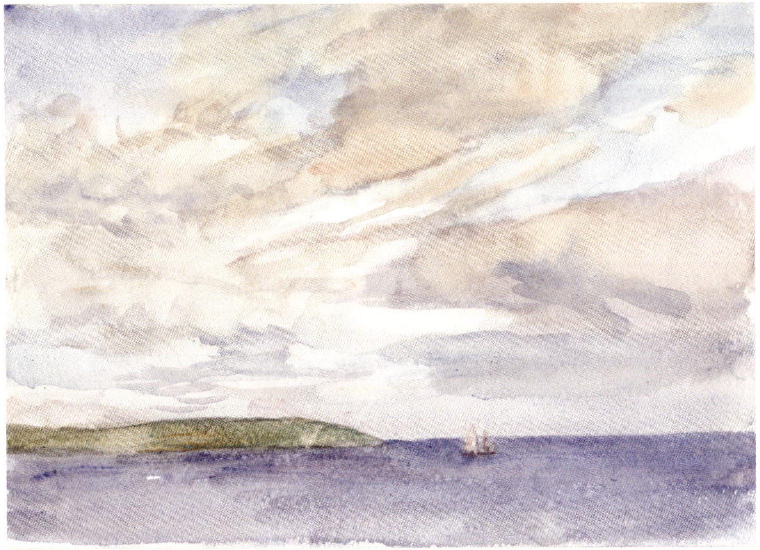

Coastal Scene

Watercolour, 17.8 x 25cm
Provenance: Given to Tuke Collection by Hester Sainsbury 27 June 1964 from a dismembered sketch book
RCPS Tuke Collection A222

A view of the Roseland Peninsula at the mouth of Falmouth harbour with a small sailing boat at sea.

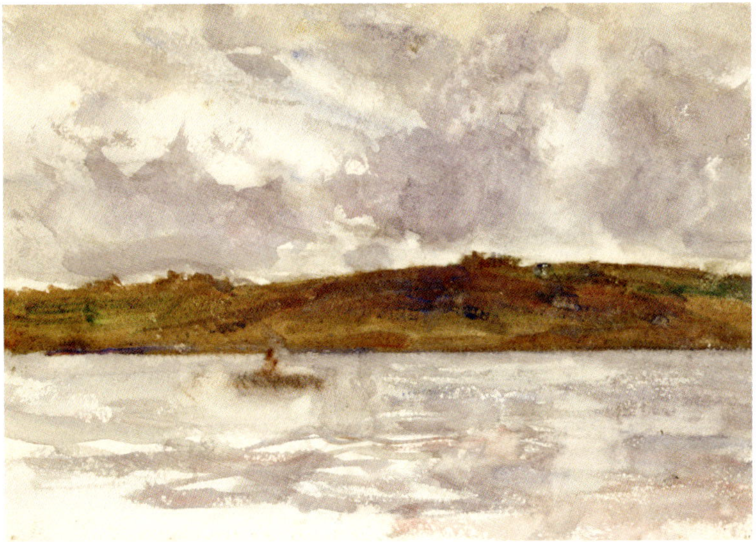

Coastal Scene

Watercolour, 17.9 x 25.1cm
Provenance: Given to Tuke Collection by Hester Sainsbury 27 June 1964 from a dismembered sketch book
RCPS Tuke Collection A223

A view of one of the headlands around Falmouth.

Coastal Scene

Watercolour, 17.9 x 24.9cm
Provenance: Given to Tuke Collection by Hester Sainsbury
27 June 1964 from a dismembered sketch book
RPCS Tuke Collection A221

A view of Rosemullion Head, Falmouth, probably painted from the coast just outside Falmouth.

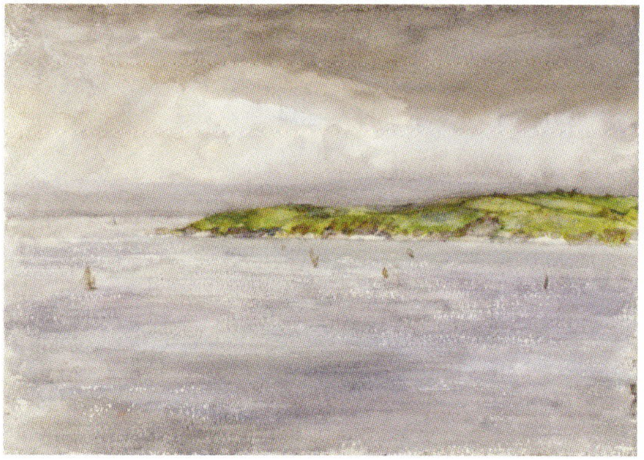

Cliff Scene

Watercolour, 17.9 x 25.5cm
Provenance: Given to Tuke Collection by Hester Sainsbury
27 June 1964 from a dismembered sketch book
RCPS Tuke Collection A224

The white cliffs in this view suggest the south coast of England, rather than Cornwall.

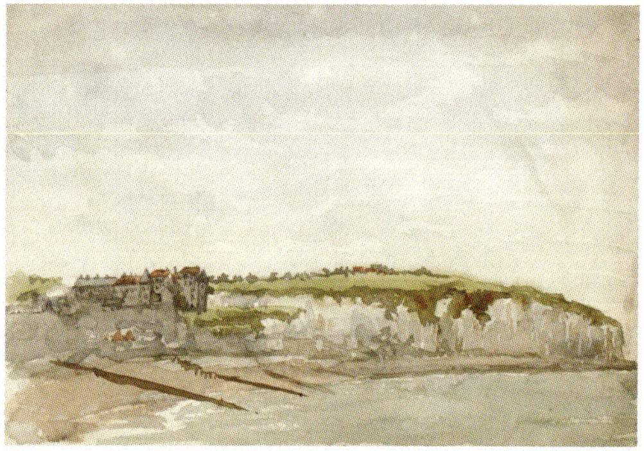

Rocky Coast, 1899

Watercolour, 17.5 x 24.9cm
Initialled and dated bottom right: H.S.T 1899
Provenance: Purchased from Geoffrey Sainsbury
14 December 1967
RCPS Tuke Collection A212

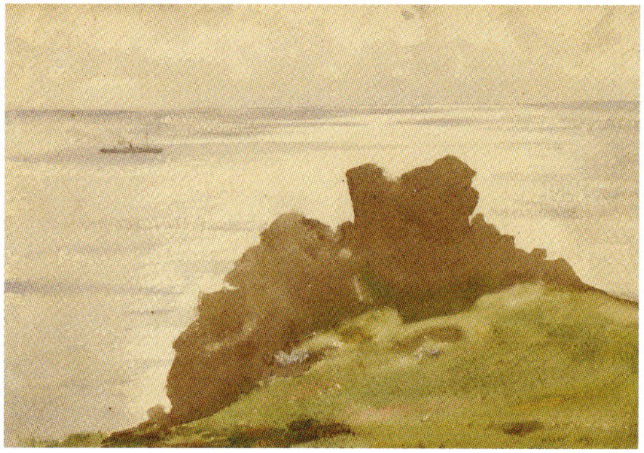

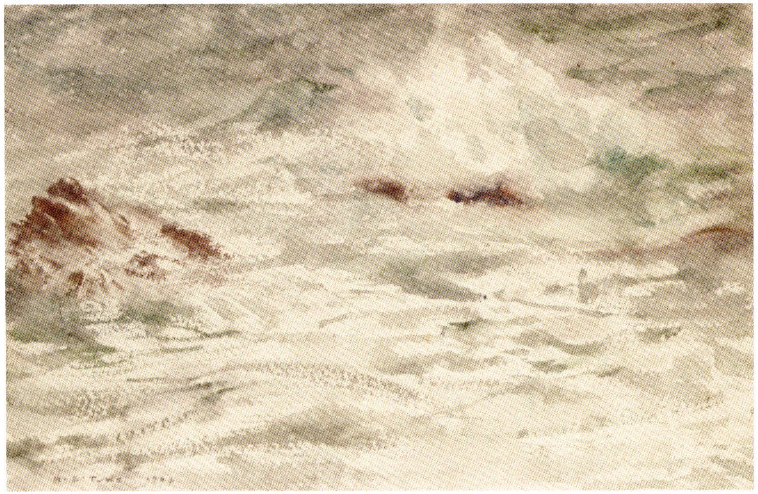

Sea and Rocks, 1903
Watercolour, 13.4 x 21.4cm
Initialled and dated bottom left: H.S.T. 1903
Provenance: Purchased from Geoffrey Sainsbury
30 April 1967
RCPS Tuke Collection A219

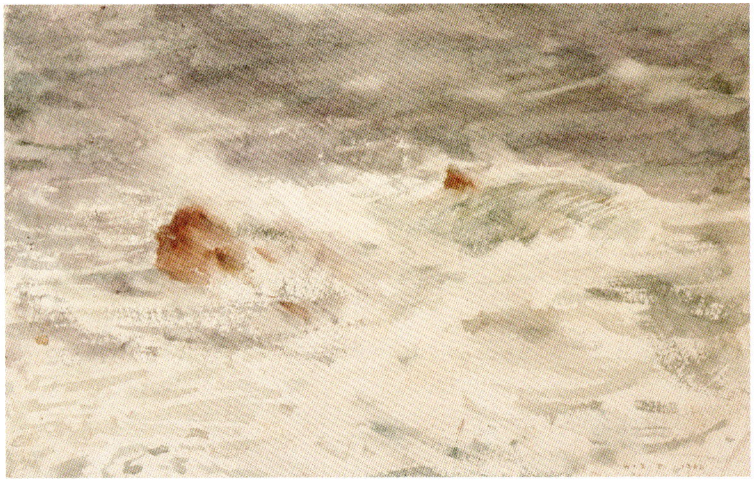

Sea and Rocks, 1903
Watercolour, 13.8 x 21.4cm
Initialled and dated bottom right: H.S.T.1903
Provenance: Purchased from Geoffrey Sainsbury
30 April 1967
RCPS Tuke Collection A220

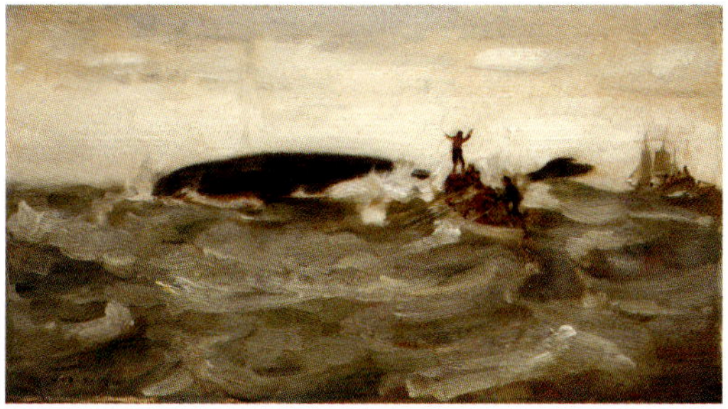

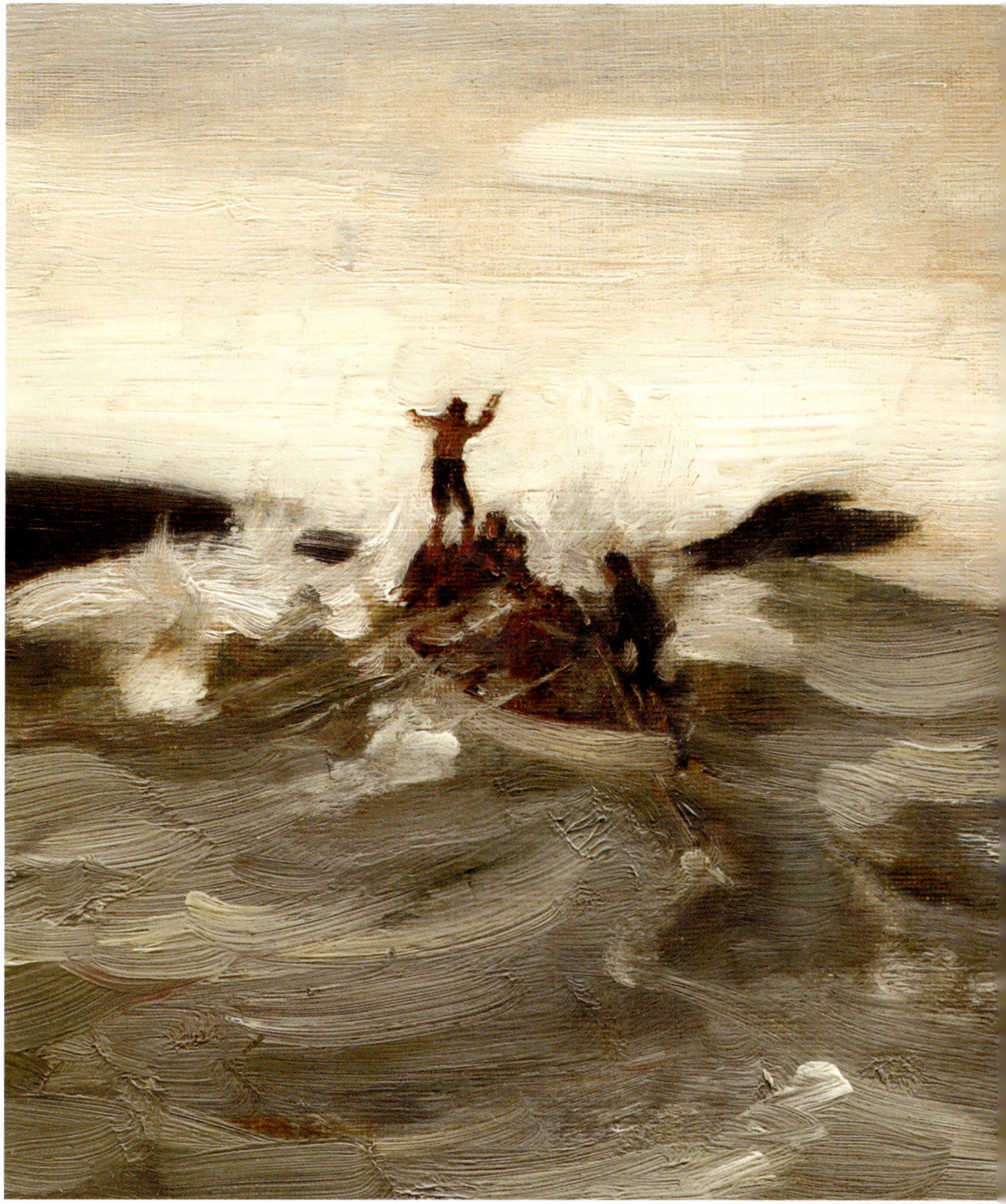

Whale Blowing, 1910

Oil on canvas, 25.5 x 46cm
Initialled and dated bottom left: H.S.T. 1910
Provenance: Purchased from Geoffrey Sainsbury
9 October 1966
RCPS Tuke Collection A86

This unique painting of a whale blowing, with a small boat crewed by sailors who are chasing it for the kill, could have been something Tuke witnessed on one of his many sailing trips. He may have made sketches on the spot and worked it up into a painting in the studio. It certainly has all the vigour of an action he could have seen and wanted to capture on canvas.

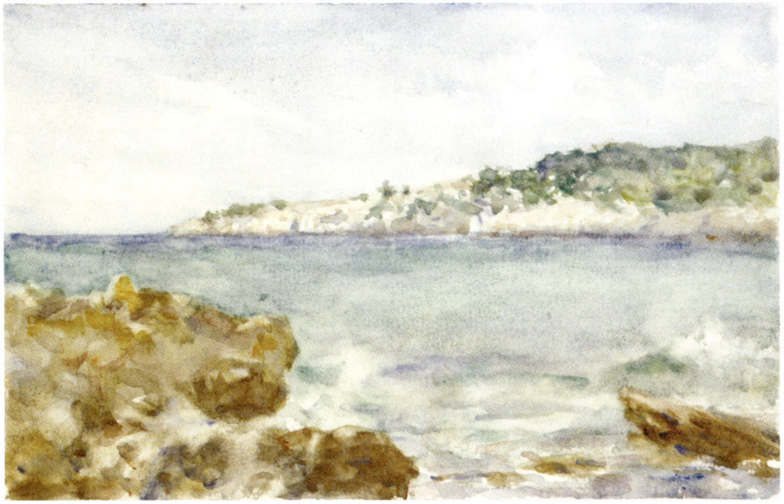

Coastal Scene

Watercolour, 13.7 x 21.5cm
Provenance: Purchased from Geoffrey Sainsbury
8 September1968
RCPS Tuke Collection A194

This watercolour of a sea inlet, with rocks in the foreground and a rocky coast with aqua blue/green sea, seems to be made with a similar palette to the West Indies watercolours of 1923/24. If not the West Indies, it is probably a view from the Mediterranean coast.

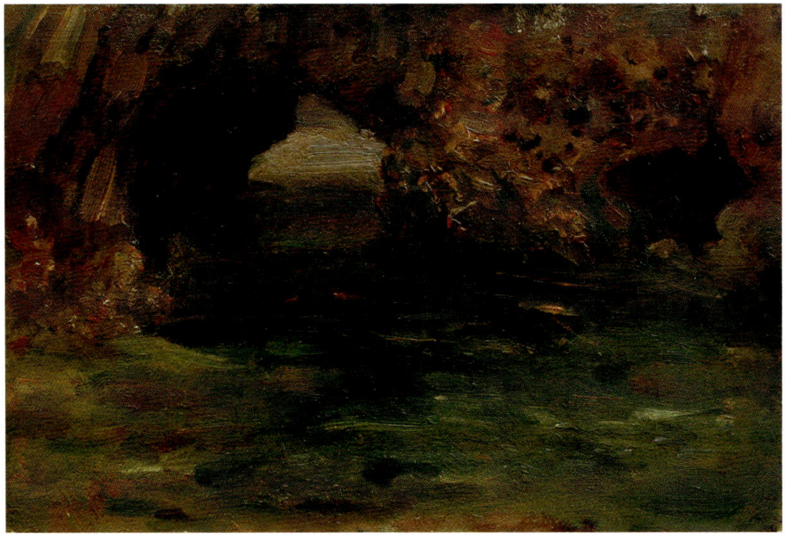

Archway in Rock Pool, c.1925

Oil on panel, 20 x 29cm
Provenance: Purchased from Henry Shemilt
17 January 1964
RCPS Tuke Collection A129

Painted on Newporth beach, Falmouth. Diary entry 8 June 1925 reads, 'Newporth every day making new studies for picture by the natural arch with green water through.' This would probably have been a study for *Green Waterways* (R1179, 1926) which features a rock arch as a backdrop to the bathing figures and is in The Grundy Art Gallery, Blackpool.

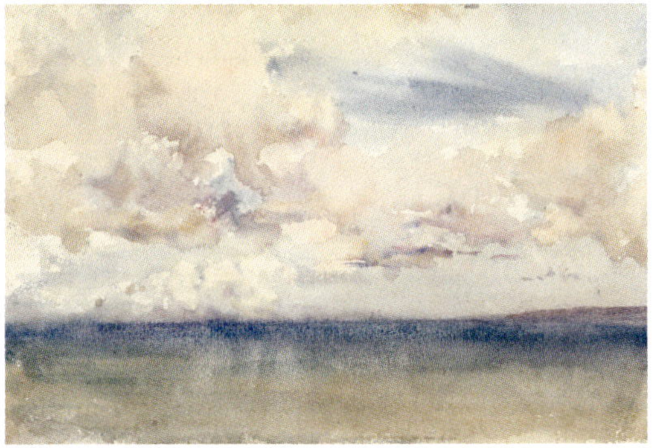

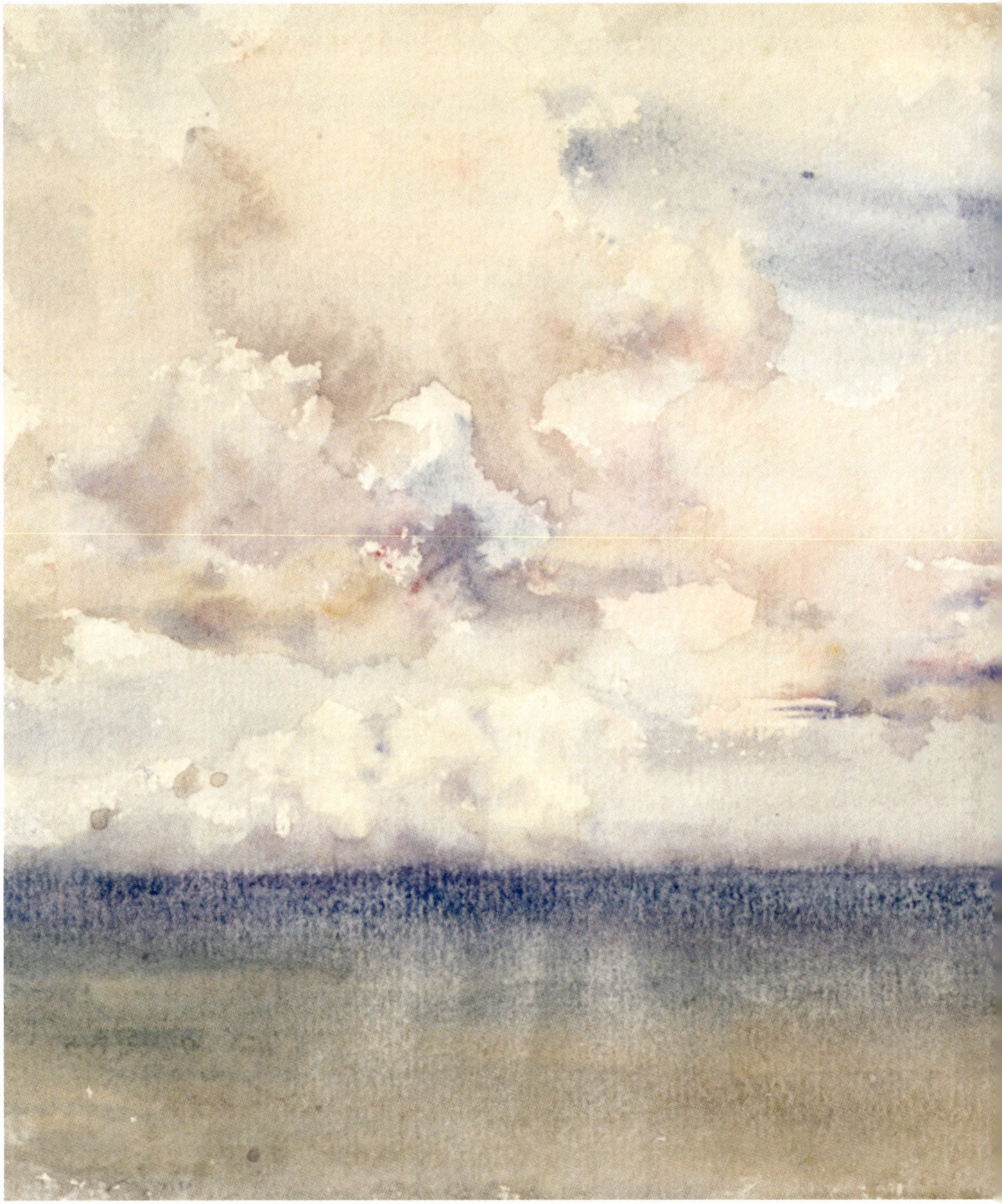

Study of Sea and Sky
Watercolour, 17.7 x 25.5cm
Inscribed on reverse in Tuke's hand:
Study of Sea and Sky
Provenance: Purchased from W. Dyer
20 August 1968
RCPS Tuke Collection A148

North Berwick Sketches 1891

In August 1891 Tuke was invited to visit Sir Walter Dalrymple (1854-1920) at his house in Scotland. Tuke had met the 8th Baronet of North Berwick at the Slade. He was commissioned to undertake portraits of Sir Walter's wife, Lady Hamilton Dalrymple (R166), his mother the Dowager Lady Dalrymple (R167), and his daughter Molly (R168). The latter two paintings were exibited at the Royal Academy in 1892. These portraits were painted at The Lodge in Quality Street, North Berwick, just one of the Dalrymples' properties, also known as the Wall Tower. Tuke also painted portraits of John Parrott's children at the Marine Hotel in North Berwick. John Parrott was from San Mateo, San Fancisco.

During his 3 month stay in North Berwick, Tuke kept a sketchbook and this series of ten sketches is taken from it. They are quite loose in style.

After an initial dislike of North Berwick, Tuke wrote to his sister to complain that 'at first I thought the place an awful fraud, and still think it blasphemy to compare it with Falmouth. But with the finer weather much more beauty has appeared and the long stretches of sand and wide horizons are lovely.' MTS p.96. This is evident in the sketches of the North Berwick landscape and coast. It is clear that the dramatic light of the area also appealed to Tuke's impressionist style. According to his sister Maria, on the first Sunday he was there he attended mass at the Roman Catholic church 'but each Sunday after he seems to have escaped, to walk up the Law, or to call on Laidlay, who was at Tantallon.' MTS p.96.

The golf course featured in the sketches is the West Links at North Berwick. The Dalrymples owned Bass Rock and Tantallon Castle (as they do to this day) and Tuke's friend Laidlay lived at Seacliff just along the coast from North Berwick, which allowed Tuke access to the views of Bass Rock and Tantallon Castle. In 1894 Sir Walter gave land to the town to build another golf course called the Rhodes Course, which was extended in 1907 and became the North Berwick East Links. He also helped to secure the ruins of Tantallon Castle and prevent further deterioration.

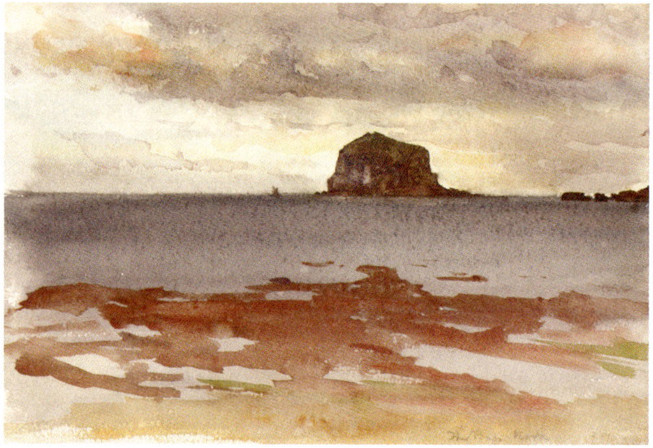

The Bass Rock, Scotland, 1891
Watercolour, 17.7 x 25.3cm
Inscribed bottom right: The Bass Rock
Provenance: Purchased from Geoffrey Sainsbury 30 April 1967
RCPS Tuke Collection A244

North Berwick, 1891

Watercolour, 17.7 x 25.5cm
Provenance: Purchased from Geoffrey Sainsbury
30 April 1967
RCPS Tuke Collection A250

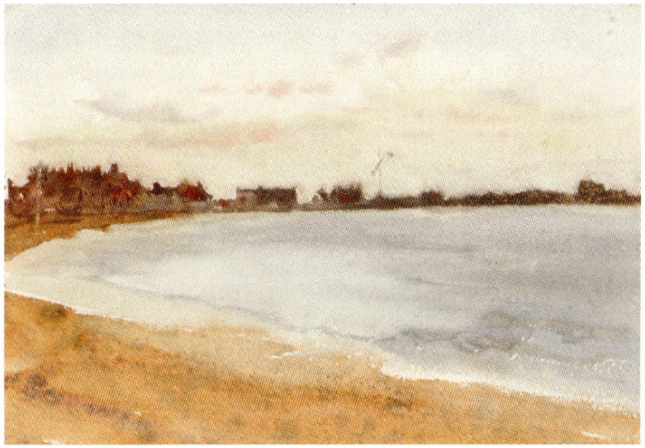

North Berwick Law, 1891

Watercolour, 17.8 x 25.5cm
Inscribed bottom left: N.Berwick Law
Provenance: Purchased from Geoffrey Sainsbury
30 April 1967
RCPS Tuke Collection A245

North Berwick Law is a 187m (613ft) lump of volcanic rock located just to the south of the town of North Berwick. It is visible for many miles in every direction.

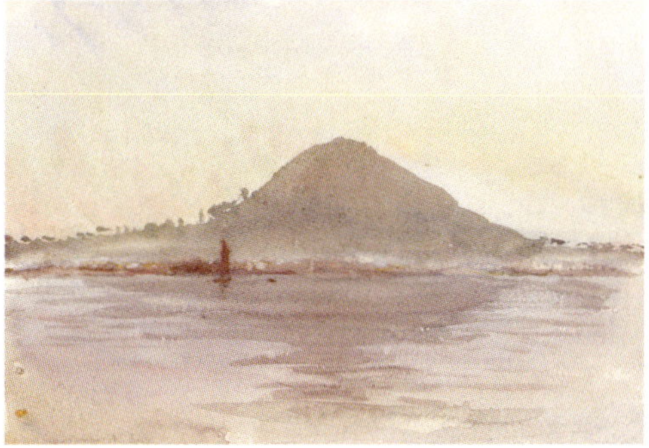

North Berwick Seascape, 1891

Watercolour, 17.5 x 25.5cm
Provenance: Purchased from Geoffrey Sainsbury
30 April 1967
RCPS Tuke Collection A242

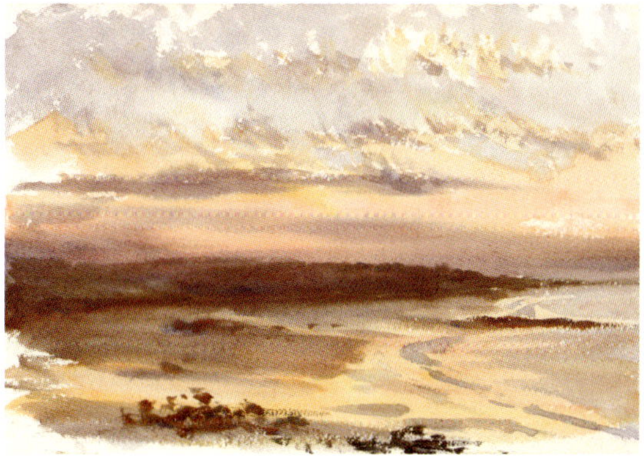

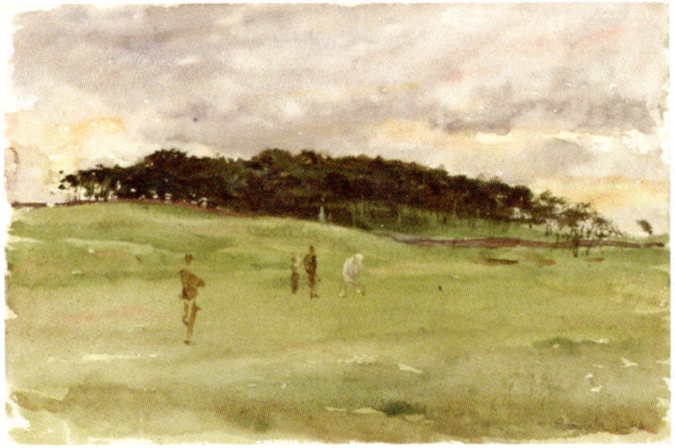

North Berwick Links, 1891
Watercolour, 17.6 x 25.5cm
Inscribed bottom right: N. Berwick Links
Provenance: Purchased from Geoffrey Sainsbury
30 April 1967
RCPS Tuke Collection A248

This is a picture of the 4th hole on the West Links golf course.

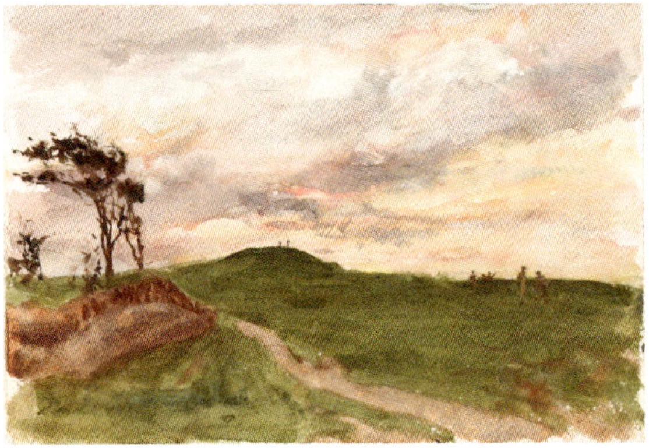

North Berwick Golf Links, 1891
Watercolour, 17.5 x 25.5cm
Provenance: Purchased from Geoffrey Sainsbury
30 April 1967
RCPS Tuke Collection A243

A view of the West Links at North Berwick.

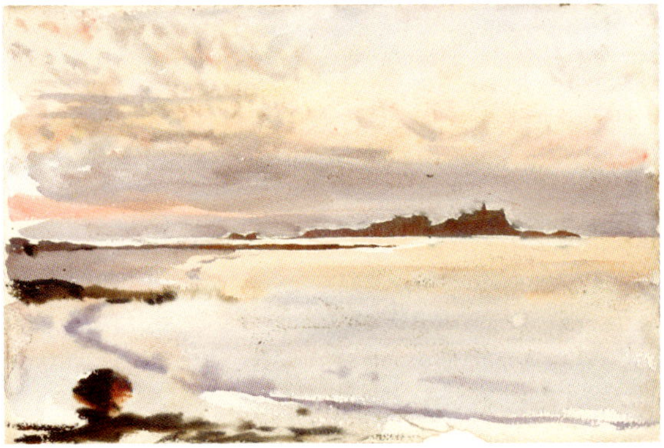

Fidra Island (previoulsy known as Futura), 1891
Watercolour, 17.8 x 25.5cm
Provenance: Purchased from Geoffrey Sainsbury
30 April 1967
RCPS Tuke Collection A251

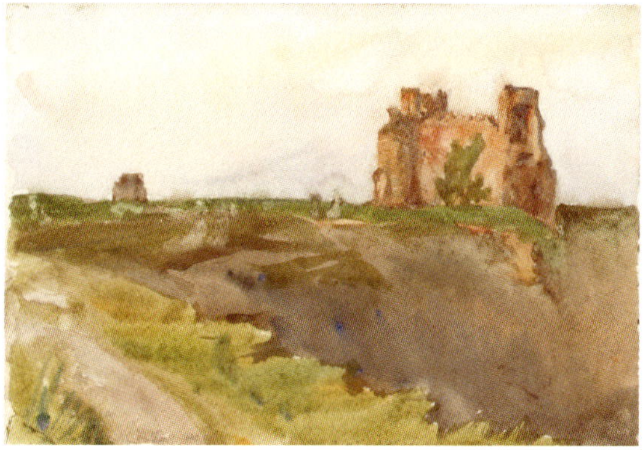

Tantallon, 1891

Watercolour, 17.8 x 25.7cm
Initialled and inscribed bottom left: Tantallon HST
Provenance: Purchased from Geoffrey Sainsbury
30 April 1967
RCPS Tuke Collection A247

Tantallon Castle stands on the cliff edge and looks out towards the Bass Rock. It was built c.1350 by William the 1st Earl of Douglas. It was besieged and destroyed in the mid –17th century and was left to decay until the end of the 19th century, when Sir Walter Dalrymple carried out work to stabilise the ruins.

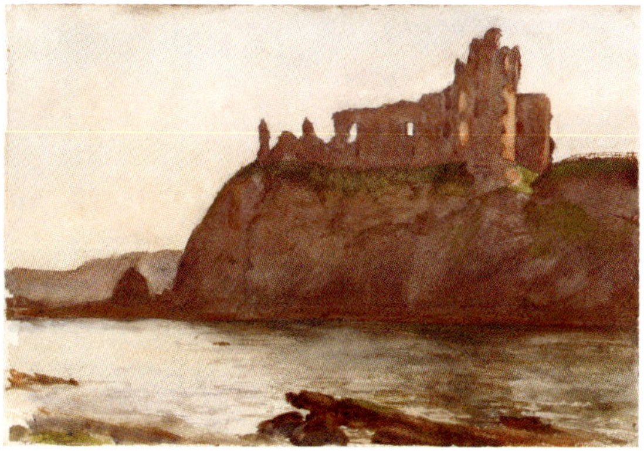

Tantallon Castle, 1891

Watercolour, 17.9 x 25.5cm
Provenance: Purchased from Geoffrey Sainsbury
30 April 1967
RCPS Tuke Collection A246

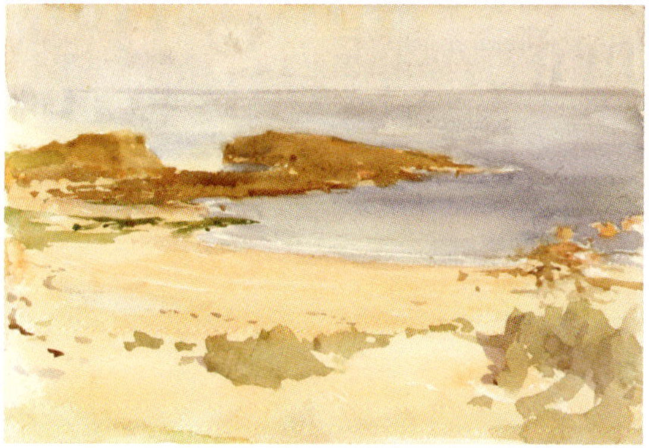

Beach Scene, North Berwick, 1891

Watercolour, 17.7 x 25.5cm
Provenance: Purchased from Geoffrey Sainsbury
30 April 1967
RCPS Tuke Collection A249

This is a picture of The Leithies, East Bay at North Berwick.

Other British Landscapes

Tuke loved to travel, whether it was by sailing ship or by train and car, or push-bike. He used the train to get from Cornwall to the family home, Lyndon Lodge in Hanwell, near Hammersmith, London. His mother and father and sister had moved there after the death of his brother William in 1883. They had previously lived in Charlotte Street, Bedford Square at No 5 from 1874-1878, and No 4 from 1878-1883. Tuke was to use Lyndon Lodge as his second home, and the Tuke Collection has several oils of the garden there. Tuke made many friends in Hanwell including the Bakers, the Charlton Bastians, Dr Henry Rayner, and the Bishops. He also frequently painted the viaduct at Hanwell and the trains going across it. From Hanwell, Tuke could take his bicycle and the train to many different places, as reflected in the watercolour sketches in the Collection. Eton and Windsor were places he frequently visited from 1897 to 1902, having friends such as Dawson and Vaughan to visit there. Having a home in London allowed Tuke to undertake many of his society portraits, and initially he had the use of studios lent to him by friends such as Mrs Donald Smith, a fellow portrait painter, until he rented his own in Clareville Grove, South Kensington.

The second family home was at Hill House, Saffron Walden where Tuke's aunt, Elizabeth Tuke Gibson (1821-1890), lived with her husband George Stacey Gibson (1818 -1883). The Gibsons were a long-established Quaker family in Saffron Walden. George Stacey Gibson was elected mayor twice in 1875 and in 1876, and he made many generous gifts of land and properties to the town. Elizabeth's brothers James (1819-1926) and William Murray (1822-1903) also lived in Saffron Walden. William was a partner in his brother-in-law George Stacey Gibson's banking firm, Gibson, Tuke and Gibson, which became Barclay's Bank in 1896 and William became a local director. These relatives were lifelong friends to Tuke and his sister Maria. Most Christmas holidays were spent at Saffron Walden. The Tuke Collection has an interesting watercolour of the Dutch Garden which was part of the Bridge End Gardens at Saffron Walden. Tuke also used to visit Cambridge, in particular the Fitzwilliam Museum, and further afield to Ely and its cathedral.

Another uncle, James Hack Tuke (1819-1896), who lived in Hitchin, was also frequently visited by Tuke, as was his grandmother Stickney in Hull and his cousins the Rheams at Freshfield and Southport. Harry was particularly close to his eldest cousin Henry Meynell Rheam (1859-1920), who was also a painter and lived in Newlyn and Penzance in Cornwall for a time.

The Collection includes sketches from other visits to Yorkshire, probably made when visiting relatives there.

In the summer of 1908 Tuke visited Shillinglee in Sussex with his friend Charlie Mitchell. They stayed in a house rented by the Indian cricketer Prince Ranjitsinjhi, and while there Tuke painted his portrait. The Tuke Collection has a watercolour sketch Tuke undertook of the park at Shillinglee. It is also where he painted the portrait of A.J. MacLaren (A120). Chithurst in West Sussex was where the Marshall family lived, and Tuke was great friends with Kenneth Marshall who married Edith Stanton and became a major in the army. His son Leo Marshall modelled for Tuke. The two works *On the Rother* (A44) and *The Abbey House Chithurst* (A45) were probably done while visiting the Marshall family.

Hanwell Viaduct, GWR

Watercolour, 17 x 22.3cm
Provenance: Purchased from Geoffrey Sainsbury
13 July 1963
RCPS Tuke Collection A28

Tuke's family moved to Lyndon Lodge, Hanwell, Middlesex in 1883. Lyndon Lodge remained in the family until 1923. Tuke used it as his London base for all those years, and he stayed there for 3 months in 1915 from 1 March, when he had a serious fever and nearly died and was nursed back to health by his sister Maria. This is one of two watercolours of a steam train going over Hanwell viaduct.

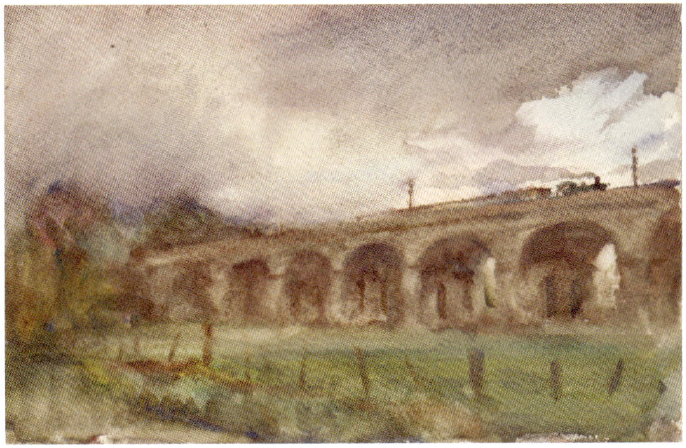

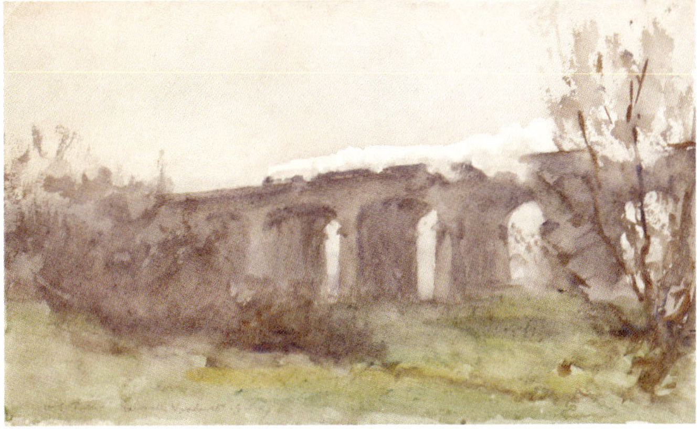

Hanwell Viaduct, GWR

Watercolour, 13.6 x 21.5cm
Signed bottom left: H.S.Tuke
Provenance: Purchased from Geoffrey Sainsbury
8 September 1968
RCPS Tuke Collection A196

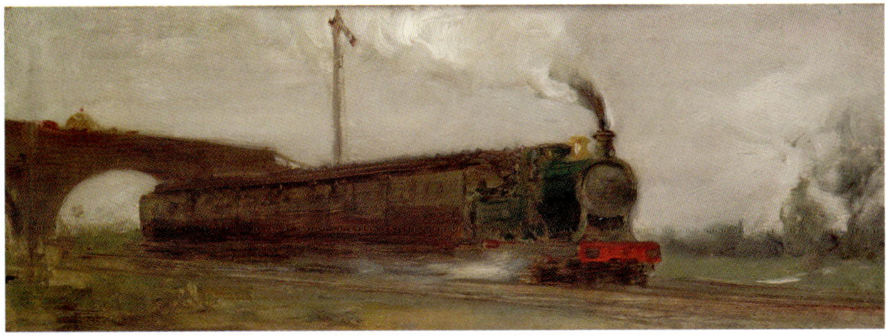

Railway Train

Oil on board, 14.2 x 38.1cm
Provenance: Purchased from Henry Shemilt
24 December 1963
RCPS Tuke Collection A38

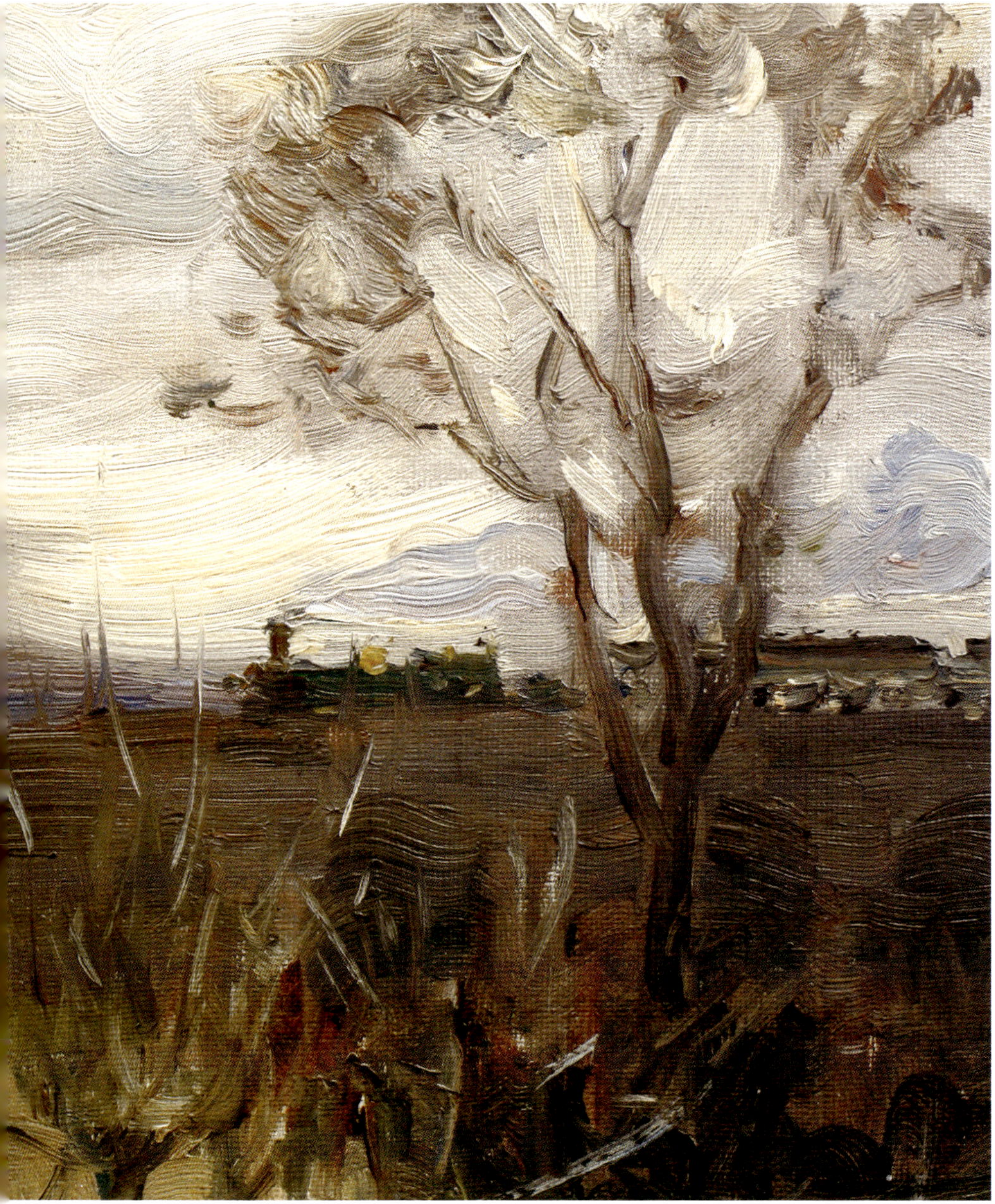

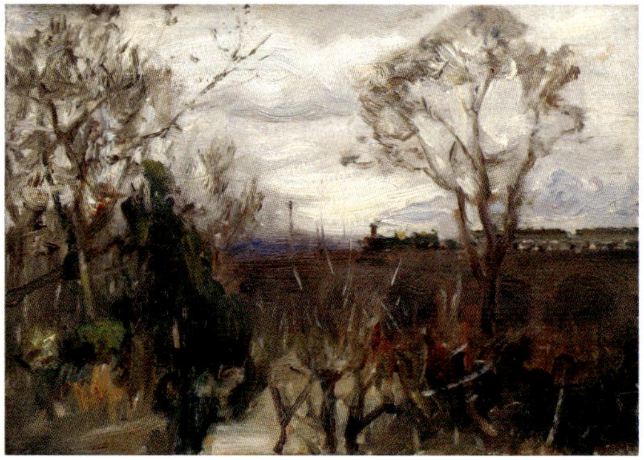

Trees and Hanwell Viaduct
Oil on canvas board, 24 x 33cm
Inscribed on reverse: H.S.Tuke R.A. 1858-1929
Provenance: Purchased from Henry Shemilt
24 December 1963
RCPS Tuke Collection A63

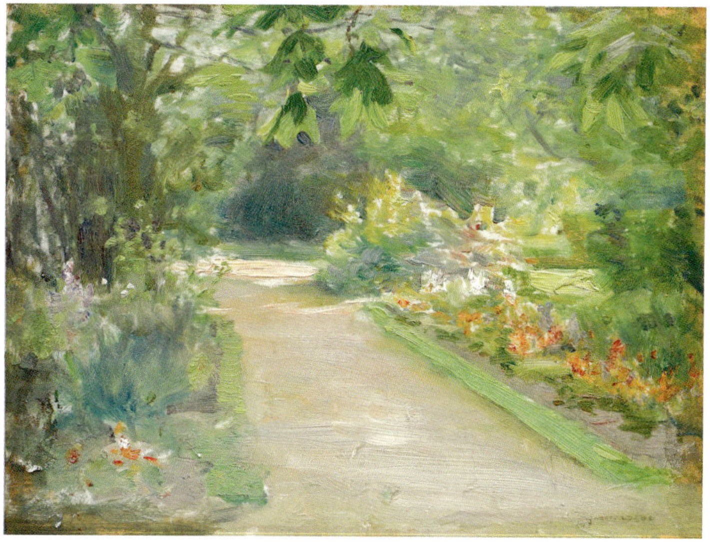

Lyndon Lodge

Oil on board, 26.6. x 35cm
Inscribed in pencil bottom right: Lyndon Lodge
Provenance: Purchased from Henry Shemilt
17 January 1964
RCPS Tuke Collection A64

Lyndon Lodge was Tuke's family home in Hanwell, London. He used to spend a good deal of each year there, often using it as a base for undertaking portrait commissions, attending the Royal Academy openings, visiting other galleries, going to the theatre, watching cricket at Lord's, and catching up with his society friends and family.

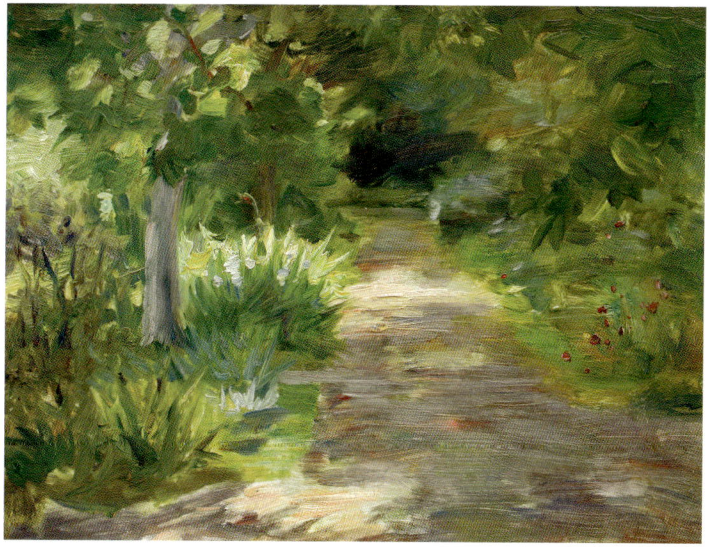

Lyndon Lodge Garden

Oil on board, 26.8 x 35.2cm
Provenance: Purchased from Henry Shemilt
17 January 1964
RCPS Tuke Collection A65

In March 1915 Tuke happened to be staying at Lyndon Lodge when he came down with a 'fearful attack of erysipelis'. His sister Maria recalls she 'stayed at Lyndon Lodge for three months, with two nurses... when in May he crept out of bed for the first time he found he was quite unable to walk. However he soon progressed when he was allowed to lie out in the garden.' MTS p.154-155.

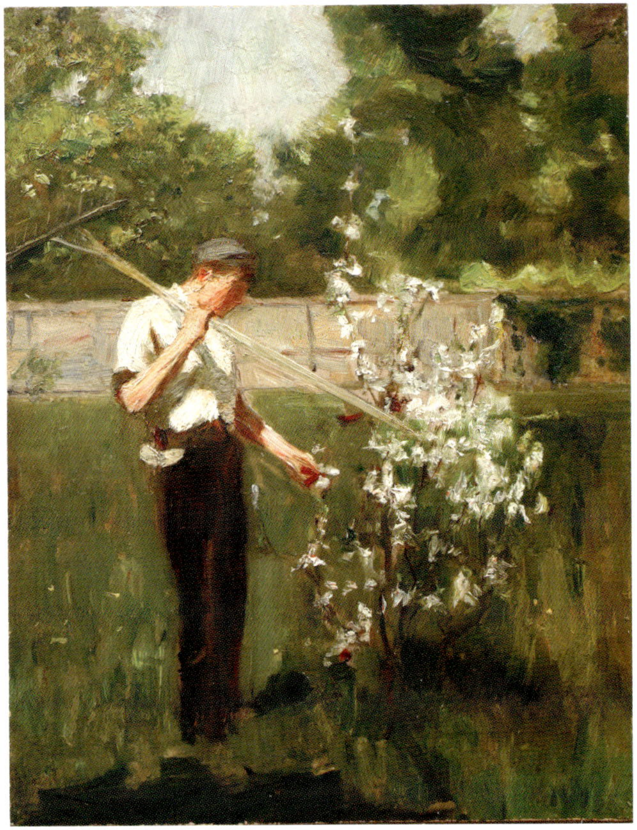

Boy with Grass Rake

Oil on canvas, 37 x 28cm
Provenance: Purchased from Henry Shemilt
24 December 1963
RCPS Tuke Collection A107

According to Brian Price this is probably a portrait of Henry Allen (b.1886) in the garden at Lyndon Lodge in Hanwell. There are several diary entries for May 1903 where Tuke describes painting in the garden, and on 2nd May, 'Did a study from Allen. He got faint from standing.' Henry Allen was the son of a local vicar and was 17 when Tuke first met him. They used to go cycling together and play cricket and go to Lord's. Allen came to Swanpool one summer for six weeks before he returned to London, and became a clerk for London City Council.

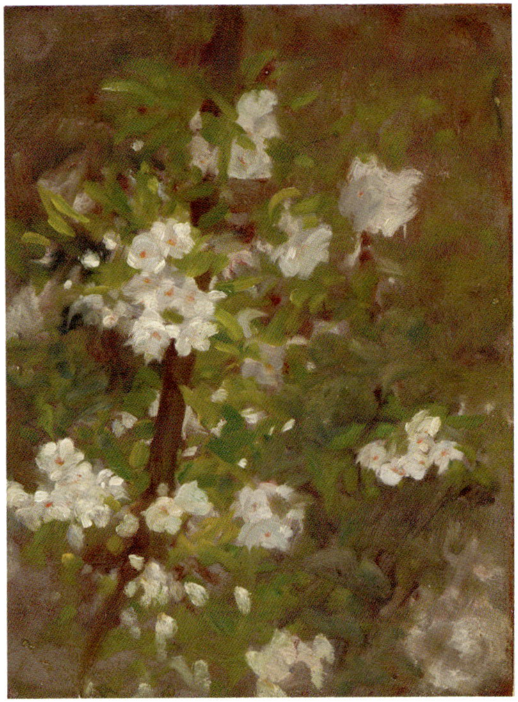

White Blossom

Oil on wood panel, 33 x 24cm
Provenance: Purchased from Henry Shemilt
24 December 1963
RCPS Tuke Collection A34

A study of tree blossom probably painted in the garden at Lyndon Lodge, Hanwell.

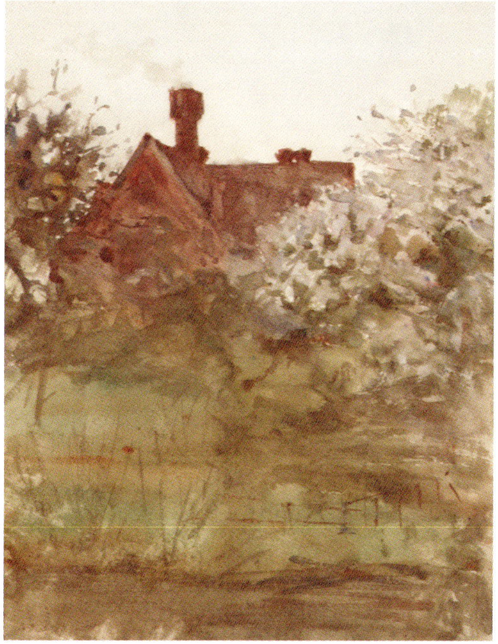

The Abbey House, Chithurst

Watercolour, 23.4 x 17.7cm
Signed on old mount: The Abbey House, Chithurst by H.S.Tuke
Provenance: Purchased from Miss Barbara Marshall
21 November 1964
RCPS Tuke Collection A45

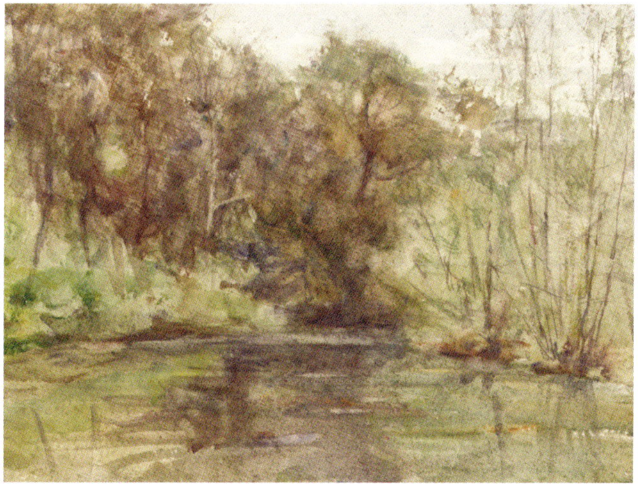

On the Rother, 1893

Watercolour, 17 x 22cm
Initialled, dated and inscribed on the reverse: Up the river Rother, near Chithurst, by H.S.T 21 April 1893
Provenance: Purchased from Miss Barbara Marshall
21 November 1964
RCPS Tuke Collection A44

This watercolour was probably painted while Tuke was on one of his many visits to Chithurst, West Sussex, the home of the Marshall family. He recalls in his diary of 1899 on 16 June cycling to Chithurst from Hanwell, 'Off at 6 for Chithurst. Good passage over Hindhead and arrived at C[hithurst] by midday. Out in the punt with Mrs D.[olly Marshall].' Going punting on the river Rother was probably the inspiration for this watercolour.

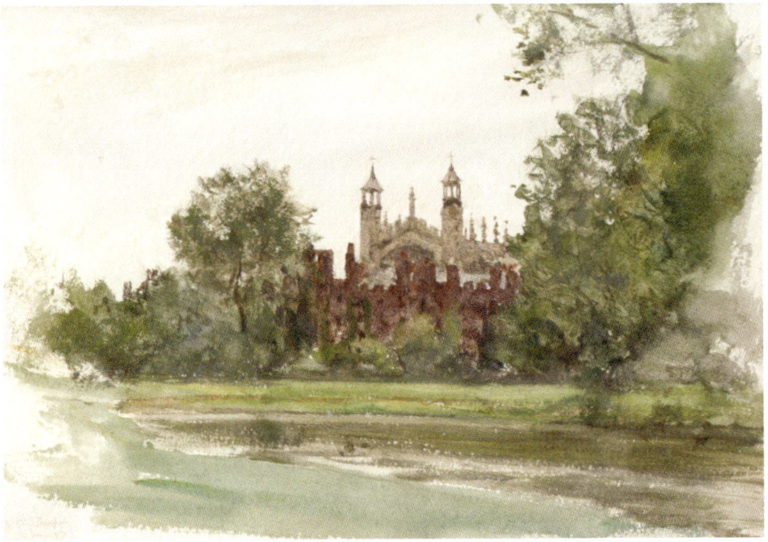

Eton Chapel, 1897

Watercolour, 17.9 x 25.9cm
Dated and inscribed bottom left: Eton Chapel 2 June 97
Provenance: Purchased from Geoffrey Sainsbury
29 May 1968
RCPS Tuke Collection A200

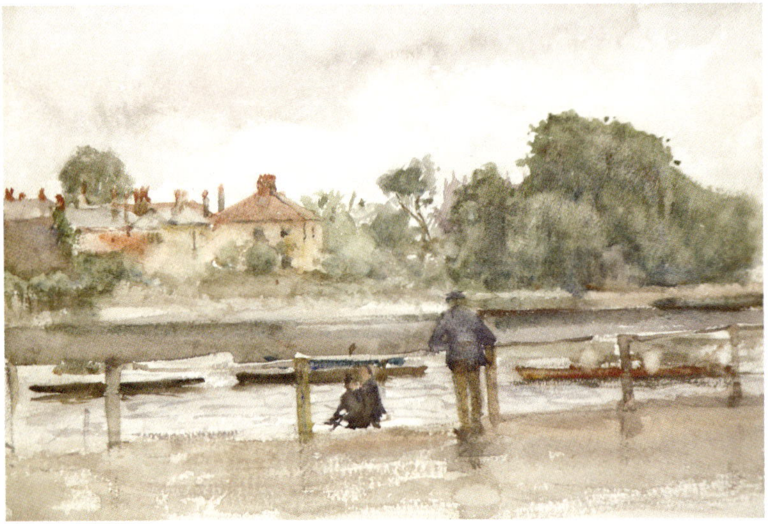

Thames at Windsor

Watercolour, 17.9 x 26cm
Provenance: Purchased from Geoffrey Sainsbury
19 December 1963
RCPS Tuke Collection A57

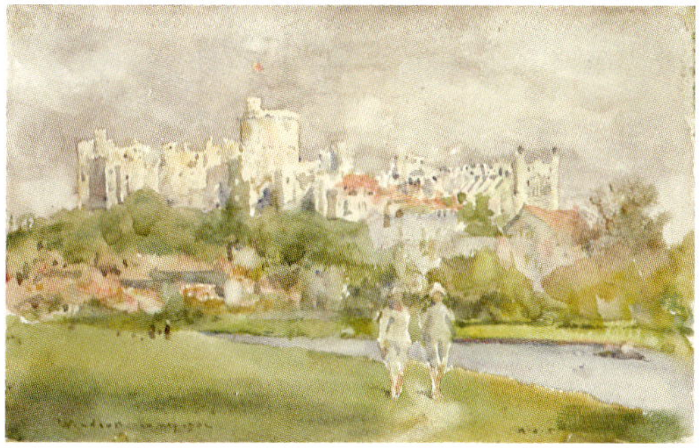

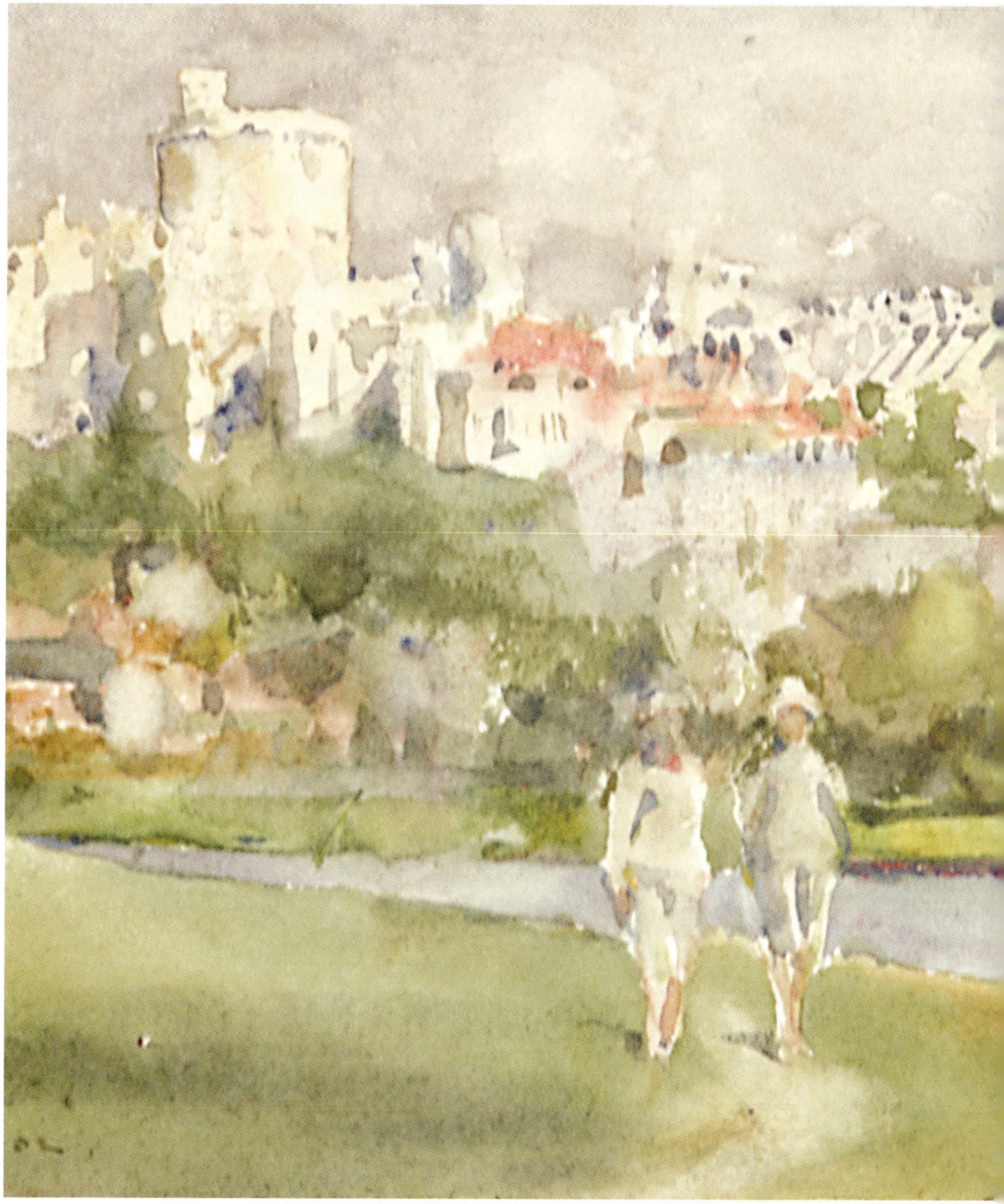

Windsor, 1902

Watercolour, 13.9 x 21.3cm
Signed bottom right: H.S.T.
Inscribed bottom left: Windsor 10 May 1902
Provenance: Purchased from Brian Wells
14 May 1967
RCPS Tuke Collection A53

This picture of Windsor shows the castle in the background and the river in the foreground. On May 10 1902 Tuke wrote in his diary, 'Afternoon at Windsor and Eton, cricket and sketch of the castle.' The sketch is unusual in that it shows two women walking or posing by the river in tunics which stop at the knee, wearing sun hats, which was not in keeping with the fashions of 1902, unless it was some kind of swimwear.

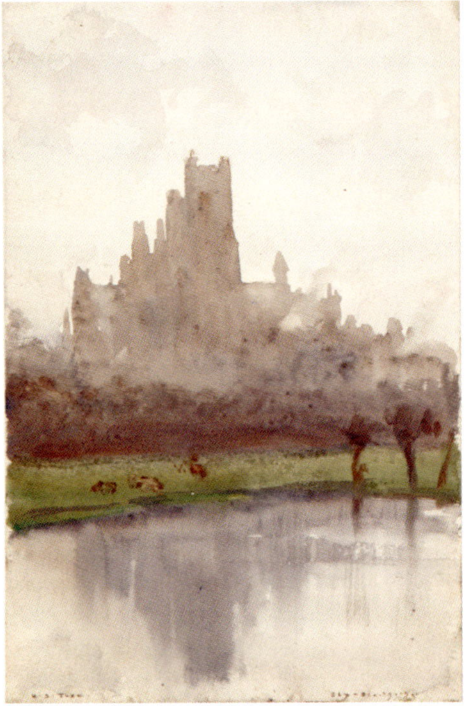

Ely Cathedral, 1903

Watercolour, 21.4 x 13.6cm
Signed, inscribed and dated bottom right: H.S.Tuke Ely Dec.29 1903
Provenance: Purchased from Geoffrey Sainsbury
8 September 1968
RCPS Tuke Collection A182

Tuke mentions Ely Cathedral in his diary of 30 December 1903, while he was staying with his family at Saffron Walden: 'A lovely bright frosty day. Biked to Ely. Revisited the Fitzwilliam Museum at Cambridge and the Cathedral at Ely. Train back to Cambridge and bike from there.'

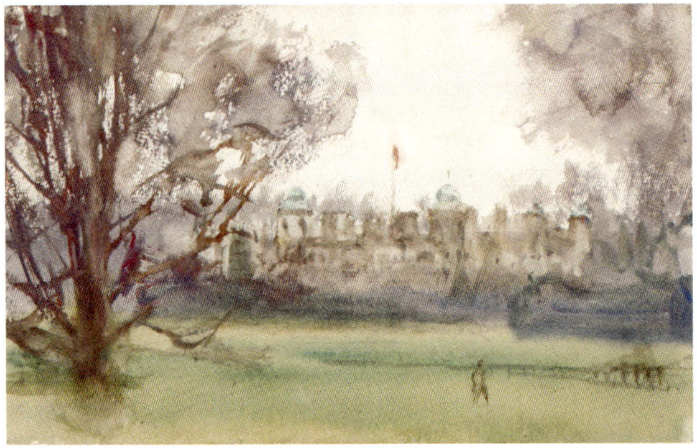

Castle

Watercolour, 13.6 x 21.4cm
Provenance: Purchased from Geoffrey Sainsbury
8 September 1968
RCPS Tuke Collection A198

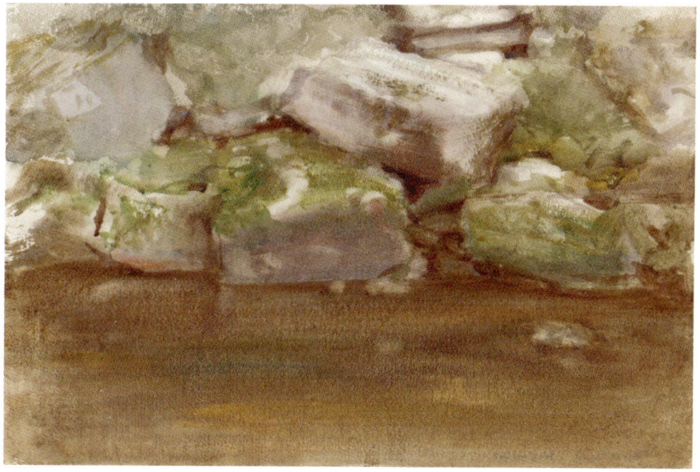

Salmon Pool, Dartmeet

Watercolour, 18.2 x 26.8cm
Provenance: Purchased from Geoffrey Sainsbury
19 December 1963
RCPS Tuke Collection A241

Gilling Castle, Yorks, 1908

Watercolour, 13.8 x 21.4cm
Initialled and dated on reverse: H.S.T. 1908
Inscribed on reverse: Gilling Castle, Yorks
(W.S. Hunter's place)
Provenance: Purchased from Geoffrey Sainsbury
8 September 1963
RCPS Tuke Collection A197

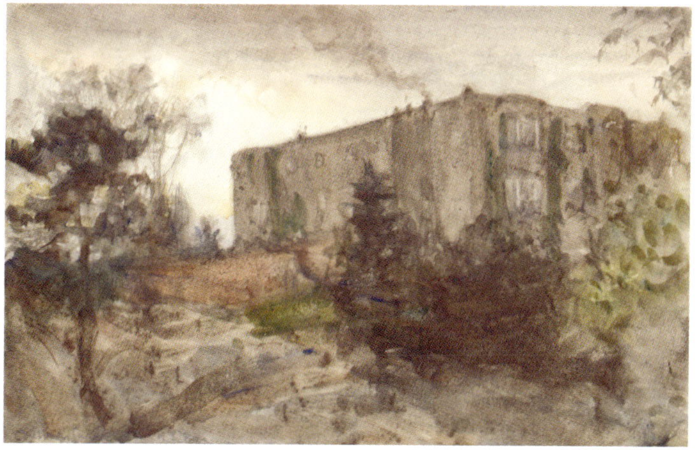

This was probably painted in May 1908 when Tuke visited the castle with the cricketer Prince Ranjitsinjhi, the Jam Sahib of Nawanager, after Tuke had been watching him play at Old Trafford. 'After this Harry went with the Jam Sahib to the Hunters at Gilling Castle for a week-end, where he "dined in the beautiful panelled Elizabethan dining room."' MTS p.144
Mr William Slingsby Hunter bought Gilling Castle in 1904. He made considerable modifications, making it a more comfortable place in which to live. Tuke may have known Hunter through family connections in Yorkshire.

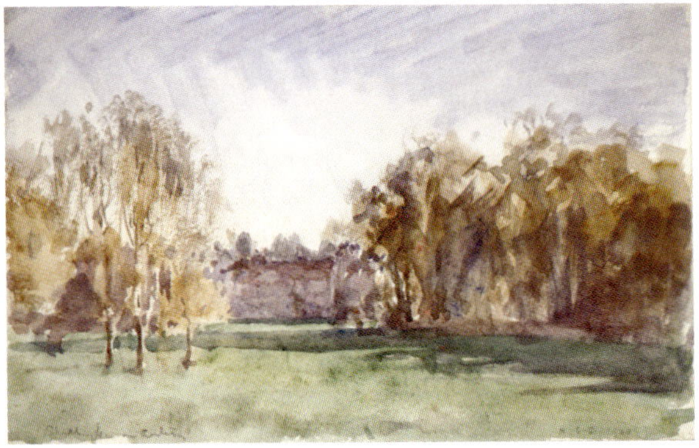

Shillinglee in Autumn, 1908

Watercolour, 13.7 x 21.5cm
Initialled and dated bottom right: H.S.T. 1908
Inscribed bottom left: Shillinglee in Autumn
Provenance: Purchased from Geoffrey Sainsbury
29 May 1968
RCPS Tuke Collection A139

Tuke was at Shillinglee Park for several months in the summer – autumn of 1908 as he was painting the portrait of the cricketer Prince Ranjitsinjhi, who was renting Shillinglee from the Earl of Winterton. Archibald MacLaren, who was a cricketer and great friend of Tuke, was acting as the Prince's private secretary and probably introduced Tuke to Ranji who bought several paintings including *Return from fishing* (R566) and *The Mid-day Rest* (aka) *Sailor's Yarning* (R544). According to Maria, he also invited Tuke out to India but nothing came of it.

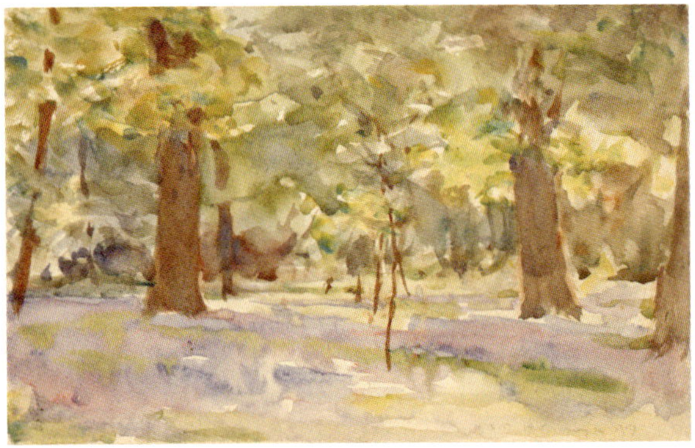

Woodland Scene, 1917

Watercolour, 13.9 x 21.4cm
Initialled and dated bottom right: H.S.T. May 24 1917
Provenance: Purchased from Geoffrey Sainsbury
8 September 1968
RCPS Tuke Collection A184

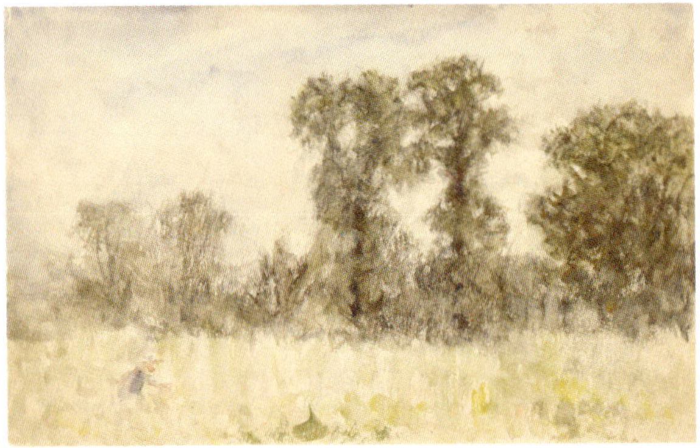

Landscape with Trees

Watercolour, 14.2 x 22.2cm
Provenance: Purchased from Geoffrey Sainsbury
8 September 1968
RCPS Tuke Collection A183

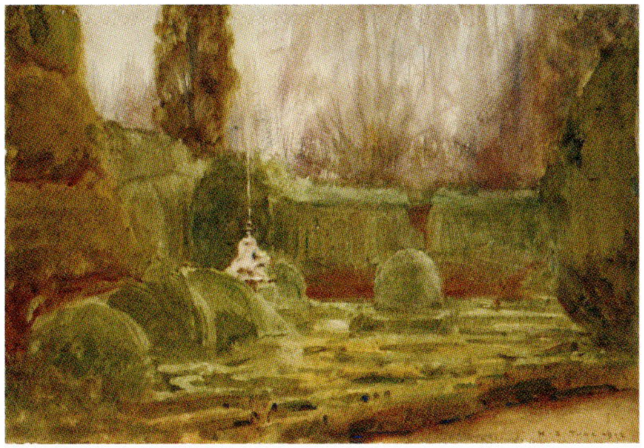

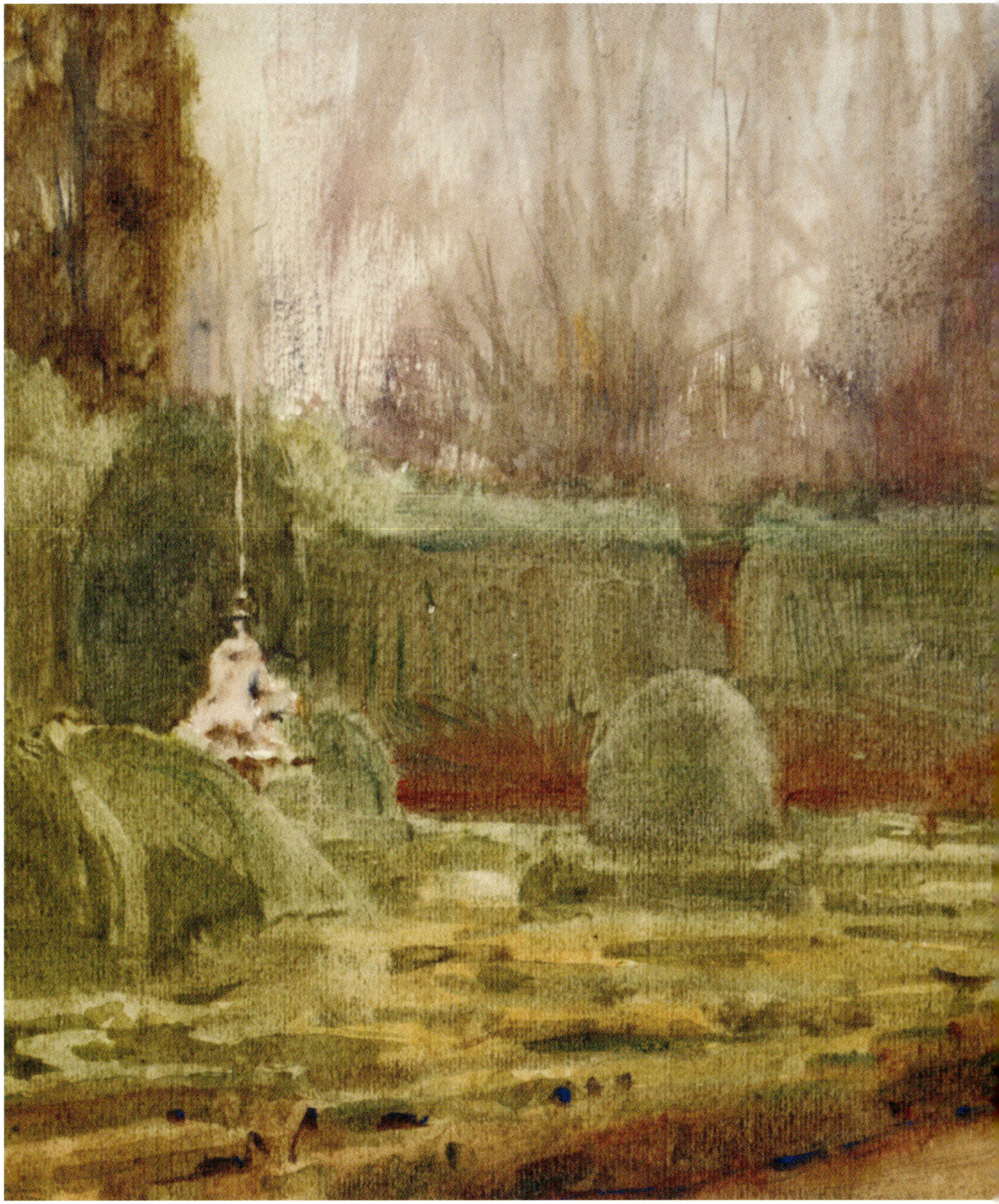

The Dutch Garden - Bridge End, Saffron Walden,1912

Watercolour, 18.4 x 26.2cm
Signed and dated bottom right: H.S.Tuke 1912
Provenance: Purchased from Geoffrey Sainsbury
29 May 1968
RCPS Tuke Collection A171

The Dutch garden was built as part of Bridge End gardens by the Gibsons at Saffron Walden c.1840. Attached to the garden was a gallery holding Francis Gibson's art collection, which passed by descent to his grandson, the painter Lewis George Fry (1860 – 1933). Tuke spent most Christmas holidays with the Gibsons, his aunt and uncle, and in his diaries he mentions visiting the Dutch garden. 2nd January 1901, 'Mag and I to Lewis Fry's beautiful Dutch garden. Returned after lunch and did a little sketch.' He again mentions visiting the Dutch garden on 7 Jan. 1905. Gertrude Jekyll, the garden designer, also visited the garden in 1912 and made a plan of it - such was its significance.

Foreign Travels

Tuke travelled abroad extensively throughout his life. His main purpose was to paint, and he filled many sketchbooks on these journeys, predominantly in watercolour. It also allowed him to indulge in one of his favourite activities, sailing. The Tuke Collection has several works that Tuke undertook on a sailing trip to Nordenham in 1908 on board the *'Grace Harwar'*. His longest and most adventurous voyage was to the West Indies from late 1923 to March 1924. The Tuke Collection has a substantial number of works from this visit, mainly in watercolour.

Tuke also travelled to Europe on many occasions to paint and to visit friends. His love affair with Italy lasted all his life, from his early days studying there as an art student. His longest visit to the South of France, Italy and Corfu was in 1892 when he spent five months in the Mediterranean, firstly staying with the Dowager Lady Dalrymple[1] at Monte Carlo, then in Venice with Horatio Brown[2], and finally travelling from Italy to the Greek island of Corfu. The Tuke Collection has a sensitive study of a lemon tree in a Corfu garden from this visit. On his next trip to France in May 1899, Tuke was accompanied by the artist Fred Millard. He then went on alone to Venice by train, where he painted a portrait of his friend Horatio Brown. Tuke thought Venice was 'the loveliest place in the world, but so difficult to attack. To do much it would be essential to settle down for six months or so and feel there was plenty of time.' May 31 1899 letter to Maria, M.T.S. p.125.

He was back in France and Italy again in February 1904, visiting Paris and Marseilles, before arriving in Monte Carlo where he again stayed with the Lady Dowager Dalrymple. He then went to Livorno and on to Genoa in northern Italy, where he stayed on Captain Dowman's ship the *'Lynton'*. He also stayed in Alassio at his friend Sir Walter Dalrymple's Villa de la Pergola for several weeks. The Tuke Collection contains three outstanding watercolours from this trip, one of Cervo, another of a Riviera village, and one of Livorno. In June 1904 Dowdeswell's Gallery in New Bond Street hosted *'Along the Italian Riviera'*, a one-man show of 55 watercolours undertaken earlier in the year.

Tuke returned to Italy in 1912 when he revisited some of his old haunts; he found them much altered in eight years, and thought many had been ruined. He stayed once again with Sir Walter Dalrymple at Alassio.

After the epic voyage to the West Indies from late 1923 to spring 1924, Tuke made annual pilgrimages to his favourite painting spots on the French and Italian Riviera, such as Rapallo, St. Tropez and Genoa. In February 1925 he went as far as North Africa where he visited the ruins at Carthage.

These trips were made possible for Tuke by having many friends to accompany him, and an equal number such as Captain Dowman and the Dalrymples to play host when he arrived. Tuke loved to travel by sea and it is easy to understand the pleasure and excitement gained from these voyages. His excursions to the Mediterranean were also an obvious attraction artistically because of the quality of light and the variety of shipping.

His last foreign excursion was in February 1927 when he again visited his old haunts such as St. Tropez, still finding the colours and atmosphere an inspiration, producing stunning watercolours such as St. Tropez (A73).

1. Sophia Dalrymple née Pattle (1829-1911), mother of Sir Walter Dalrymple, whom Tuke had met while a student at the Slade.

2. Horatio Forbes Brown (1854-1926) was employed by the British Government to edit Venetian State Papers and their relation to British history. Author of Sketches and Studies in Italy and Greece, 1914 edited by John Addington Symonds.

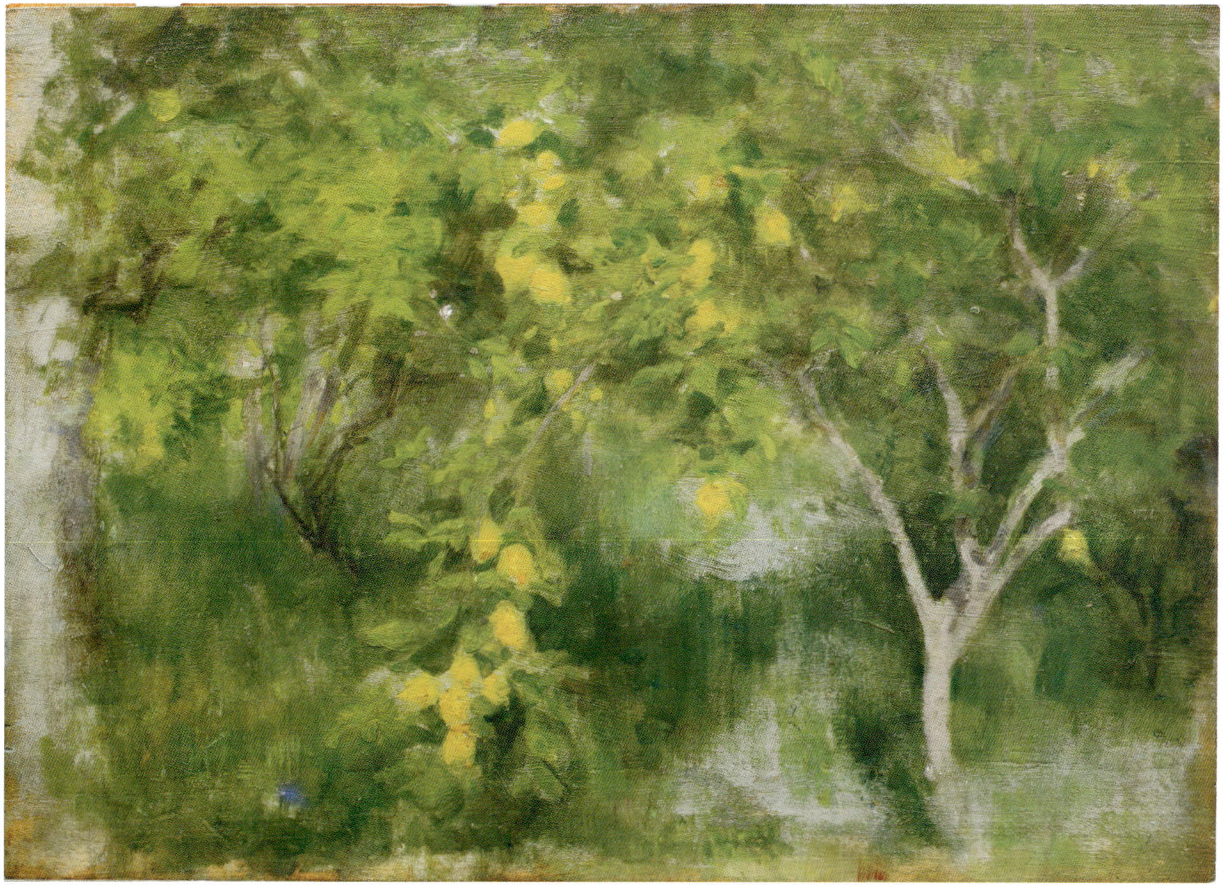

Study for *A Corfu Garden*, c.1892
Oil on board, 26 x 35.6cm
Provenance: Purchased from Henry Shemilt 24 December 1963.
RCPS Tuke Collection A17

A study sketch for R187 *A Corfu Garden* which was painted in Theotocky's garden at Benitza. Tuke went to Corfu from Italy in 1892, a journey which took twelve hours. He met Arthur Tanner and Tom Mostyn (1864-1930) who were there for the Easter festivities, and stayed with them in their place at Benitza. 'We are very well off as the country is charming and the sea ten yards off. We have the run of a lemon garden to paint in, lemons and olives are the principal trees, lots of wild flowers but nothing to equal primrose.' MTS p.102. *A Corfu Garden*, a.k.a. *The Lemon Tree* (R187) is in Bradford City Art Galleries and Museums collection.

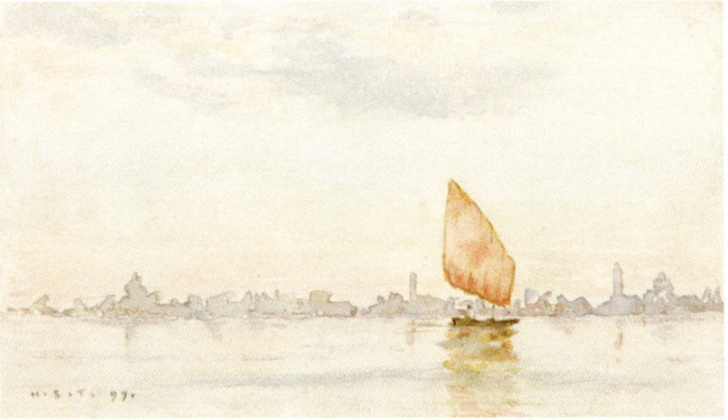

Greetings Card of Venice, 1899

Watercolour, 9 x 15.6cm
Initialled and dated bottom left: H.S.T. 99
Provenance: Given by Commander D. Clift
16 September 1964
RCPS Tuke Collection A46

This watercolour sketch of Venice was sent as a card to Tuke's Aunt Jeanette Clift in 1899. It is a memento of his trip of May that year when he painted a portrait of his friend Horatio Brown. He was out bathing in the Lido or dining with friends the rest of the time and sketching the various boats.

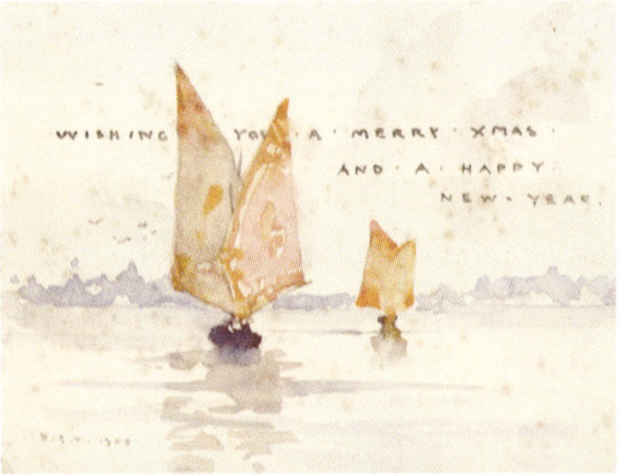

Christmas and New Year Card, 1905

Watercolour, 8.8 x 11.3cm
Initialled and dated bottom left: H.S.T. 1905
Inscribed: 'Wishing you a Merry Xmas and A Happy New Year'
Provenance: Given to Tuke Collection by Geoffrey Sainsbury
RCPS Tuke Collection A206

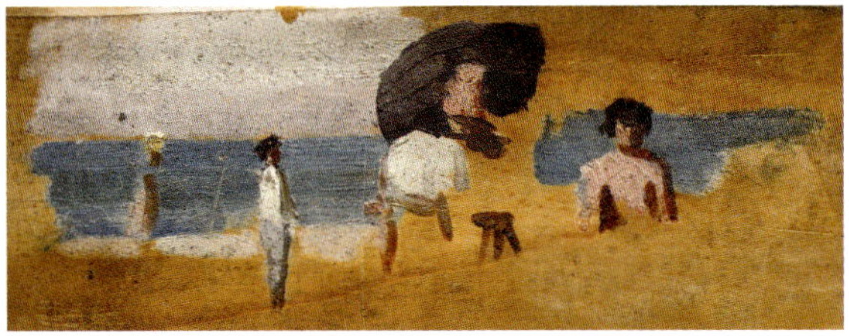

People on a beach

Oil on panel, 14.1 x 23.1cm
Provenance: Purchased from Brian Wells
14 May 1967
RCPS Tuke Collection A131a

This is the sketch on the reverse side of *Under the Jetty* (A131).

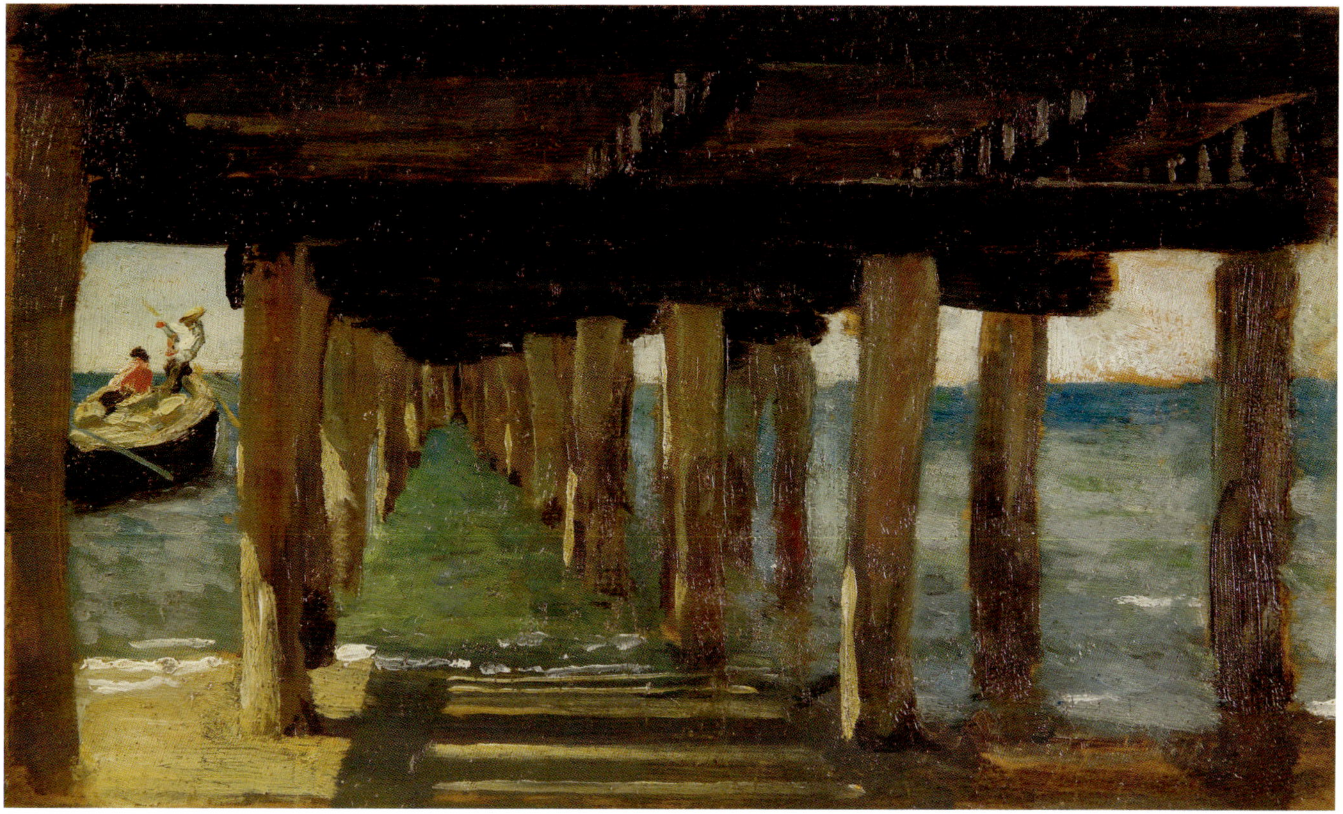

Under the Jetty

Oil on panel, 14.1 x 23.1cm
Provenance: Purchased from Brian Wells
14 May 1967
RCPS Tuke Collection A131

This scene is possibly of Venice or somewhere near, due to the gondola type boat on the left of the picture.

The image of people on a beach on the reverse of this picture also looks like a Mediterranean scene as opposed to a British seaside. It has previously been suggested that this is a view beneath the Submarine pier at Falmouth.

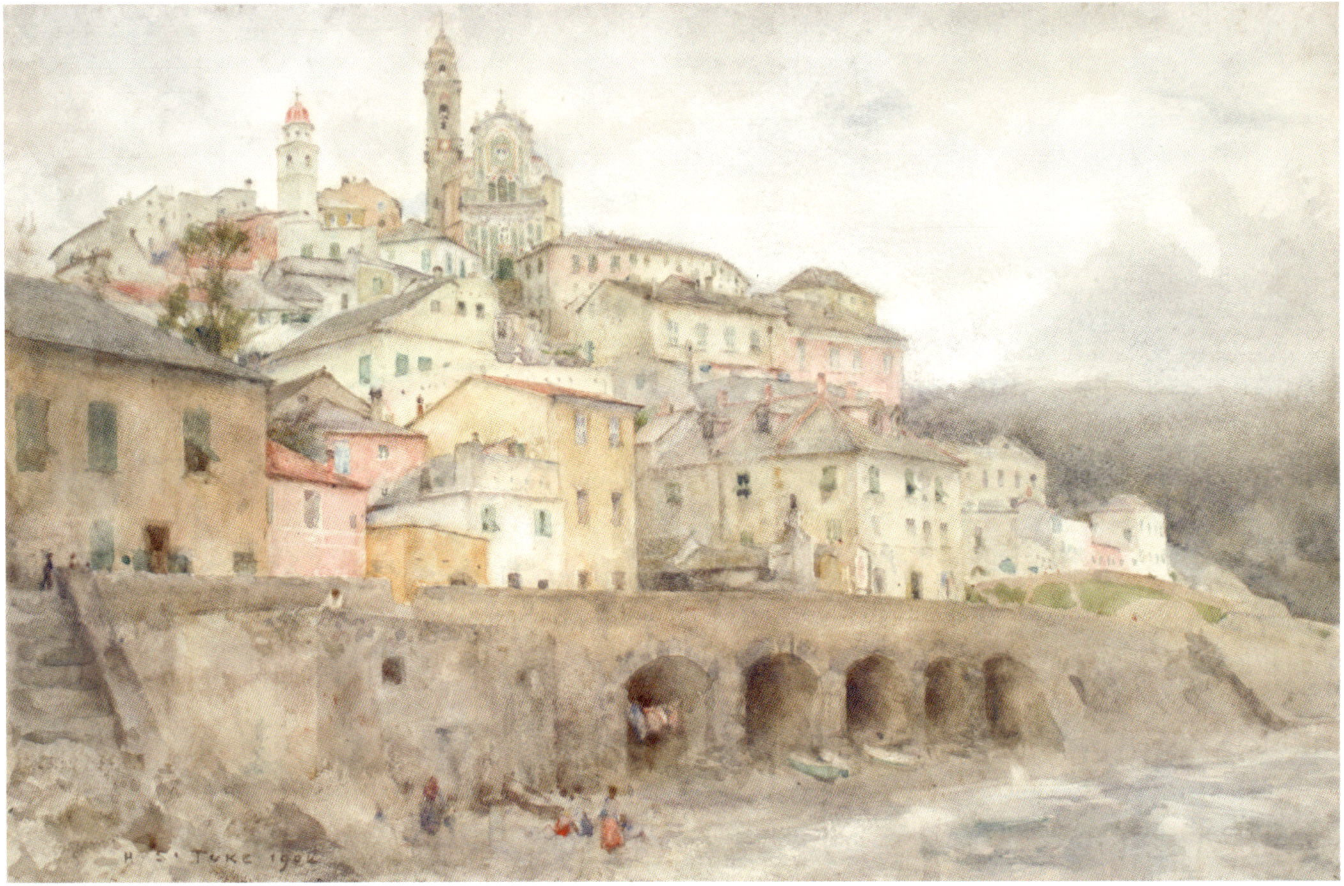

Cervo, A Ligurian Rock Village, 1904

Watercolour, 30.4 x 45.7cm
Signed and dated bottom left: H.S.Tuke 1904
Exhibited: *'Along the Italian Riviera'* at Dowdeswells' Galleries June 1904, No. 23.
Provenance: Purchased from Geoffrey Sainsbury 30 April 1967
RCPS Tuke Collection A172, R431

This fine watercolour was painted on Tuke's visit to the South of France and Northern Italy in April 1904.
Tuke wrote in his diary, April 14, 'To Cervo, by train and began a larger sketch of one of the finest places I have seen yet.'
April 16, 'By bike to Cervo for the day and did pretty well.'
April 20, 'To Cervo again, too bright for my pic. but a wonderful sight, the town against a blue sky.'
By April 25th Tuke went for the last time to Cervo and finished the painting.

Riviera Village (near Menton), 1904

Watercolour, 25.8 x 36cm
Signed and dated: H.S.Tuke 1904 bottom left
Provenance: Purchased from Geoffrey Sainsbury
30 April 1967
RCPS Tuke Collection A145

This watercolour was probably painted in February when Tuke was staying near Monte Carlo at the Dowager Lady Dalrymple's villa. From here he probably ventured over to Menton and the surrounding villages. This picture could have appeared in the Dowdeswell's exhibition in New Bond Street *'Along the Italian Riviera'* June/July, 1904, but has not been clearly identified in Tuke's register.

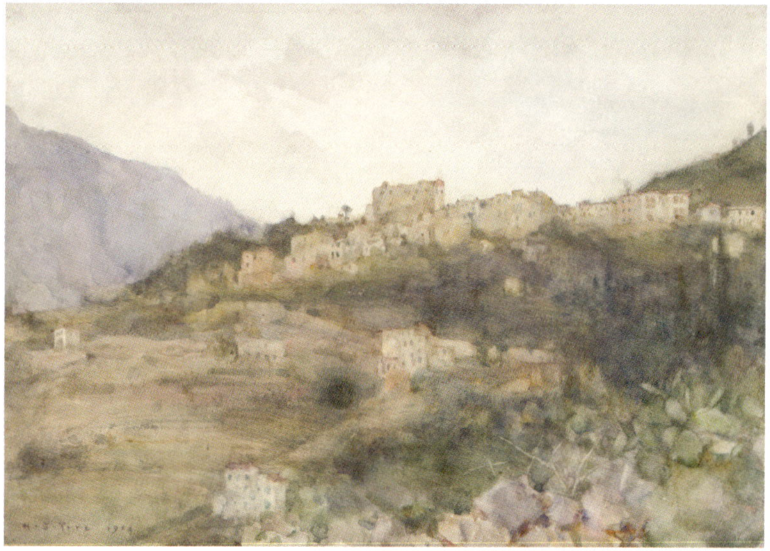

Livorno, 1904

Watercolour, 27.7 x 36.6cm
Signed, inscribed and dated bottom right: H.S.T.
Livorno 1904
Inscribed on reverse of mount: Charlie Mit.
Provenance: Purchased from John Maggs 14 July 1962
Reputedly from Charlie Mitchell's brother
RCPS Collection A112

On 21 March 1904 Tuke had travelled into northern Italy on the coast, where he went to Livorno from Porto Venere via Carrara. He had stayed near Carrara previously in 1881 when studying in Florence. On March 22 Tuke wrote to his sister, 'This is a wonderful place, quite one of the best I have seen, and perhaps quite the best for old shipping, and wonderfully coloured boats.' In his diary he wrote, 'At Livorno, put up at the Hotel Campari. Down to the port before dinner and saw lots of vessels and steamers.' The next day, 'Took a boatman and began on a group of small vessels.'

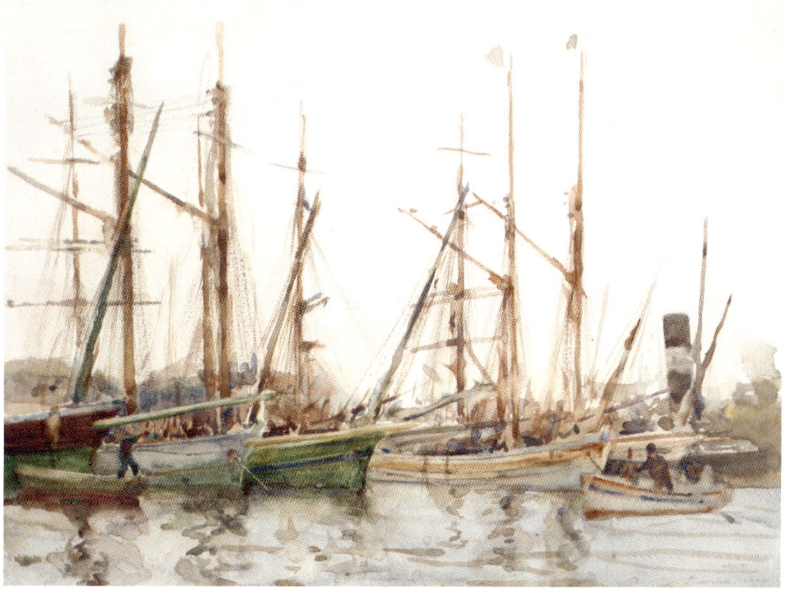

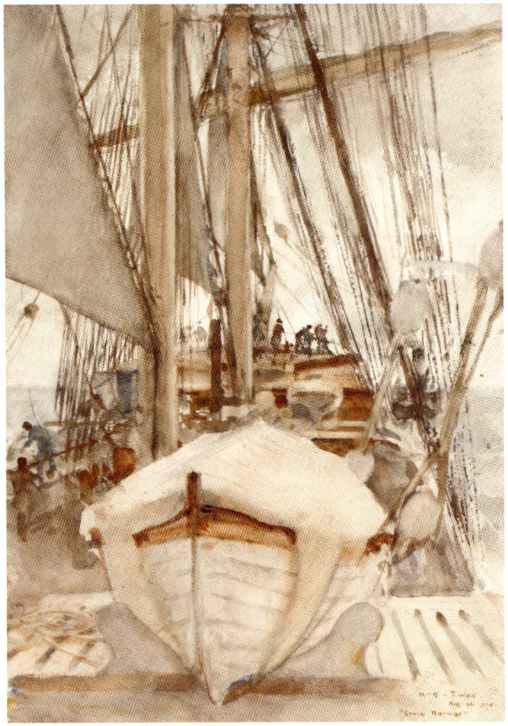

A Fair Wind, August 1908

Watercolour, 45.6 x 30.5cm
Signed, dated and inscribed bottom right: H.S.Tuke Aug 26 1908
'Grace Harwar'
Exhibited: Royal Watercolour Society winter 1908
Provenance: Purchased from D.W. Dobbs
10 May 1964
RCPS Tuke Collection A178 R605

Painted on the *'Grace Harwar'*. In August 1908 Tuke was invited by Captain James to sail on her from Falmouth to Nordenham in Germany, which took five days. His diary entry for 25 and 26 August reads, 'Anchors up and off in tow of the Triton. Soon got the canvas on her in a rising SW breeze. About 10pm took in everything except top sails, and at 12 it was blowing a whole gale, with some rain and a lot of phosphorescent sea coming on board. Stood up on the poop deck until 3.am.... Woke up to find the sun shining, with a strong west wind. Running along all day with royals set, signalled St. Catherine's, and saw the lights of Hastings abeam.' M.T.S. p.147.

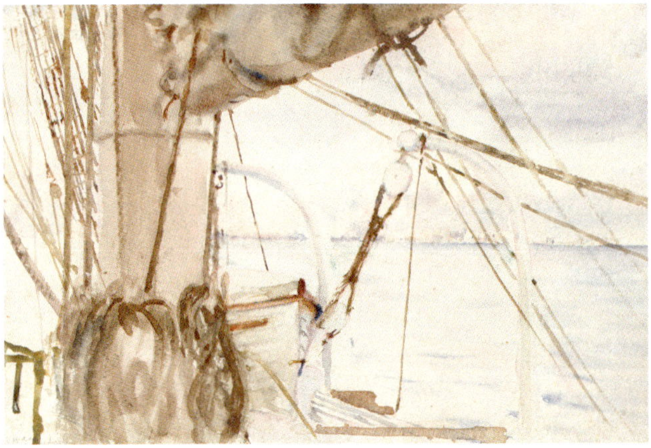

From the Deck of The *'Grace Harwar'*, c.1908

Watercolour, 17.6 x 26cm
Signed and inscribed bottom left: H.S.Tuke, Bremerhaven from Nordenham from the deck of the Grace Harwar.
Provenance: Purchased from Geoffrey Sainsbury
29 May 1968
RCPS Tuke Collection A141

The Look-Out (aka The Lookout Man), 1908

Watercolour, 50.8 x 35.8cm
Signed and dated bottom left: H.S.Tuke 1908,
Provenance: Purchased for Tuke Collection by A.E. Hookham 28 October 1962
Exhibited: The Royal Watercolour Society 1908
RCPS Tuke Collection A116 R604

This picture was painted as a souvenir of the *'Grace Harwar'*[1] for Mrs. Alfred Draper, but painted on the *'Braemar'* which was laid up in St. Just Pool. Tuke obviously used this watercolour as the basis of a later oil painting called *All's Well,* (R658) which was exhibited at the Royal Academy in 1910 and shows the same posed figure with sou'wester standing with his hands in his pockets in the same position on the deck of a rigged sailing ship.

1.The voyage Tuke took from Falmouth to Nordenham on the *'Grace Harwar'*.

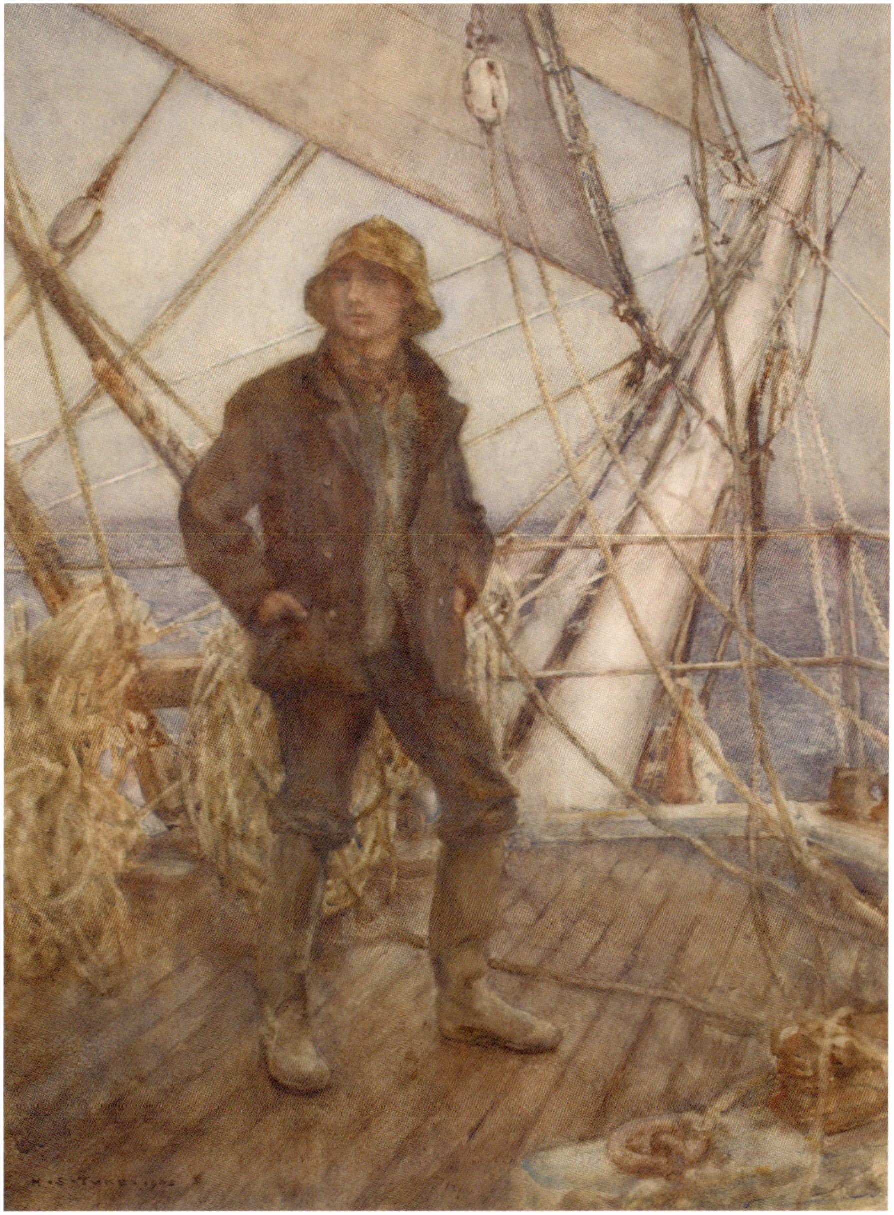

The West Indies 1923-24

Tuke went on an expedition on 26th November 1923 to the West Indies with friends Frederick Albert Mitchell-Hedges (1882-1959), an explorer whom he met in Falmouth, Lady Richmond Brown, who funded the expedition for Mitchell-Hedges, and Miss MacBeth, in a sailing and steam vessel the *'SS Coronado'*. There are 18 watercolours and an oil of this trip in the Tuke Collection. It is a unique record of the longest expedition and possibly the most hazardous Tuke ever undertook. The first stop on the journey was Jamaica where he made numerous sketches in watercolour, and some in oil of the Black River. There were frequent fishing excursions, when Tuke would get up at 5.30am and go with Mitchell-Hedges to catch a variety of fish from conger eels to sting rays. They recruited local lads to help with these trips and Ralph, Robbie and Samwel became models for many of Tuke's paintings. The party then went to Belize in British Honduras on 18th February 1924. 'Here they were joined by "Dr. Gann, the Maya archeologist," and a schooner was chartered in which they all embarked for Tobacco Caye (island) thirty-six miles away...They sailed by larger islands, Glover's Reef... and Wild Cave Caye, to the little town of Punta Gorda on the mainland, which they reached on March 8th.' M.T.S. p166. This was quite a wild adventure for Tuke who was 66 years old by this time. The rich colours of the Caribbean inspired him, and his palette of colours used in both watercolours and oils is bold and bright. The market-place at Belize was a centre of activity, and Tuke painted it with the same concentration as he did the azure blue sea and numerous boats at anchor in the harbours.

On the 10th March he set off with Mitchell-Hedges, Dr. Gann and the rest of the party on an expedition up the Rio Grande to see the Maya ruined city. It was an ill-fated trip, and after one of the dugout canoes that contained much of the Doctor's equipment and the party's food capsized, they got caught in a tropical storm with heavy rain and had to make camp with only a fire to keep the mosquitoes and ticks away. Tuke was severely bitten, and although he does not mention feeling ill in his diary until 29th March when he is about to set sail for home, Mitchell-Hedges wrote in his autobiography *Danger My Ally* that on their return to Punta Garda, 'Tuke was seriously ill. The doctor informed us that we must get him away... he has malaria and his heart is badly affected.' p.173. Despite this, Tuke's accounts of his return journey to the UK are full of playing bridge with fellow passengers and crew, undertaking portraits commissioned by those on board, selling some of the work he had done on the trip to fellow passengers, and enjoying the good weather they had for most of the time. Little did he know he would never really recover from this foreign adventure.

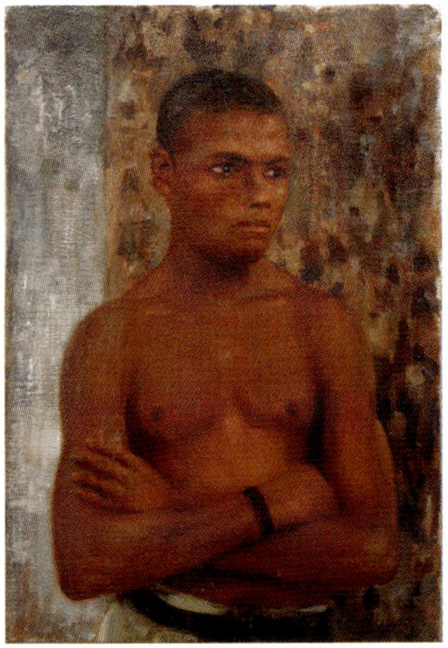

Half Length of Ralph, 30 December 1923
Oil on canvas board, 45 x 30.4cm
Provenance: Given to Tuke Collection by Geoffrey Sainsbury
16 September 1962
RCPS Tuke Collection A104 R1266

This study was undertaken in 1923 on Tuke's West Indies tour. His diary entry for 30 December 1923 reads, 'Got my oil box out and did a half-length of Ralph against the palings, starting about 4.30, moon and starlight'. This was probably painted at night as it was too hot for the models during the heat of the day.

Turk's Island, 8 December 1923
Watercolour, 14 x 21.7cm
Provenance: Purchased from Geoffrey Sainsbury
14 December 1967
RCPS Tuke Collection A208

Dated from diary entry 8 December 1923: 'About 3 sighted Turk's Island, passed quite near. Soon after ran into heavy rain clouds.'

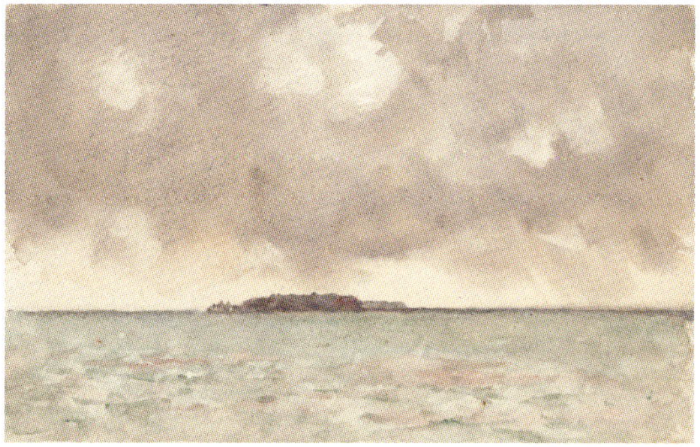

Sunrise off Hayti, 9 December 1923
Watercolour, 14 x 21.9cm
Inscribed and initialled bottom right: Sunrise off Hayti HST
Provenance: Purchased from Geoffrey Sainsbury
29 May 1968
RCPS Tuke Collection A168

Dated from diary entry 9 December 1923: 'Just before sunrise looked out and saw Hayti, a gorgeous sight, volcanic rocks up against the rising sun. Ran up on deck and did a sketch.'

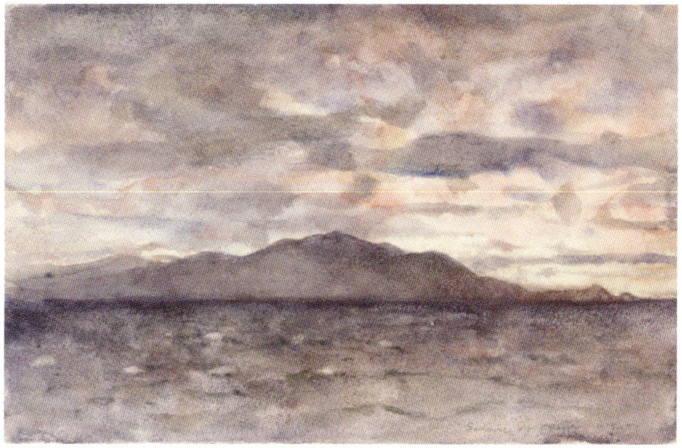

Kingston Harbour, 11 December 1923
Watercolour, 18.8 x 26.1cm
Dated, inscribed and initialled bottom left:
Dec 11 1923, Kingston Harbour, HST
Provenance: Purchased from W. Dyer of Camborne
28 October 1967
RCPS Tuke Collection A211

On 10 December, Tuke and his party arrived at Port Royal, Jamaica. Tuke's diary entry for 11 December 1923 reads, 'After lunch hired a boat with melancholy nigger and pulled off in the harbour. Sketched the nigger and later a line of mountains.'

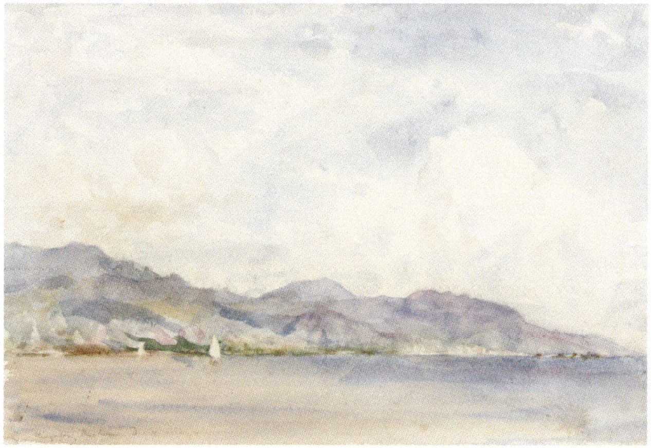

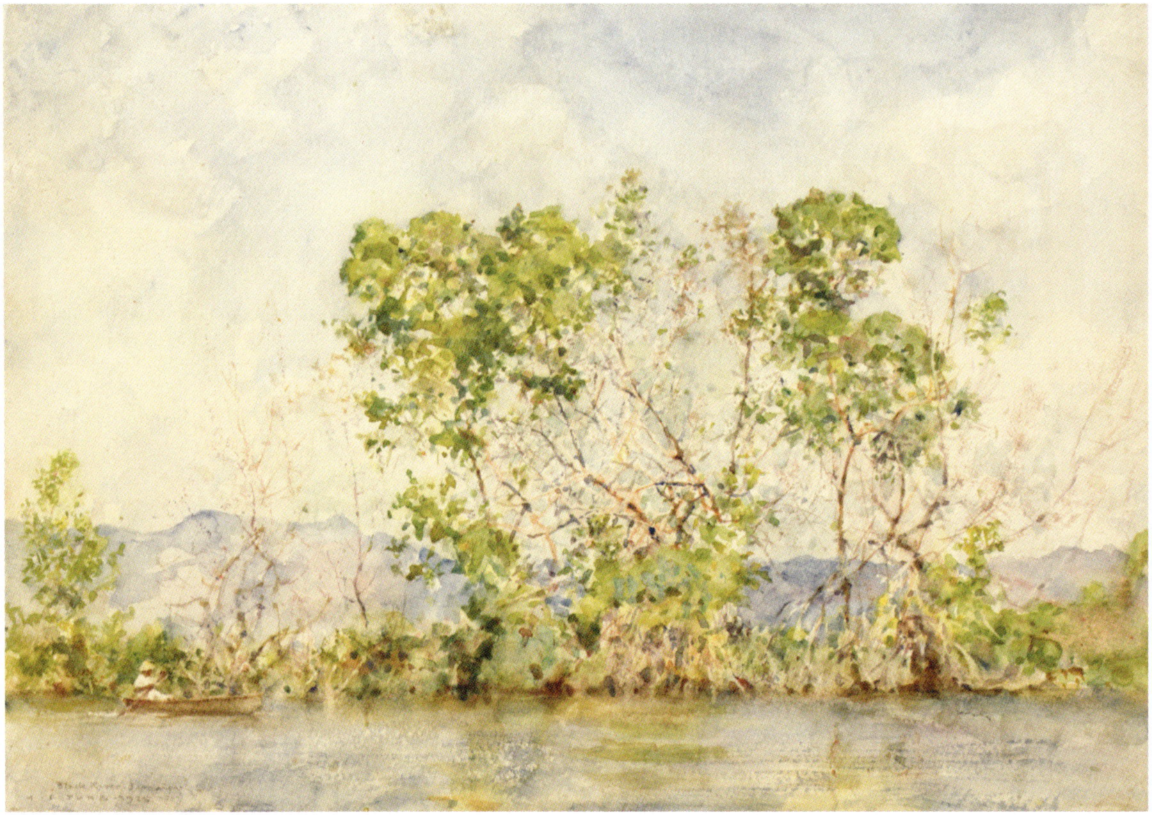

Black River, Jamaica, 1924

Watercolour, 26 x 36cm
Inscribed, signed and dated bottom left: Black River, Jamaica, H.S.Tuke 1924
Exhibited at the Royal Watercolour Society, Winter 1924
Provenance: Purchased from Geoffrey Sainsbury
29 May 1968
Tuke Collection A138 R1068

On 13 December 1923, Tuke arrived 'at the famous Black River where received by Mrs. Levy at Waterloo House.' There he stayed for Christmas and New Year. On 6 January, after setting off on an expedition along the Black River, he realised he had left his bag on the quay and on his return his watercolour box was missing. It seems it failed to be recovered and Tuke had to improvise. On 14 January, 'Sent for the tin-smith and gave him instructions with rough cardboard model, how to make a watercolour box. This he completed with no little skill and delivered in the afternoon.' He must have replaced the watercolours by 23 January as he notes, 'Up the river and began watercolour of the same group of trees I did in oil.' The work done after 6 January, which uses a different range of colours from Tuke's normal watercolour palette, implies he had to make do with whatever colours were available.

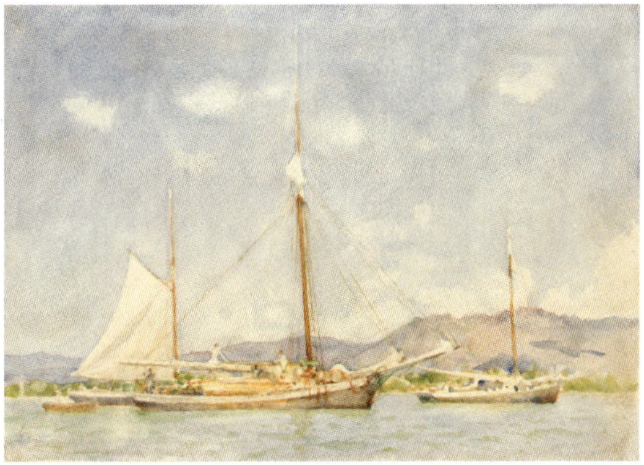

Three Sloops at Black River, 22 January 1924

Watercolour, 26 x 36cm
Initialled bottom right: H.S.T
Provenance: Purchased from Geoffrey Sainsbury
8 September 1968
RCPS Tuke Collection A150

Although there are no titles on this painting, it has been deduced by B.D. Price that from the black hills in the distance and the colours used, this is one of Tuke's paintings undertaken on the Black River in Jamaica. His diary of 22 January 1924 reads, 'A group of three sloops including Massa Dory's *'Energy'*, did rather a successful sketch.'

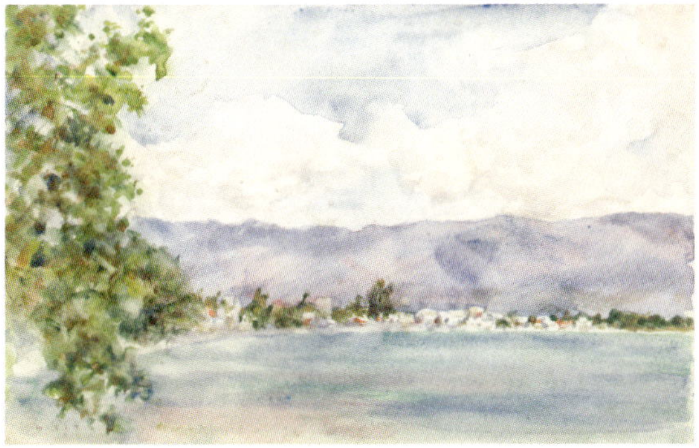

Black River from West Beach, 9 February 1924

Watercolour, 14.2 x 21.6cm
Initialled bottom left: H.S.T.
Provenance: Purchased from Geoffrey Sainsbury
29 May 1968
RCPS Tuke Collection A167

Dated from Tuke's diary 9 February 1924: 'After lunch went along to the West Beach and did a small sketch of the village.' Picture shows a bay with buildings on the shore and tree foliage on left hand side.

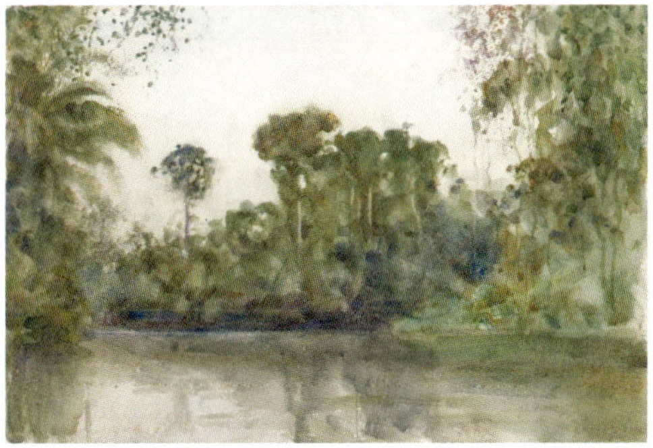

Group of Trees, Black River, 1924

Watercolour, 17.7 x 26cm
Initialled bottom right: H.S.T.
Provenance: Purchased from Geoffrey Sainsbury
29 May 1968
RCPS Tuke Collection A137

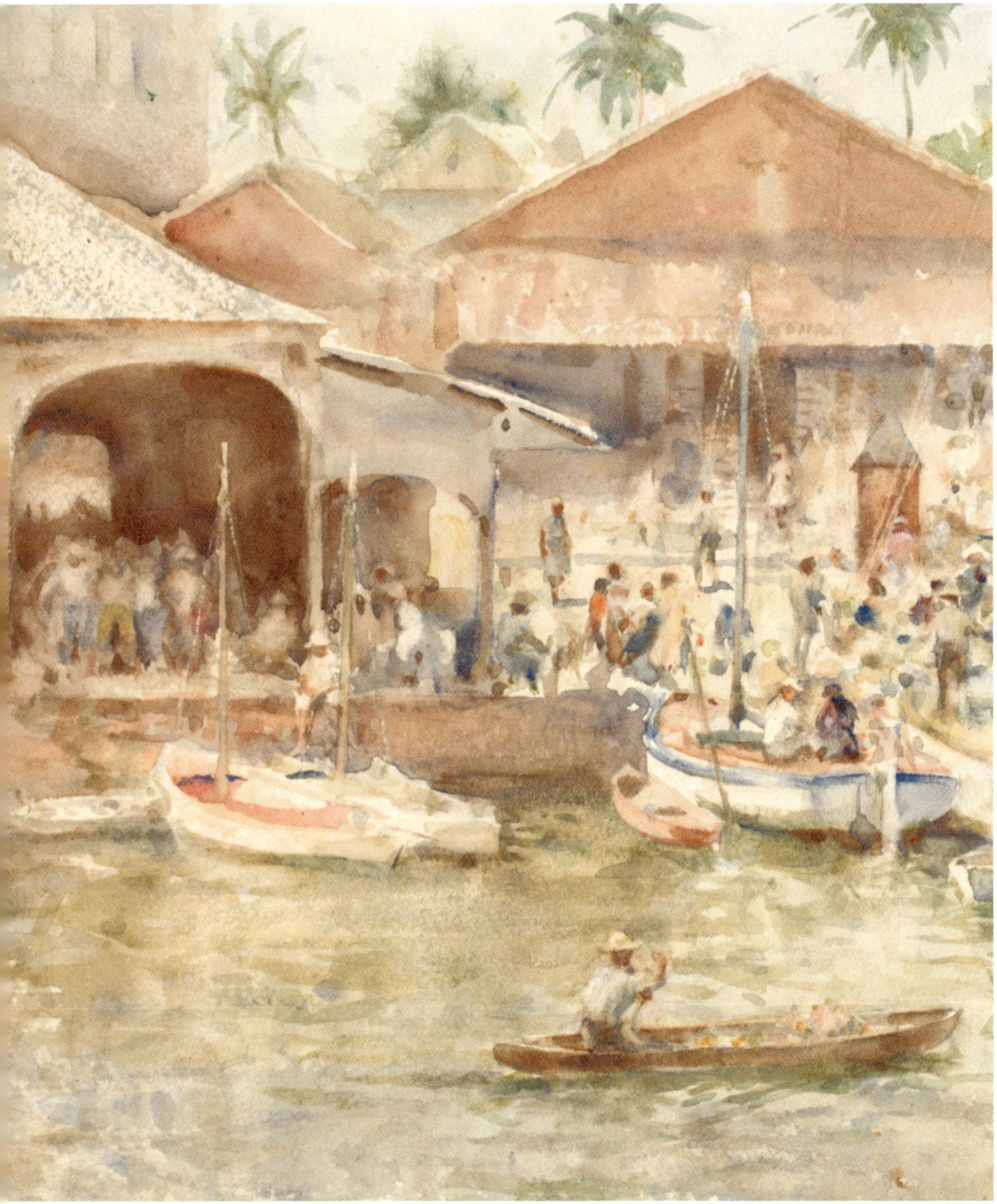

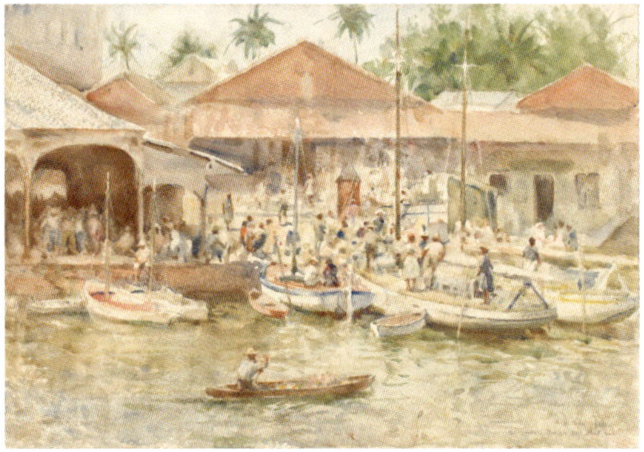

The Market, Belize,
British Honduras, 1924

Watercolour, 26 x 36.3cm
Signed, dated and inscribed bottom right: H.S.Tuke
1924, The Market, Belize, British Honduras
Exhibited: The Empire Exhibition, Wembley, 1924
Provenance: Purchased from Geoffrey Sainsbury
29 May 1968
RCPS Tuke Collection A163 R1047

Tuke's diary entry for 19 February 1924 reads, 'Looked around early and started a small sketch looking across the river to the fish market with boats. After breakfast Mr. Newcombe of the stores arranged a table and chair for me to paint from a balcony and I began a larger one of the market with boats.'

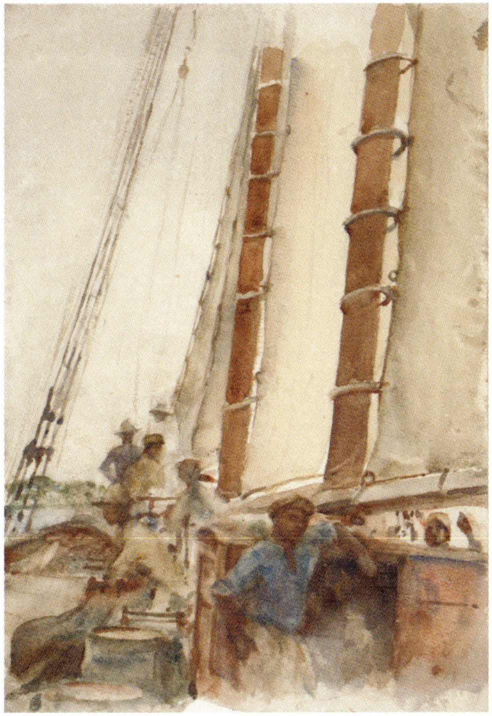

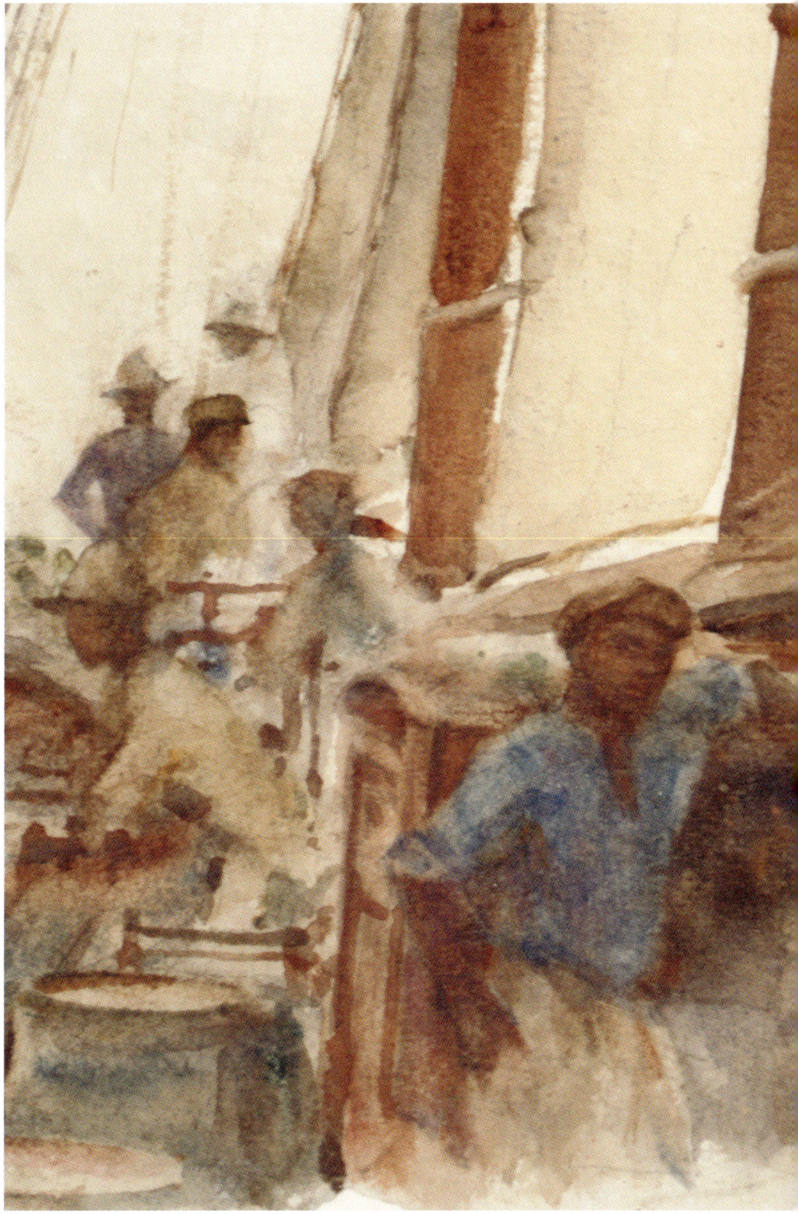

On the Schooner W.W. 22 February 1924

Watercolour, 23.5 x 18cm
Provenance: Purchased from Geoffrey Sainsbury
19 December 1963
RCPS Tuke Collection A56

Painted on the way to Tobacco Caye. Tuke's diary entry for 22 Feb 1924 reads, 'Packed up everything, leaving a good deal behind in the Hotel, and embarked on the schooner W.W., let go from the wharf just before 11 and started under sail and motor. Crew seven with captain, all negroes, the captain a fine slim fellow, and most of them a picturesque lot. In addition we had Tom Gibb as fishing expert, and Dr. Gann brought his Mexican servant "Muddy". A fine breeze came up about 1, but unluckily brought heavy rain and interrupted a promising sketch on the deck looking forward.'

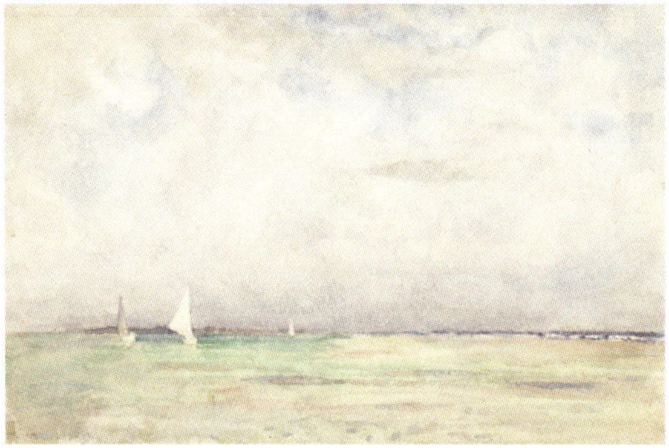

Tobacco Caye, 24 February 1924

Watercolour, 17.5 x 26cm
Inscribed bottom left: Tobacco Caye
Provenance: Purchased from W. Dyer
20 August 1968
RCPS Tuke Collection A147

Tuke left for Tobacco Caye on 22 February. On Sunday 24th he notes in his diary, 'A sketch of the reef and green water with big clouds.'

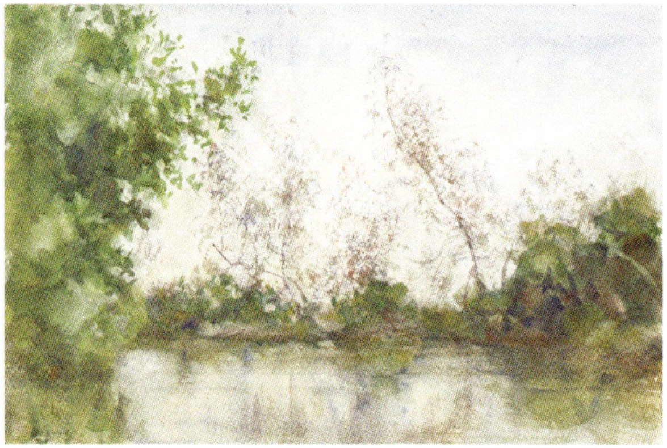

Mangrove Swamp, 1924

Watercolour, 17.4 x 26cm
Signed bottom left: H.S.Tuke
Provenance: Purchased from Geoffrey Sainsbury
29 May 1968
RCPS Tuke Collection A169

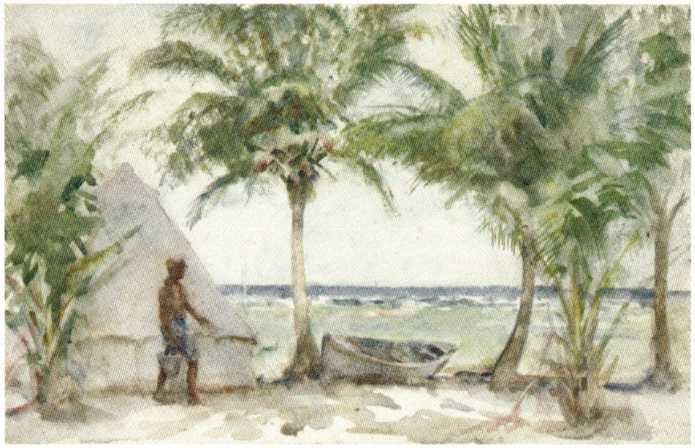

Robbie's Tent, Tobacco Caye, c. Feb.1924

Watercolour, 14 x 21.5cm
Initialled bottom right: H.S.T.
Inscribed on mount: Robbie's Tent, Tobacco Caye B-H
Provenance: Purchased from Geoffrey Sainsbury
31 March 1964
RCPS Tuke Collection A42

On arriving at Tobacco Caye, Tuke described 'The island is covered in cocoanut (sic) trees with reefs running north and south.'
His diary entry for 24 February 1924 reads, 'Afternoon began a small one of the tent and trees and the breaking water beyond.'

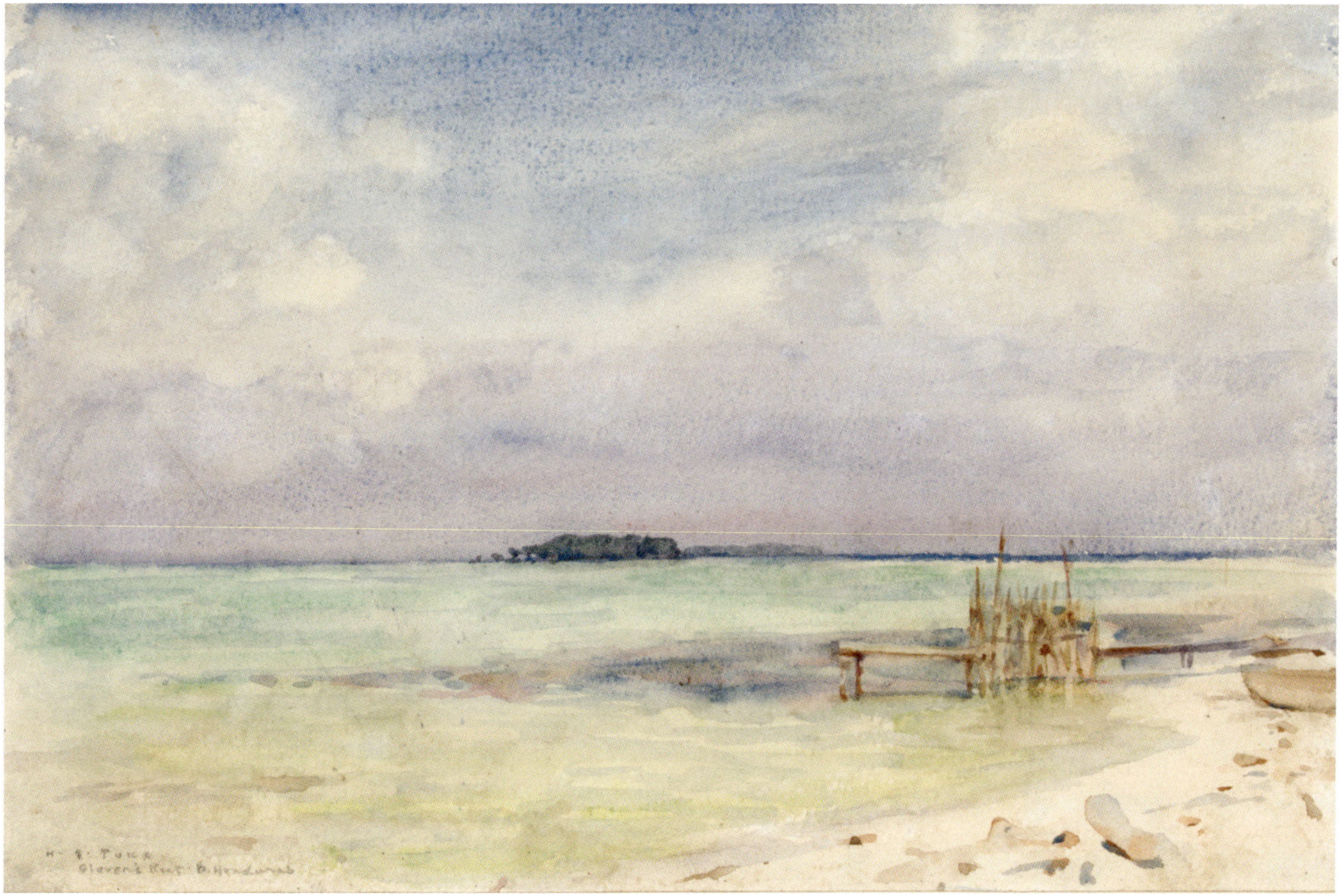

Glover's Reef, British Honduras, 2 March 1924
Watercolour, 17.5 x 26cm
Signed and Inscribed bottom left: H.S.Tuke Glover's Reef B.Honduras
Provenance: Purchased from Geoffrey Sainsbury
29 May1968
RCPS Tuke Collection A164

On 29th February Tuke went on the schooner to Glover's Reef which was 18 miles from Tobacco Caye, which they achieved in two hours. Tuke describes Glover's Reef as 'a bigger island than Tobacco with many cocoanuts (sic) and nice water for bathing, which is considered safe here though sharks come in when they are cleaning fish.' His diary entry for 2nd March 1924 notes, 'The weather good again, some lovely skies and green seas... After lunch another sketch of green water etc.'

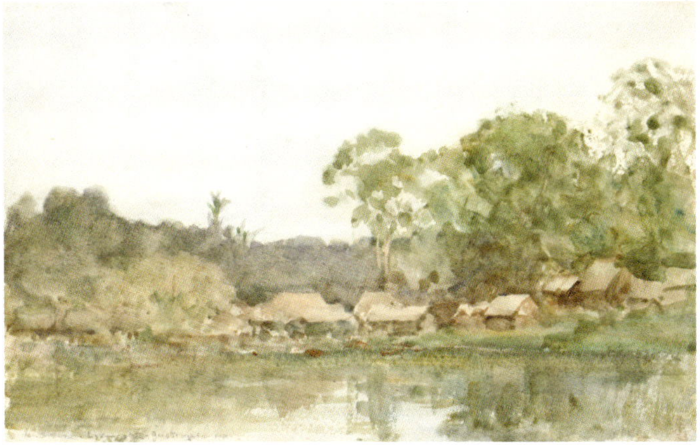

Livingston, Guatemala, Central America,

March 1924
Watercolour, 14.2 x 21.9cm
Signed and inscribed bottom left: H.S.Tuke Livingston, Guatemala C.A
Provenance: Purchased from Geoffrey Sainsbury 29 May1968
RCPS Tuke Collection A202

After surviving a night out in the rain and being bitten by mosquitoes and ticks, Tuke and the ladies of the expedition party left Mitchell-Hedges and Dr. Gann and boarded the schooner for Livingston, Guatemala on 14th March. 'Arrived there – a numerous crowd, custom house officers, the Commandante, the doctor all came aboard. The first trouble was we should have had the Guatemalan flag on the foremast as well as the red ensign on the poop – Then trouble with passports, finally the ship's papers were out of order. Eventually we were allowed to land, first visited the British Consul Reed, a seedy old chap, who assured us everything w[ould] be easy. Then we bought some coloured hammocks and other things and went aboard again for the night, the ladies sleeping in hammocks.' Diary entry 13 March 1924.

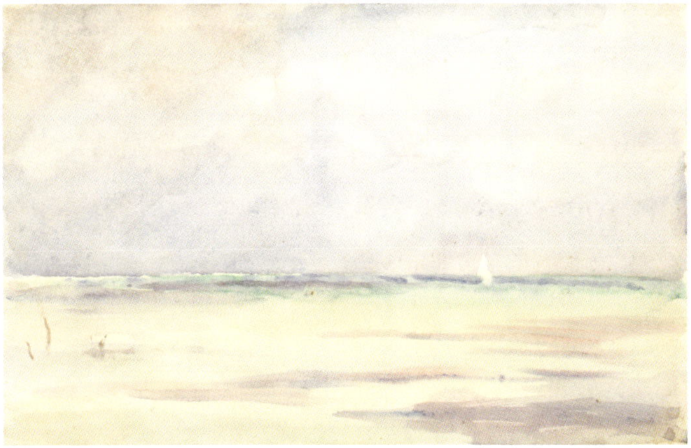

St. George's Caye, British Honduras,

23 March 1924
Watercolour, 14 x 21.6cm
Inscribed on reverse: St George's Caye
Provenance: Purchased from Geoffrey Sainsbury 8 September 1968
RCPS Tuke Collection A189

Tuke notes in his diary for 23 March 1924, 'Arranged with Claud to take me in the motor dory to St. George's Caye, the popular weekend bathing place. It was over ten miles but the engine ran well and we had a delightful bathe in the one near a great shallow sandy patch. Did a small colour note.'

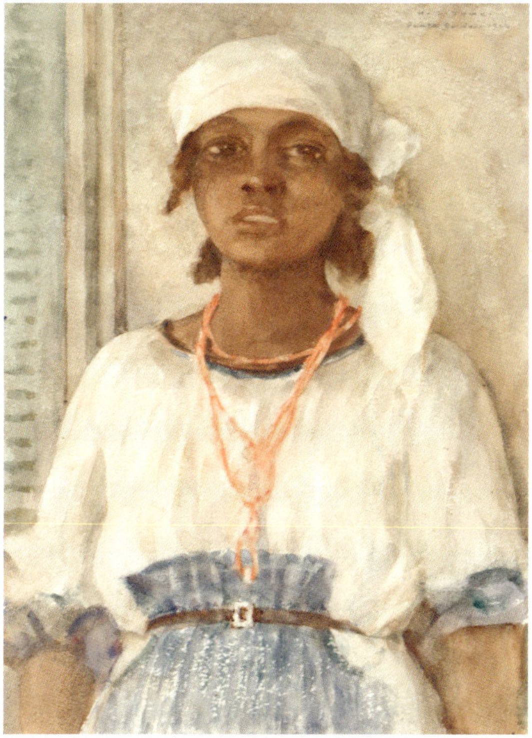

Jane Flowers, 17 March 1924
Watercolour, 25.8 x 17.9cm
Signed, inscribed and dated top right: H.S.Tuke
Punta Gorda 1924
Exhibited: Royal Watercolour Society Winter 1924
Provenance: Purchased from Geoffrey Sainsbury
31 March 1964
RCPS Tuke Collection A41 R1072

Tuke's diary entry for 17 March 1924 refers to this model and painting: 'Through Catrina, the Heatherington's servant, got hold of a nice Carib girl and did a good head and shoulder of her in the verandah. She was disappointed as she could not have the picture as well as her pay.' In Tuke's register (R1072 Carib Indian Girl) he writes, 'Painted in the verandah at Heatherington's house at Punta Gorda, British Honduras.'

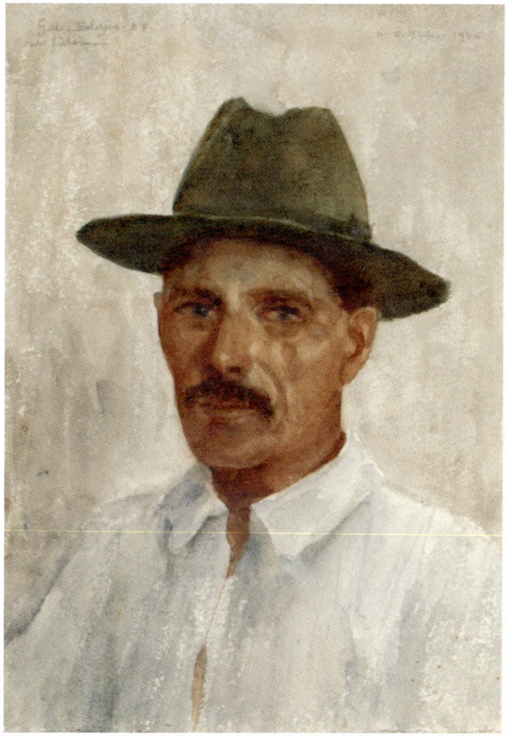

Gill, Our Fisherman, 24 March 1924
Watercolour, 26 x 18cm
Signed and dated top right: H.S.Tuke 1924
Inscribed top left: Gill, Belize, B.H. Our fisherman
Provenance: Purchased from Geoffrey Sainsbury
18 December 1964
RCPS Tuke Collection A87

Tuke's diary entry for 24 March 1924 notes, 'Painted a sketch head of Stanley Gill.' Stanley was the fishing expert taken on the trips from Belize.

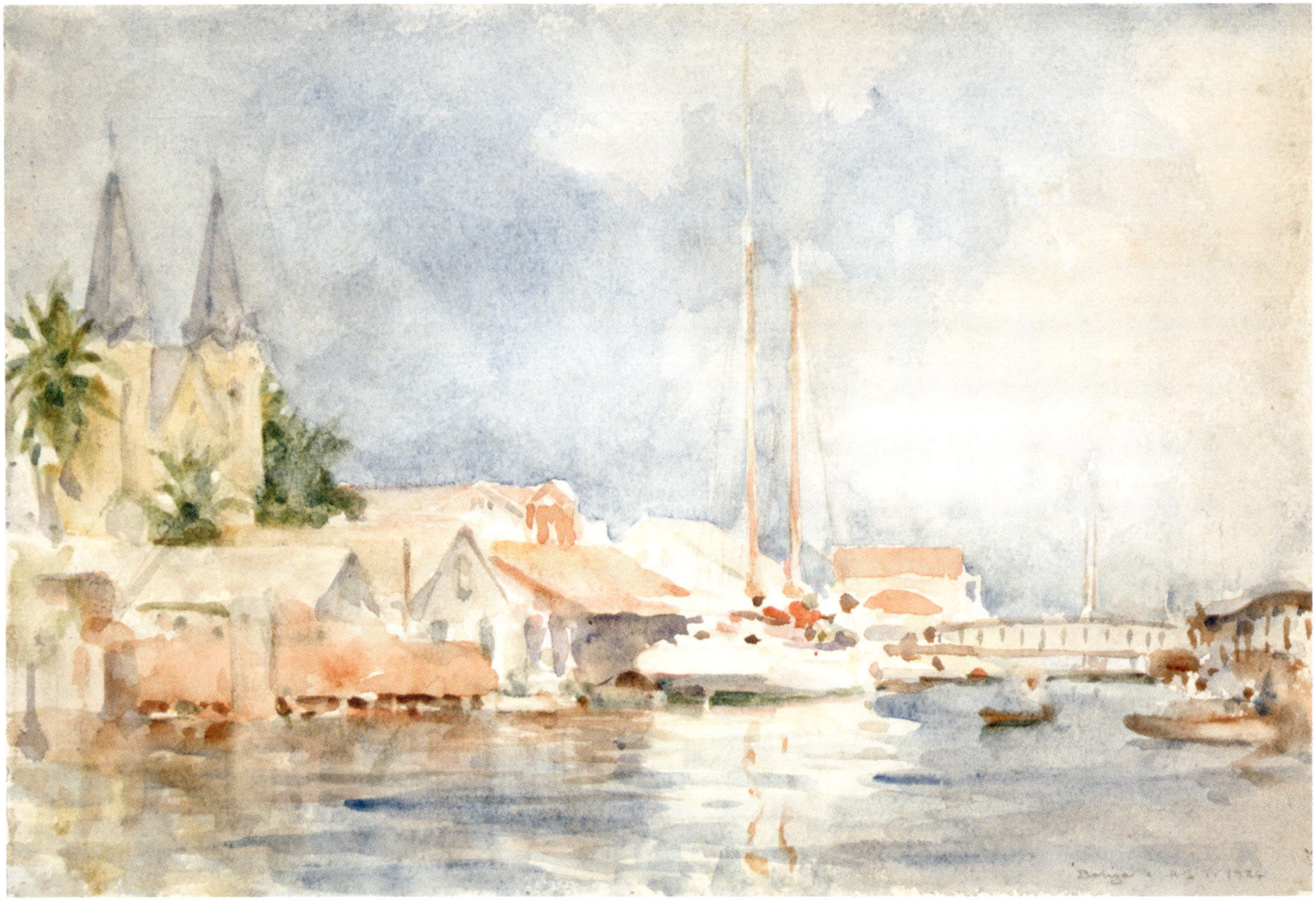

Belize, 1924
Watercolour, 17.7 x 26cm
Initialled, dated and inscribed bottom right: HST, 1924, Belize
Provenance: Purchased from Geoffrey Sainsbury
27 February 1966
RCPS Tuke Collection A95 R1268

Tuke's diary entry 27 March 1924 states, 'Anchored in the river with Claud and got a good view looking towards the bridge with the schooner W.W and the RC Church.'

Mediterranean and North Africa 1925-27

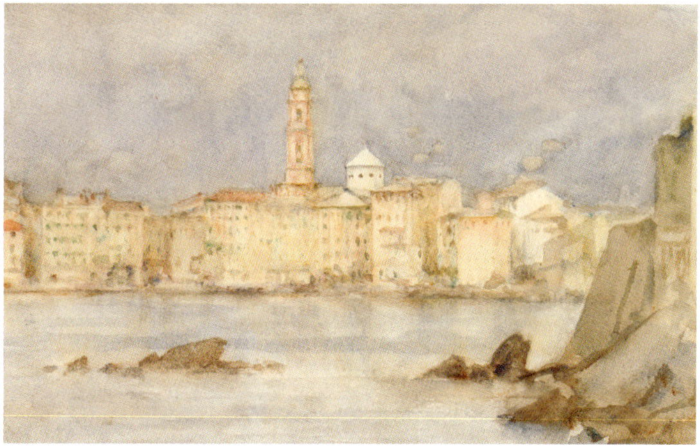

Rapallo, c.1925
Watercolour, 17.8 x 28cm
Provenance: Purchased from Geoffrey Sainsbury
13 July 1963
RCPS Tuke Collection A60 R112

Tuke travelled abroad again in 1925, stopping in Paris at Julian's studio and the Louvre on his way to Rapallo via Turin, where he stayed with Captain Dowman. His diary entry for 18 January 1925 reads, 'Started a view from the unfinished ruins near the Hotel Bristol, looking across to Rapallo about a mile away. The sun almost oppressively hot. Another small note looking from my balcony.'

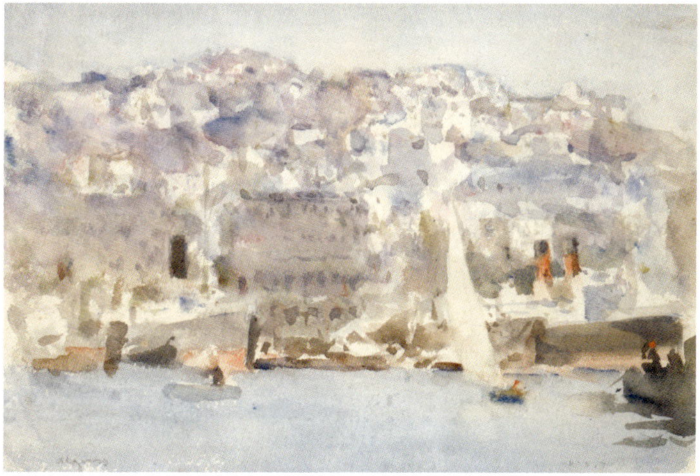

Algiers, c.1925
Watercolour, 17.9 x 26cm
Initialled bottom right: H.S.T.
Inscribed bottom left: Algiers
Provenance: Purchased from Geoffrey Sainsbury
29 May1968
RCPS Tuke Collection A153

'Out with the boatman again and did a useful note of the town in sunlight making as little as possible of the near houses which are ugly and modern.' Diary entry 10 February 1925.

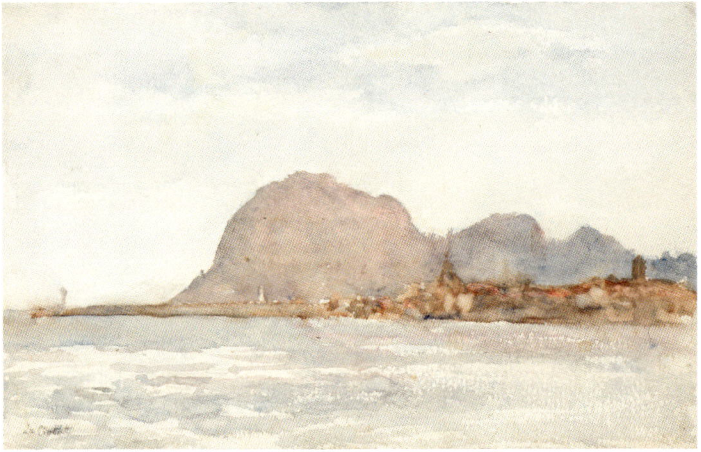

‘La Ciotat’

Watercolour, 13.7 x 21.5cm
Inscribed bottom left: La Ciotat
Provenance: Purchased from W. Dyer of Camborne
28 October 1967
RCPS Tuke Collection A210

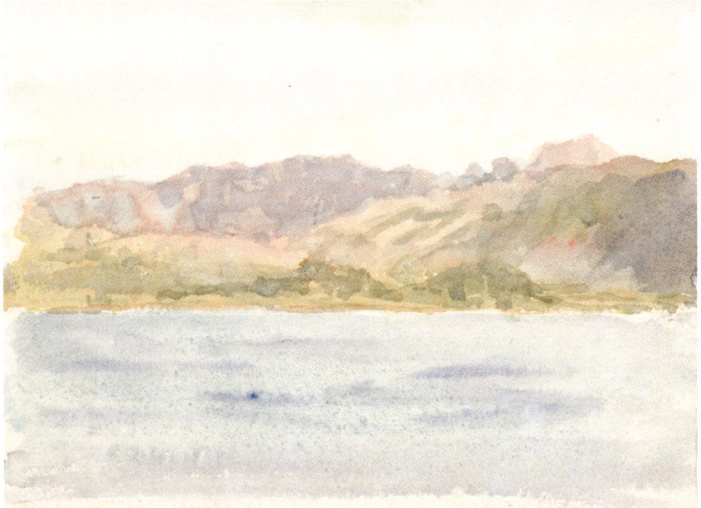

Coastal Scene

Watercolour, 12.6 x 17.8cm
Provenance: Purchased from Geoffrey Sainsbury
14 December 1967
RCPS Tuke Collection A207

This work is very similar in colour and terrain to *Ruins at Carthage* (A89) dated 1925.

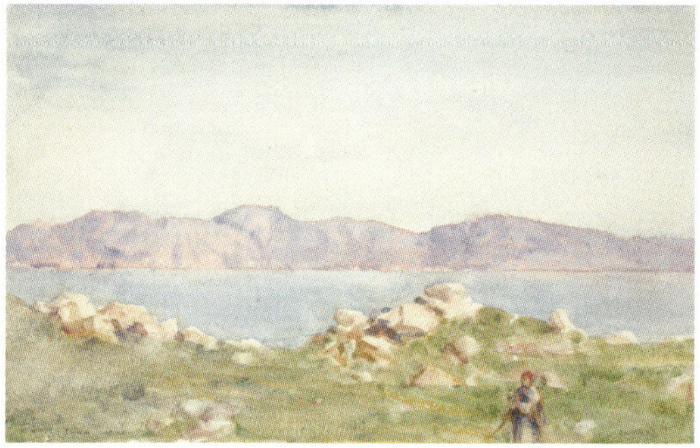

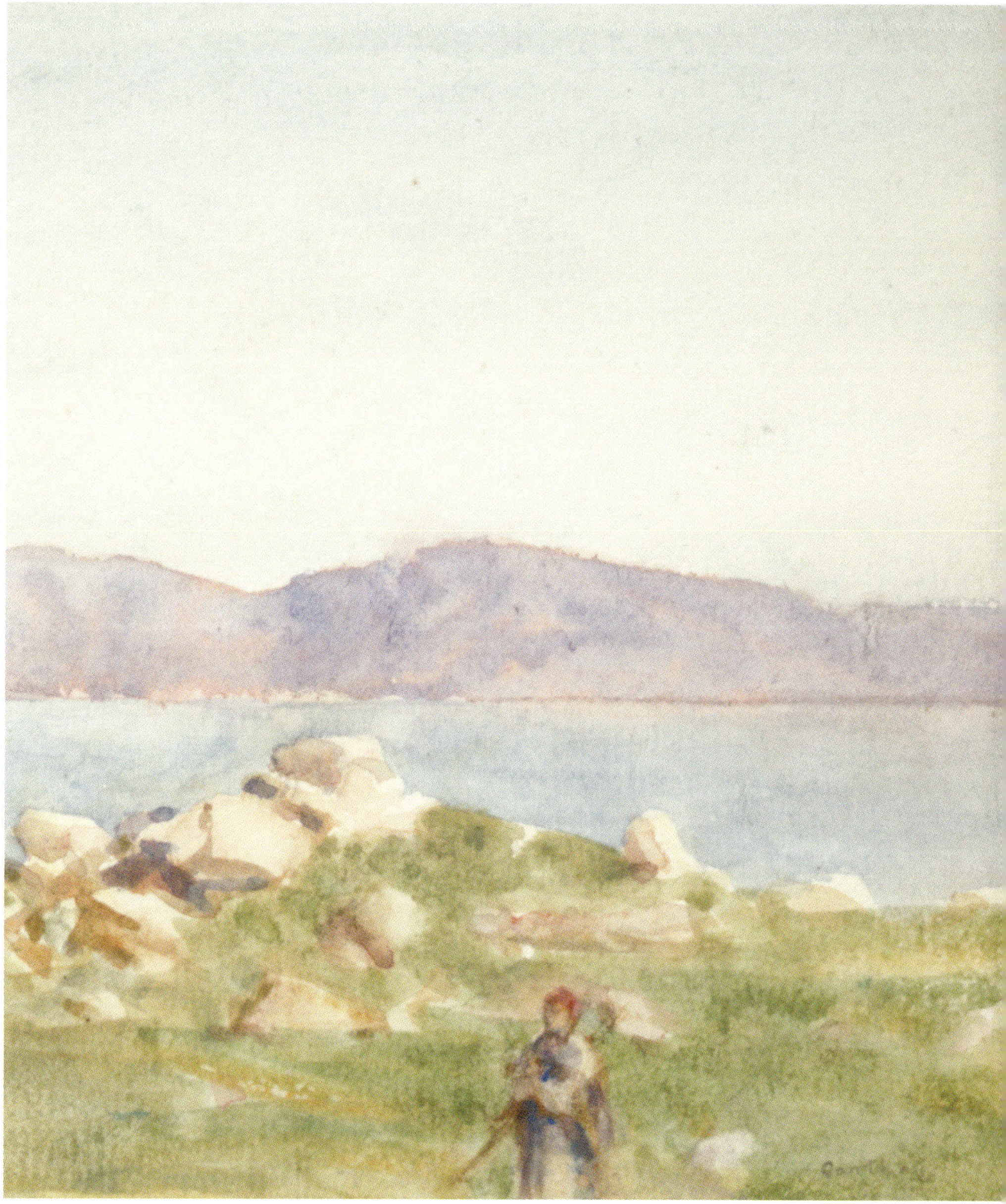

Ruins of Carthage, 1925

Watercolour, 14 x 21.8cm
Signed and dated bottom left: H.S.Tuke 1925
Inscribed bottom right: Carthage
Exhibited: The Royal Watercolour Society, Spring 1925
Provenance: Purchased from Geoffrey Sainsbury
27 February 1966
RCPS Tuke Collection A89

Tuke ventured to Carthage after spending a night vomiting and having diarrhoea in Tunis where he had been staying from 16-18th February 1925. By the morning of 19th he writes in his diary, 'Felt practically all right again. Up to see the Souks and native quarter and after lunch took a train out by La Goulette to Carthage. A most perfect day of fresh sunshine. A lovely site, not much left, but most of the things are in the Museum. Did a note looking across to the lovely hills across the bay.'

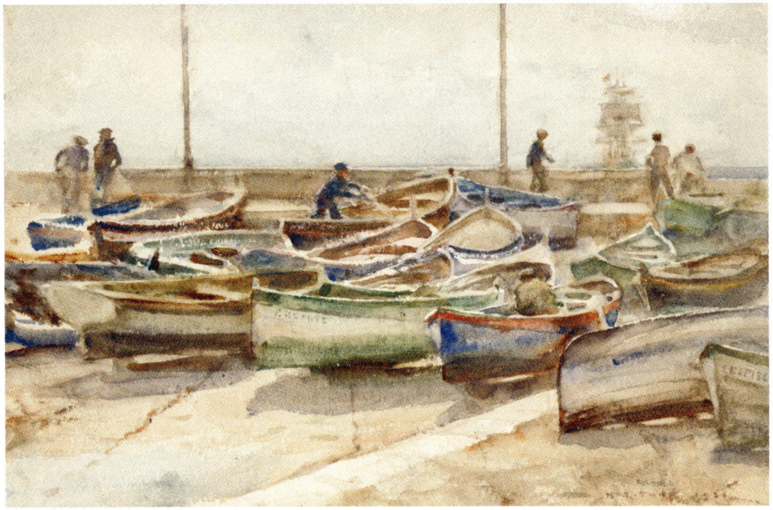

Boats at Cassis, 1926

Watercolour, 16.5 x 25cm
Inscribed, signed and dated bottom right:
Cassis, H.S.Tuke 1926
Provenance: Given to Tuke Collection by Glyn Ward
17 November 1962
Previously owned by Geoffrey Sainsbury
RCPS Tuke Collection A9

Tuke returned to the South of France and Italy in 1926. He went to Captain Dowman's new Villa Roborati at Rapallo in January and then on 16 February he wrote, 'Stradling is very anxious for me to join him at Cassis. It takes me about 14 hours from here to Toulon, and Cassis is 15 miles further on... there are some good sketching bits and lots of artists, but I am very disappointed with it and doubt if I shall stay long... The boats I hoped to find are all motor driven, and only occasionally put up a small auxiliary sail.' On February 21 he wrote, 'This trip will be a failure as far as painting goes, I shall bring home only a few slight sketches. That is owing in great measure to me having a cold, but there is very little for me to paint here.' M.T.S. p.175-176.

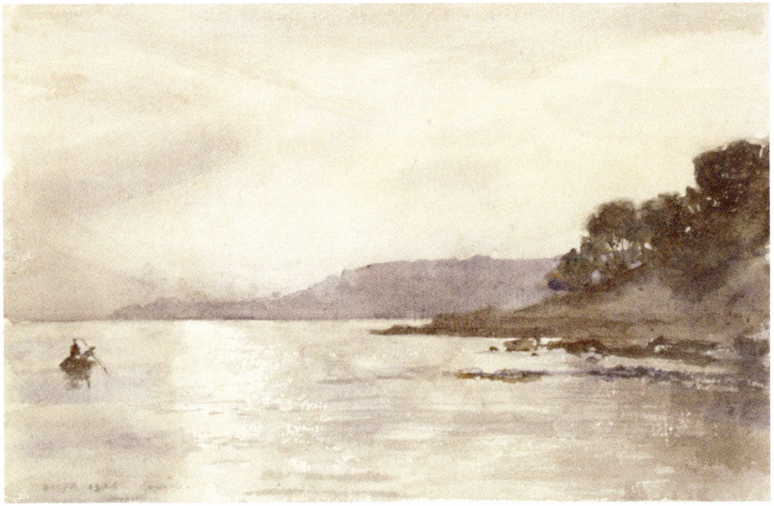

Coast at Cassis, 1926

Watercolour, 14 x 21.7cm
Initialled, dated and inscribed bottom left: H.S.T.
1926, Cassis Provenance:
Purchased from Geoffrey Sainsbury
8 September 1968
RCPS Tuke Collection A187

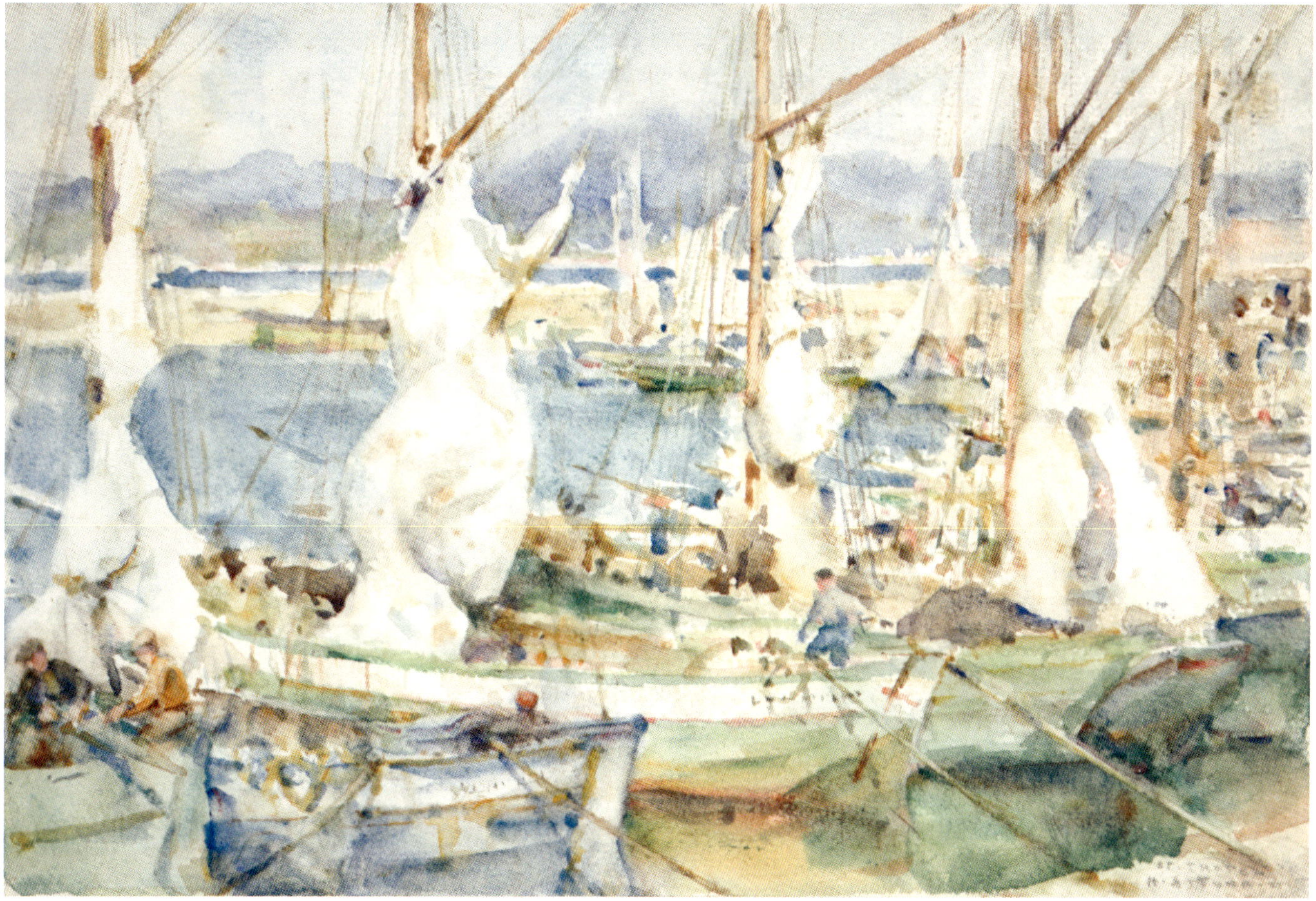

St. Tropez, 1927

Watercolour, 17.7 x 25.5cm
Inscribed, signed and dated bottom right: St.Tropez, H.S.Tuke '27
Provenance: Purchased from Geoffrey Sainsbury
31 March 1964
RCPS Tuke Collection A73

In February 1927 Tuke headed off to Europe for the last time – first to Cassis, stopping with his friend Stradling, then driving together to St. Tropez. He wrote to his sister on February 21, 'We came on here by car, about 74 miles, through Toulon and Hyeres and various small towns. This place is just as paintable as I found last year, only no sailing ships for the moment, but lots of the big sailing boats laden with barrels of wine. They are moored right in front of the hotel so I can sit on my balcony and paint all day long, but we go out as well on the Quays. The boats are all colours and are quite distractingly beautiful.' M.T.S. p.177.

Self Portraits – 1927

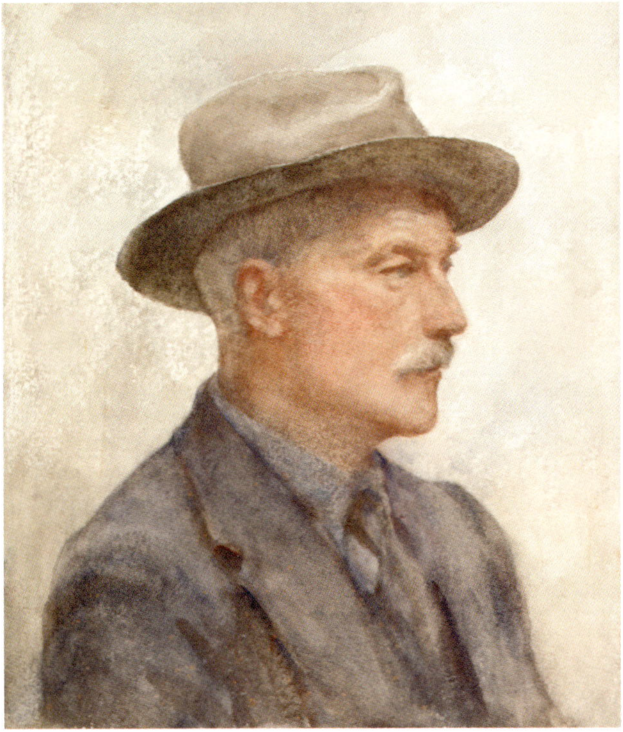

Self Portrait, c.1927
Watercolour, 25.3 x 21.4cm
Provenance: Purchased from Geoffrey Sainsbury
13 March 1965
RCPS Tuke Collection A72

This self-portrait was probably done at the same time as A77.

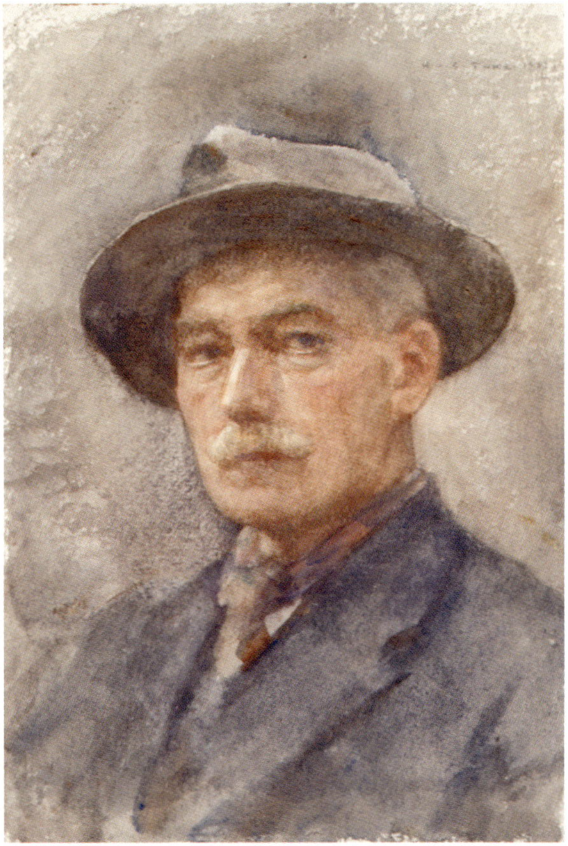

Self Portrait, 1927
Watercolour, 25.4 x 17.7 cm
Signed and dated top right: H.S.Tuke 1927
Provenance: Purchased from Geoffrey Sainsbury
13 March 1965
RCPS Tuke Collection A77

This self portrait in his trilby hat was painted in 1927, the last year of travel, reasonable health and painting, according to his sister Maria, and the beginnings of that ill health which was to follow from December 1927 until his death in March 1929.

Still Lifes and Miscellaneous

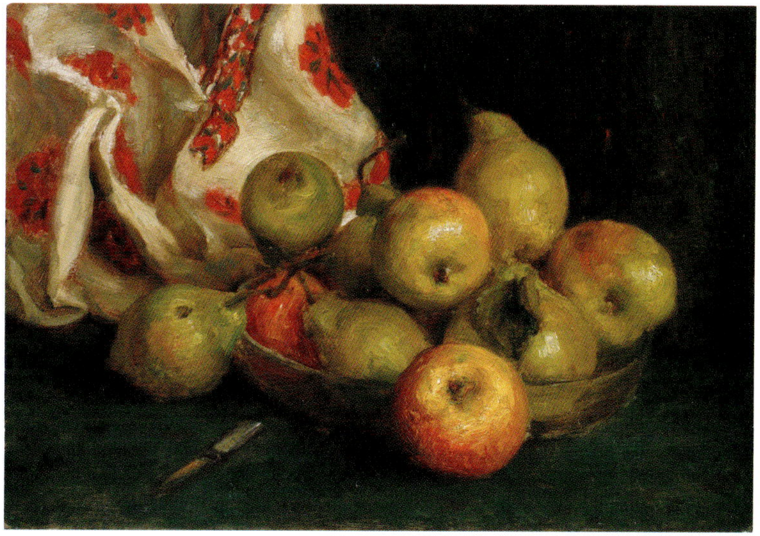

Dish of Fruit with Cloth
Oil on board, 27.5 x 28.5cm
Provenance: Purchased from Henry Shemilt
17 January 1964
RCPS Tuke Collection A70

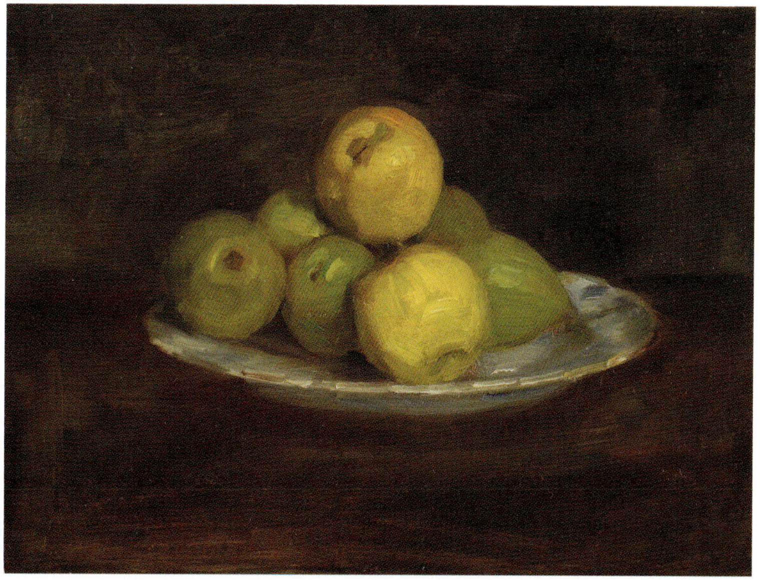

Still Life, Fruit
Oil on panel, 26.7 x 35cm
Provenance: Purchased from Henry Shemilt
17 January 1964
RCPS Tuke Collection A12

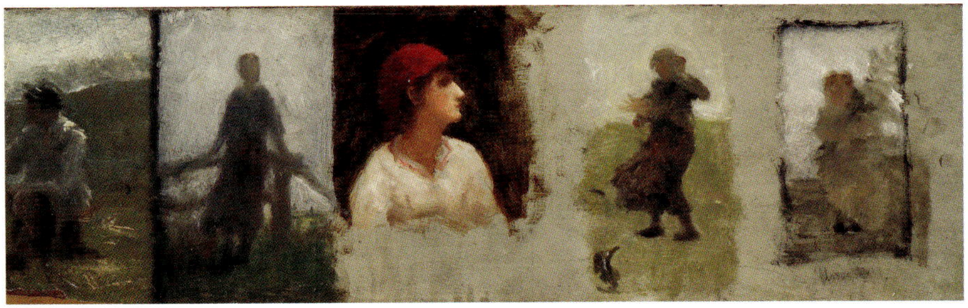

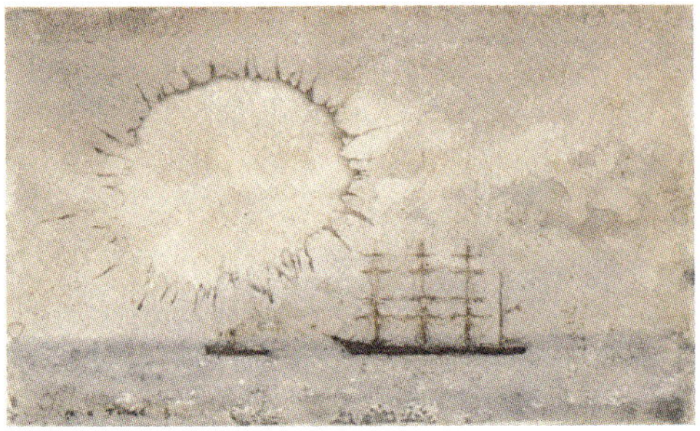

Italian Sketches
Oil on panel 13 x 42cm
Pencil inscription bottom right: Alassio, 27
Provenance: Gift to Tuke Collection by Geoffrey Sainsbury in 1965
RCPS Tuke Collection A126

Although the inscription reads 'Alassio 27', it is thought that this is a much earlier study of Italian figures from Tuke's earlier trips to Italy.

Tug towing ship
Watercolour, 7.9 x 12.7cm
Signed bottom left: H.S.Tuke
RCPS Tuke Collection A408

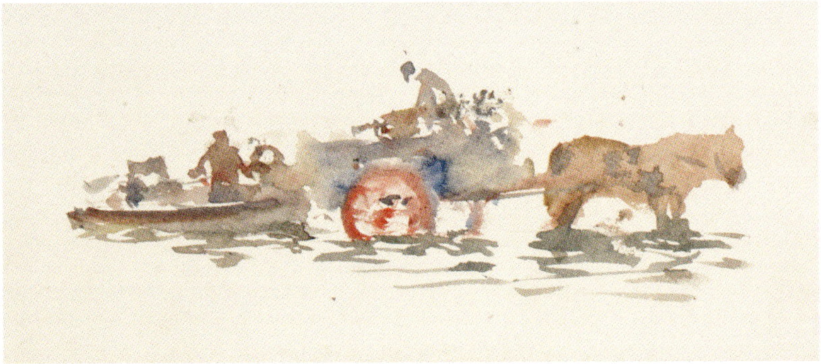

New Year's Card, 1902
Watercolour, 8.6 x 12.5cm
Initialled and dated: H.S.T. 1902
Inscribed: A Happy New Year 1902 from H.S.T
Provenance: Gift to Tuke Collection by Norman Hall in 1966
RCPS Tuke Collection A204

Cart and Boat
Watercolcour, 10 x 21.9cm
Inscribed: With all good wishes from
Antoinette and Geoffrey Sainsbury Christmas 1966
Provenance: Sent to Brian Price by Antoinette and Geoffrey Sainsbury,
cut out from one of Tuke's sketch books
RCPS Tuke Collection A199

Verso Images

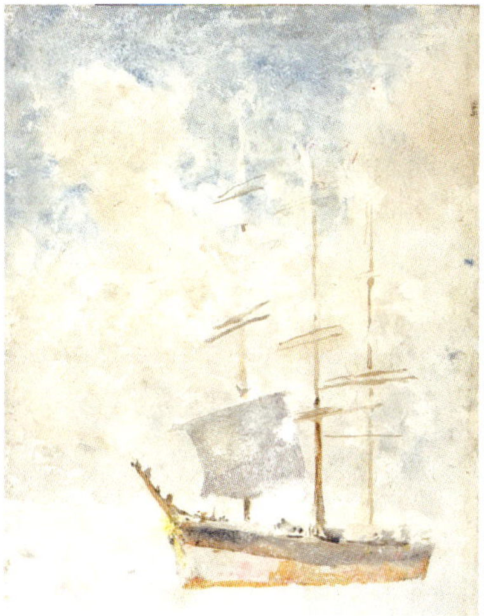

Study of a ship
Watercolour, 35.5 x 25.3cm
Provenance: Purchased from Geoffrey Sainsbury
29 May 1968
RCPS Tuke Collection A170a (Verso of A170)

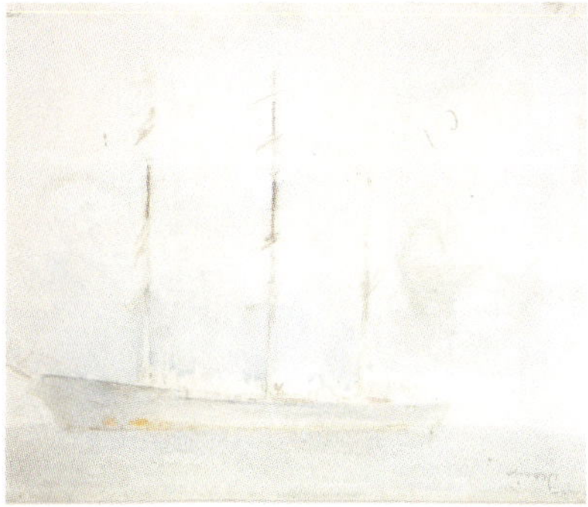

Study for *'Desaix'*, c.1920
Watercolour, 30.6 x 36cm
Provenance: Purchased from Geoffrey Sainsbury on
8 September 1968
RCPS Tuke Collection A154a

Sketch of shipping
Watercolour, 17.5 x 25cm
Provenance: Purchased from Geoffrey Sainsbury
29 May 1968. Previously Willy Sainsbury's
RCPS Tuke Collection A156a (Verso of A156)

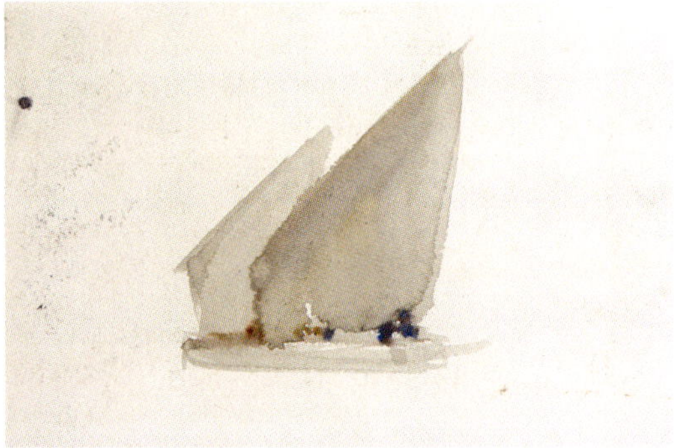

Sketch of two sailing boats

Watercolour, 21.5 x 13.8cm
Provenance: Purchased from Geoffrey Sainsbury
8 September 1968
RCPS Tuke Collection A191a (Verso of A191)

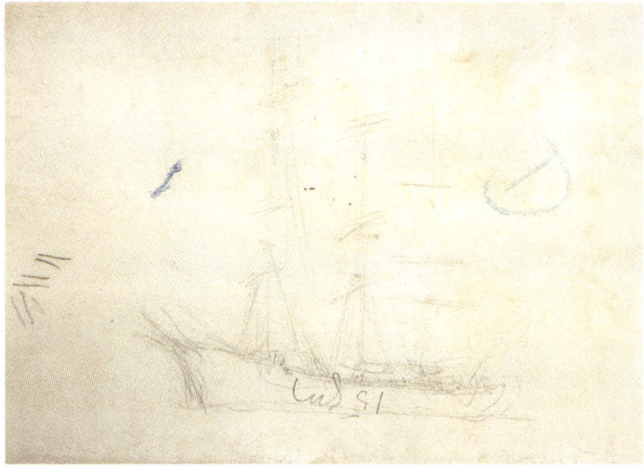

Sketch of Sailing ship

Pencil, 30.3 x 45.6cm
Provenance: Purchased from Geoffrey Sainsbury
30 April 1967
RCPS Tuke Collection A177a (Verso of A177)

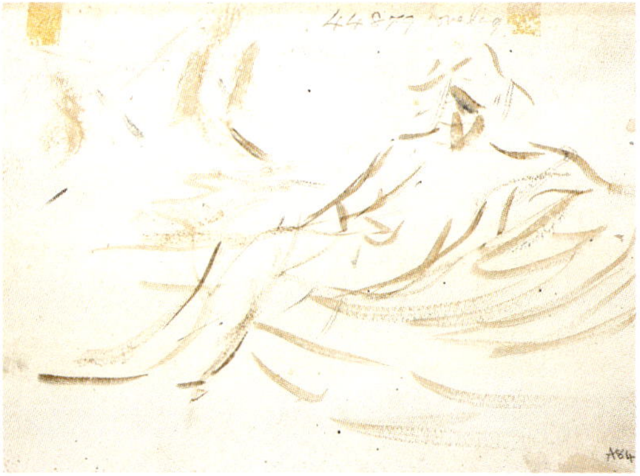

Sketch of Boy leaning on a boat

Watercolour wash, 17.8 x 25cm
Provenance: From the sketchbook given by
Hester Etchells to the Tuke Collection
27 June1964
RCPS Tuke Collection A84a (Verso of A84)

Sketch of a boat on the water
Charcoal, 14 x 25.9cm
Provenance: Purchased from Geoffrey Sainsbury
14 December 1967
RCPS Tuke Collection A209a (Verso of A209)

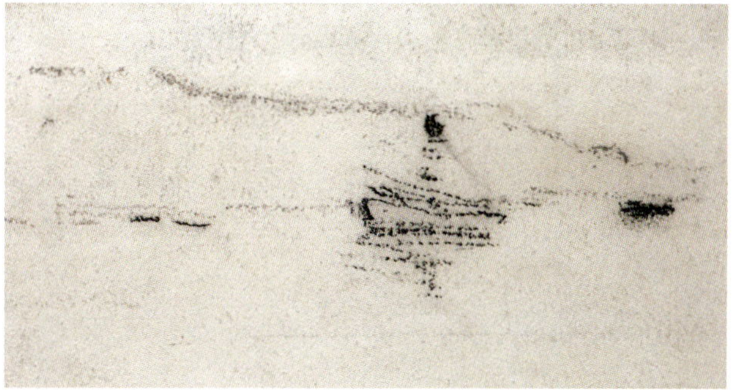

Study of Bass Rock, 1891
Watercolour, 17.5 x 25.5cm
Provenance: Purchased from Geoffrey Sainsbury
30 April 1967
RCPS Tuke Collection A250a (Verso of A250)

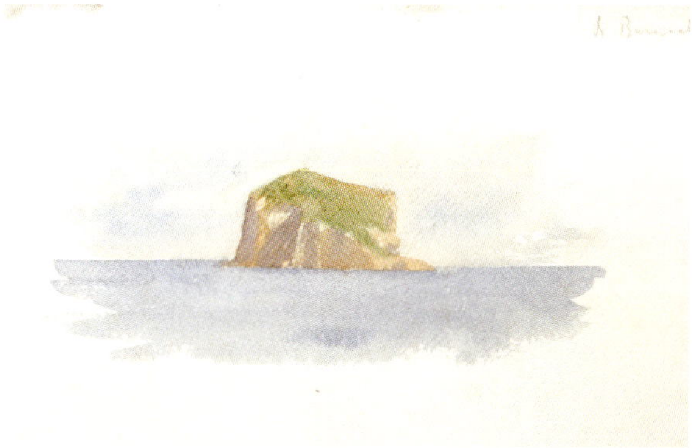

Sketch of Tantallon Castle, 1891
Watercolour, 17.5 x 25.5cm
Provenance: Purchased from Geoffrey Sainsbury
30 April 1967
RCPS Tuke Collection A249a (Verso of A249)

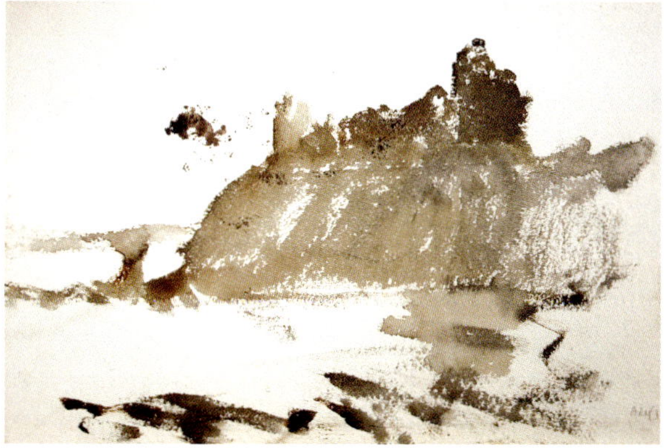

Maria Tuke Sainsbury (1861-1947)

Maria Tuke was the third child of Daniel Hack Tuke and Esther Maria Stickney. She was born in Woodlane, Falmouth on 24 February 1861.

Maria practised art at home with her brother Henry. She went to a Quaker school in Reigate which was run by the Sharp sisters. They were the sisters of Irwin Sharp who ran the Quaker School in Weston–Super-Mare which Harry and her other brother Willy attended. Maria describes the Sharp sisters as 'two of the best and kindest women.' She learnt art there and became an accomplished watercolourist. She wished to attend the Slade School of Art like her brother Henry but her parents refused to allow it. She also had hopes of going to the Queen's Square School for Ladies, but to no avail.

Henry Scott Tuke always supported his sister in the pursuit of her art and would send her materials so she could continue with her work. On Henry's return from Italy in the summer of 1881, Maria accompanied him to Clifton where their mother and brother Willy were staying. Tuke then helped to take Willy to Bournemouth for the good of his health, and this is where Maria undertook her portrait of Henry that is in the Tuke Collection (A181). He was 23 years old. He was to return the compliment and paint a major oil of her at the same age in 1884.

Maria got to know all Tuke's friends at the Slade including Thomas Cooper Gotch to whom she was briefly engaged, but he withdrew and left Maria deeply hurt; but it was a friend of Willy Tuke's, a medical student Harrington Sainsbury (1853 - 1936), that Maria did marry on March 26 1889. The small watercolour of a *'Pilchard Look Out'* (A254) is inscribed 'MS to GES' which would have been her new sister-in-law Gertrude Sainsbury. Maria exhibited her work from 1885-1911 at the Royal Academy four times, at the Royal Institute of Painters in Water Colour three times, once at the New English Art Club and once at the Grosvenor Gallery. In 1887 and 1888 she loaned two of her works to the South London Fine Art Gallery. She also exhibited her work at the Royal Society of British Artists in 1889, alongside her brother.

She went on to have four children, Hester Margaret (1890 – 1936) who married the architect and artist Frederick Etchells, William Tuke Sainsbury (1891 – 1960), Geoffrey Sainsbury (1893 - 1973) who married twice the second time to Antoinette Greusard (1893 - 1983), and Philip Sainsbury (1899-1937). Maria is best known for her biography of her brother *'H.S.Tuke, A Memoir'* published by Martin Secker in 1933.

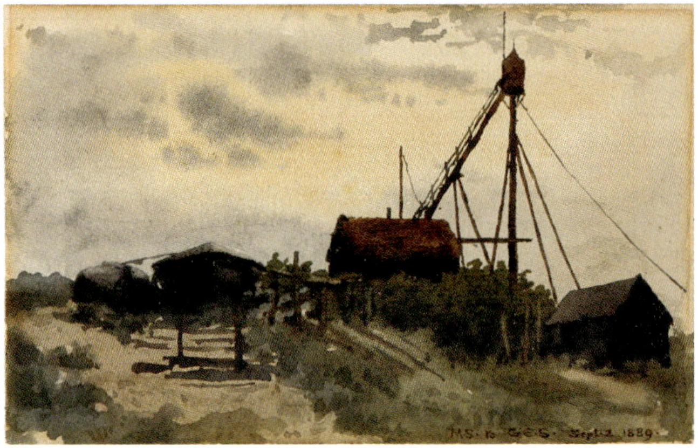

Maria Tuke Sainsbury (1861-1947)
Pilchard Look-Out, Sept. 2 1889
Watercolour, 10 x 15.5cm
Initialled bottom right: MS to GES, Sept. 2 1889
Provenance: Given to the Tuke Collection by B.D. Price February 2006
RCPS Tuke Collection A407

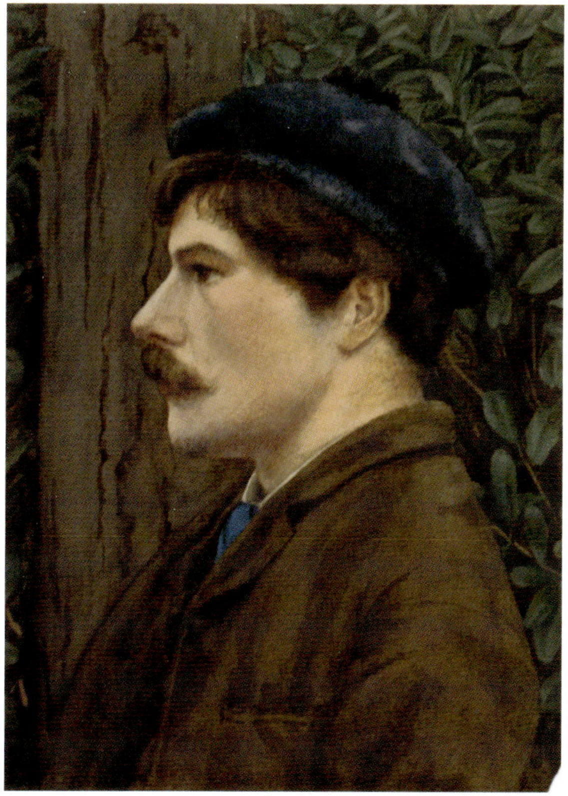

Maria Tuke Sainsbury (1861-1947)
Portrait of Henry Scott Tuke, Sept.1881
Watercolour25.2 x 17.7cm
Inscribed on reverse in Maria's hand: H.S.Tuke Sept. 81
Provenance: Purchased from Geoffrey Sainsbury
8 September 1968
RCPS Tuke Collection A181

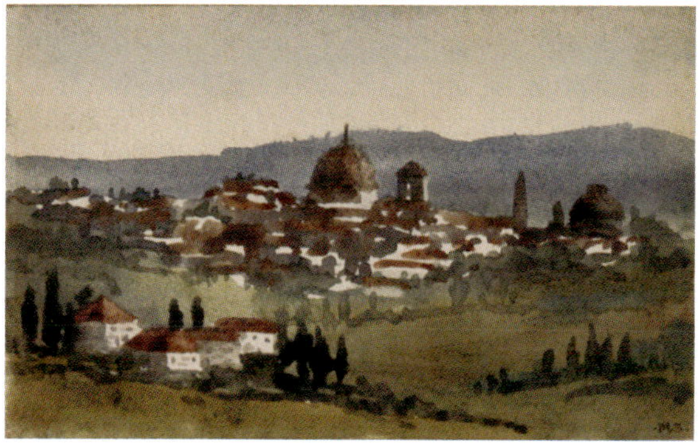

Maria Tuke Sainsbury (1861-1947)
Italian Town (Florence), c.1890
Watercolour 6.8 x 11cm
Initialled bottom right: M.S
Inscribed on the reverse: Watercolour by Maria Tuke (sister of Henry Scott Tuke) in scrapbook of Mrs Marshall, Chithurst, Sussex. circ. 1890
Provenance: Given to the Tuke Collection by B.D.Price February 2006
RCPS Tuke Collection A406

Henry Scott Tuke RA RWS (1858-1929)

A brief biography

1858: 12 June. Born in Lawrence Street, York, second son of Dr. Daniel Hack and Esther Maria Tuke (neé Stickney) who were Quakers.

1860: After a year in Clevedon, Tuke family move to Falmouth for Daniel's ill health; Henry and his brother William (born 1856) are educated by a governess.

1861: Maria Tuke, Henry's sister and author of his biography, is born.

1872-74: Henry and his brother William study at a Quaker School in Weston–Super–Mare.

1875: Henry enters the Slade School of Art, University of London. Studies under Poynter and then Alphonse Legros.

1877: Wins 3 years scholarship - travels to Antwerp, Bruges, Brussels and Paris with A.H. Wallis, becomes friends with T.C. Gotch and W. Dalrymple.

1878: Travels to Normandy with artist Arthur Tanner and with his mother to Paris.

1879: *The Good Samaritan* (RCPS Tuke Collection) is his first painting to be accepted at the Royal Academy, London. Leaves the Slade.

1880-81: Studies in Florence, Italy and meets Arthur Lemon and travels to the Italian coast where he paints the nude outdoors for the first time.

1881: He moves to Paris where he attends the studio of Jean Paul Laurens.

1883: Henry's brother William dies. Henry returns to England and visits Falmouth with T.C. Gotch before taking rooms in Newlyn.

1884: Becomes associated with the Newlyn School of painters - meets Stanhope Forbes.

1885: Leaves Newlyn for Falmouth where he rents rooms in Pennance Cottage, Swanpool.

1886: Purchases the French brigantine the '*Julie of Nantes*' which he uses as a floating studio and is the setting for many of his paintings over the next few years.

Becomes a Founder Member of the New English Arts Club.

Purchases his first boat the '*Lily*' and meets Jack Rolling in Falmouth - his model for several years.

1889: *All Hands to the Pumps!* painted on the '*Julie*' is purchased by the Chantrey Bequest.

A Sailors Yarn is purchased by Sydney National Gallery (Art Gallery of New South Wales).

1890: *The Message* featuring Mrs Fouracre and her two sons and Tuke's postman William Martin is exhibited at Dowdeswell's Cornish Exhibition.

Bathers, 1888 bought by Leeds Municipal Art Gallery.

1891: To North Berwick where he paints portrait commissions of the Dalrymple family and the Parrott family.

1892: First long trip to Europe, visits Paris and Venice and on to Corfu.

1894: *The Fisherman* purchased by Nottingham Municipal Gallery.

Euchre or *The Dog Watch* purchased by the Bavarian Government, Germany.

Tuke establishes an Art Gallery in Falmouth with William Ayerst Ingram as a commercial outlet, mainly for their own paintings.

Tuke's sailing boat '*Firefly*' is built.

1895: *August Blue* purchased by the Chantrey Bequest for the nation.

Tuke's father dies.

The '*Red-Heart*' sailing boat is designed and built in Jackett's Yard, Falmouth.

Article published on Tuke in The Studio and in *The Windsor Magazine*.

1899: Travels to Venice to paint Horatio Brown's portrait.

Elected Vice President of the Royal Cornwall Polytechnic Society.

1900: Elected Associate of the Royal Academy. A banquet is held in Tuke's honour at the Royal Cornwall Polytechnic Society Hall.

1902: *Ruby, Gold and Malachite* bought by the Guildhall Gallery, London

Article published on Tuke in The Magazine of Art by C. Kains-Jackson.

1903: *Noonday Heat* along with the *'The Run Home'* exhibited at the Royal Academy.

Tuke's sailing boat '*The Flamingo*' is designed and built in Jackett's Yard, Falmouth.

1904: Visits the Italian Riviera, undertakes many watercolours.

Is elected to the Royal Society of Painters in Watercolour.

Holds solo show at Dowdeswell's, *'Along the Italian Riviera'*.

Takes on a ten year lease of a small office on Customs House Quay which acts as a store and studio.

1907: *To the Morning Sun* bought by Hugh Lane Gallery, Dublin.

1908: Sails to Nordenham in Germany on the '*Grace Harwar*'.

Goes to Shillinglee Park to paint a portrait of the cricketer Prince Ranjitsinjhi.

Also paints the portrait of A.J. McLaren (RCPS Tuke Collection)

1909: Article on Tuke appears in *The Yachting and Boating Monthly*.

1911: Elected a full member of the Royal Society of Painters in Watercolour.

1912: To Italy including Careggi, Assisi, Leghorn, Genoa and Alassio.

1914: Elected Royal Academician.

Paints on board the captured German ship the '*Ponape*' at King Harry Ferry.

1915: Is seriously ill for 3 months with erysipelas at Lyndon Lodge and takes until November to recover, nursed back to health by the Henderson Bulls at Marlborough House, Falmouth.

1917: Tuke's mother dies.

1923: *The Message* along with other works by Tuke are donated to Falmouth Municipal Art Gallery by Alfred de Pass.

1923-4: Visits the West Indies by ship with the explorer F.A.Mitchell-Hedges, Lady Richmond Brown and Miss MacBeth, stopping at Jamaica, Belize, Tobacco Caye, Glover's Reef and Guatemala. Undertakes many watercolours (see RCPS Tuke Collection)

1925: Returns to Italy, visits Rapallo and travels to Algiers, North Africa.

1926: To Italy and France visits Rapallo and Cassis.

1927: Last works shown at the Royal Society of Painters in Watercolour.

Final visit to the Mediterranean, visits Cassis and St.Tropez.

1929: March 13, Tuke dies at Pennance Cottage, Falmouth and is buried in Falmouth cemetery.

Memorial exhibition including many works from Tuke's estate sold at The Cooling Galleries, New Bond Street, London.

The Run Home presented to the RIC Truro by Alfred de Pass.

1965: Donation made by Brian Price of his Tuke collection to the Royal Cornwall Polytechnic Society, Falmouth.

Index of Works

Index

Numbers in **bold** refer to illustrations and *n* refers to notes.

E

F

G

M

N

P

Q

U

V

W

Y